Technology in Healthcare

Introduction, Clinical Impacts, Workflow Improvement, Structuring and Assessment

Brian Pickering, Roland Roller,
Holmer Hemsen, Gerrit J. Noordergraaf,
Igor Paulussen and Alyssa Venema
(Editors)

now
the essence of knowledge

Published, sold and distributed by:
now Publishers Inc.
PO Box 1024
Hanover, MA 02339
United States
Tel. +1-781-985-4510
www.nowpublishers.com
sales@nowpublishers.com

Outside North America:
now Publishers Inc.
PO Box 179
2600 AD Delft
The Netherlands
Tel. +31-6-51115274

ISBN: 978-1-63828-236-5
E-ISBN: 978-1-63828-237-2
DOI: 10.1561/9781638282372

Suggested citation: Brian Pickering, Roland Roller, Holmer Hemsen, Gerrit J. Noordergraaf, Igor Paulussen and Alyssa Venema (eds.). (2024). *Technology in Healthcare: Introduction, Clinical Impacts, Workflow Improvement, Structuring and Assessment*. Boston–Delft: Now Publishers

Table of Contents

Editors and Contributing Authors

The Author Affiliation reflects their participation during the project, and may no longer be up-to-date.

Board of Editors

Chairman:

Brian Pickering
Electronics and Computer Science,
University of Southampton,
Southampton. SO17 1BJ. UK

Coordinating members:

Igor Paulussen
Philips Research, Eindhoven (NL),
Department of Anaesthesiology,
Resuscitation and Pain Management,
Elisabeth-TweeSteden Hospital,
Tilburg, The Netherlands

Gerrit Jan Noordergraaf
Department of Anaesthesiology,
Resuscitation and Pain Management,
Elisabeth-TweeSteden Hospital,
Tilburg, The Netherlands

Members:

Roland Roller
German Research Center for Artificial
Intelligence (DFKI), Berlin, Germany

Holmer Hemsen
German Research Center for Artificial
Intelligence (DFKI), Berlin, Germany

Alyssa Venema
Department of Anaesthesiology,
Resuscitation and Pain Management,
Elisabeth-TweeSteden Hospital,
Tilburg, The Netherlands

Further queries about the book may be addressed to Philips Research Europe, Department Europartners, Eindhoven (NL), or to the Board of Editors via BML-Handbook@gmail.com

Chapter 1

Supriyo Chatterjea
Philips Research, Eindhoven (NL),
The Netherlands

Chapter 2

Brian Pickering
Electronics and Computer Science,
University of Southampton,
Southampton. SO17 1BJ. UK
j.b.pickering@soton.ac.uk

Chapter 3

Anne Marie Weggelaar-Jansen
Erasmus University Rotterdam – Erasmus School of Health Policy & Management Tilburg University — Tranzo
j.w.m.weggelaar@tilburguniversity.edu

Sandra Sülz
Erasmus University Rotterdam – Erasmus School of Health Policy & Management Tilburg University — Tranzo
sulz@eshpm.eur.nl

Rik Wehrens
Erasmus University Rotterdam – Erasmus School of Health Policy & Management Tilburg University — Tranzo
wehrens@eshpm.eur.nl

Chapter 4

Ricard Martínez Martínez
Associate Professor of Constitutional Law and Director of the Microsoft Chair of Privacy and Digital Transformation at the University of Valencia. Universitat de València. Avinguda dels Tarongers, s/n 46022 València
ricard.martinez@uv.es

Ghost writer

Brian Pickering
Electronics and Computer Science,
University of Southampton,
Southampton. SO17 1BJ. UK
j.b.pickering@soton.ac.uk

Chapter 5

Brian Pickering
Electronics and Computer Science,
University of Southampton,
Southampton. SO17 1BJ. UK
j.b.pickering@soton.ac.uk

Chapter 6

Anca Mihalache
AXA Group, Health Office, Paris,
France
anca.mihalache@axa.com

Marcin Detyniecki
AXA Group Operations, GETD
Research, Paris, France; Sorbonne
Universite, LIP6/CNRS, Paris, France;
Polish Academy of Science, IBS PAN,
Warsaw, Poland
marcin.detyniecki@axa.com

Chapter 7

Igor Paulussen
Philips Research, Eindhoven (NL),
Department of Anaesthesiology,
Resuscitation and Pain Management,
Elisabeth-TweeSteden Hospital,
Tilburg, The Netherlands

Alyssa Venema
Department of Anesthesiology,
Resuscitation & Pain Management,
Elisabeth-TweeSteden Hospital,
Tilburg, NL, Department of
Traumatology, Radboudumc,
Nijmegen, NL, Network Emergency
& Acute Care for the Province of
North Brabant, Elisabeth-TweeSteden
Hospital, Tilburg, The Netherlands

Gerrit Jan Noordergraaf
Elisabeth-TweeSteden Hospital,
Tilburg, The Netherlands
g.noordergraaf@gmail.com

Chapter 8

José-Ramón Navarro-Cerdán
Instituto Tecnológico de Informática,
Universitat Politénica de Valéncia,
Spain
jonacer@iti.es

Manuel Sánchez-Gomis
Instituto Tecnológico de Informática,
Universitat Politénica de Valéncia,
Spain

Patricia Pons
Instituto Tecnológico de Informática, Universitat Politénica de Valéncia, Spain

Santiago Gálvez-Settier
Instituto Tecnológico de Informática, Valencia, Spain
sgalvez@iti.es

Francisco Valverde
Instituto Tecnológico de Informática, Universitat Politénica de Valéncia, Spain

Ana Ferrer-Albero
INCLIVA Health Research Institute, University of Valencia, Spain

Inmaculada Sauri
INCLIVA Health Research Institute, University of Valencia, Spain

Antonio Fernández
INCLIVA Health Research Institute, University of Valencia, Spain

Josep Redon
CIBERObn, Instituto de Salud Carlos III, Madrid, Spain, INCLIVA Research Institute. University of Valencia, Spain
josep.redon@uv.es

Chapter 9

Wiebke Duettmann
Charitéé – Universitätsmedizin Berlin, Medical Department of Nephrology and Medical Intensive Care, Berlin, Germany, Berlin Institute of Health, Berlin, Germany
wiebke.duettmann@charite.de

Roland Roller
German Research Center for Artificial Intelligence (DFKI), Berlin, Germany
roland.roller@dfki.de

Bilgin Osmanodja
Charité – Universitätsmedizin Berlin, Medical Department of Nephrology and Medical Intensive Care, Berlin, Germany
bilgin.osmanodja@charite.de

Verena Graf
Charité – Universitätsmedizin Berlin, Business Division IT, Berlin, Germany
verena.graf@charite.de

Matthias Pfefferkorn
Charité – Universitätsmedizin Berlin, Medical Department of Nephrology and Medical Intensive Care, Berlin, Germany
matthias.pfefferkorn@charite.de

Danilo Schmidt
Charité – Universitätsmedizin Berlin, Business Division IT, Berlin, Germany
danilo.schmidt@charite.de

Anne Schwerk
IU International University, Department IT & Engineering, Extended Artificial Intelligence Germany;

Berlin Institute of Health, Berlin, Germany

Marcel G. Naik
Charité – Universitätsmedizin Berlin, Medical Department of Nephrology and Medical Intensive Care, Berlin, Germany
marcel.naik@charite.de

Klemens Budde
Charité – Universitätsmedizin Berlin, Medical Department of Nephrology and Medical Intensive Care, Berlin, Germany
klemens.budde@charite.de

Chapter 10

Margherita Grossi
Huawei German Research Center, Riesstrasse 25, 80992, Munich, Germany
margherita.grossi@huawei.com

Brian Pickering
Electronics and Computer Science, University of Southampton, Southampton. SO17 1BJ. UK
j.b.pickering@soton.ac.uk

Chapter 11

Brian Pickering
Electronics and Computer Science, University of Southampton, Southampton. SO17 1BJ. UK
j.b.pickering@soton.ac.uk

Chris Duckworth
Electronics and Computer Science, University of Southampton, Southampton. SO17 1BJ. UK
c.j.duckworth@soton.ac.uk

Michael Boniface
Electronics and Computer Science, University of Southampton, Southampton. SO17 1BJ. UK
m.j.boniface@soton.ac.uk

Alison Blythin
my mhealth Limited
alison.blythin@mymhealth.com

Tom Wilkinson
Professor of Respiratory Medicine, Clinical and Experimental Sciences, Faculty of Medicine, University of Southampton, Southampton General Hospital, Southampton SO16 6YD
t.wilkinson@soton.ac.uk

Chapter 12

Gabriele Spini
TNO (Dutch Organization for Applied Scientific Research), P.O. Box 96800, 2509 JE, the Hague, The Netherlands
gabriele.spini@tno.nl

Marie Beth van Egmond
TNO (Dutch Organization for Applied Scientific Research), P.O. Box 96800, 2509 JE, the Hague, The Netherlands
marie_beth.vanegmond@tno.nl

Thijs Veugen
TNO (Dutch Organization for Applied Scientific Research), P.O. Box 96800, 2509 JE, the Hague, The Netherlands; University of Twente, P.O. Box 217, 7500 AE Enschede, The Netherlands; Cryptology Research Group, Centrum Wiskunde & Informatica (CWI), P.O. Box 94079, 1090 GB, Amsterdam, The Netherlands
thijs.veugen@tno.nl

Alex Sangers
TNO (Dutch Organization for Applied Scientific Research), P.O. Box 96800, 2509 JE, the Hague, The Netherlands
alex.sangers@tno.nl

Chapter 13

Brian Pickering
Electronics and Computer Science, University of Southampton, Southampton. SO17 1BJ. UK
j.b.pickering@soton.ac.uk

Chapter 14

Per Henrik Vincent
Department of Molecular Medicine and Surgery, Karolinska Institutet and Department of Pelvic Cancer, Karolinska University Hospital, Stockholm, Sweden
per.vincent@regionstockholm.se

Pieter C. Vos
Philips Healthcare
pieter.vos@philips.com

Erik Rönmark
Department of Pelvic Cancer, Karolinska University Hospital, Stockholm, Sweden
erik-peder.ronmark@regionstockholm.se

Olof Akre
Department of Molecular Medicine and Surgery, Karolinska Institutet and Department of Pelvic Cancer, Karolinska University Hospital, Stockholm, Sweden.
olof.akre@regionstockholm.se

Ralf Hoffmann
Philips Healthcare
ralf.hoffmann@philips.com

Ghost writer

Brian Pickering
Electronics and Computer Science, University of Southampton, Southampton. SO17 1BJ. UK
j.b.pickering@soton.ac.uk

Chapter 15

Dimitrios Vogiatzis
National Centre for Scientific Research "Demokritos"; The American College of Greece, Deree
dimitrv@iit.demokritos.gr

Alejandro Rodriguez Gonzalez
Universidad Politécnica de Madrid
alejandro.rg@upm.es

Ernestina Menasalvas
Universidad Politécnica de Madrid (UPM), Spain

Fotis Aisopos
National Centre for Scientific Research "Demokritos"
fotis.aisopos@iit.demokritos.gr

Anastasia Krithara
National Centre for Scientific Research "Demokritos"
akrithara@iit.demokritos.gr

Georgios Paliouras
National Centre for Scientific Research "Demokritos"
paliourg@iit.demokritos.gr

Samaneh Jozashoori
Leibniz University of Hannover, L3S Research Center, TIB Leibniz Information Centre for Science and Technology
samaneh.jozashoori@gmail.com

Ariam Rivas
Leibniz University of Hannover, L3S Research Center, TIB Leibniz Information Centre for Science and Technology
ariam.rivas@tib.eu

Ahmad Sakor
Leibniz University of Hannover, L3S Research Center, TIB Leibniz Information Centre for Science and Technology
ahmad.sakor@tib.eu

Maria-Esther Vidal
Leibniz University of Hannover, Germany

Maria Torrente
Puerta de Hierro University Hospital, Servicio Madrileño de Salud
mtorrente80@gmail.com

Mariano Provencio Pulla
Puerta de Hierro University Hospital, Servicio Madrileño de Salud
mprovenciop@gmail.com

Anna Triantafillou
Innovation Lab, Athens Technology Center
a.triantafillou@atc.gr

Athanasios Dalianis
Innovation Lab, Athens Technology Center
T.Dalianis@atc.gr

Chapter 16

Simona Rabinovici-Cohen
IBM Research – Israel, Mount Carmel, Haifa 3498825, Israel
simona@il.ibm.com

Chapter 17

Igor Paulussen
Philips Research, Eindhoven (NL), Department of Anaesthesiology, Resuscitation and Pain Management, Elisabeth-TweeSteden Hospital, Tilburg, The Netherlands

Bart Spruijt
Department of Anesthesiology, Resuscitation & Pain Management, Elisabeth-TweeSteden Hospital, Tilburg, NL; Philips Research, Eindhoven, NL; Network Emergency & Acute Care for the Province of North Brabant, Elisabeth-TweeSteden Hospital, Tilburg, The Netherlands
b.spruijt@etz.nl

Gerrit Jan Noordergraaf
Elisabeth-TweeSteden Hospital, Tilburg, The Netherlands
g.noordergraaf@gmail.com

Chapter 18

Igor Paulussen
Philips Research, Eindhoven (NL), Department of Anaesthesiology, Resuscitation and Pain Management, Elisabeth-TweeSteden Hospital, Tilburg, The Netherlands

Frederick Callebaut
Department of Anaesthesiology, Resuscitation and Pain Management, Elisabeth-TweeSteden Hospital, Tilburg, The Netherlands
f.callebaut@etz.nl

Gerrit Jan Noordergraaf
Elisabeth-TweeSteden Hospital, Tilburg, The Netherlands
g.noordergraaf@gmail.com

Chapter 19

Sebastian Roehrich
Department of Biomedical Imaging and Image-guided Therapy, Medical University of Vienna
sebastian.roehrich@meduniwien.ac.at

Helmut Prosch
Department of Biomedical Imaging and Image-guided Therapy, Medical University of Vienna
helmut.prosch@meduniwien.ac.at

Mia Ilic
contextflow GmbH, Vienna, Austria
mia.ilic@contextflow.com

Allan Hanbury
Vienna University of Technology, Vienna, Austria
allan.hanbury@tuwien.ac.at

Georg Langs
Computational Imaging Research Lab, Department of Biomedical Imaging and Image-guided Therapy, Medical University of Vienna, Vienna, Austria. Contextflow GmbH, Vienna, Austria
georg.langs@meduniwien.ac.at

Markus Krenn
Contextflow GmbH, Vienna, Austria
markus.krenn@contextflow.com

Chapter 20

Igor Paulussen
Philips Research, Eindhoven (NL), Department of Anaesthesiology, Resuscitation and Pain Management, Elisabeth-TweeSteden Hospital, Tilburg, The Netherlands

Gerrit Jan Noordergraaf
Elisabeth-TweeSteden Hospital, Tilburg, The Netherlands
g.noordergraaf@gmail.com

Ana Leitão
Philips Research, Eindhoven, (NL), The Netherlands
anajleitao@gmail.com

J.H. van Tuijl
Department of Anaesthesiology, Resuscitation and Pain Management, Elisabeth-TweeSteden Hospital, Tilburg, The Netherlands

Ben P. W. Jansen
Department of Neurology Elisabeth-TweeSteden Hospital, Tilburg, The Netherlands

Frederick Callebaut
Department of Anaesthesiology, Resuscitation and Pain Management, Elisabeth-TweeSteden Hospital, Tilburg, The Netherlands
f.callebaut@etz.nl

Supriyo Chatterjea
Philips Research, Eindhoven (NL), The Netherlands

Chapter 21

Ana Leitão
Philips Research, Eindhoven, (NL), The Netherlands
anajleitao@gmail.com

Pau Redon
CIBERObn, Instituto de Salud Carlos III, Madrid, Spain
paredlur@gmail.com

José-Ramón Navarro-Cerdán
Instituto Tecnológico de Informática, Universitat Politénica de Valéncia, Spain
jonacer@iti.es

Santiago Gálvez-Settier
Instituto Tecnológico de Informática, Valencia, Spain
sgalvez@iti.es

Evert van Loenen
PHILIPS Research, Eindhoven, The Netherlands

Josep Redon
CIBERObn, Instituto de Salud Carlos III, Madrid, Spain, INCLIVA Research Institute. University of Valencia, Spain
josep.redon@uv.es

Ghost writers

Igor Paulussen
Philips Research, Eindhoven (NL), Department of Anaesthesiology, Resuscitation and Pain Management, Elisabeth-TweeSteden Hospital, Tilburg, The Netherlands

Gerrit Jan Noordergraaf
Elisabeth-TweeSteden Hospital, Tilburg, The Netherlands
g.noordergraaf@gmail.com

Chapter 22

Job Gutteling
OLVG
jwa.gutteling@gmail.com

Heleen Nelissen
OLVG
h.e.nelissen@olvg.nl

Marijke Vulink
OLVG
m.vulink@olvg.nl

Ghost writers

Igor Paulussen
Philips Research, Eindhoven (NL), Department of Anaesthesiology, Resuscitation and Pain Management, Elisabeth-TweeSteden Hospital, Tilburg, The Netherlands

Gerrit Jan Noordergraaf
Elisabeth-TweeSteden Hospital, Tilburg, The Netherlands
g.noordergraaf@gmail.com

Chapter 23

Roland Roller
German Research Center for Artificial Intelligence (DFKI), Berlin, Germany
roland.roller@dfki.de

Chapter 24

Holmer Hemsen
German Research Center for Artificial Intelligence (DFKI), Berlin, Germany
holmer.hemsen@dfki.de

Roland Roller
German Research Center for Artificial Intelligence (DFKI), Berlin, Germany
roland.roller@dfki.de

Supriyo Chatterjea
Philips Research, Eindhoven (NL), The Netherlands

Anne Marie Weggelaar-Jansen
Erasmus School of Health Policy Management, Rotterdam, The Netherlands
j.w.m.weggelaar@tilburguniversity.edu

Alexandra Muñoz-Oliver
INCLIVA Health Research Institute, University of Valencia, Spain

Chapter 25

Roland Roller
German Research Center for Artificial Intelligence (DFKI), Berlin, Germany
roland.roller@dfki.de

Anne Marie Weggelaar-Jansen
Erasmus School of Health Policy Management, Rotterdam, The Netherlands
j.w.m.weggelaar@tilburguniversity.edu

Ricard Martínez Martínez
Associate Professor of Constitutional Law and Director of the Microsoft Chair of Privacy and Digital Transformation at the University of Valencia. Universitat de València. Avinguda dels Tarongers, s/n 46022 València
ricard.martinez@uv.es

Sven Schmeier
German Research Center for Artificial Intelligence (DFKI), Berlin, Germany

Holmer Hemsen
German Research Center for Artificial Intelligence (DFKI), Berlin, Germany
holmer.hemsen@dfki.de

Supriyo Chatterjea
Philips Research, Eindhoven (NL), The Netherlands

Chapter 26

Brian Pickering
Electronics and Computer Science, University of Southampton, Southampton. SO17 1BJ. UK
j.b.pickering@soton.ac.uk

Chapter 27

Roland Roller
German Research Center for Artificial Intelligence (DFKI), Berlin, Germany
roland.roller@dfki.de

Supriyo Chatterjea
Philips Research, Eindhoven (NL), The Netherlands

Holmer Hemsen
German Research Center for Artificial Intelligence (DFKI), Berlin, Germany
holmer.hemsen@dfki.de

Dimitrios Vogiatzis
National Centre for Scientific Research "Demokritos"; The American College of Greece, Deree
dimitrv@iit.demokritos.gr

Ricard Martínez Martínez
Associate Professor of Constitutional Law and Director of the Microsoft Chair of Privacy and Digital Transformation at the University of Valencia. Universitat de València. Avinguda dels Tarongers, s/n 46022 València
ricard.martinez@uv.es

Georg Langs
Computational Imaging Research Lab, Department of Biomedical Imaging and Image-guided Therapy, Medical University of Vienna, Vienna, Austria. Contextflow GmbH, Vienna, Austria
georg.langs@meduniwien.ac.at

Simona Rabinovici-Cohen
IBM Research, Israel
simona@il.ibm.com

Wiebke Duettmann
Charitéé – Universitätsmedizin Berlin, Medical Department of Nephrology and Medical Intensive Care, Berlin, Germany, Berlin Institute of Health, Berlin, Germany
wiebke.duettmann@charite.de

Alex Sangers
TNO (Dutch Organization for Applied Scientific Research), P.O. Box 96800, 2509 JE, the Hague, The Netherlands
alex.sangers@tno.nl

Maria-Esther Vidal
Leibniz University of Hannover, Germany

Ernestina Menasalvas
Universidad Politécnica de Madrid (UPM), Spain

Marga Martin Sanchez
Huawei, Germany

Josep Redon
CIBERObn, Instituto de Salud Carlos III, Madrid, Spain, INCLIVA Research Institute. University of Valencia, Spain
josep.redon@uv.es

Ana Ferrer-Albero
INCLIVA Health Research Institute, University of Valencia, Spain

Alexandra Muñoz-Oliver
INCLIVA Health Research Institute,
University of Valencia,
Spain

Gerrit Jan Noordergraaf
Elisabeth-TweeSteden Hospital,
Tilburg, The Netherlands
g.noordergraaf@gmail.com

Igor Paulussen
Philips Research, Eindhoven (NL),
Department of Anaesthesiology,
Resuscitation and Pain Management,
Elisabeth-TweeSteden Hospital,
Tilburg, The Netherlands

Per Henrik Vincent
Karolinska Insitutet, Stockholm,
Sweden
per.vincent@regionstockholm.se

Arne IJpma
Erasmus Medical Center Rotterdam,
The Netherlands

José-Ramón Navarro-Cerdán
Instituto Tecnológico de Informática,
Universitat Politénica de Valéncia,
Spain
jonacer@iti.es

Santiago Gálvez-Settier
Instituto Tecnológico de Informática,
Valencia, Spain
sgalvez@iti.es

Brian Pickering
Electronics and Computer Science,
University of Southampton,
Southampton. SO17 1BJ. UK
j.b.pickering@soton.ac.uk

Preface to the BigMedilytics Handbook

By Alina Senn

As the longest-serving Project Officer who followed the BigMedilytics project (Big Data for Medical Analytics), I now have the privilege to write the preface to the handbook you have in front of you.

The project was funded by the European Commission (EC), more specifically by the Data Policy and Innovation Unit, which aims at advancing data policies, research, and innovation. To achieve this goal, the Unit funds research and innovation projects and issues legal acts, such as Open Data Directive, Data Governance Act, Data Act, and High-Value Data Sets Implementing Act.

The BigMedilytics project, running for 45 months altogether, covered an exceptionally large scope and a very ambitious research and development program. Led by Philips, it received nearly EUR 15 million of EC funding and brought together 35 partners from different Member States of the European Union. Philips coordinated a dedicated and well-run project team working on the biggest EC-funded project so far to demonstrate the potential of Big Data in healthcare (a Lighthouse Project).

BigMedilytics covered the most important and costly strands of healthcare. The pilots focused respectively on the following three strands split into 12 pilots:

1. Population health and chronic disease management:
   - Comorbidities
   - Kidney disease
   - Diabetes
   - COPD/asthma
   - Heart failure
2. Cancer:
   - Prostate cancer

  - Lung cancer
  - Breast cancer
3. Industrialization of health services:
  - Stroke management
  - Sepsis management
  - Asset management
  - Radiology workflows

I, therefore, wholeheartedly welcome the publication of the handbook. It represents a post-project outcome, which shows once again the commitment of project partners to their work. The handbook constitutes a much needed compilation of the most important lessons and insights gained in the course of implementing the project's 12 pilots. Thanks to the publication of the handbook, many stakeholders will now be able to benefit from the body of knowledge on Big Data in healthcare created in the course of the project. Decision-makers, researchers, companies, and anyone else dealing with the subject will find something of interest here.

The area of healthcare addressed by the project could not be more relevant and in need of urgent action. Just as in many other sectors today, healthcare faces many opportunities and challenges arising from digital transformation. The stakes are high, because it is very often a question of life and death for patients whether they will receive treatments that are timely and well targeted. Big Data, if used effectively, can be a real game changer. It can enable more personalized and reliable interventions for patients. It can make hospitals more efficient through better workflows. It can support healthcare professionals (doctors and nurses) with decision support systems. Finally, and significantly, it can bring substantial cost savings for healthcare providers.

However, the challenges are equally significant. The high quality of the source data is not always easy to guarantee. Data interoperability at technical and semantic levels often remains an unsolved question. Ethical issues, including both the ethical treatment of individuals and data protection, are very complex and must be handled appropriately to avoid potentially compromising security via breaches of health data. Furthermore, the workings of AI underpinning decision support systems must be sufficiently transparent, trustworthy, and understandable to healthcare professionals and patients – if not, there is a high risk that they may not be accepted.

The landscape is not static either and continues to evolve. As regards the situation in healthcare, two very important developments took place during the project's lifetime: the first was the entry into force of the General Data Protection Regulation (GDPR) in May 2018. While this highly important piece of legislation marked a turning point for the protection of personal data in the European Union, the GDPR also left open to Member States the possibility of complementing its provisions with their own national regulations in relation to the processing of health data.

As a result, different legal bases are applied across Europe for secondary health data processing, and the regulatory landscape has a crucial impact on the use of Big Data for research. The project brought this fact to the attention of the political policymakers. It also stressed the need for harmonizing data-sharing policies and ethical requirements across Member States. A noteworthy outcome of the project in this area is, therefore, the infographics on regulations for Big Data technologies in the healthcare sector in several European countries.

The introduction of the GDPR also affected the work on BigMedilytics itself. In the first months after the new regulation entered into force, time was needed to understand how its specific provisions should be translated into concrete steps, actions, and safeguards on the ground. All across Europe, ethical committees were established to provide guidance on the application of the GDPR in healthcare practice. This process, however, took some weeks or even months and consequently slowed down the implementation of the BigMedilytics project, leading to an extension of its duration.

The second hurdle the project encountered was the outbreak of the COronaVIrus Disease of 2019 (COVID-19) pandemic. One of its many side effects was that it made access to hospitals across Europe more difficult for BigMedilytics researchers following the introduction of restrictions. However, the pandemic itself dramatically demonstrated the vital importance of using Big Data for developing new vaccines, finding effective treatments, and supporting healthcare professionals in their work in all possible ways. Everyone will probably agree that unlike any other event, the pandemic showed the necessity for sharing health data more effectively than before and for applying AI to develop digital tools, technologies, and applications. These can increase patients' and healthcare professionals' health, safety, and self-efficacy in situations of greater exposure to the risk of dangerous infection. The pandemic also completely changed the perception of professions in healthcare, demonstrating how many human lives depend in an emergency on these "key workers", highlighted the importance of agile, well-prepared, and well-functioning hospitals, and made clear the need to protect vulnerable patients with comorbidities by strengthening remote care, thus relieving the burden on hospitals. In this context, the work of BigMedilytics gained a new dimension and acquired even stronger relevance than before.

With hindsight, we can conclude that even though it might have been difficult and time-consuming, the project successfully dealt with both hurdles of very different natures: the new regulatory landscape created by the GDPR and the more challenging conditions in hospitals following the outbreak of the pandemic.

The project was reviewed by the EC three times during its lifetime with the help of external experts. Each review showed an upward trend in the project's research and development and other work, while the final review confirmed the successful outcome of the project. I allow myself to quote here some passages of the final review report submitted by the experts to the EC:

> *The results presented during the final review were impressive, live demos were presented of representative pilots demonstrating that they had clearly met or exceeded their objectives. Also, the project dissemination was very successful in terms of both communications and important publications. The consortium was able to establish a solid narrative around the 12 pilots and they could show the purpose of the project for different stakeholders through the interactive blueprint. All pilots have been successfully achieved and tested in real-world conditions (e.g. the telemedicine pilots, with certifications and accreditations as well as asthma and kidney transplant).*
>
> *The consortium had devoted extra resources to the development of the Big Data Healthcare Analytics Blueprint, which was requested in the previous review. The Blueprint was presented as an interactive web portal, including an extensive and valuable repository of experiences from the 12 pilots.*

One of the greatest challenges for EC-funded projects is to make their work, research findings, lessons, and insights available to as broad an audience as possible. It is extremely important because effectively sharing a project's "lessons learned" means enabling other researchers, innovators, policymakers, and any other possible stakeholders in the field to build on the newly produced body of knowledge. If this is accomplished well, it also leads to avoiding duplication of effort and can greatly accelerate further scientific and technological progress.

Let me use a metaphor for this task. Pioneers in any given field are like a team moving through deep snow with difficulty but already leaving a well-trod path behind them. If they manage to share their knowledge with other teams, then they are making it possible for others to walk faster, more comfortably, with less effort, and following an already established path. Failing to share the acquired know-how and expertise might in turn be compared to a situation where one team has invested a lot of effort and left a well-trod path in the snow, but others have not been told that it exists or have not seen it. They now expend much effort to explore and make progress across the field, which could so easily have been crossed with the benefit of knowing what others who went before found.

With that in mind and given that all the BigMedilytics pilots dealt with large amounts of data generated by patients and/or healthcare workers, the project developed a Big Data Healthcare Analytics Blueprint (defining platforms and components) based on open Big Data technologies. The blueprint allows BigMedilytics concepts to be replicated across Europe. Apart from an interactive web portal, including an extensive and valuable repository of experiences from the 12 pilots, you now have the possibility of using this handbook. Just like the blueprint, it illustrates how to make use of large, complex datasets for healthcare even in settings outside the project. It is in the interest of everybody to see the results of the project adopted on a large scale and integrated into a wide range of hospitals and other entities across Europe.

Therefore, I hope you will decide to study this handbook in detail, and I wish you many fruitful insights from reading through the experiences of its contributors. I also hope you will replicate them in practice and thus advance the field of digital health in Europe.

Acknowledgements

Implementing Technology to Support Healthcare

By Bart Spruijt, Alyssa Venema, Igor Paulussen and Gerrit J. Noordergraaf

1 Introduction Into BigMedilytics and This Handbook

As part of the Horizon 2020 project, the European Commission granted project 780495 to a large consortium of institutions, including healthcare institutions, technology corporations, and other entities, with the focus of making technology and big data more available to support healthcare and reduce costs while improving quality. The project ran from January 2018–2021, including a cost-neutral extension of 6 months due to delays resulting from the COVID-19 pandemic. Including this extension, the project lasted a total of 45 months.

The objectives of BigMedilytics (BML) were:

- To improve chronic disease management and cancer outcomes using big data
- Optimize workflows through industrialization of healthcare services using big data
- Guarantee replicability of big data concepts in healthcare
- Increase market share through data integration
- Establish secure and privacy-preserving cross-border and cross-organization healthcare services, thus strengthening the European Union (EU)'s digital market strategy

- Define best big data practices
- Enable knowledge transfer

BML was a consortium of 35 partners, led by Mr. Supriyo Chatterjea, PhD, of Philips Research (Eindhoven, The Netherlands), in which healthcare providers, technology companies, pharma, research institutes, and universities from 12 different countries participated. The countries spanned Europe, from Scandinavia to the Mediterranean. The Netherlands and Germany, with eight members each, were the countries with the largest number of partners, followed by Spain with five and the United Kingdom with three. France, Austria, and Greece participated in the project with two partners each. Finally, there is the collaboration with one participant from Finland, Ireland, Israel, Serbia, and Sweden.

The final report of the 12 studies, and the outcomes of consortium as a whole, was accepted by the European Commission in January of 2022.

Although the project was finished early in 2022, based on an initiative by Philips Research and the current members of the Board of Editors, an ad hoc project was set up to bundle and make readily accessible the insights and outcomes from the BML project. This initiative has reached fruition in this Handbook.

It is with great satisfaction that we, on behalf of all the project participants and the Board of Editors for the Handbook, are able to offer you this Handbook, reporting in an open access environment on the developments, thoughts, progress, outcomes, and learnings of the BML project.

2 The Participating and Supporting Institutions

We would like to recognize the participating organizations for all their contributions to the success of the BML project and honour their willingness to continue their participation in making this Handbook a reality (Table 1). We are particularly proud of the 100% participation of the institutions and the quality of their input for the Handbook.

Table 1. Alphabetical listing of participating organizations in the consortium.

No	Participant organization name	Short name	Country
1	Achmea BV	ACH	NL
2	AOK Nordost – die Gesundheitskasse	AOK	DE
3	AstraZeneca UK Limited	ASZ	GB
4	Athens Technology Center SA	ATC	GR
5	Atos Spain S.A.	ATOS	ES

(Continued)

Table 1. Continued

No	Participant organization name	Short name	Country
6	Charité – Universitätsmedizin Berlin	CHA	DE
7	ContextFlow GmbH	CON	AT
8	Deutsches Forschungszentrum für Künstliche Intelligenz GmbH	DFKI	DE
9	Erasmus Universitair Medisch Centrum Rotterdam	EMC	NL
10	Erasmus Universiteit Rotterdam	BMG	NL
11	Fundación para la Investigación del Hospital Clínico de la Comunidad Valenciana, Fundación Incliva	INC	ES
12	Instituto Tecnológico De Informática	ITI	ES
13	GIE AXA	AXA	FR
14	Hassno-Plattner-Institut für Softwaresystemtechnik GmbH	HPI	DE
15	HUAWEI Technologies Düsseldorf GmbH	HUA	DE
16	IBM Israel – Science and Technology LTD	IBM	IL
17	Institut Curie	CUR	FR
18	Medische Universität Wien	MUW	AT
19	My mHealth Limited	MYM	GB
20	National Centre of Scientific Research "Demokritos"	DEM	GR
21	Nederlandse Organisatie voor Toegepast-Natuurwetenschappelijk Onderzoek	TNO	NL
22	Onze Lieve Vrouwe Gasthuis	OLV	NL
23	Optimedis AG	OPTI	DE
24	Philips Electronics Nederland B.V.	PHI	NL
25	Privredno Drustvo za Pruzanje Usluga Istrazivanje i Razvoj Nissatech Innovation Centre DOO	NISS	RS
26	Rheinische Friedrich-Wilhelms-Universität Bonn	UNIB	DE
27	Royal College of Surgeons in Ireland//Rotunda Hospital	RCSI	IE
28	Servicio Madrileño de Salud	HUP	ES
29	Stichting Elisabeth-TweeSteden Ziekenhuis	ETZ	NL
30	Stockholms läns landstings	KAR	SE
31	Technische Universiteit Eindhoven	TUE	NL
32	Teknologian tutkimuskeskus VTT Oy	VTT	FI
33	Universidad Politécnica De Madrid	UPM	ES
34	Universitätsklinikum Essen	ESS	DE
35	University of Southampton	UNIS	GB

These 35 partners were the BML consortium. In addition to these 35 partners, there were 56 supporting partners who made major contributions and without whom the project would not have become such a great success (Table 2). The Board of Editors wants to thanks these supporting partners for their dedication to the project and their contributions.

Table 2. Alphabetical listing of the supporting organizations.

No	Organization	Country
1	Assuta	IL
2	Barcelona Supercomputing Center	ES
3	BDVA	ES
4	Bellvitge University Hospital and Research Institute (IDIBELL)	ES
5	BIOIATRIKI S.A., bioMed	GR
6	Catholic University of Milan	IT
7	CeADAR	IE
8	Clinical Research Consultants	FR
9	Competence Center Machine Learning Rhein/Ruhr ML2R	DE
10	Complejo Hospitalario Universitario de Badajoz	ES
11	CRG	ES
12	EGI Foundation	NL
13	European Alliance Partners Company AG	SE
14	Everis Spain S.L.U.	ES
15	Ferrer	ES
16	Foundation 29	ES
17	Fraunhofer-Gesellschaft zur Förderung der angewandten Forschung Ev	DE
18	Fundación Empresa Universidad Gallega	ES
19	Fundación Vicomtech	ES
20	GEN inCode	ES
21	GMV Soluciones Globales Internet S.A.U.	ES
22	Helsinki Biobank	FL
23	Hospital Niño Jesús (SERMAS)	ES
24	Hospital Universitario de Tarragona Joan XXIII	ES
25	Hospital Universitario y Politecnico LA FE	ES

(*Continued*)

Table 2. Continued

No	Organization	Country
26	I2CAT	ES
27	IGENOMIX	ES
28	Instituto de Biomecánica de Valencia	ES
29	Instituto de Salud 'Carlos III' (OTRI)	ES
30	Instituto de Salud 'Carlos III' (OPE)	ES
31	INTERAMERICAN	GR
32	IRCCS Istituto Auxologico Italiano – Milano	IT
33	Know-Center GmbH	AT
34	Quibim S.L.	ES
35	Leids Universitair Medisch Centrum	NL
36	Maasstad Ziekenhuis (Business Intelligence Department)	NL
37	Maasstad Ziekenhuis (Information Management Department)	NL
38	Madrimasd	ES
39	Medical School of Hannover	DE
40	MediRisk Organisatie BV	NL
41	Microsoft Ibérica S.R.L.	ES
42	Mondragon Goi Eskola Politeknikoa J.M.A.S. Coop	ES
43	OLVG	NL
44	Oxford Academic Health Science Network	UK
45	P3 Group	DE
46	St Antonius Ziekenhuis	NL
47	Stichting ZorgTTP	NL
48	Treelogic SL	ES
49	TU/Eindhoven	NL
50	Turku University Hospital	FI
51	University Hospital of Tarragona Joan XXIII	ES
52	University Medical Center Mainz	DE
53	University of Groningen/Academic Medical Centre	NL
54	Visual Limes	ES
55	Wings ICT solutions	GR
56	Zorginstituut Nederland	NL

3 COVID-19

The COVID-19 pandemic started at the end of 2019 and was declared a pandemic in January 2020. Formally, it was as late as May 2023 before the WHO declared the global health emergency over.

For BML, most of the institutions were in the formalization phase of prospective studies in clinical settings. Interventions for patient and caregiver safety impacted these studies, but in general, progress, though limited and requiring extensive efforts, was able to continue.

We would like to recognize the unusual dedication to the BML project, both by Philips as well as all the participating institutions and their staff, in continuing to strive for success and excellence under these mitigating circumstances. Research and innovation clearly wait for no man, including COVID-19!

4 The Handbook (Implementing Technology to Support Healthcare) and the Board of Editors

While the idea to produce an open-access book was readily made, progressing from concept to completion was a herculean task. Participants in the BML project had changed positions or institutions, or had new, demanding tasks.

We would particularly like to name the chair and members of the Board of Editors:

Dr. Brian Pickering, of the University of Southampton (UK), Chairman of the Board of Editors; Dr. Roland Roller and Dr. Holmer Hemsen of the Deutsches Forschungzentrum für Künstliche Intelligenz, DFKI, Berlin (D); Dr. Gerrit J. Noordergraaf and Alyssa Venema of the Elisabeth-TweeSteden Hospital, Tilburg (NL); Igor Paulussen of Philips Research, Eindhoven (NL) and the Elisabeth-TweeSteden Hospital, Tilburg (NL) for their enthusiasm, persistence, (semi-) gentle prodding, and systematic approach to getting the job done.

Members of the Board of Editors not only coordinated but also authored, reviewed, ghost-wrote where needed, and extensively used the teleconferencing skills learned during COVID-19, to make the Handbook a whole and representative of the intentions of the EU.

The Board of Editors would like to expressly thank all the physicians, nurses, patients, managers and technical staff in the many institutions who participated in the BigMedilytics project and who cared the load tirelessly. An impressive effort which has generated a timely product on the road to further improving healthcare.

We would also like to thank Anesthesiologist Rob Tolboom, MD, PhD, who supported the Board of Editors in the final review with his usual exacting, detailed, and consistent approach. His interest and expertise in Artificial Intelligence was invaluable in helping get the Handbook done.

The Handbook will be open access and available free of cost online, and it can be ordered in its physical form. Each of the contributing groups will receive one book per chapter submitted.

5 Proceeds

In close collaboration with the publisher, the Board of Editors also decided to dedicate the proceeds of the sale of printed copies to the UNICEF Office of Innovation (Global Office of Innovation, United Nations Children's Fund, Box 8161, 104 20 Stockholm, Sweden) to support the development of AI and technologies.

Now Publishers can be reached via Mike Casey, Lange Geer 44, 2611 PW Delft, +31 6 511 152 74, www.nowpublishers.com.

Further queries about the book may be addressed to Philips Research Europe, Dept. Europartners, Eindhoven (NL), or to the Board of Editors via BMLHandbook@gmail.com.

In late 2024, the book will be presented to the EU as a tangible recognition of all those who have participated in the BML project and this Handbook.

Glossary

A

AC - *AChmea*. 165, 166, 169

ACG - *Adjusted Clinical Groups*. 94, 103

ADC - *Apparent Diffusion Coefficient*. 189, 221, 224

ADSS - *Automated Decision Support Systems*. 120

AEPD - *Spanish Data Protection Agency*. 336

AI - *Artificial Intelligence*. xxxii, xxxiii, 2, 9, 37, 51–55, 59, 60, 67, 80, 120, 123, 138, 183, 218, 221, 222, 226, 227, 232, 233, 247, 248, 252, 256, 258, 259, 313, 315, 317–319, 321, 325, 327, 328, 331–333, 336–339, 342, 343, 347, 351, 352, 354, 357–360, 368, 369, 373, 374, 376

ANE - *ANEsthesiology*. 265

ANOVA - *ANalysis Of VAriance*. 348

API - *Application Programming Interface*. 112, 114, 189, 255

AUC - *Area Under the Curve*. 119, 120, 193–196, 219, 222–224, 226

AUROC - *Area Under the Receiver Operating Characteristic*. 147, 149

B

BLE - *Bluetooth Low Energy*. 238

BMI - *Body Mass Index*. 95, 132, 133, 171, 225

BML - *BigMedilytics*. xxxvii, xxxviii, xl, xlii, xliii, 17–21, 24–27, 29, 51–60, 63–68, 87, 231, 232, 238, 247–250, 257, 279, 342, 343, 347–355

BMMR2 - *Breast Multiparametric MRI for prediction of NAC Response*. 221, 226

BP - *Blood Pressure*. 283

BSL - *Blood Sugar Level*. 128

C

CAD - *Computer-Aided Diagnosis*. 255, 257

CAPABLE - *CAncer PAtients Better Life Experience*. 227

CAS - *Community-Acquired Sepsis*. 277, 278

CAT - *COPD Assessment Test*. 142, 143, 146, 148–156

CBIR - *Content-based Image Retrieval*. 247, 249, 252

CDS - *Clinical Decision Support*. 186–188, 191, 192, 197–202

CDSS - *Clinical Decision Support System*. 119, 120

CE - *Conformité Européenne (French for European Conformity)*. 239

CEO - *Chief Executive Officer*. 359

CI - *Confidence Intervals*. 146–149, 219

CIRS - *Cumulative Illness Rating Scale*. 93, 103

CNIL - *National Commission on Informatics and Liberty*. 336

CNN - *Convolutional Neural Networks*. 223, 252

COPD - *Chronic Obstructive Pulmonary Disease*. 88, 89, 97, 141–143, 148–150, 153, 156, 344, 358

COVID-19 - *COronaVIrus Disease of 2019*. xxxiii, xxxvii, xlii, 1, 15, 22, 24, 38, 71, 79–81, 116, 118, 122, 133, 138, 139, 157, 161, 187, 191, 198, 258, 268

COW - *Computers On Wheels*. 235, 293, 294, 296, 299, 307, 308

CRISP-DM - *CRoss-Industry Standard Process for Data Mining*. 314, 331, 333, 336

CT - *Computerized Tomography*. 55, 59, 183, 227, 232, 240, 242, 247–251, 255–259, 342, 367, 369

CT/CTC/CTCa - *Computed Tomography, Also CT scan, CTC (Cerebrum), CTCa (angiography of the Cerebrum)*. 264, 265, 268–272

CTa - *CT-angio*. 242

CTG - *CardioTocoGram*. 295, 301

CTR - *Clinical Trials Regulation*. 48

CVA - *Cerebrovascular accident*. 241, 242, 269

D

DARPA - *Defense Advanced Research Projects Agency*. 352

DCE - *Dynamic Contrast-Enhanced*. 224

DCE-MRI - *Dynamic Contrast-Enhanced Magnetic Resonance Imaging*. 220, 221

DGA - *Data Governance Act*. 40, 45

DL - *Deep Learning*. 218, 220–224, 226

DOI - *Diffusion Of Innovations*. 341, 343, 353–355

DP - *Data Points*. 116, 117

DPIA - *Data Protection Impact Assessment*. 37, 129, 143

DRE - *Digital Rectal Exam*. 189

DRG - *Diagnosis-Related Groups*. 94, 103

DSA - *Donor-Specific Antibodies*. 110, 122

DSS - *Decision Support Systems*. 129

DTN - *Door-To-Needle*. 242

E

EAU - *European Association of Urologists*. 192, 193

EC - *European Commission*. xxxi, xxxiv, 2, 317

ECG - *Electrocardiogram*. 235, 265

ED - *Emergency Department*. 233, 234, 240–244, 262–266, 268–270, 272, 273, 278, 279, 282, 287, 288, 371

EDPB - *European Data Protection Board*. 40–42, 44, 333

EHDS - *European Health Data Space*. 34, 40, 44, 45

EHR - *Electronic Health Record*. 103, 104, 116, 206, 208–210, 212, 213, 369

EMA - *European Medicines Agency*. 227, 259, 373

EMC - *Erasmus MC*. 165, 166, 169

EMR - *Electronic Medical Record*. 75, 88, 112, 123, 188, 189, 191, 233–235, 243, 263, 265, 266, 268–273, 278–280, 282, 285, 287, 288, 358, 370

EMS - *Emergency Medical Services*. 270, 271

EPE - *ExtraProstatic Extension*. 196

ER - *Emergency Room*. 206, 212, 213

ETZ - *Elisabeth-TweeSteden Hospital*. 264

EU - *European Union*. xxxvii, xlii, xliii, 1–3, 7, 13, 14, 31, 40, 46, 120, 128, 185, 227, 248, 313, 317, 318, 334–336, 358, 360, 364

F

F - *Fasting threshold*. 136

FCC - *Federal Communications Commission*. 239

FDA - *Food and Drug Administration*. 227, 259, 373

FHIR - *Fast Healthcare Interoperability Resources*. 112–115, 120, 122, 189

FN - *False Negatives*. 193

FP - *False Positive*. 193

G

GBRT - *Gradient Boosted Regression Trees*. 116, 117

GD - *Gradient Descent*. 167

GDM - *Gestational Diabetes Mellitus*. 89, 127–130, 133, 135–139, 325

GDP - *Gross Domestic Product*. 1, 3, 8, 333

GDPR - *General Data Protection and Regulation*. xxxii, xxxiii, 13, 14, 26, 31–37, 40–42, 74, 90, 111, 114, 121, 128, 129, 161, 163, 208, 218, 266, 282, 318, 333, 334, 338, 360, 362, 364, 365, 372

GGG - *Gleason Grade Group*. 189

GP - *General Practitioner*. 320, 321, 325, 327

GPS - *Global Positioning System*. 238, 264

GPU - *Graphic Processing Unit*. 218, 258, 338, 360

GUI - *Graphical User Interface*. 338, 339

H

HBM - *Health Belief Model*. 56, 341, 343, 344

HC - *Hospital-based Clinics*. 136, 137

HDFS - *Hadoop Distributed File System*. 96

HDL - *High-Density Lipoprotein*. 97

HIPAA - *Health Insurance Portability and Accountability Act*. 161

HIV - *Human Immunodeficiency Virus*. 163

HL7 - *Health Level 7*. 112, 114, 120, 122

HPRA - *Health Products Regulatory Authority*. 128

HRG - *Healthcare Resource Groups*. 94, 103

HTML - *HyperText Markup Language*. 267, 320

HUPHM - *Hospital Universitario Puerta de Hierro Majadahonda*. 206, 208

I

IADPSG - *International Association of Diabetes and Pregnancy Study Groups*. 127

IAT - *Intra-Arterial Thrombectomy*. 265, 266, 268–270

ICED - *Index of CoExisting Disease*. 93, 103

ICT - *Information and Communication Technology*. 3, 191, 232, 244

ID - *IDentifier*. 115, 208, 239, 241, 264, 266, 267

INR - *International Normalized Ratio*. 265

IoT - *Internet of Things*. 2, 5, 38, 309

IQR - *Inter-Quartile Range*. 135, 136

IR - *InfraRed*. 232, 238–241, 264, 266, 294, 295, 303, 309

IRB - *Institutional Review Boards*. 53, 58, 66, 68

ISO - *International Organization for Standardization*. 372

ISPM - *IntelliSpace Precision Medicine*. 186, 188, 189, 191, 197, 198, 200–202

IT - *Information Technology*. 8, 43, 81, 111, 139, 208, 233, 255, 258, 321, 325, 339, 360, 372

IV - *IntraVenous*. 265, 268, 282, 291

IVT - *IntraVenous Thrombolysis*. 265, 266, 268–270

K

KAR - *Karolinska University Hospital*. 186–189, 191, 192, 196–198

KarDa - *Kar Datalake*. 188, 189

KPI - *Key Performance Indicators*. 287, 288, 337, 339, 373, 374

KTR - *Kidney Transplant Recipients*. 109, 110, 116–118, 121–123

L

Lasso - *Least Absolute Shrinkage and Selection Operator*. 167

LC - *Lung Cancer*. 205–209, 211–213

LDL - *Low-Density Lipoprotein*. 97

LNI - *Lymph Node Involvement*. 190–196

LOINC - *Logical Observation Identifier Names and Codes*. 120, 368

M

MDT - *MultiDisciplinary Team*. 182, 183, 186, 187, 189, 193, 197–203

MeSH - *Medical Subject Headings*. 208

MG - *MammoGraphy imaging*. 220–224, 227

MIMIC-III - *Medical Information Mart for Intensive Care*. 120

ML - *Machine Learning*. 218, 219, 226

MPC - *Multi-Party Computation*. 162, 163, 168, 170, 174, 363, 364, 366, 372

mpMRI - *multiparametric Magnetic Resonance Imaging*. 224

MR - *Magnetic Resonance*. 248

mRCC - *metastatic Renal Cell Carcinoma*. 227

MRI - *Magnetic Resonance Imaging*. 182, 189, 193, 221–225, 227, 241, 248, 367, 369

N

NAC - *NeoAdjuvant Chemotherapy*. 182, 217–219, 222, 223, 226

NAFLD - *NonAlcoholic Fatty Liver Disease*. 97

NASSS - *Non-adoption, Abandonment, Scale-up, Spread, Sustainability*. 347, 352, 354, 355, 368

NEU - *NEUrology*. 265

NHS - *National Health Service*. 142, 143, 150, 343, 372

NICU - *Neonatal Intensive Care Unit*. 127, 135–137

NIHSS - *National Institutes of Health Stroke Scale quantifies stroke severity based on weighted evaluation findings*. 265

NIS - *National (Nationwide) Inpatient Sample*. 278

NLP - *Natural Language Processing*. 184, 196, 201, 202, 209, 210, 319, 335, 369

NPCR - *National Prostate Cancer Register*. 189

NPT - *Normalisation Process Theory*. 354, 355, 368

O

OBO - *Open Biological and Biomedical Ontology*. 208, 209

OECD - *Organization for Economic Co-operation and Development*. 1, 8, 334

OGTT - *Oral Glucose Tolerance Test*. 135

OLVG - *Onze Lieve Vrouwe Gasthuis*. 235, 292–294, 296, 299, 306

OMOP - *Observational Medical Outcomes Partnership*. 373

OR - *Operating Room*. 241, 264, 265

OVD - *Operative Vaginal Delivery*. 136

P

PACS - *Patient Related Outcome Measurements*. 250, 251, 253, 255

PCR - *Polymerase Chain Reaction*. 118

pCR - *pathologic Complete Response*. 218–222, 226

PET - *Privacy-Enhancing Technologies*. 363

pGGG - *pathologic Gleason Grade Group*. 190

PI-RADS - *Prostate Imaging Reporting And Data System*. 189, 193, 195, 196

PLND - *Pelvic Lymph Node Dissection*. 190, 192, 193

PMC - *PubMed Central*. 208, 209

pN - *pathologic lymph Node involvement*. 190

PoC - *Point of Care, bedside laboratory analysis*. 265

PP - *PostPrandial threshold*. 136

PPIE - *Patient and Public Involvement and Engagement*. 344, 354, 368

PR - *Precision/Recall*. 120

PR - *Pulmonary Rehabilitation*. 142

PROM - *Picture Archiving and Communication System*. 120

PROMS - *Patient Reported Outcome Measures*. 368

PSA - *Prostate-Specific Antigen*. 188, 189, 193

PSM - *Post-Surgical tumour-positive resection Margins*. 197

pT - *pathologic T stage*. 190

Q

qSOFA - *quick SOFA*. 279

R

RAD - *RAdiology Department*. 241

RCT - *Randomized Controlled Trial*. 122

REC - *Research Ethics Committees*. 53, 58, 66, 68

REST API - *Representational State Transfer Application Programming Interface*. 96, 212

RF - *Radio-Frequency*. 232, 238, 239, 241, 264, 266, 280, 294, 309

RN - *Registered Nurse*. 268, 269

ROC - *Receiver Operating Characteristic*. 119, 120, 135, 148, 193, 219, 223

ROI - *Region Of Interest*. 249–253

RPM - *Remote Patient Monitoring*. 342

RTLS - *Real-Time Location System*. 232–241, 243, 244, 263, 264, 266, 268–273, 278–280, 282, 285, 288, 292–297, 299, 301–309, 371

S

SCU - *Stroke Care Unit*. 265

SD - *Standard Deviation*. 283, 284, 287

SHAP - *SHapley Additive exPlanations*. 224, 225, 227

SJR - *Scimago Journal Rank*. 370

SM - *Surgical resection Margin*. 190

SNOMED CT - *Systematized NOmenclature of MEDicine Clinical Terms*. 120, 368

SOFA - *Sequential Organ Failure Assessment*. 277

SPARQL - *SPARQL Protocol And RDF Query Language*. 210

SQL - *Structured Query Language*. 188, 267

T

TAD - *Diastolic Arterial Pressure*. 97

TAM - *Technology Acceptance Model*. 341, 343, 355

TAS - *Systolic Arterial Pressure*. 97

TN - *True Negatives*. 193

TNM - *Tumour, Node, Metastasis*. 209

TNO - *The Netherlands Organization for Applied Scientific Research*. 90, 162, 175

TP - *True Positive*. 193

tPA - *tissue Plasminogen Activator*. 242

TRE - *Trusted Research Environment* . 365

TRL - *Technology Readiness Level*. 372

U

UCSF - *University of California at San Francisco*. 226

UK - *United Kingdom*. 53, 56, 72, 79, 81, 127, 143, 152, 153, 343, 344, 365

UMAP - *Uniform Manifold Approximation and Projection*. 103

UMLS - *Unified Medical Language System*. 206, 209

US - *United States*. 72

UTAUT - *Unified Theory of Acceptance and Use of Technology*. 341, 343, 355

UWB - *Ultra-WideBand*. 238

UX - *User Experience*. 122

V

VC - *Virtual Clinics*. 136, 137

VPN - *Virtual Private Network*. 116

W

WHO - *World Health Organization*. xlii, 181

Wi-Fi - *Wireless Fidelity*. 238, 240, 294, 309, 371

DOI: 10.1561/9781638282372.ch1

Chapter 1

Introduction

By Supriyo Chatterjea

1.1 Background

Healthcare systems around the world are grappling with major challenges such as the growing prevalence of chronic diseases, rising healthcare costs, and a shortage of healthcare workers. Chronic diseases account for 80% of the European Union (EU) healthcare budget of €700 billion, leading to a significant economic impact [1]. Absence due to illness results in a loss of €240 billion in productivity in the EU, equivalent to 2% of gross domestic product (GDP). Without action, the Organization for Economic Co-operation and Development (OECD) has estimated that the average public spending on healthcare costs will increase to 10% of GDP [1].

The shortage of healthcare workers has been a long-standing issue in Europe, even before the COVID-19 pandemic. The overall shortfall of healthcare workers was estimated to be 1.6 million in 2013 [2]. Such shortages have resulted in longer waiting times for patients, increased workload and stress for healthcare workers, and a lower quality of care for patients [3].

It is clear that the healthcare sector needs to undergo radical changes to ensure that future generations have easy access to quality care that is also affordable. One way to achieve this is by leveraging the increasing use of digitization in the sector. According to the World Economic Forum, hospitals produce 50 petabytes of data every year [4]. The question then is how can we leverage the insights that lie within this vast amount of data to transform the healthcare sector and address its most pressing issues, namely cost, quality, and accessibility of care?

This book captures the learnings from the BigMedilytics project, funded by the EC from 2018 to 2021. The project aimed to transform Europe's healthcare sector by using state-of-the-art big data technologies to achieve breakthrough productivity in the sector by reducing cost, improving patient outcomes, and delivering better access to healthcare facilities, covering the entire healthcare continuum – from prevention to diagnosis, treatment, and home care throughout Europe. The €15 million project executed 12 real-life, hospital-related big data pilots across three different themes: (1) population health and chronic disease management, (2) oncology, and (3) industrialization of healthcare (which focused on improving the efficiency of hospitals by optimizing various hospital-related workflows). The pilots spanned eight European countries, the health data of 11 million patients, involved 35 consortium partners, and incorporated diverse data sets originating from the public health sector, insurance companies, Internet of Things (IoT) devices, pharmaceutical industry, and public data sets.

While the BigMedilytics project used advanced data analytics techniques such as machine learning, deep learning, and natural language processing to analyze large amounts of healthcare data, including electronic health records, medical imaging data, and genomic data, what sets it apart is its multi-disciplinary approach. A key learning from the project was that successfully implementing Big Data and AI-driven solutions in a healthcare setting requires a multi-disciplinary approach that focuses not only on developing state-of-the-art technologies but also on a multitude of other aspects such as ethics, privacy, public policy, business models, the experience of care personnel, and, of course, the patient and their family. It is this holistic approach that is critical to breaking down the barriers of the iron triangle (quality, access, and costs) of healthcare and ensuring that big data solutions can scale effectively across different health systems and countries [5].

1.2 BigMedilytics Project Overview

BigMedilytics (Big Data for Medical Analytics) is the largest EU-funded initiative to transform the region's healthcare sector by using state-of-the-art big data technologies to achieve breakthrough productivity in the sector by reducing cost, improving patient outcomes, and delivering better access to healthcare facilities simultaneously.

There are three main reasons to apply big data technologies in healthcare:

- An improvement in health leads to economic growth through long-term gains in human and physical capital, which ultimately raise productivity and per capita GDP.
- In 2019, on average, healthcare accounted for 8.3% of the EU's GDP over all countries. It is continuously becoming more expensive due to a rapidly aging population, rising prevalence of chronic diseases, and costly developments in medical technology. In fact, compared to 2014, the EU-28's total healthcare expenditure is expected to increase to 30% by 2060. This is clearly not sustainable.
- As healthcare is traditionally very conservative when adopting ICT, while big healthcare data is becoming available, the expected impact of applying big data technologies in healthcare is enormous.

The expected increase in healthcare expenditure results in the need to improve the sustainability of current health system models. The effectiveness of a healthcare system depends on quality (determined by efficacy, value, and outcome), access (who can receive care when needed), and cost (the actual expense of patient care) (Figure 1.1).

To improve the productivity of the healthcare sector, it is necessary to reduce costs while maintaining or improving the quality of care provided. The fastest, least costly, and most effective way to achieve this is to use the knowledge that is hiding within the already existing large amounts of generated medical data, currently estimated at around 3 zettabyte. The current trend is toward the digitalization of these large amounts of data, resulting in what is known as big data.

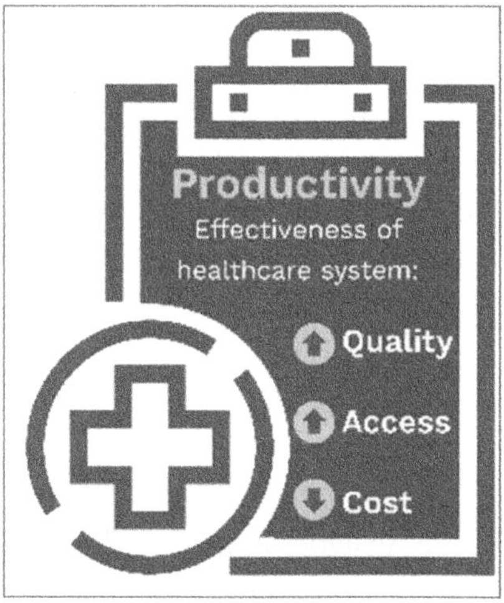

Figure 1.1. Effectiveness of healthcare systems (iron triangle).

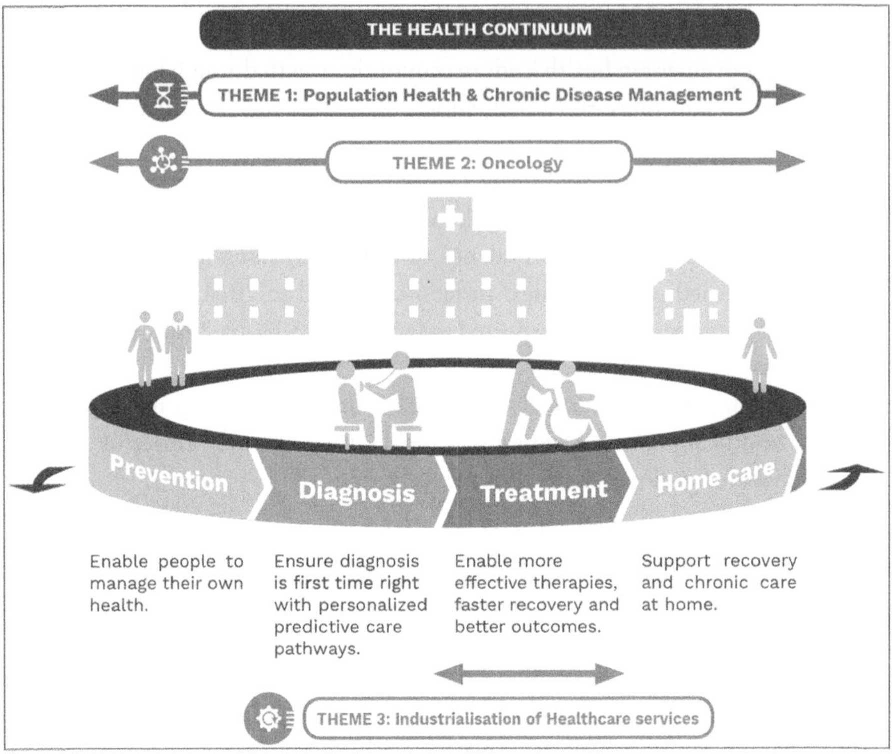

Figure 1.2. The three BigMedilytics themes.

1.2.1 Overview

The BigMedilytics project addressed three themes with the greatest impact on the sector: population health and chronic disease management (described in section II of this book), oncology (described in section III of this book), and industrialization of healthcare services (described in section IV of this book), and deals with the entire healthcare continuum from prevention to diagnosis, treatment, and home care (Figure 1.2). These themes contained separate pilots (called studies in this book). In total, the project was composed of 12 pilots (Figure 1.3). Each pilot was led by a BigMedilytics participant, and other participants took part in the execution of the studies (Table 1.1).

1.2.2 BigMedilytics Deliverables

The BigMedilytics project aimed to deliver the following:

- A Big Data Healthcare Analytics Blueprint (defining platforms and components) based on open Big Data technologies that enable secure collaborative innovation.

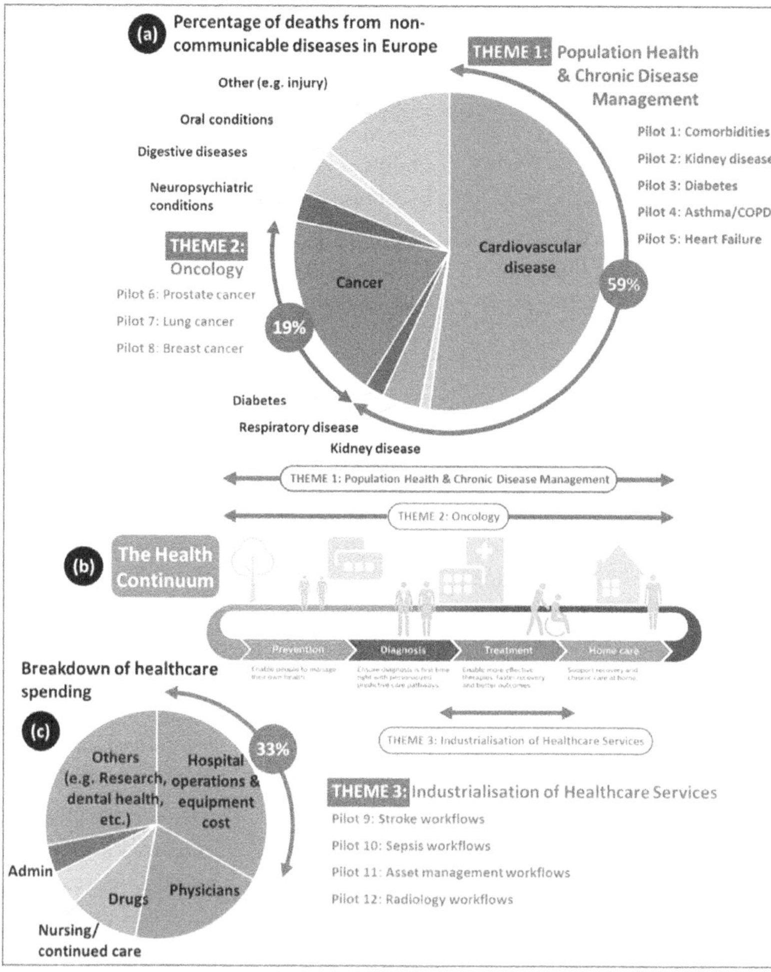

Figure 1.3. The 12 pilots (studies) in the BigMedilytics project.

- Instantiations of the Blueprint are used to replicate BigMedilytics concepts across the 12 large-scale studies, accounting for an estimated 86% of deaths and 77% of the disease burden in Europe.
- The Best "Big Data technology and Healthcare policy" practices take into account aspects related to Big Data technologies, new business models, and European and national healthcare data policies and regulations.

1.2.3 Characteristics of Datasets Used

BigMedilytics used the health records of more than 11 million patients across eight countries in Europe, streaming data from IoT-connected devices at more than a million records per hour and patient-generated data from mobile apps. It also

Table 1.1. BigMedilytics pilot linked to book chapters.

Pilot	Topic	Leader	Participants	Chapter
1	Comorbidities	Incliva	Atos, ITI, OptiMedis, Philips, TU Eindhoven	Chapter 8 (Effects of comorbidities (chronic illness) on hospitalization and mortality risks)
2	Kidney disease	Charité Hospital	AOK, DFKI, HPI, Universitätsmedizin Essen	Chapter 9 (eHealth and telemedicine for risk prediction and monitoring in kidney transplantation recipients)
3	Diabetes	Huawei	Nissatech, Rotunda hospital	Chapter 10 (Remote monitoring to improve gestational diabetes care)
4	COPD/ Asthma	University of Southampton	AstraZeneca, my mHealth	Chapter 11 (Monitoring wellness in chronic obstructive pulmonary disease using the myCOPD app)
5	Heart failure	Erasmus MC	Achmea, TNO	Chapter 12 (Privacy-preserving techniques for analysis of medical data)
6	Prostate cancer	Karolinska	Philips	Chapter 14 (Usability of enhanced decision support and predictive modeling in prostate cancer)
7	Lung cancer	Demokritos	ATC, Politécnica, Hospital Universitario Puerta de Hierro Majadahonda, Leibniz Universität Hannover	Chapter 15 (Monitoring and decision support in treatment modalities for lung cancer)
8	Breast cancer	IBM	InstitutCurie, VTT	Chapter 16 (Artificial Intelligence to support chooses in neoadjuvant chemotherapy in breast cancer patients)

(Continued)

Table 1.1. Continued

Pilot	Topic	Leader	Participants	Chapter
9	Stoke management	ETZ	Politécnica, Philips, TU Eindhoven	Chapter 20 (Innovative use of technology for acute care pathway monitoring and improvements)
10	Sepsis management	Incliva	Politécnica, ETZ, Philips, TU Eindhoven	Chapter 21 (Monitoring sepsis patients in the emergency department)
11	Asset management	Philips	OLVG, TU Eindhoven	Chapter 22 (Technological support for paramedical asset management in a hospital setting)
12	Radiology workflows	Contextflow	Atos, Hospital Universitario Puerta de Hierro Majadahonda, Medizinische Universitat Wien	Chapter 19 (Implementation and impact of AI for the interpretation of lung diseases in chest CTs)

ensured that the security and privacy of personal data were guaranteed and managed within national and EU regulatory frameworks.

The BigMedilytics project was an initiative that originated from the Big Data Value Association with the intention to implement a part of the program related to the large-scale projects. The project was formed by a consortium of 35 entities led by Philips.

1.2.4 Objectives

The BigMedilytics project had seven objectives:

Objective 1: Improve chronic disease and cancer outcomes using big data
Objective 2: Optimize workflows through industrializing healthcare services using big data
Objective 3: Guarantee the replicability of big data concepts for healthcare
Objective 4: Increase the activity through data integration
Objective 5: Establish secure and privacy-preserving cross-border and cross-organization healthcare services, thus strengthening the EU's Digital Market Strategy
Objective 6: Define Best "Big Data" practices
Objective 7: Enable knowledge transfer

1.2.5 Impact

BigMedilytics aimed to have a transformational impact on the healthcare sector by ensuring that big data technologies will be routinely used throughout the healthcare sector in delivering high-quality care while reducing costs. In this sense, the project aimed to:

- Demonstrate an increase in healthcare productivity between 20% and 63% across the 12 studies covering the most prevalent and expensive disease groups across Europe. Evidence suggests that by improving the productivity of the healthcare system, public spending savings would be large, approaching 2% of GDP on average in the OECD, which would be equivalent to €330 billion in Europe based on GDP figures for 2014.
- Enable collaborative innovation across the key players in the healthcare and data value chains.
- Increase in the market share of big data technology providers by at least 25% in the oncology, cardiology, radiology, hospitals logistics, and healthcare IT security market segments.
- Create a lasting impact of big data in the healthcare sector, even after project completion, due to the investment of €78 million by the consortium.
- Contribute to 40–70 times reduction in carbon emissions due to the usage of telehealth driven by big data technologies, thus contributing to Europe's 2020 emission targets.
- Be instrumental in training Europe's next generation of healthcare data innovators.

1.3 Structure of the Book

The goal of this book is "translational", from project to application. There are five major sections (Sections I–V).

Section I contains cross-project themes, including policy (Chapter 3: using causal diagrams to understand and deal with hindering patterns in the uptake and embedding of big data technology), privacy and legal (Chapter 4: lessons learned in the application of the General Data Protection Regulation to the BigMedilytics project), ethics (Chapter 5: ethics: a checklist for investigators, ethics boards and reviewers), and platform businesses (Chapter 6: health platform businesses – from investigations to platforms).

In Section II, five studies (Pilots 1–5) in the population heath domain are presented: comorbidities (Chapter 8: effects of comorbidities (chronic illness) on hospitalization and mortality risks), kidney disease (Chapter 9: eHealth and telemedicine for risk prediction and monitoring in kidney transplantation recipients), diabetes (Chapter 10: remote monitoring to improve gestational diabetes care), COPD/asthma (Chapter 11: monitoring wellness in chronic obstructive pulmonary disease using the myCOPD app), and heart failure (Chapter 12: privacy-preserving techniques for analysis of medical data).

Section III elaborates on three studies (Pilots 6–8) in the oncology domain: prostate cancer (Chapter 14: usability of enhanced decision support and predictive modeling in prostate cancer), lung cancer (Chapter 15: monitoring and decision support in treatment modalities for lung cancer), and breast cancer (Chapter 16: artificial Intelligence to support chooses in neoadjuvant chemotherapy in breast cancer patients).

Industrialization of healthcare is the common topic of the studies (Pilots 9–12) in Section IV. This section contains chapters about stroke management (Chapter 20: innovative use of technology for acute care pathway monitoring and improvements), sepsis management (Chapter 21: monitoring sepsis patients in the emergency department), asset management (Chapter 22: technological support for paramedical asset management in a hospital setting), and radiology workflows (Chapter 19: implementation and impact of AI for the interpretation of lung diseases in chest CTs).

Section V elaborates on the BigMedilytics project itself and its learnings: the BML website (Chapter 24: the interactive BigMedilytics website), the blueprint (Chapter 25: data processing in healthcare using CRISP), technology acceptance (Chapter 26: technology acceptance in healthcare), and the general learnings (Chapter 27: general learnings from the Horizon 2020 project BigMedilytics).

1.4 Conclusion

The authors hope that those rolling out big data/AI solutions in hospitals or health systems can benefit from the learnings captured in this book and also embark on the multi-disciplinary approach that we have both pursued and benefited from, thus scaling such solutions across a variety of health systems and countries.

References

[1] POLITICO (2017) Tackling the tough problem of European health care sustainability. Available at: https://www.politico.eu/sponsored-content/tackling-the-tough-problem-of-european-health-care-sustainability/.

[2] Michel, J-P., and Ecarnot, F. (2020) The shortage of skilled workers in Europe: its impact on geriatric medicine. Eur Geriatr Med. 11(3): 345–347. https://doi.org/10.1007/s41999-020-00323-0.

[3] The World Health Organisation (2022) Ticking timebomb: Without immediate action, health and care workforce gaps in the European Region could spell disaster. Available at: https://www.who.int/europe/news/item/14-09-2022-ticking-timebomb--without-immediate-action--health-and-care-workforce-gaps-in-the-european-region-could-spell-disaster.

[4] Global Health (2019) 4 ways data is improving healthcare. Available at: https://www.weforum.org/agenda/2019/12/four-ways-data-is-improving-healthcare/.

[5] Kissick WL. Medicine's dilemmas: infinite needs versus finite resources. London, UK: Yale University Press. 1994.

Section I

Policy, Ethics, Privacy, Legal

DOI: 10.1561/9781638282372.ch2

Chapter 2

Introduction Section I: Setting the Scene for Collaborative Healthcare Research

By Brian Pickering

The BigMedilytics project was ambitious right from the start. With 35 partners across European Union (EU) Member States and beyond, including clinicians, data scientists, technologists, and social scientists, as well as commercial enterprises, the logistics of coordinating the project alone were a significant challenge. But we need to step back at this point. The project did not only depend on successful cross-disciplinary communication between experts in their own fields; this was healthcare, involving vast amounts of special-category personal data shared across organizations and borders. The regulatory landscape alone required careful navigation at a time when the General Data Protection Regulation (GDPR) was still relatively new, increasing the sensitivity of healthcare providers and researchers still trying to understand how to identify and mitigate risks within their control.

Against such a backdrop, the four chapters in this section provide insights to support all future collaborations of this type, no matter how complex. Based on an extensive set of interviews and observational work, Chapter 3: Using causal models to understand and deal with hindering patterns in the uptake and embedding of big data technology introduces a well-known technique from the social sciences (causal modeling) to encapsulate and make sense of the collaboration experiences of the various project stakeholders in attempting to navigate not only regulatory constraints – avoiding the trap of overly cautious elephant paths – but also to see the ambitious nature of such complex projects realized. The authors identified three causal models, including the Information Road, the Golden Mountain, and the Swamp of Rules, in each case summarizing the main recommendations for targeting the introduction of complex and advanced technologies into an established field (healthcare) where the stakes are high, especially for public trust. While these recommendations provide practical pointers in support of the successful completion of complex projects of this nature, reflection on the causal models themselves provides a valuable technique for all project managers and project teams.

The third causal model, the Swamp of Rules, recognizes the challenges of multidisciplinary collaboration across domains, involving different sets of regulatory constraints. At the same time that researchers in all relevant disciplines were waking up to the potential of big data for healthcare, the GDPR brought in increased nervousness about exploiting that potential. How could researchers get the most out of the data routinely collected as part of existing care pathways in such a risk-averse environment? Taking an explicitly pragmatic approach to support the ambitious nature of the project, Chapter 4: Lessons learned in the application of the General Data Protection Regulation to the BigMedilytics project signposts stakeholders through the complexity of relevant regulation. Indeed, responding to the call for "experts in privacy, security, safety, ethics, and law on the team [to] advise health care professionals and data scientists how they can comply with different rules" from Chapter 3, Chapter 4 is not about 'no, you can't' because of regulation, but rather 'this is how you can do it'. Furthermore, based on the real-life objectives and results of the BigMedilytics, it takes us from existing regulation forward toward the regulatory frameworks proposed by the EU.

Chapter 4 finishes with a set of recommendations for an appropriate governance model akin to the proposals in the academic literature for Trusted Research Environments. Chapter 5 Ethics: A checklist for investigators, ethics boards, and reviewers picks up on the recommendation to appoint an ethics committee and explores the consent fallacy in Chapter 4 within the context of academic research. Interrogating empirical data from three surveys (two within BigMedilytics and a third from a subsequent project) against the background of research ethics, this chapter suggests 12 points that a Research Ethics Committee (or Institutional Research Board) should consider when evaluating research proposals from Big Data and advanced technologies such as machine learning based on such data. Contextualizing these 12 points against existing trust relationships between patient and clinician on the one hand and participant and researcher on the other, the chapter shifts research consent away from "fully informed" decision-making on the part of the patient/research participant toward an ongoing trust-based negotiation between the main parties.

The final chapter, Chapter 6: Healthcare platforms businesses – From investigations to platforms, returns to the enterprise focus of the project to provide a synthesis of competing requirements in support of the commercialization of healthcare service provision. For the results of projects like BigMedilytics to be converted into successful healthcare delivery, there is a need to establish suitable business models and delivery contexts, while respecting governance. So, although the main focus of the studies in Sections II to IV was to demonstrate the potential of Big Data in healthcare, from diagnosis, treatment, and self-management to efficient operational delivery, there is a significant need to reap the rewards of those studies. Chapter 6 begins by describing what platform business models entail, including well-known examples from different industries such as Uber, eBay, and Zoom. It then asks if and how such models might apply if the findings of the individual studies are to be exploited in maximizing benefit within healthcare. It picks up on issues such as the core interactions that both Chapter 3 and, to some extent, Chapter 5 present for projects and research, respectively, the governance challenges explained in Chapter 4, and then shows the path to successful commercialization while appreciating the challenges of the domain. As such, Chapter 6 effectively offers a demonstration of meeting the quadruple aims of healthcare – containing costs, improving healthcare outcomes, supporting productivity, and respecting patient expectations – based on tried and tested practice in other enterprise domains.

Section I, therefore, brings together some of the learnings from BigMedilytics to benefit all stakeholders across healthcare. Each of the chapters answers one or more of the implicit challenges of those trying to navigate their way through complex research and innovation in an area often fraught with constraints but which affects us all individually. While the COVID-19 pandemic highlighted all these aspects – collaboration across multiple disciplines, the pragmatic interpretation and compliance with regulation, meeting private citizen expectations around research, and the sustainable commercialization of service delivery – the chapters here provide evidence-based answers to fellow researchers and innovators for them to build on and take these findings forward to improve all aspects of healthcare.

DOI: 10.1561/9781638282372.ch3

Chapter 3

Using Causal Diagrams to Understand and Deal with Hindering Patterns in the Uptake and Embedding of Big Data Technology

By Anne Marie Weggelaar-Jansen, Sandra Sülz and Rik Wehrens

3.1 Introduction

In this chapter, we explain the interdependencies between actors and factors that influence the uptake of big data technology and provide more insights into the adoption and spread of big data technologies [1]. The systematic literature review by Günther *et al.* revealed that to advance our understanding of big data technology, [2] research should move beyond BigMedilytics (BML) study levels and examine how work practices, organizational models, and stakeholder interests interact with big data technology practices. In the BML project, we had a unique opportunity to review 12 study projects using different big data technologies aimed at different goals in several European countries. The studies:

> *cover three themes with the greatest impact on the sector. Population Health & Chronic Disease Management and Oncology comprise the 78% of deaths [in non-communicable] diseases. The third theme represents operations and equipment cost, covering the 33% of the expenditure in the sector.*[i]

---

i. BigMedilytics on: https://www.bigmedilytics.eu/ Accessed on August 29th, 2022.

Where possible, we captured interactions during the development of concrete BML studies, the organizations in which they took place, and the healthcare systems to which the organizations belong.

Our study contributes in two ways to gain more insights in the uptake of big data technology. First, we outline what policymakers should consider when developing public policy for big data in healthcare. Second, we give directions to management and healthcare professionals aiming to use big data technologies for the benefit of their patients and efficient processes.

The study presented here involved three single, yet aligned, multidisciplinary studies. The overarching aim was to examine how stakeholders in the 12 BML study projects worked on the performance, embedding, legitimation, and value creation of their big data application [3]. We include three broad categories: normative barriers (including cultural and ethical norms), market failures, and technocratic barriers (related to technological issues and government processes and regulations) [4].

First, we studied governance approaches, regulatory challenges, ethical dilemmas, and societal debates about big data technology. We conducted 145 semi-structured interviews in eight European countries: Austria, France, Germany, Ireland, the Netherlands, Spain, Sweden, and the United Kingdom. Respondents were identified via desk research and via our partners in BML. Respondents were: (1) healthcare professionals and management involved in big data studies; (2) ethical and legal experts knowledgeable about the key discussions in their country; (3) technology developers and data scientists; (4) representatives of patient and professional associations; (5) visible actors in the public debate to capture public perspectives on big data; and (6) policymakers and additional policy experts. Interview data were triangulated with policy documents, news articles, scientific papers, presentations, and gray literature provided by the respondents and a supplementary analysis of online documents. All interview transcripts and documents were analyzed abductively by qualitatively (open, thematic, and axial) coding [5].

Second, we monitored the performance of big data technology value over time with BML study-specific key performance indicators. For each BML study, workshops were organized to select relevant indicators and tailor these to the specific patient cohort, big data technology, and the aim of the BML studies. In these workshops, study team members and researchers developed the indicators based on an adopted version of the Balance Business Score Card to reflect the multidimensionality of performance: patient satisfaction [6], process outcomes, patient outcomes, and financial outcomes. Next, for most of the studies, a baseline measurement taken in the period before the implementation of the big data technology was followed by 6-monthly measurements during and after the implementation of the big data technology. The data collected were displayed on a digital dashboard available to all project team members.

Third, we studied via interviews on the dynamic processes involved in embedding big data technology in the daily work practices of healthcare professionals, organizations, and sometimes even societies. We developed insights into the underlying mechanisms, including how big data applications do or do not become embedded in organizational routines. Based on insights from normalization process theory [7], we include the different actor dimensions: (1) sense-making work: interpretations of what technology can add to work processes; (2) relational work: efforts in building a community of practice around the application; (3) operational work: the work involved in establishing new task divisions; and (4) appraisal work: formal and informal assessments conducted to assess the value [8].

During the BML project, we collected data on three levels: macro (as described before, e.g., ethical and legal experts, representatives of patient and professional associations, policymakers, policy experts, and public opinion makers), meso (organizational), and micro (professional interactions) levels. We included 'hard' data on structures, strategies, and procedures, and 'soft' data regarding stories, conflicts, and values as these point toward underlying patterns about 'the way things are'. The latter were collected through in-depth interviews with project members and stakeholders on both national and European levels as well as regular feedback moments with key actors in the BML project. Additionally, we conducted observations during general assemblies and study project meetings, and collected relevant policy and information documents.

After two and a half years, based on a thorough understanding of our data, we distilled a list of relevant factors and actors that influenced each other. Next, we drafted diagrams showing the interdependencies and patterns between actors and factors. Using arrows and loops in the causal models, we visualized patterns and identified underlying dynamics. These initial visualizations represent causal models (see Section 3.2) that were validated and improved in five workshops involving key actor groups: clinicians, technicians and data scientists, vendors, managers, policymakers, and funders. The draft models were adjusted and refined based on feedback and insights gathered in the workshops.

3.2 Findings

We present the three most important mechanisms for the uptake and embedding of big data technologies derived from our studies. We used causal modeling to synthesize our findings on the interpretations of our respondents on the uptake of big data technologies. This is especially relevant as causal models not only depict the actors and factors reinforcing patterns, but also focus on identifying leverage points where intervention is possible.

Causal models[ii] derive from a tradition of systems thinking in organizational studies, which focuses on examining the interdependencies between parts to understand the whole dynamic, interconnected system. Causal models are a powerful tool to deal with organizational change issues characterized by content complexity (the multidimensional and ambiguous character of organizational problems) and process complexity (the large number of people involved in the organizational problem, all with different viewpoints and interests) [3]. A typical characteristic of causal models is discerning feedback mechanisms (both positive and negative). These important mechanisms help to explain why some organizational issues tend to persist, despite many efforts to address them. These mechanisms are often invisible, as causes can be subtle and far removed from the consequences, often producing delayed effects [9].

In the following paragraphs, we present three causal models – The Information Road, The Golden Mountain, and The Swamp of Rules – which encapsulate the result of our interviews and engagement with the BML study projects. In each case, we provide a description of the particular causal model and summarize a set of recommendations for relevant stakeholders.

3.2.1 The Information Road

Measuring the impact of big data innovations is equivalent to identifying and quantifying the causal effect. We want to be able to quantify how much the quality of care (or other performance dimensions) would differ if a big data innovation had not been present compared with if it were present. This requires a clear understanding of the mechanisms of cause and effect. Without that understanding, we can still measure various indicators for monitoring or learning purposes, but we cannot attribute a causal meaning to the measurements.

How can big data impact healthcare? The central claim is that deploying big data does not improve healthcare directly. But big data innovations can help contribute by changing the information upon which decisions are made. This translates into a sequence of cause-and-effect relations, outlined in the conceptual model in Figure 3.1. We subsequently zoom in to the various cause and effect relations depicted in the model: we face a dynamic environment in which data are generated continuously. Mobile apps record our physical activities, smart devices keep track of our lifestyle, and eHealth technology increasingly monitors clinical alarms. Facilitated by technology, this continuous data-generating process is coupled with a growing belief that combining and analyzing that data can improve decision-making. For

ii. See for an explanation of this methodology: https://www.youtube.com/watch?v=cH4ybsGN2lA&t=375s.

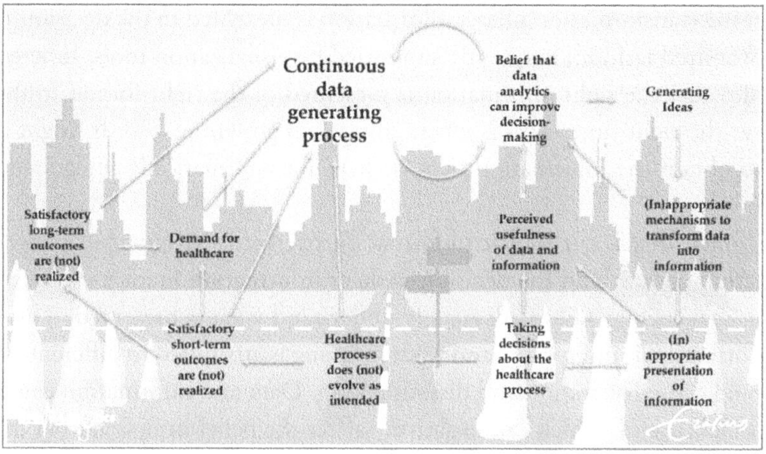

Figure 3.1. Causal model of how to measure the impact of big data technology.

instance, data-driven prediction models can alert to the potential deterioration in a patient's condition. These prediction models are expected to help clinicians to decide whether and when to intervene. Notably, the data-generating process and the belief in data analytics go hand in hand and reinforce each other. An increase in data availability leads to a stronger belief that there is something useful in the amount of data. And at the same time, the more the belief is verbalized, communicated, and debated, the more new data are generated. With an ever-increasing amount of data and technology, data scientists and healthcare practitioners generate new ideas on how data technology can help to improve decision-making. For instance, one of the BML teams was wondering whether the integration of real-time weather data can actually improve the accuracy of the prediction models. Data scientists and healthcare practitioners are jointly exploring how these ideas can be developed further and implemented in routine care.

The ideas that are generated affect the transformation process from data to information. To transform data into information, mechanisms and algorithms are in place to extract and pool relevant data. Inherent here is the idea that adequate mechanisms and algorithms are deployed that extract the right data from the right place at the right point in time and are provided to the right person at the right time in the right format/visualization.

This requires effort and a lot of unseen work such as 'cleaning' and correctly annotating data that can be used to develop algorithms. Importantly, the data transformation phase is not free from errors since integrating data can introduce bias if any data are incomplete or inaccurate. For instance, sometimes synthetic data are generated for testing a model or demonstration purposes, and this needs to be filtered out during the analytics. Such efforts affect the belief in big data technologies and can either reinforce or diminish that belief.

After the transformation phase, information is presented to the decision-makers in a customized fashion, frequently supported by visualization tools. Inherent here is the idea that the right information is presented in the right format to the right person at the right time. This is where things can go wrong, too. It might require effort to obtain the information because it is not automatically integrated in the workflow.

Too much detail can lead to information overload. Mismatches between the information context and the decision-maker's information literacy can occur, and decision-makers may fail to adequately understand what is presented. This affects how information is interpreted and what meaning is attributed to different options. This could cause frustration and dissatisfaction. Data and information can be perceived as less useful, which can negatively affect the belief in how far big data and data analytics can improve decision-making.

The way information is interpreted affects the decision-making process and which decisions are taken. Prediction models, for instance, have fuzzy decision points. Patients are more or less likely to respond to chemotherapy, and for some patients, this is not a clear-cut decision. Clinicians and patients might respond differently to the uncertainty in the information, which might cause differing decisions about the patient's health trajectory.

Once decisions are taken, health processes may not go as intended. The patient's condition might deteriorate unexpectedly during treatment, making ad hoc adjustments necessary. Or other exogenous challenges like the COVID-19 pandemic can cause disruptions and force rearrangements in health service processes. For instance, during the pandemic, in-house consultations had to be postponed or replaced by remote consultations, which affected the cost-of-service delivery. But was this change in cost attributable to the big data technologies or rather a consequence of the COVID-19 pandemic?

The way the health trajectory evolves affects how far we can achieve satisfactory short-term outcomes such as a reduction in hospitalizations. It also affects the data that are gathered at this stage. And it affects whether new demand for healthcare is generated if, for instance, patients are readmitted to the hospital. Therefore, whether satisfactory long-term outcomes are achieved and what type of new healthcare demand and data are generated all depend on a sequence of decisions and exogenous factors. Mortality, for instance, is affected not only by how well an algorithm supports clinical decision-making but also by the patient's underlying health condition. The extent to which changes in long-term outcomes can causally be attributed to big data, therefore, depends on how rigorously we can establish the counterfactual scenario of what might have happened if the big data innovation had not been developed and implemented. Also, the rigor and relevance of the data provided to the data scientists are influencing this.

In sum, the most important lesson learned:

- Data scientists and healthcare professionals need to define together feasible, acceptable, measurable, and informative indicators.

If data scientists and healthcare professionals intend to measure patient satisfaction, professional satisfaction, costs, and population health, the time period needs to be sufficiently long to track these in a proper way.[iii]

3.2.2 The Golden Mountain

This causal model explains how the innovative nature of big data fosters several processes that undermine the uptake of big data.

Due to the innovative nature of big data technology in the healthcare sector, healthcare reimbursement systems do not cover the entire data chain. This chain starts with data collection, combining various data sets, goes on to data storage, analysis, and developing an algorithm all the way through until the algorithm is eventually used for the benefit of the patient, professional, or organization. Given that there are no financial systems in place for big data technology, if you want to develop or apply an algorithm, you would need a grant to fund your work on, for example, developing a machine-learning-based decision-support system in precision medicine or preventive healthcare or a deep-learning-based algorithm for care prediction or real-time alerts. Alternatively, you might start a research project without additional funding.

Healthcare professionals and data scientists need to work together to write the grant application or start the research. To receive a grant, the proposal must contain specific, measurable goals expressed in tangible, appealing deliverables. The tendency is to have ambitiously high hopes for what will be developed, and this might lead to overpromising. This applies especially to big data technologies: what will be developed and how they will affect healthcare are promises, which can be seen as the "golden mountain" we all strive toward. However, it is hard to reach this golden mountain for four reasons.

First, the whole process of grant application is time-consuming. For instance, the reviewing committee takes time to decide, legal arrangements must be made, and partners need to hire staff. Meanwhile, knowledge of big data technologies increases, and before you know it, the ideas expressed in the grant might make less sense.

---

iii. See explanation of the Information Road causal model: https://www.youtube.com/watch?v=RrYvtg0_508&t=2s

A second reason is that daily practice can change even before the project starts. For example, a healthcare organization could restructure or develop a new care pathway that changes daily operations. The COVID-19 pandemic saw many changes that heavily influenced the set-up of big data projects. How can we collect valid, reliable data when the whole system is unstable and the results could be dubious? Can we use machine-learning algorithms based on data from old processes in the same way as from new processes? And sometimes daily operations change during a project. For example, the problem one BML study was designed to address vanished entirely after data collection. Understanding the problem showed that there was no need to develop an algorithm. Simply rearranging the processes was enough to solve the issue.

The third reason concerns the amount of work that needs to be done. This is often underestimated in grant proposals. Think, for example, about the work required to collect and clean the data, build the algorithm, and implement it in the daily practice of healthcare professionals. We noticed many BML projects did not consider how much additional work was needed before anything concrete could be shared.

The fourth aspect, common in innovation, is also worth mentioning. As explained above, you need to adapt your ideas to tailor them to a new situation, and this requires flexibility. However, the promises made in the grant proposal regarding the aims and methodology cannot easily be changed. By having to stick to the agreements made, you do not have the flexibility to meet the requirements of committed deliverables, and, as a result, means and ends are decoupled. It is tempting to proceed with the methodology agreed upon, but in the end, these projects get stuck in the middle of nowhere as they will not produce the results practice needs, and stakeholders – especially healthcare professionals – will be disappointed. One might argue that this inflexibility should be changed. However, this is usually not possible in the arrangements made with the funder. Changing things without the funder's agreement could lead to credibility issues, which will decrease the chance of future funding.

The slippery slope to the top of the golden mountain has many unexpected turns. If you take the other road and conduct a research project without additional funding, the same problems will occur. Researchers cannot simply change their methodology, as doing so will compromise the validity and reliability of their study. Additionally, no short-term results can be expected, as people cannot devote much time to the big data technology project. In some BML studies, big data research was a kind of hobby for healthcare professionals, next to patient care and organizational tasks. Again, the lack of short-term results is a disappointment for all involved, but especially for the data scientists.

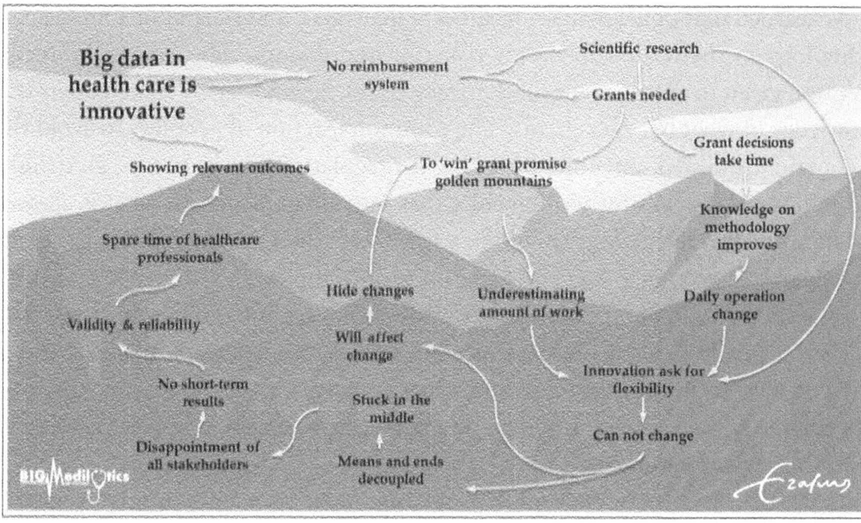

Figure 3.2. Causal model of how to measure the impact of big data technology.

In BML, we learned that to keep things on track, it is important to show the relevant short-term outcomes that prove that big data technologies are innovative and can be useful for daily practice (Figure 3.2). Even modest outcomes align healthcare professionals with data scientists. Discussing the methodology, data set, and outcomes leads to a shared understanding that helps to get and keep people engaged.

In sum, the most important lessons learned are:

- Data scientists and health professionals need to reflect on the promises they make in grant proposals.
- Grant proposals should include a description of all the work (not just the deliverables) that needs to be done to develop and employ big data technologies.
- Grant-funded projects need to have room to adjust the aims and adapt the plan to develop and employ big data technologies.[iv]

3.2.3 The Swamp of Rules

This causal model explains the interdependencies between actors possessing different expertise and their aligned rules and regulations. It explains how the innovative nature of big data slows down its uptake.

iv. See explanation of the Golden Mountain causal model: https://www.youtube.com/watch?v=aSmQTueUt0o&t=5s

We learned that policymakers, healthcare managers, and the public find big data technology in the healthcare sector risky for two reasons. The first is the media attention given to data breaches and privacy issues. Second, many stakeholders lack knowledge of what big data entails. The common reaction of people is to avoid risk or contain unwanted outcomes by asking for regulations, laws, norms, guidelines, and policies. This calls for written rules that provide guidance on what is allowed and how big data technology should be used. These rules should apply to the entire data chain (see Section 3.2.2) and focus on various topics, such as privacy, security, safety, ethics, and legal aspects. These diverse topics require different experts, such as lawyers in the field of big data, privacy and security officers, medical ethical advisers, data protection officers, and cyber security experts. Consequently, new jobs emerge with their own language and perspectives on the rules that need to be set for big data in healthcare.

As big data is a fuzzy concept, experts have their own opinions as to what it involves. For example, in the BML projects, some teams used an eHealth application or a medical device for data collection. Experts argued that eHealth and medical devices were big data, and thus the team had to comply with specific big data rules, which resulted in new approval procedures. The wide variety of new experts, who all focus on subsets of rules for big data, leads to project teams being confronted with a range of individual opinions on what is allowed or not allowed. This is because experts working in different fields are often not in close contact with one another. Thus, their expertise gets lost in knowledge silos.

As each knowledge silo makes their own rules, big data study teams can get bogged down in a misalignment between the rules set by the different experts, something we call "the Swamp of Rules." This misalignment creates uncertainty about which rules should be met before the big data project can start. Rule misalignment is especially troublesome when data are shared beyond the borders of organizations or even countries and whenever diverse experts in different organizations have differing opinions on which rule matters or should be prioritized.

We noticed in projects that were sharing data across nations that differences popped up in the interpretation of rules, despite legal attempts at harmonization, such as the General Data Protection Regulation (GDPR). Moreover, in addition to European legislation, every country has its own rules and specific derogations. Not only must big data projects comply with different rules, but the rules are also still developing rapidly. For instance, in one project, new national rules put the whole project on hold until the new privacy application was approved. In another project, the vendor of the data collection device was sold to a company in another country, which heavily influenced the progress of their project.

We noticed that, in general, the people involved in the BML project felt stuck in a cumbersome swamp of rules. Healthcare professionals and data scientists needed advice on how to comply with the different rules, especially when they appeared contradictory or open to different interpretations. Yet, in some projects, the role of the experts was only in checking compliance with the rules of the big data practice. In this context, unintentional mistakes can happen. Such unintended mistakes gain much media attention, which influences public opinion and, in turn, confirms the idea that big data in healthcare is risky.

We observed people using three 'steppingstones' to escape from or avoid the Swamp of Rules. The first steppingstone involved inviting all the experts in the project team to share their ideas on how to solve any rule misalignment or any other practical issues related to the set rules. The second steppingstone involved 'workarounds' and 'elephant paths' that project teams used as a form of knowledge brokering between the silos. For instance, patients in one study were asked retrospectively to give consent for using their data. Physicians made home visits to explain the reason. The third steppingstone placed the project in a context that permitted 'learning by doing', naturally with the consent of all the stakeholders involved. As a result, the innovative nature of big data was no longer seen as a risk, and the whole project team gained the opportunity to learn how to avoid problems caused by the set rules.

Figure 3.3 ties all the pieces together to reveal the opportunities to change aspects that sometimes hinder big data uptake.

In sum, the most important lessons learned are:

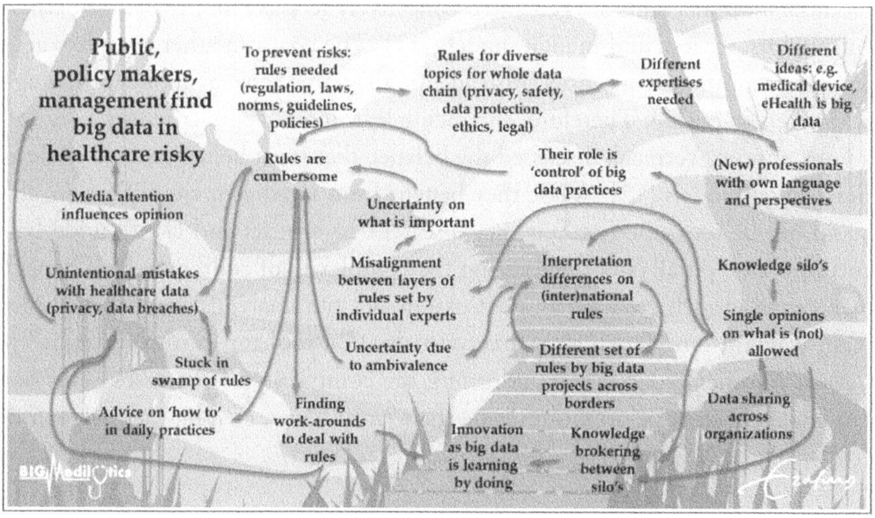

Figure 3.3. Causal model of influences that slow down uptake of big data innovations.

- Experts in the fields of privacy, security, safety, ethics, and law should work together and align their (expertise) work in big data technology projects.
- The experts in privacy, security, safety, ethics, and law on the team should advise healthcare professionals and data scientists on how they can comply with different rules.
- The experts in privacy, security, safety, and ethics on the team should inform the healthcare professionals and data scientists how to use 'workarounds' and 'elephant paths' that will enable them to follow the rules.[v]

3.3 Reflection on the Use of Causal Models

We have shown in this chapter that causal models are helpful to understand how to break self-enforcing patterns and how doing this can bring about change. Tying the pieces together in a causal diagram visualizes the obstructive and supportive actors and factors, and this in turn is helpful to understand when and how to intervene to overcome the problems revealed. In his work, Vermaak distinguished three main approaches to causal loop diagrams [9]. In the rationality-oriented approach, the emphasis is on making a solid causal loop diagram that represents 'reality' as accurately as possible. The aim is to produce a diagram that is as precise, objective, and valid as possible [10]. Second, the commitment-oriented approach focuses on building support to facilitate change. Such diagrams function as tools to bring diverging opinions closer together. Rather than accuracy and objectivity, the focus is on recognition and support. Finally, the development-oriented approach prioritizes learning and exploring.

Causal loop diagrams are generated collectively to share and exchange observations, points of view, and mental models [11]. The goal is neither complete accuracy nor unanimous consensus. Instead, the diagrams serve as input for dialogue and awareness-raising. Therefore, enhancing learning is a core criterion.

Furthermore, Vermaak discussed the balance that must be maintained in developing causal models [12]. While they benefit from intelligent simplification, they should not be too superficial, as they also seek to unravel and clarify underlying processes. One pitfall is not addressing the complexity of content, which happens when causal models are used as a discussion aid, but analytical rigor is discarded. Then, diagrams are drawn as a 'fuzzy visualization tool for intuitive insights' [9, p. 232]. Another pitfall is not addressing the complexity of processes. This happens when experts operate from inside their ivory tower, locking themselves away

v. See explanation of the Swamp of Rules causal model: https://www.youtube.com/watch?v=B3NCbg__4_4&t=28s.

to achieve research rigor. Causal loop diagrams therefore need to fulfill various criteria. "They need to be rich enough to capture underlying mechanisms, precise enough to spot leverage but also simple enough so that most important dynamics clearly stand out" [9, p. 233].

Our study applied the development-oriented approach to creating causal diagrams, as our aim was to support the study teams' activities and facilitate their efforts to embed big data technology in broader organizational routines. However, this approach may have biased our findings, especially because the data we used was derived mainly from BML project members and other actors involved in the project on national and European levels. On the other hand, we included many actors involved in the uptake and embedding of big data technology in organizations. Additionally, we realize that making and testing causal loop diagrams are interventions on their own. The awareness developed through these diagrams can empower early adopters, shift power balances, and so forth. Thus, our causal diagrams contributed in various ways to the uptake of big data technologies and hence the overall results of the BML project.

References

[1] Sweeney LB, Meadows D. The systems thinking playbook: exercises to stretch and build learning and systems thinking capabilities. Chelsea Green Publishing. 2010.

[2] Günther WA, Mehrizi MHR, Huysman M, Feldberg F. Debating big data: a literature review on realizing value from big data. The Journal of Strategic Information Systems. 2017. 26(3), 191–209. DOI: 10.1016/j.jsis.2017.07.003.

[3] Wehrens R, Sihag V, Sülz S, Van Elten H, van Raaij E, de Bont A, Weggelaar-Jansen AM. Understanding the uptake of big data in health care: protocol for a multinational mixed-methods study. JMIR Research Protocols. 2020. 9(10), e16779. DOI: 10.2196/16779.

[4] Heitmueller A, Henderson S, Warburton W, Elmagarmid A, Pentland AS, Darzi A. Developing public policy to advance the use of big data in health care. Health Affairs. 2014. 33(9), 1523–1530. DOI: 10.1377/hlthaff.2014.0771.

[5] Tavory I, Timmermans S. Abductive analysis: theorizing qualitative research. University of Chicago Press. 2014.

[6] Kaplan RS, Norton DP. The balanced scorecard: measures that drive performance. Harvard Business Review. 2005. 83(7), 172. URL: https://hbr.org/2005/07/the-balanced-scorecard-measures-that-drive-performance.

[7] May CR, Mair F, Finch T, MacFarlane A, Dowrick C, Treweek S, *et al.* Development of a theory of implementation and integration: normalization process theory. Implementation Science. 2009. 4(1), 1–9. DOI: 10.1186/1748-5908-4-29.

[8] Murray E, Treweek S, Pope C, MacFarlane A, Ballini L, Dowrick C, *et al.* Normalisation process theory: a framework for developing, evaluating, and implementing complex interventions. BMC Medicine. 2010. 8(1), 1–11. DOI: 10.1186/1741-7015-8-63.

[9] Vermaak H. Using causal loop diagrams to deal with complex issues: mastering an instrument for systemic and interactive change. Consultation for Organizational Change Revisited: Research in Management Consulting. 2016. 23, 231–254.

[10] Richardson GP. Problems in causal loop diagrams revisited. System Dynamics Review: The Journal of the System Dynamics Society. 1997. 13(3), 247–252. DOI: 10.1002/(SICI)1099-1727(199723)13:3<247::AID-SDR128>3.0.CO;2-9.

[11] Kim DH. Gui delines for drawing causal loop diagrams. The Systems Thinker. 1992. 3(1), 5–6. URL: https://www.cs.toronto.edu/~sme/SystemsThinking/GuidelinesforDrawingCausalLoopDiagrams.pdf.

[12] Vermaak H. Working interactively with causal loop diagrams: intervention choices and paradoxes in practical applications. Intervening and Changing: looking for meaning in interactions. John Wiley & Sons. 2007. 175–194.

DOI: 10.1561/9781638282372.ch4

Chapter 4

Lessons Learned in the Application of the General Data Protection Regulation to the BigMedilytics Project

By Ricard Martínez Martínez

This chapter outlines the challenges faced by the BigMedylitics project for the design of big data research projects with health data. The solutions adopted advanced compliance methodologies aligned with the Data Governance Act and the proposed European Health Data Space Regulation. The lessons learned are especially useful for the future development of health data repositories for research purposes.

4.1 Introduction

The BigMedilytics project (the Project) posed significant challenges from the point of view of the implementation of Regulation (EU) 2016/679 of the European Parliament and of the Council of April 27, 2016, on the protection of natural persons with regard to the processing of personal data and on the free movement of such data [General Data Protection Regulation (GDPR)] [1]. In fact, a study conducted in the context of the project itself showed that there was a general consensus among experts regarding the barriers and difficulties posed by the GDPR.

Although the regulation strongly claims to create a favorable ecosystem for health research, the practical reality proves to be very different. For that reason, the main objective of this chapter is to share with the scientific and legal communities the set of difficulties that the Project had to face in this area, as well as the lessons learned. In order to do so, it is necessary to point out our ethical and scientific starting points. In our experience supporting different research projects in the field of health, the influence of the GDPR has led to a distortion of the criteria and values that should govern research activity.

A reading of several recitals of the GDPR offers an apparent positive view. First, the regulation states that the use of data is subordinate to the pursuit of the common good of our society (Recital 4; see also Recital 128). Second, it expressly affirms the public interest that exists in research and invokes the existence of a sufficient legal basis to allow the deployment of big data techniques (for instance, Recital 159). Following the argumentation of the GDPR, we should understand that health research in the European Union has a favorable and competitive ecosystem. The regulation guarantees patients' fundamental rights and, apparently, favors the development of particularly competitive research based on their data.

However, this was not the reality we faced during the deployment and execution of BigMedilytics. Using the language of clinical trials, we might say that the GDPR has undoubtedly produced some adverse effects that would merit an observational study. The studies promoted by the European Commission, and its legislative position on the creation of the European Data Space, prove the obvious: the existence of significant asymmetries in national legislation. Therefore, the sharing of personal data for health research is a risky activity in the European Union.

Before going deeper into an initial diagnosis of the situation, it is necessary to advance a clear conclusion drawn from our experience in the Project. Usually, both research staff and institutions act in a defensive manner, subordinating research interests to compliance with the GDPR. And because of this, the natural order that procedures should follow when applying the so-called data protection principle by design and by default is distorted.

It is natural for scientists to focus their expertise on designing their research. In this gestation phase, the GDPR support team is integrated from the very beginning. The role of this team is to provide adequate support for compliance. Methodologically speaking, this should provide the design of the investigation plan with a sequential filtering process. First, what is prohibited is eliminated; it is an unattainable objective due to a lack of legal basis or due to the increased risk of noncompliance. Second, the risk analysis – and the data protection impact assessment – provides the measures to be implemented to make the investigation possible. Finally, the data protection by design and by default phase allows designing the context of the processing operations. However, the GDPR has promoted 'defensive' research in which decisions on the processing of personal information are subordinated to compliance guarantees due to the undefined legal framework applicable.

In practice, there are at least two adverse effects. The first of these consists of self-censorship on the part of the researcher, who, fearing the rejection of his or her research by legal teams, restricts the definition and scope of the investigation. On the other hand, the data protection officer is placed in a position that is alien to the role defined by the GDPR itself. Not infrequently, he or she is set up as the judge who decides which data or which processing operations are viable and which must be avoided. The aim is to protect the reputation of institutions that carry out research in the field of health and, on more than a few occasions, to ensure that the organization is shielded against particularly dissuasive sanctioning legislation. In practice, this introduces a new competitive gap for European institutions, which usually lack the financial muscle that allows large American multinational groups to take risks in the belief that they will be able to cope with the damage caused by the so-called regulatory risk.[i]

This conclusion is self-evident. It would make sense to apply the risk-based approach that defines the methodology of the data protection impact assessment. Once the risks are verified, the research conditions would operate by applying data protection by design and by default. However, this virtuous circle ends up becoming a loophole that restricts the possibilities for research. GDPR methodologies are applied with a risk-based approach that aims to avoid receiving a sanction from a data protection authority.

The reasons for the above assertions can be found in the GDPR and, above all, in the way in which it is interpreted and applied. If this regulation was born with the aim of defining a common regulatory framework, it makes little sense to delegate to national law the development of the conditions enabling the processing of personal data for research purposes and particularly the authorization for the processing of special categories of data in this area. In other words, while the systematic interpretation of the GDPR leads to a clear preference of the European legislator for harmonized and cross-border use of data, its practical results make this extremely difficult. It is impossible to reconcile profoundly divergent legislation when regulating health research using personal data. The GDPR may consider research to be in the public interest, and it may define it as a compatible processing activity. But the fact is that its mandate is very clear: it is essential to anonymize data for health

i. Mayer-Schönberger and Range consider that "...despite its noble intentions, GDPR has in fact helped digital superstar companies enlarge their informational power and expand their centrally planned digital economies" [2, p. 15].

research. Anonymization would have undoubted advantages insofar as it apparently excludes the application of the GDPR. As will be pointed out below, nothing could be further from the truth.

BigMedilytics, by its very nature, was a trans-European research project with health data that faced a highly complex regulatory ecosystem that imposed significant barriers to the deployment of research activity. This forced the search for functional solutions that were also experimented with in other contemporary projects. It might seem that the main result of the project and its main contribution in terms of regulatory compliance was the ability to find robust alternatives to make research possible. This would certainly be an incorrect conclusion. The main lesson learned, and one that we should undoubtedly share honestly, is the opposite. Research in health using personal data is, in practice, an obstacle course that must overcome very significant administrative and technical barriers.

At the time of this writing, the European Union is facing the biggest challenge to health research in our history with the Proposal for a Regulation of the European Parliament and of the Council on the European Health Data Space (EHDS) [3]. The GDPR has been ineffective and does not offer adequate solutions. Repeating its mistakes could undoubtedly lead to a research ecosystem that appears to be particularly self-satisfied but not very competitive. By sharing the lessons learned in this project, we hope not only to narrate the experience of such an exciting research project but also to contribute to the debate about the future of health data research.

In the following paragraphs, I look first at how collaborative research projects need to address regulatory compliance with regard to the GDPR (Section 4.2). This provides the initial background against which data governance and regulatory compliance need to be developed. In Section 4.3, I turn to specific examples from BigMedylitics, including a reference to the implementation of the GDPR in Spain (Section 4.3.1), some considerations around the challenges for data protection consent (Section 4.3.2), and the practical considerations associated with the provision of large data repositories (Section 4.3.3). Finally, in Section 4.4, I propose a functional model for dealing with health data within Europe based on the experiences from BigMedylitics.

4.2 Managing the Complexity: The Working Flow in Data Protection

The definition of a data protection compliance framework should focus on the concept of processing personal data. Therefore, it is recommended to apply the GDPR to each processing operation by following an orderly procedure for the implementation of the compliance framework. Usually, in the deployment of a cross-border research project, the task is complicated by the need to ensure:

- the reliability of each partner; and
- the roles that are deployed in the different processing activities.

This process should be appropriate to the needs of the project. Usually, in the deployment of a project, we have to consider the steps in Table 4.1.

It should be noted that proactive accountability (Article 5(2) of the GDPR) is the overarching goal of compliance. It attaches substantial importance to documentation and evidence of compliance. It is therefore essential to have an adequate record of evidence (Table 4.2).

Each of the tasks defined in Table 4.2 is deployed for the activities that usually integrate the management of a Horizon 2020 project: human resource management, dissemination, and research. The essential challenge that BigMedilytics had to address in many of its research studies consisted of resolving two essential issues: sizing the categories and volume of data, and ensuring adequate anonymization conditions. Because of its relevance, we will consider the second one in particular.

4.3 New Scenarios for Research: Focusing in Anonymization

The most demanding of the various research studies developed at BigMedilytics in terms of regulatory compliance was the comorbidities study (Chapter 8: Effects of comorbidities (chronic illness) on hospitalization and mortality risks). In order to achieve its goals, it was necessary to process thousands of medical records. Population medicine is based on the handling of enormous amounts of data, which may well amount to petabytes or exabytes, and combining those data from medical records with non-personal data relating to pollution, climate, mobility, or socio-economic aspects, among others, which may increase re-identification risk.

From the point of view of preventive and predictive medicine, data analytics adds correlation to causation. In areas such as comorbidity, it can offer opportunities for the doctor and the patient themselves to design strategies, adapting their behavior to make it possible to prevent and avoid not only the exacerbation of their diseases, but also the appearance of concurrent or successive pathologies.

Personalization is another possibility offered by data analytics. Using data analytics, lessons learned from a population perspective in the treatment of a disease can help to fine-tune and personalize therapeutic targets. In its most applied dimension, this type of approach is effective in cases of poly-medicated patients when it is necessary to adjust their medication. Finally, the evolution of the Internet of Things

Table 4.1. Workflow for GDPR compliance.

Initial Requirements	
Relations between project partners	• Definition of a framework of trust relationships/coordination of data protection officers • Definition of GDPR relationships (controller-processor-processors-joint controllers) and relationships in case of use of anonymized data (data-sharing agreements)
⇓	
Description and contextualization of each processing activity	
Notification process/ self-declarations of processing activities	• Description of the processing activity • Purpose • Data, data subject categories, uses, etc.
⇓	
Risk analysis	
Risk-based approach	• Data protection impact assessment • Risk analysis • Risk management (measures, residual risk, etc.)
⇓	
Data protection by design and by default	
Technical design/ development	• Article 5 Principles: data minimization • Proper implementation of GDPR-compliant systems and procedures
⇓	
Measures to adapt the legal design of the processing to the requirements of the GDPR	
Legal design	• Relations with third parties (processors and joint controllers) • Lead supervisory authority • International data transfers • Transparency • Record of processing activities
⇓	

(Continued)

Table 4.1. Continued

Specific requirements	• Cookies • Social networks • Anonymization
	⇓
	Accountability
Evidence	• Risk analysis reports • Data protection impact assessment reports • Technical documentation in the development of applications (data protection by design, functionalities, and security) • Legal documents • Audit reports

Table 4.2. Evidence summary.

	Document	
Paragraph	**Prospective**	**Paragraph**
1. Description of the research	☐	☐
2. Ethical requirements		
2.1 Protocol/research design	☐	☐
2.2 Ethical protocol	☐	☐
2.3 Ethics Committee Approval	☐	☐
2.4 Informed consent	☐	☐
2.5 AI impact assessment	☐	☐
3. GDPR evidence		
3.1 Data flow and/or description	☐	☐
3.2 Roles/relationship between parties	☐	☐
3.3 Risk analysis, DPIA, data protection by design and by default	☐	☐
3.4 Security measures	☐	☐
3.5 Anonymization or pseudonymization	☐	☐
3.6 Transparency	☐	☐
3.7 Record of processing activities	☐	☐

(IoT) and mobile applications enables the design of digital environments in which patient engagement can be particularly relevant. Wearables and connected objects, such as glucometers and blood pressure monitors, that help monitor patients' heart rates, diabetes, and physical activity, are available on the market. Alongside these, there is a huge range of products that can create patient interaction environments. These can provide new ways of collaboration and participation that involve a new understanding of the patient's relationship with the healthcare system.

The scenario we have just described clearly leads to a connected health environment. The COVID-19 disease highlighted the extent to which connected medicine, telemedicine, and remote patient healthcare may be critical for the future of healthcare, and this emerging model cannot be confused with a regular system of patient check-ups via telephone conversations. In fact, these are monitoring, interaction, and participation scenarios that require the development of particularly complex information systems. In these systems, data analytics and decision-making processes assisted by specific-purpose artificial intelligence will transform the way in which healthcare is delivered to the population. From a technological point of view, this implies an increase in the complexity of information systems, and necessarily requires appropriate design in terms of data quality, robustness, and reliability.

On the other hand, the above scenario defines a context for data use that is developing new perspectives from the point of view of purpose. In the past, health research approaches focused on clinical trial methodologies. The scope of the research was limited in terms of both the object pursued and the number of patients involved. In this model, the legal framework regulating data processing was fully consistent and appropriate. Thus, access to data was based on the patient's informed consent and was permitted for very specific purposes limited to specific research. However, this is not the reality that is pointed out by the use of data analytics methodologies in retrospective and prospective studies.

The first difference between these models is the volume of data used. For example, completely unlike traditional clinical trials, a retrospective study with data in the field of comorbidity could include millions of medical records. The second appreciable difference results from the gap between correlation and causality. Traditionally, scientific research sought to establish a cause–effect relationship, whereas one of the results of using data analytics is the drawing of inferences from correlations. It is obvious that, from a scientific point of view, not every correlation implies a causal relationship. Moreover, it is not desirable to treat correlations as sacred. However, it is no less true that, thanks to this methodology, the researcher can obtain inferences and results that were previously unsuspected and that must now be verified.

That being said, this has a particularly strong effect from a legal point of view in relation to aspects such as determining the purpose. This type of research is particularly open to incidental findings and results whose interest may need to be validated. On the other hand, the combination of strictly clinical sources with datasets from other areas may generate new data and new models of analysis. In practice, the new data, conceptual models, or inferences that are generated, far from being situated in the framework of a specific investigation, can be open, from a conceptual point of view, to nearby or related areas and, in theory, to any dimension of patient health or to additional dimensions (social, economic, or public policy).

There are thus significant differences between the scenario that was regulated in the past and the current scenario. The background experience of the legislator, the law enforcer, and the data protection authorities has focused on the clinical trial model that defines a very precise patient target, with a limited volume of subjects and data in the context of a specific research study. In contrast, the use of data analytics, by its very nature, tends toward a holistic approach to the patient in the context of a population.

Finally, in a description that by no means pretends to be exhaustive, there is a second contribution made by the new data analytics tools to health research models. These tools provide a dimension that adds to the traditional objectives and approaches of the fundamental research elements that are clearly oriented toward the care dimension of health. Thus, we can add to the secondary uses of data for basic research purposes a primary use specifically aimed at improving the quality of care and the management of the health system.

4.3.1 Spanish Data Protection Law: A Highly Efficient Model for Big Data Research

The development of a predictive model for the evolution of the health of patients with comorbidities faces very demanding requirements to ensure regulatory compliance in this area. The first of these was to find an adequate basis to legitimize the data processing. It should be stressed that, in this context, our research project had a competitive advantage. In the framework of Spanish law, the 17th Additional Provision of Law 3/2018 offers three possibilities for the processing of data [4]. Each of these options can be applied to both retrospective and prospective studies.

First, it is possible to process data by obtaining the patient's informed consent under the terms of Article 9.2(a) of the General Data Protection Regulation. Spanish law allows this type of manifestation of will. However, it is not an efficient solution since, especially in prospective studies, it is impossible to target tens of thousands of people and there is no public or private register of data donors (data altruism). Spanish law provides a legal basis for the processing of data for health research purposes when the data are anonymized or pseudonymized with appropriate safeguards.

Although BigMedilytics opted for anonymization, it was considered relevant to design the processing to incorporate the following guarantees of Spanish law:

- Technical and functional separation between the research team and those who carry out the pseudonymization and keep the information that enables re-identification.
- Express commitment to confidentiality and not to carry out any re-identification activity. This may be supported by a data sharing agreement.
- Specific security measures were adopted to prevent re-identification and access by unauthorized third parties.
- A data protection impact assessment identifying the risks arising from the processing in the cases provided for in Article 35 of Regulation (EU) 2016/679 or those established by the supervisory authority was implemented.
- Previous approval from the research ethics committee was obtained.

The rationale for this decision is different. First, the nature of the project did not require the identification of the subjects whose data were studied. The essential aim was to access a wide volume of medical records and reach a wide range of relevant clinical data. In this regard, the risk-based approach required by the GDPR clearly offers anonymization as the best possible technique. Moreover, it can be deduced from the principles established by Article 89 of the GDPR that the European law proposes by default this technique as the ideal one for research with data insofar as it is the least harmful from any perspective. This interpretation is confirmed by the European Health Data Space (EHDS), [5, 6] which in its current wording establishes anonymization as the preferred technique, admitting that in the case of rare diseases, this will be difficult to achieve, and pointing out that the cases in which data processing by means of pseudonymization must be justified.

4.3.2 The Consent Fallacy

On the other hand, a structural problem exists in the collection of personal data by means of consent, which the Data Governance Act (DGA) defines as data altruism [7]. Historically, research projects with health data have used the methodology of informed consent. Usually, the number of subjects was easily manageable, and consent was given for a specific purpose. The clearest example is clinical trials involving pharmaceutical drugs. There has been no systematic planning to promote data collection with consent at all levels of health systems. Indeed, to the extent that consent has traditionally been obtained for the conduct of specific research, there have always been severe difficulties in re-using the data, as well as a model of research purposes that is not functional for research through data analytics. It is not surprising that this issue has had to be addressed by the European Commission, following a report by the European Data Protection Board (EDPB) [8, 9].

If we consider Recital 33 of the GDPR, we could conclude that the consent regime would have been relaxed, as it states that:

> *(33) It is often not possible to fully identify the purpose of personal data processing for scientific research purposes at the time of data collection. Therefore, data subjects should be allowed to give their consent to certain areas of scientific research when in keeping with recognised ethical standards for scientific research. Data subjects should have the opportunity to give their consent only to certain areas of research or parts of research projects to the extent allowed by the intended purpose.*

However, the EDPB has not abandoned a strict concept of consent that is not consistent with the intention of the GDPR. Thus, in its Guidelines 05/2020, [10] the EDPB points out that:

> *153. The definition of scientific research purposes has substantial ramifications for the range of data processing activities a controller may undertake. The term 'scientific research' is not defined in the GDPR. Recital 159 states "(...) For the purposes of this Regulation, the processing of personal data for scientific research purposes should be interpreted in a broad manner. (...)", however [STET] the EDPB considers the notion may not be stretched beyond its common meaning and understands that 'scientific research'* ***in this context means a research project set up in accordance with relevant sector related methodological and ethical standards, in conformity with good practice****. (My emphasis)*

In practice, these approaches mean that, even if compatible uses are allowed, the specificity of the research or the link to a specific research project significantly hinders all research based on data analytics that seeks a general purpose or covers general areas of action or clinical research[ii] [11]. In conclusion, consent can never be an adequate functional methodology for the use of big data in health research, since its collection implies a management effort that can be projected to include tens or hundreds of thousands of people. On the other hand, as long as

ii. This is not the criterion of Spanish law nor of the Spanish Data Protection Authority, which is an exception in the European Union as a whole. This authority considers: ‹It follows from all this that the requirements of specificity and unambiguousness for the provision of consent should not be interpreted in the field of scientific research in a restrictive manner, limited to a specific piece of research on which all available information is provided, but should be considered to be met in cases where consent is given in relation to a specific field of research, This consent can be extended in the future, without this vitiating it in any way, even to "purposes" or areas of research that could not even have been determined at the time it was given, without it being necessary to seek a new consent from the source subject, taking into account the benefits for individuals and society as a whole that may arise from such unforeseen research. Thus, for example, in order to guarantee the unambiguous and specific nature of consent, it would not be necessary for it to be given for the conduct of specific research; nor even for the conduct of research in a narrowly defined field, such as a particular type of cancer, but, taking into account the interpretation derived directly from the Regulation itself, consent given in relation to a broad field of research, such as cancer research, or even for more extensive areas, would be sufficiently unambiguous and specific.› See [11].

the dominant criterion does not change, this effort will not compensate either the patient or the healthcare system. If we are asking for consent to be issued for each research project, we will cause tiredness and click fatigue. On the other hand, the investment required for such an information system would not be cost-effective in proportion to the modest benefits that could be expected.[iii]

4.3.3 The Creation of Repositories Based on Controlled Anonymity

Anonymization is not problem-free. The position of the data protection authorities,[iv] on data anonymization is particularly strict in requiring irreversible anonymization. In practice, the former Article 29 Working Party, now the EDPB, gives a broad interpretation of the scope of application of the GDPR. One might think that anonymizing data excludes it from the Regulation. This is not the case. For the working party and the EDPB, anonymization is a processing operation in itself. It must therefore be consistent and compatible with the purposes for which the data were collected. On the other hand, data subjects have an expectation of transparency. That is, privacy policies should incorporate clear information regarding the possible anonymization of data and its use for research purposes. This implies, in practice, the theoretical possibility for patients to exercise a right to object to such processing.

Both Directive 95/46/EC and the GDPR define anonymization as a process that should achieve two objectives [1, 13]. First, to proportionately eliminate the risks of re-identification through singling out, inference, or linking. Second, the anonymization process should be of such a nature that any third-party external to the data controller would not be able to identify the individuals concerned with reasonable effort. In order to consider both the risks and the level of effort, a prospective exercise that takes into account the state of the art and a predictive exercise that considers the future or possible evolution of the technology within a reasonable period of time seemed or appears reasonable. These criteria have been interpreted restrictively by the working party, which, in its opinion, calls for anonymization to be irreversible, equivalent to erasure, and suggests extreme rigor in the verification of risk in relation to future technologies.

This extreme position determined for BigMedilytics research was the adoption of a set of guarantees inspired by the Spanish regulation on the processing of

iii. On the other hand, the diversity of national regulations significantly complicates any cross-border consent-based research initiative. See [12].

iv. https://ec.europa.eu/justice/article-29/documentation/opinion-recommendation/files/2014/wp216_en.pdf.

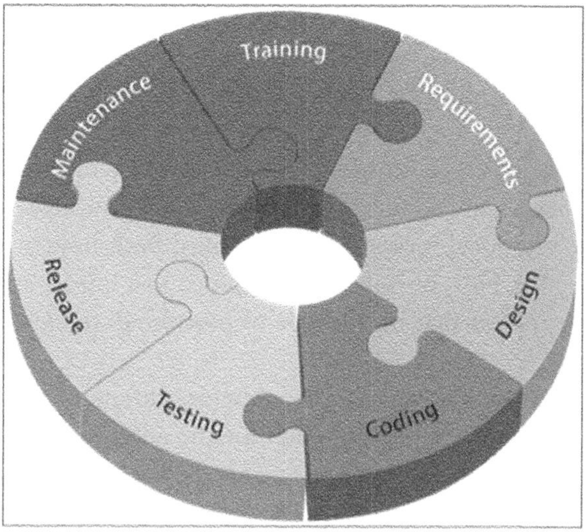

Figure 4.1. Source: Guidelines on Software development with Data Protection by Design and by Default [14].

pseudonymized data and which would operate as additional guarantees for processing in the sense attributed to them by Article 89 of the General Data Protection Regulation. These measures were inspired by the methodology of data protection by design and by default proposed at the time by the Norwegian Data Protection Authority and suitably adapted to the characteristics of the project. These measures are shown in Figure 4.1.

4.3.3.1 Training of the research team

Practically from the launch of the project, a process of team training on data protection by design was undertaken. This involved operational, work package, and consortium meetings. The training approach covered all aspects relevant to the project. For example, a specific workshop was dedicated to third-party relationships, which were involved in the development of IT applications or mobile applications. This methodology enabled all the project teams to be empowered from a scientific, technical, development, and management perspective.

4.3.3.2 From requirements to release

During the design phase, the specific needs of the project were taken into account. At this point, a set of strategic decisions was taken, aimed at defining in a very precise way what the conditions for the deployment of the data processing would be. It should be noted that the risk-based approach is applied from this point onward and in all phases of development. The conclusions reached were the following.

Although the data had been delivered in an anonymized format by the healthcare system, a decision was taken to verify the dataset to ensure that it complied with the specifications defined by EDPB Opinion 5/2014. The analysis of the data revealed clear risks of re-identification by singularization and linking. This inevitably led to a process of elimination of specific records and the use of a script with the aim of verifying possible linkages and eliminating data that could generate some kind of risk.

The need for additional measures was identified both from a compliance and a security perspective. First, obviously, a data protection impact assessment had to be carried out. It is clear that in this type of processing, the main risk is that of re-identification.

However, an element inherent to the corporate culture of the Spanish public health system provided very relevant clues for the adoption of decisions involving the implementation of additional safeguards. Public hospitals in Spain perceive health data to be in the public domain. In this sense, patient data would not only belong to the data subject. To the extent that they are integrated into the information systems aimed at the provision of the public health service, they constitute a public good that is ordered to the satisfaction of the common good of society.

In practice, this does not prevent the private sector or any third party from using the data – on the contrary. However, this use of data cannot be confused with either a disclosure and renouncement of data ownership or a loss of control. It should not be forgotten that during the lifetime of BigMedilytics, the Open Data Directive had not been published [6], nor was there a draft EHDS regulation.[v] Therefore, while biomedical legislation provided a reliable framework for research, legislation on the reuse of special categories of data was inconsistent. This was a barrier to the widespread reuse of these data, including the possibility of developing commercially exploitable products. Consequently, in (Chapter 8: Effects of comorbidities (chronic illness) on hospitalization and mortality risks), the hospital's position was to facilitate the use of the data for the specific purposes of the project but not to transfer possession of the data to a partner or third party under any circumstances.

This required two measures, one technological and one legal. From a technological point of view, a processing system was designed with a software intermediary model to ensure that the processing would always take place under the control of the hospital and that under no circumstances would it be possible to copy or download data [13, 15–17]. From a legal point of view, an attempt was made to establish a set of safeguards regarding the sharing, access, and use of the data by drafting a data sharing agreement.

---

v. Though see: https://digital-strategy.ec.europa.eu/en/policies/legislation-open-data.

4.4 Lessons Learned: A Functional Model for the Proposed European Health Data Space

The BigMedilytics project identified and documented the regulatory compliance decisions that were functional to the needs of the project. The primary scheme of the project allowed the definition of a secure processing ecosystem that was later applied in the project 'Notebook de la Fundación 29', awarded by the Spanish Data Protection Agency [19, 20].

The EHDS Proposal and the DGA subsequently confirmed the wisdom of designing ecosystems for the controlled processing of anonymized health data [18, 21]. It is an appropriate methodology for research that can be combined with data space federation technologies. This approach offers two major benefits. First, the framework is suitable for managing the risk of re-identification of both participants in the processing and any third parties. Furthermore, it makes it possible to generate data lakes while respecting the legal framework of each member state and maintaining the data holder's[vi] control over its information systems.

However, the maturity model required by EHDS implies the design of a technological and legal governance model that needs to integrate different strategies. In our opinion, it would make sense for repositories that integrate health data for research purposes to have a certain structure that would include membership from the following:

(a) A corporate governance body
Understood as an oversight body for the repositories to which substantial decisions can be attributed in terms of defining policies and controlling operation.

(b) A data access committee (see [22])
A body that would be assigned the task of final approval of the processing of data in any of its aspects.

---

vi. DGA defines this concept as:

> (8) "data holder" means a legal person, including public sector bodies and international organizations, or a natural person who is not a data subject with respect to the specific data in question, which, in accordance with applicable Union or national law, has the right to grant access to or to share certain personal data or non-personal data;

The EHDS proposal defines it with a more accurate approach:

> (Y) "data holder" means any natural or legal person, which is an entity or a body in the health or care sector, or performing research in relation to these sectors, as well as Union institutions, bodies, offices, and agencies who have the right or obligation, in accordance with this regulation, applicable Union law or national legislation implementing Union law, or in the case of non-personal data, through control of the technical design of a product and related services, the ability to make available, including to register, provide, restrict access, or exchange certain data.

(c) An ethics committee
At the ethics level, different alternative or complementary operational criteria could be considered:

1. To have its own ethics verification body.
2. Include a catalogue of committees, e.g., hospital and/or university committees, whose decisions are recognized.
3. To agree the assessment of applications with a competent external committee.
It should be noted that only in the fields of university research and/or health research are there such bodies. At least one risk must be identified in this area. Both from a strict ethical point of view and from the point of view of the future EU Regulation on Artificial Intelligence, [23] different ethical variables can be identified depending on the nature of the data processing. This implies, in the case of recognition of positive reports from other ethics committees, the need to consider the possibility of reserving review powers regarding these issues.

(d) An advisory committee
A body of consultative nature could provide guidance, participate in the definition of strategic lines, promote interaction with all public and private sectors, including the so-called third sector, and propose programs, actions, or new developments. The actors concerned by public policies on data reuse can be of varied types, such as:

1. Patient organizations
2. Professional experts in data protection, security, ethics, and humanities
3. Universities

(e) Adequate and well-dimensioned management
In terms of day-to-day management, there is a clear need to have a particularly specialized team and to define an agile and efficient application management procedure. Finally, control procedures will be very important in this area. In particular, it is considered essential to have auditing procedures in aspects related to algorithmic ethics, data protection, and information security, as well as the opening of internal and external whistleblowing channels to ensure integrity, good governance, and the appropriate use of information.

The challenge to be met goes far beyond the limited scope of this chapter. Nevertheless, it is a process that must begin without delay and with a commitment to guaranteeing both fundamental rights and the common good.

4.5 Conclusion

In this chapter, I have provided a perspective on the data protection space in Europe as operationalized via legislative instruments as well as opinions from the European Commission and its bodies. The motivation to review these instruments and attempt to provide practical advice came from the various stakeholders involved in projects like BigMedylitics who, as discussed in (Chapter 2: Using causal diagrams to understand and deal with hindering patterns in the uptake and embedding of big data technology), would otherwise be overwhelmed by the apparent complexity of the relevant legislation. Within an already risk-averse environment like healthcare, the danger then becomes that researchers and clinicians feel constrained and therefore unable to innovate. Although the perspective in this chapter is only just beginning to be validated in other projects, the hope is that what is presented here will guide research and innovation in exploiting the available data for the common good. Furthermore, in identifying appropriate governance structures, as outlined in the previous paragraph, the experience reported here may well inform initiatives such as the European Health Data Space and similar Trusted Research Environments.

References

[1] European Commission. Regulation (EU) 2016/679 of the European Parliament and of the Council of 27 April 2016 on the protection of natural persons with regard to the processing of personal data and on the free movement of such data. 2016. https://eur-lex.europa.eu/legal-content/EN/TXT/?uri=CELEX%3A02016R0679-20160504&qid=1532348683434

[2] Mayer-Schönberger V, Ramge T. Access rules: freeing data from big tech for a better future. University of California Press: Oakland, CA, USA. 2022.

[3] Proposal for a Regulation of the European Parliament and of the Council on the European Health Data Space. Available at: https://eur-lex.europa.eu/legal-content/EN/TXT/HTML/?uri=CELEX:52022PC0197&from=EN.

[4] Organic Law 3/2018, of 5 December, on the Protection of Personal Data and the guarantee of digital rights. Available at: https://www.boe.es/buscar/act.php?id=BOE-A-2018-16673&p=20230221&tn=1#da-17.

[5] Recital 64 of the Proposal for a Regulation of the European Parliament and of the Council on the European Health Data Space. Available at: https://eur-lex.europa.eu/legal-content/EN/TXT/HTML/?uri=CELEX:52022PC0197&from=EN.

[6] European Commission. Proposal for a regulation – The European Health Data Space. COM. 2022. 197/2. Available at: https://health.ec.europa.eu/publications/proposal-regulation-european-health-data-space_en.

[7] Article 2 of DGA. Regulation (EU) 2022/868 of the European Parliament and of the Council of 30 May 2022 on European data governance and amending Regulation (EU) 2018/1724 (Data Governance Act). Available at: https://eur-lex.europa.eu/legal-content/EN/TXT/?uri=CELEX%3A32022R0868.

[8] European Data Protection Board. Opinion 3/2019 concerning the Questions and Answers on the interplay between the Clinical Trials Regulation (CTR) and the General Data Protection regulation (GDPR) (art. 70.1.b). 2019. Available at: https://edpb.europa.eu/our-work-tools/our-documents/opinion-art-70/opinion-32019-concerning-questions-and-answers_en.

[9] European Commission Directorate-General for Health And Food Safety Health Systems And Products Medical products – quality, safety and innovation. Question and Answers on the interplay between the Clinical Trials Regulation and the General Data Protection Regulation. 2019. Available at: https://health.ec.europa.eu/system/files/2019-04/qa_clinicaltrials_gdpr_en_0.pdf.

[10] European Data Protection Board. Guidelines 05/2020 on consent under Regulation 2016/679. Version 1.1. 2020. Available at: https://edpb.europa.eu/sites/default/files/files/file1/edpb_guidelines_202005_consent_en.pdf.

[11] INFORME: 073667/2018. Available at: https://www.aepd.es/es/documento/2018-0046-investigacion-biomedica.pdf.

[12] de Sutter E, Meszaros J, Borry P, Huys I. Digitizing the informed consent process: a review of the regulatory landscape in the European Union. *Frontiers in Medicine, Sec. Family Medicine and Primary Care.* 2022. Volume 9. https://doi.org/10.3389/fmed.2022.906448.

[13] European Commission. Directive 95/46/EC of the European Parliament and of the Council of 24 October 1995 on the protection of individuals with regard to the processing of personal data and on the free movement of such data. 1995. Available at: https://eur-lex.europa.eu/legal-content/EN/TXT/?uri=CELEX%3A31995L0046.

[14] Norwegian Data Protection Authority. Guidelines on Software development with Data Protection by Design and by Default. 2017. Available at: https://www.datatilsynet.no/en/about-privacy/virksomhetenes-plikter/data-protection-by-design-and-by-default/.

[15] European Parliament. Directive (EU) 2019/1024 of the European Parliament and of the Council of 20 June 2019 on open data and the re-use of public sector information. 2019. Available at: https://eur-lex.europa.eu/legal-content/EN/TXT/?uri=CELEX%3A32019L1024.

[16] van Haaften W. Sangers A. Engers T, Djafari S. Coping with the general data protection regulation; anonymization through multi-party computation technology. 23rd International Legal Informatics Symposium, Salzburg, Austria. 2020. Available at: https://enablingpersonalizedinterventions.nl/2020-08-09/2020-08-09.pdf.

[17] Wörm D, Sangers A. "Secure multi-party computation." Available at: https://www.tno.nl/en/technology-science/technologies/secure-multi-party-computation/.

[18] European Data Protection Board. EDPB-EDPS Joint Opinion 03/2022 on the Proposal for a Regulation on the European Health Data Space. 2022. Available at: https://edps.europa.eu/system/files/2022-07/22-07-12_edpb_edps_joint-opinion_europeanhealthdataspace_en_.pdf.

[19] Foundation 29. Award from the AEPD for our work with the Playbook and HealthData 29. Available at: https://www.foundation29.org/news/Award%20from%20the%20AEPD%20for%20our%20work%20with%20the%20Playbook%20and%20HealthData%2029/13.

[20] Martínez R, López G, Padín A, Del Hoyo I. HealthData 29: un modelo de compartición de datos de investigación en salud en el contexto del futuro Espacio Europeo de Datos de salud. Comunicaciones en propiedad industrial y derecho de la competencia. N°. 93 (mayo-agosto). 2021. ISSN 1579-3494, 5–30.

[21] European Parliament. Directive (EU) 2019/1024 of the European Parliament and of the Council of 20 June 2019 on open data and the re-use of public sector information. 2019. Available at: https://eur-lex.europa.eu/legal-content/EN/TXT/?uri=CELEX%3A32019L1024.

[22] Yeong Cheah P, Piasecki J. Data Access Committees. BMC Medical Ethics. 2020. 21(12). https://doi.org/10.1186/s12910-020-0453-z.

[23] European Commission High-Level Expert Group on Artificial Intelligence. The Assessment List for Trustworthy Artificial Intelligence. 2020. Available at: https://digital-strategy.ec.europa.eu/en/library/assessment-list-trustworthy-artificial-intelligence-altai-self-assessment.

DOI: 10.1561/9781638282372.ch5

Chapter 5

Ethics: A Checklist for Investigators, Ethics Boards, and Reviewers

By Brian Pickering

The BigMedilytics (BML) project involved a series of exploratory studies aimed at understanding how advanced, Artificial Intelligence (AI)-enabled and big data technologies might be introduced into different healthcare scenarios and whether such inclusion would be acceptable to patients and clinicians, and institutions. This is in the first place because of the target cohort – namely, patients who are intrinsically vulnerable – and the sensitivity of their personal data. Therefore, these studies require appropriate oversight from a regulatory as well as an ethical perspective. Against the backdrop of what has already been written on ethics, big data, and AI, BML offers a unique opportunity to explore stakeholder attitudes toward the ethical treatment of their data and the effects advanced technologies might have on what they expect from healthcare usage thereof.

This chapter reports the findings of several surveys, including with the BML partners, which provide insight into stakeholder attitudes and concerns regarding the use of advanced technologies. Homing in specifically on the ethical principles of justice and respect for the individual, the chapter considers three ethical theories as they relate to assessing the benefit of research using advanced technologies, followed by a review of the different types of informed consent. This leads to a set of proposed review questions to guide researchers, ethics committees, and institutions when evaluating research proposals involving advanced technologies in healthcare.

5.1 Introduction

In the previous chapter of this book (Chapter 4: Lessons learned in the application of the General Data Protection Regulation to the BigMedilytics project), the focus was specifically on data protection and regulatory governance. Understandably, privacy is a significant part thereof. Martínez acted as Data Protection Officer for the BigMedilytics (BML) project and published on regulatory compliance relating to developing advanced, data-driven technologies [1].[i] Privacy, however, is problematic. Although the first paragraph of Article 8 of European Court of Human Rights states that "Everyone has the right to respect for his private...life," [2] the second paragraph adds the caveat:

> *...except such as is in accordance with the law and is necessary in a democratic society ...for the protection of health or morals, or for the protection of the rights and freedoms of others.* [2, Art. 8]

Data protection legislation makes some provision for this, effectively increasing the responsibility of researchers as data controllers [3]. At the same time, though, it is unclear whether data subjects are able to understand and make informed decisions about the potential use of their data, given their regulatory rights [4]. Furthermore, citizen attitudes to privacy and how they behave in reality may be at odds [5], even vary depending on context [6].

Turning to research ethics, however, there is much more to consider than privacy alone [7], and a balance needs to be struck between data protection and the needs of research [8, 9]. So, respect for the individual research participant is much broader [10]. They have a right to be seen and heard for who and what they are: protests and demonstrations will generally involve the loss of privacy in support of a given cause such as the Black Lives Matter movement and regular Pride marches usually involve public self-disclosure. Risk of re-identification may also depend on the research method itself [11].

---

i. Note that the terms advanced technology, AI-enabled technology, and data-driven technology are all used to refer to big data technologies that use techniques such as machine learning to develop models of behaviors or characteristics based on patient or healthcare operational data.

In this chapter, I review some of the issues around the exploitation of big data in research and innovation projects such as BML based on some empirical studies. The aim is to develop some guidance for research ethics reviewers to evaluate research on large datasets. Since existing guidance is often based on the Belmont report, I also consider different aspects of the ethical principles of: respect for the individual, beneficence/non-maleficence, and justice as they relate to some of the experiences in BML [10], with the intention of providing explicit guidance for those from multiple disciplines and roles who need to judge the acceptability of a study from a research ethics perspective.

This is particularly challenging given that, as BML has demonstrated, studies will involve researchers and practitioners from many different disciplines. In this way, I will propose additional checks to be taken into account by Institutional Review Boards (IRBs) or Research Ethics Committees (RECs) when assessing big data projects in healthcare.

5.2 Background

The commercial exploitation of extensive collections of personal data on clients has been well-attested for over a decade [12], with the Netflix Prize, for instance, reporting a little over 10% improvement in prediction accuracy [13]. At the same time, there is increasing public concern about big data analytics [14]. There is anecdotal evidence of life-threatening mistakes: when an operator was forced to go through a script based on the modeling of typical patient calls, a man in the UK died even though his condition would have been easy to diagnose and treat [15]. Nevertheless, the sheer volume of healthcare data represents an under-utilized resource that might improve outcomes for multiple stakeholders, including the patients themselves, clinicians, and the associated ecosystem of planning and resource allocation [16, 17]. While appropriate tools are required to exploit the available data [18], not least because of its amount and complexity, there is also a need for caution. If both diagnostic and predictive exploitation of big data analytic technologies are envisaged, then there must also be some ethical governance framework against which to evaluate what's being attempted.

The Toronto Declaration and some European governments have begun to produce guidance on the use of personal data for advanced, AI-enabled technologies [19–22], and an EU-based interest group has developed a checklist for those developing such technologies [23]. In their review, Jobin and her colleagues highlight transparency, justice and fairness, non-maleficence, responsibility, and privacy, as the main guiding principles for the ethical development of AI [24]. These restate Belmont's principles, although highlighting responsibility introduces the concept of liability rather than the shared responsibility, which also pervaded the BML studies and seems to rely on different stakeholders accepting vulnerability, while acting with integrity rather than bound by a contract.

Focusing on ethnography and fieldwork, Sula has proposed a framework of ethical principles for researchers [25]. He focuses specifically on power relations between researcher and participant, geared toward protecting them against harm, but also sharing data and findings. This coincides largely with the CARE principles [26]. Power distribution between researcher and participant needs to be considered during the ethical review, therefore. Neither Sula nor the CARE principles include specific guidance for reviewers, though, especially when faced with cross-disciplinary applications for approval. Leslie provides helpful suggestions for the AI researcher for the design and execution of AI- and big-data-centered studies [27]. Hand also introduces useful checks, though again more suited to the individual researcher than multiple stakeholders and those trying to evaluate particular studies [28]. Such guidance needs to be translated for reviewers into specific pointers to assess the ethical appropriateness of proposed work.

In the discussion below, therefore, I focus more specifically on the needs of research ethics reviewers. This is largely based on the reported experience of BML partners as well as related engagement with healthcare app users in the general public.

The upper portion of Figure 5.1 shows four actors: a Patient clearly expects treatment from a Clinician. The clinician's activities are monitored by an appropriate

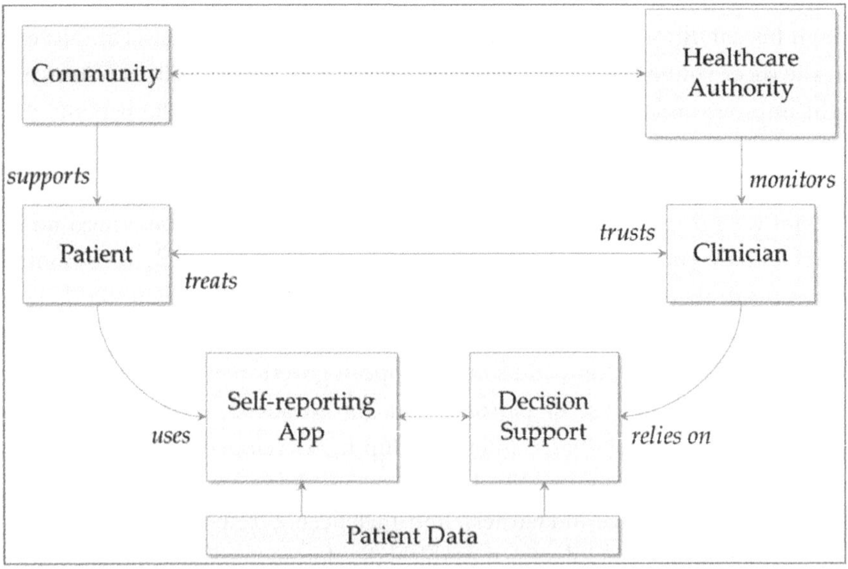

Figure 5.1. A schematic representation of a simple healthcare network.

body, here labeled Healthcare Authority. For instance, they may be expected to oversee medical training, including ongoing career development, as well as monitoring everyday practice. They may also include peers who share experience and information. In parallel, a patient might give feedback to and get support from the wider Community. This may include patient advocates or similar groups, but also the general public, who may respond following press coverage or other media exposure. The clinician cannot practice without agreement from the healthcare authority, and similarly, patients trust that decisions derive not only from the trustworthiness characteristics of the clinician but also from social norms and reputation via the community.

Extending this into an actor-network approach for healthcare delivery [29], the lower half of Figure 5.1 introduces three further constructs. As with many of the studies in BML and reported in Chapter 26 (Technology acceptance in healthcare), Patient Data is typically used in a number of contexts. First, patients (app users) may provide data via a Self-reporting app (see Chapter 10 (Remote monitoring to improve gestational diabetes care) and Chapter 11 (Monitoring wellness in chronic obstructive pulmonary disease using the myCOPD app), for instance). In addition, such data may be used in developing a decision support system for the clinician based on advanced, AI-enabled technology (such as in Chapter 16 (Artificial Intelligence to Support Choices in Neoadjuvant Chemotherapy in Cancer Patients) and Chapter 19 (Implementation and impact of AI for the interpretation of lung diseases in chest CTs)). Furthermore, the self-reporting app may be integrated with the decision support system in receiving alerts, for instance, or providing other data such as location, app usage, and so forth.

Adding these constructs means that the trust relationship between patient and clinician has changed. The patient may be influenced by societal perceptions of technology, including the fashion to use healthcare gadgets such as wearables. Data from those may not reach the clinician to help them treat their patient. At the same time, the clinician may receive decision support beyond what he gets from his training and peers from an AI-enabled system. The clinician will therefore be reliant on a system that they perhaps do not fully understand or at least do not perceive how a decision was made (for them), and they must then integrate that decision with what they know and have experienced with the patient. The patient may or may not know or understand the decision support system, just as the clinician may not receive data directly from a self-reporting app. This makes the patient–clinician relationship more complex.

At the same time, though, there is currently little mandatory oversight for advanced technology development or deployment. For this reason, we must consider the implications for the ethical governance surrounding the advanced technology development as informed by the BML project in this case.

5.3 The Stakeholder Perspectives

Three BML-related surveys provide a useful perspective on stakeholder attitudes and understanding toward healthcare technologies. Survey 1 and Survey 2 were run as part of the BML project. The former, reported in more detail in Chapter 26 (Technology acceptance in healthcare), used constructs from the health belief model (HBM) to query the general public's views on self-reporting app usage as part of their healthcare. The latter, also reported in Chapter 26 (Technology acceptance in healthcare), was aimed at different stakeholder types within the BML project to establish their views on the introduction of big data-driven technologies into healthcare. Survey 3 was an independent, anonymous online survey developed as part of a follow-up project to BML. Themes identified from a set of workshops with members of the general public were used to develop a questionnaire to explore the general public's attitudes toward privacy and about sharing their data with different institutions.[ii] In the following paragraphs, I highlight some of the findings that are particularly relevant for those reviewing the risks associated with big data projects.

Survey 1

We ran an anonymous online survey targeted at the general public in the UK, including both existing app users and non-app users (N = 400). Highlights include the following: "I'm worried about my privacy when using healthcare apps"; 53% agreed, while 48% disagreed. So, there is a debate possible as to whether privacy is a concern or not when using apps. Data protection regulation, of course, should provide adequate safeguards (see also Chapter 4 (Lessons learned in the application of the general data protection regulation to the BigMedilytics project)). But this has not translated to general perceptions. Users remain unsure about their privacy when using apps.

Second, "I don't trust healthcare apps will get it right for me", 46% agree, and 54% do not. The assertion relates to bias and representation: if a model has been built with sufficient examples including the target user, then it should be able to respond as expected to all potential users (see, for instance, [30]). Users therefore want to see benefits for themselves in using apps, including the reassurance that responses will be personally relevant.

Survey 2

This was a survey of key stakeholders among the partners of BML (N = 47). Among the ethical considerations was the observation that advanced technologies

ii. This was run as part of the Dare UK PRiAM project.

require a new set of ethical norms, developed in consultation and by agreement with all relevant actors and stakeholders. In other words, it is important to involve multiple stakeholders in deciding what is ethically acceptable and what is not.

Furthermore, as well as observations about the need for transparency, where responsibility lies, and how essential advanced technologies are for the future of healthcare, responses to the assertions that I trust the person I get to talk with understands the technology they're using were equivocal. Stakeholders were unsure whether everyone using and relying on advanced technologies would be able to explain how these technologies work and how they arrive at the outcomes presented. Put another way, not all stakeholders will necessarily understand enough about the technology to make informed decisions about the validity of the outcomes.

Survey 3

An additional survey of the general public about privacy attitudes (N = 470)[iii] revealed the following: over half (58%) agreed with the statement I am concerned about my data being processed with advanced technology. This suggests some concern about personal data being used to develop or drive advanced technologies. At the same time, 71% agree that decisions are being taken about me or for me without my knowing, which seems to indicate some concern around automated decision making. 84% also disagreed that: If a company or researcher uses my data that's different from what they said originally, they don't have to tell me. They understand, therefore, that individuals have rights regarding how their data are used.

Nevertheless, 72% reported feeling overwhelmed by all the regulations, meaning ultimately that they were similarly overwhelmed by all the choices [they] have to do with privacy (to which 70% agreed). Although they know they have rights, therefore, and even though many are concerned about automated decision making and the use of data in advanced technology, they seem unable to take any action to protect their privacy themselves. In consequence, 94% believe that an independent authority should check that companies comply with the law. This is, of course, the case, though private citizens may not be aware.

Taking these results from the three surveys, it is clear that users may not feel they are indeed as empowered as data protection legislation suggests they should be; they want to understand more but do not feel their responsibilities extend beyond a decision as to whether to share their data. These conclusions need to inform the new ethics that the BML partners believe is required when considering advanced technologies and will form part of a checklist for research ethics review set out below. Table 5.1 summarizes these views. Consideration 3 should already be part

iii. The questionnaire is available at https://doi.org/10.5281/zenodo.7589522.

Table 5.1. Summary of stakeholder perspectives.

Consideration	Comment
1	Participants want to see how the research and technology are personally relevant to them
2	Participants want to understand the technology as much as possible
3	Participants want to understand how their data will be used (and potential further sharing thereof)
4	Ethical governance should be based on perspectives from multiple stakeholders
5	Privacy needs to be discussed, but is not necessarily of primary importance to participants

of the research protocol; the point here is that there needs to be a focus on data used to model an entire cohort. Consideration 5 is included to emphasize that although data protection imposes regulatory obligations regarding personal data, this is not necessarily the focus for research participants.

5.4 A Different Type of Ethics

Research ethics is based on a set of assumptions. For the research to be deemed ethical and therefore approved by IRBs or RECs, it must meet the following criteria [10]:

- Respect for the Individual: usually operationalized via the consent process (though see Section 5.5). Specifically, participants have the right to know what is expected of them, to make a decision to take part freely, and to withdraw at any time and without giving a reason;
- Beneficence: the research should directly or indirectly benefit the individual, the cohort to which the individual belongs, or society in general;
- Non-maleficence: the research should not cause any negative effect, such as physical or emotional harm; and
- Justice: everyone – again, specifically the participants themselves – should receive benefit in equal measure.

The focus understandably is on the research participant, of course. Most IRBs/RECs, though, will consider the well-being of the researcher, especially in security-sensitive work. As the BML studies illustrate, big data solutions affect multiple relationships within the healthcare ecosystem: Figure 5.1 highlights the patient–clinician relationship, which is also seen directly in Chapter 9 (eHealth and telemedicine for risk prediction and monitoring in kidney transplantation recipients), Chapter 10 (Remote monitoring to improve gestational diabetes care), and Chapter 11 (Monitoring wellness in chronic obstructive pulmonary disease using the myCOPD app). But Chapter 19 (Implementation and impact of AI for the interpretation of lung diseases in chest CTs), for instance, provides empirical evidence that there are different responses between senior and junior radiologists. So, although all would doubtless subscribe a priori to the principles of beneficence and non-maleficence (for a discussion on how these principles affect one another, see [31]), respect for the individual needs to be broadened to include not only those who contribute their data to advanced technologies, but also those who depend on the resulting technology to provide care. Similarly, justice must include benefits for both.

Herschel and Miori attempted to review ethical theories within the context of big data [32]. They provide a rigorous assessment of Kantianism and Virtue Ethics. Although they maintain that exploiting big data has little to recommend it and regardless of specific challenges to each, they conclude that evaluating big data usage really comes down to whether or not the outcomes are generally positive [32, p. 35]. Rather than revisit their critique[iv], I will focus here on the re-interpretation of "positive outcomes" for the BML stakeholders with respect to Utilitarianism and Social Contract Theory, adding Floridi's Information ethics, conceived specifically with the digital world in mind.

Respect for the Individual will be dealt with in more detail in Section 5.5 below. Here, I focus more specifically on Justice. Approaches to research ethics which deal with the distribution of benefit are summarized in Table 5.2. In Table 5.2, the focus on outcomes and the equanimity of benefit widens from Utilitarianism to Information ethics. To start with, the assumption is that benefit should be maximized. This should be made clear before work is undertaken. However, with Rawls and Social Contract Theory, there is an a priori expectation that benefit should be available to all stakeholders, not just a majority. So, as well as identifying expected benefit per se, it is also important that there is some thought given to how benefit can be maximized for as many stakeholders as possible. Finally, and notwithstanding the importance of human agents within healthcare, especially patients, what Floridi has done with Information Ethics is foreground the consideration of nonhuman agents. This does not undermine the accepted significance of human participants especially patients. But if technology is seen as an essential part of future healthcare (see Chapter ii (Foreword) and Chapter 1 (Introduction)), then that technology is

---

iv. Specifically, Kantianism is problematic for big data for its focus on individual rights, and Virtue Ethics would be based on the assumption that the data scientist should be virtuous, which is assumed prima facie anyway.

Table 5.2. Approaches to ethics (for more detail, see, for instance, [33]).

Approach	Description
Utilitarianism	Ethical judgement derives from action which maximizes the benefit across society. The BML studies targeted an improvement in healthcare irrespective of disease or of the efficiency of how healthcare is delivered. In so doing, they sought to provide empirical evidence for both Patient and Clinician in Figure 5.1, as well as inform data science in general, and public policy (affecting both the Healthcare Authority and Community perceptions in the figure). The overall benefit should be maximized, even though some individuals may miss out. In Chapter 8 (Effects of comorbidities (chronic illness) on hospitalization and mortality risks: available to clinicians through an app), for instance, if only patients presenting with a certain combination of comorbidities receive benefit would still be deemed a success, and quite rightly so.
Social Contract Theory	The idea here is that everyone in society has an equal and inalienable right to such benefit. The BML studies made no distinction across stakeholder type: although not all studies provided equal benefit to all stakeholders in each case, there was no a priori intention to favor one above the other. In Chapter 9 (eHealth and telemedicine for risk prediction and monitoring in kidney transplantation recipients), although there was clear evidence that patients benefit from the introduction of the technology, the healthcare ecosystem needed to accept additional burden in terms of cost and resource. In Chapter 19 (Implementation and impact of AI for the interpretation of lung diseases in chest CTs), by contrast, although the focus is on support for the Clinician, the benefit would also indirectly affect the Patient with improved diagnosis. This would then enhance public perception (within the Community) and could provide new standards or guidelines for the Healthcare Authority. Unlike utilitarianism, Social Contract Theory refines the notion that ethical behaviors should provide overall benefit – which allows for some to miss out so long as there is general improvement – and instead aims to provide maximal benefit to all.

(*Continued*)

Table 5.2. Continued

Approach	Description
Information Ethics	Both human agents and objects should receive equal benefit. Ethical behavior adds to the overall entropy of the Infosphere. What this means is that human agents (Patients and Clinicians) and groups and institutions (Community and Healthcare Authority), but also technologies (Self-monitoring Apps and Decision Support systems where relevant) as well as intangibles such as the algorithms and body of knowledge and experience of data science should be treated as equally worthy of receiving benefit. It is the latter concept – the body of knowledge – which makes this approach distinct. With big data and advanced technology deployment in healthcare, direct and current benefit may well have little immediate effect for human participants, but in adding to what we know about data science now, this would pay dividends for all stakeholders in the future. Furthermore, in Chapter 10 (Remote monitoring to improve gestational diabetes care), the introduction of the technology increased the accuracy of incoming data irrespective of what was derived from the data. In Chapter 11 (Monitoring wellness in chronic obstructive pulmonary disease using the my-COPD app), issues associated with the integration of environmental data highlighted the need for further work if such data are to provide benefit. In all cases (see Chapter 27 (General learnings from the Horizon 2020 project BigMedilytics)), we summarize the benefits and lessons learnt that are targeted at those engaging with advanced technology and healthcare.

Table 5.3. Summary of ethical theory perspectives.

Consideration	Comment
6	Research benefit should be maximized
7	As many stakeholders as possible should receive benefit
8	Beneficiaries may include nonhuman agents

a close second. Ethics reviewers need to weigh up how the science behind big data in healthcare is served alongside considerations of beneficence/non-maleficence to human agents.

Table 5.3 summarizes the additional considerations that need to be taken forward into research ethics review.

5.5 The Issue with Consent

In the previous chapter (Chapter 4 (Lessons learned in the application of the general data protection regulation to the BigMedilytics project)), there was a discussion of consent specifically within the context of data protection. This is not the only kind of consent, however. Requesting any of these may be deemed Respect for the Individual. In this section, I consider the different types of consent that research ethics committees are likely to encounter when asked to review research proposals. First, the question arises as to the type of consent being used and its domain, as well as whether the research participant is capable of making an informed decision about consent. This has implications for how reviewers make decisions about research ethics approval for research involving advanced technology. Although app users did not feel themselves able to make informed decisions about how their data are used as described in Section 5.2, they were still asked for consent when engaging with research, a clinical trial, or sharing their personal data. However, it is not always clear what consent means to them: the construct is very context-dependent. Table 5.4 summarizes the main types of consent that an individual may encounter.

For clinical consent, the patient is assumed to be able to reach an informed decision based on what the clinician reveals to them, but also against a background

Table 5.4. Three different types of consent.

Domain	Description
Clinical	A patient's willingness to undergo a given intervention or to take part in a clinical trial. The patient will often trust that the clinician knows what they are doing and will not intentionally harm their patient. But they will have been told of any known risks.
Research Ethics	Even where any data collected is anonymous, i.e., no individual can be identified, Consent refers to a research participant's willingness to engage in a research project or task. Like other forms of *Consent*, it is assumed to be informed: they know and understand what they are about to be asked to do. And it is freely given: participants do not feel obliged or coerced into participation. Not all research requires a full understanding of the research activities: deception may be a valid approach.
Data Protection	One lawful basis to process data. The data subject says they are happy for their data to be collected and used as stated. This comes with specific obligations and responsibilities. For instance, if some other purpose for using data is discovered, it is important to go back to each data subject and re-consent them. Therefore, always check what the original consent covered.

of public perception. One question, though, is whether the patient–clinician relationship is equal: is the patient capable of making an informed decision about their care or are they simply expecting the clinician to treat and cure them? If so, clinical consent will shift more toward paternalism rather than an autonomous, fully informed decision by the patient [34]. Second, if left to the patient alone, the clinician is prevented from satisfying their own medical goal to provide care [31].

Introducing advanced technologies, like those evaluated during BML, complicates the consent process further. As shown in Survey 2, not all stakeholders will understand the implications of working with advanced technology (see Section 5.3). The clinician may now be reliant on technology they do not fully understand, and the patient unwittingly continues to assume the same level of robustness to what the clinician tells them. At the very least, therefore, undertaking research on the integration of technology into healthcare must consider what different stakeholders – especially a patient and a clinician – can be expected to understand of the target technology and how it works. This has been highlighted to some degree in healthcare intervention frameworks (see, for instance, [35]).

Research consent is similar to clinical consent, though the potential risks may be less dramatic. It assumes an informed decision about what is expected of the research participant, including any risk during the study itself and introduced as a result of sharing research data in publications or sharing a research dataset. Some deception, of course, may be necessary when a spontaneous response is required from participants.[v] However, there is a problem specific to big data modeling. Take, for instance, Chapter 11 (Monitoring wellness in chronic obstructive pulmonary disease using the myCOPD app). First, and in common with any such modeling, it may not be clear which data items need to be used to make predictions (see Figure 11.2 of Chapter 11 (Monitoring wellness in chronic obstructive pulmonary disease using the myCOPD app) on the Gini importance of different data items). Second, irrespective of issues with velocity and so forth, integrating environmental factors effectively would involve localizing individuals. Location is considered personal data [36, Art. 4(1)]. Therefore, the researcher would need to negotiate a separate lawful basis to collect and use the data. Third, assuming location data could be used, it is dynamic: as the patient in Chapter 20 (Innovative use of technology for acute care pathway monitoring and improvements) is brought to the hospital, it would be helpful to track their progress. Tracking could potentially provide intrusive insights into participants' daily lives and activities. This risk would have to be made explicit if dynamic location data were deemed important.

---

v. See British Psychological Society Code of Human Research Ethics at https://www.bps.org.uk/guideline/bps-code-human-research-ethics.

In all, research consent is really an ongoing negotiation as the data scientist establishes what is and is not predictive for the specific study [37]. The question here for reviewers, therefore, is how much the researcher can and does share with research participants to inform them?

Finally, data protection consent is one lawful basis that permits the processing of personal data [36, Art. 6 and Art. 9]. Apart from potential confusion – whether the participant is being asked for research consent or data protection consent – consent as a lawful basis for processing can be restrictive. Specifically, a research participant may decide to withdraw their data[vi] which would require the researcher to track and remove the data. In turn, this may alter the results. If enough data subjects withdraw consent, this could skew the generalizability of any data model. Ethics reviewers should validate that the type of consent is clear to the participant from the start. Furthermore, researchers need to consider whether another lawful basis is more appropriate. For instance, if an academic institution is publicly funded to deliver research outcomes, it may be possible to rely on Public task rather than Data protection consent. This needs to be made clear to research participants.

5.6 A Question of Profiling

According to Merriam-Webster, profiling may be understood as "the act of …targeting a person on the basis of observed characteristics or behavior."[vii] For the BML studies, this translates to two sets of activity. First, using their data to identify general groupings or phenotypes (cf. Chapter 8 (Effects of comorbidities (chronic illness) on hospitalization and mortality risks: available to clinicians through an app)); and second, to make predictions for individuals (e.g., Chapter 9 (eHealth and telemedicine for risk prediction and monitoring in kidney transplantation recipients), Chapter 10 (Remote Monitoring to Improve Gestational Diabetes Care), Chapter 11 (Monitoring wellness in Chronic Obstructive Pulmonary Disease using the myCOPD app), etc.). In terms of data protection, profiling (and automatic decision-making) is clearly restricted, [36, Art. 6, Art. 22, and Recital 71] especially if the data are special-category personal data [36, Art.9(2)]. Explicit consent for data protection is a sound basis for profiling. However, as summarized in the previous paragraph, consent can be confusing for the research participant. Furthermore, for exploratory work, the researcher or data scientist may not know what data

vi. It is a moot point if they are able to understand any restrictions on this before making this decision.

vii. https://www.merriam-webster.com/dictionary/profiling Accessed on 4th Oct 2022.

they need for robust profiling. There is also concern that profiling may not lead to appropriate or generalizable outcomes [14, 15].

Data protection regulation therefore restricts profiling activities, suggesting consent as a suitable mechanism from a research participant's or data subject's perspective. This may be problematic as outlined in the previous paragraph. More generally, though, there are known issues with profiling, especially in terms of coverage [38]. This could affect public perception. Following on from the discussion of consent and whether or not it can be fully informed, it is important to consider expected accuracy and coverage. This may need ongoing negotiation as researchers interrogate data from participants.

5.7 Summary for Consent and Profiling

Thinking specifically of ethical review, Table 5.5 summarizes the final set of issues that reviewers would face based on the previous paragraphs in the context of BML. Considering both consent in this paragraph and the sharing of potential benefit from the research in relation to the BML studies has yielded 12 considerations. Some of these relate to similar issues, such as how the participant is supported to understand the implications of what the technology is trying to achieve. In the next section, Section 5.8, I use these 12 considerations to propose a set of 12 questions for research ethics reviewers when evaluating research proposals.

5.8 A Checklist for Ethics Review

In the previous paragraphs, I have highlighted some of the challenges that the BML studies faced from a research ethics perspective. Tables 5.1, 5.3, and 5.5 list a set of assertions derived from that analysis. Homing in on research activities, these assertions may be used to develop a checklist for ethics reviewers assessing research

Table 5.5. Summary of ethical issues highlighted by *Consent*.

Consideration	Comment
9	The type or types of Consent should be clear and appropriate
10	Participants need to understand what happens to their data
11	Participants need to understand who will benefit
12	Participants need to understand the purpose and limitations of any profiling

Table 5.6. Suggested checklist for research ethics reviewers.

Consideration(s)	Proposed Checklist
1, 2	How is the technology made relevant to the research participants providing data?
1, 2	How is the technology explained to the potential research participant?
3, 5	How is the use of personal data explained?
3, 5, 11, 12	Are potential research participants fully aware of what will happen to their data?
4	How is the research study publicized across other stakeholders?
6, 10	How will the proposed research benefit the community?
7, 10	How will the proposed research benefit each stakeholder?
8, 10	How will the proposed research contribute to knowledge in this area?
9	What does consent mean in the proposed research study?
9	Does the potential research participant understand what type of consent is being requested?
11, 12	Does the proposed research include profiling?
11, 12	How is the profiling explained to the potential research participants?

study proposals. Table 5.6 summarizes these points. The first column refers back to the Ref. number in Tables 5.1, 5.3, and 5.5.

Table 5.6 lists 12 items to be included in research ethics review by RECs/IRBs. Some of these should already be addressed since they are not specific to big data and advanced technology projects. For instance, How is the use of personal data explained? should already be included in a Participant Information Sheet, and where personal data are collected, the associated Privacy Notice. However, they are included in the checklist to encourage researchers when applying for ethics approval and reviewers in deciding whether the proposal meets ethical standards to consider the specific implications of big data exploitation in healthcare projects as derived from a consideration of the BML studies and experience.

Of course, identifying the specific issues that should be part of the research protocol, as listed in Table 5.6, assumes that appropriate methods are in place to communicate the relevant information among research study stakeholders. Traditionally, a participant information sheet is provided to set out the aims, potential risks, and benefits of research studies. On the basis of their understanding of the participant information sheet, research participants would decide whether or not to take part and provide informed research consent. However, it is worth considering how that

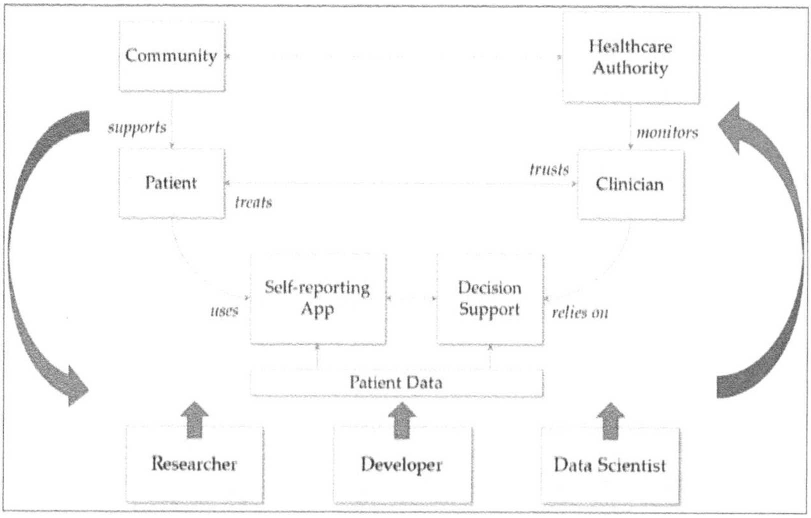

Figure 5.2. Research based on continuous negotiation.

communication can be made most effective. This requires a reconsideration of the healthcare delivery network introduced earlier (see Figure 5.1).

Overall, the experience of BML suggests how to introduce and manage the ethical governance of projects which focus on or will affect the healthcare network (see Figure 5.1). Bringing researchers, technology developers, and data scientists into the network would profit from a continual cycle of discussion: the researchers, developers, and data scientists would inform patients, clinicians, and the healthcare authority of what is happening, what has been developed and implemented, and any caveats and challenges; in return, the patients, the community at large, the clinicians, and the healthcare authority should continue to provide feedback, highlighting any concerns or issues from their side (see also Figure 5.2 [39, 40]).

5.9 Discussion and Conclusion

In this chapter, I have reviewed the ethical governance of research studies – like the study projects in BML – which seek to understand the effects of introducing advanced, AI-enabled technologies into healthcare. I have contextualized empirical survey data from BML, the experience of the study projects, and related work on privacy perceptions within two major research ethics challenges: balancing respect for the individual and the justice of sharing the benefits of the research. To some degree, this moves the cost-benefit approach forward by considering patient–clinician engagement with researchers not in financial terms but as a collaboration between all stakeholders with a common goal of improving healthcare for all [41].

On that basis, I have proposed a set of additional questions to support reviewers on IRBs/RECs when evaluating the potential benefit of research proposals against what is expected from all the stakeholders involved and especially the research participants – in BML, the patients and the clinicians – with advanced technologies.

References

[1] Martínez R. Designing artificial intelligence. Challenges and strategies for achieving regulatory compliance. Revista Catalana de Dret Public. 2019. 58: p. 64–81.

[2] Council of Europe, European Convention for the Protection of Human Rights and Fundamental Freedoms, as amended by Protocols Nos. 11 and 14, E.C.o.H. Rights, Editor. 2010. Council of Europe.

[3] Palys T, Lowman J. Defending research confidentiality "to the extent the law allows:" lessons from the Boston College subpoenas. Journal of Academic Ethics. 2012. 10: p. 271–297. DOI: 10.1007/s10805-012-9172-5.

[4] Acquisti A, Brandimarte L, Loewenstein G. Privacy and human behavior in the age of information. Science. 2015. 347(6221): p. 509–514. DOI: 10.1126/science.aaa1465.

[5] Barth S, de Jong M. The privacy paradox – Investigating discrepancies between expressed privacy concerns and actual online behavior – a systematic literature review. Telematics and Informatics. 2017. 34(7): p. 1038–1058. DOI: 10.1016/j.tele.2017.04.013.

[6] Acquisti, A., Brandimarte, L., Loewenstein, G. (2022). Privacy and Behavioral Economics. In: Knijnenburg, B.P., Page, X., Wisniewski, P., Lipford, H.R., Proferes, N., Romano, J. (eds) Modern Socio-Technical Perspectives on Privacy. Springer, Cham. https://doi.org/10.1007/978-3-030-82786-1_4.

[7] Kisselburgh L, Beever J. The ethics of privacy in research and design: principles, practices, and potential. In: Knijnenburg, B.P., Page, X., Wisniewski, P., Lipford, H.R., Proferes, N., Romano, J. (eds) Modern Socio-Technical Perspectives on Privacy. 2022. Cham: Springer International Publishing. p. 395–426.

[8] Charlesworth A. Data protection, freedom of information and ethical review committees: Policies, practicalities and dilemmas. Information, Communication & Society. 2012. 15(1): p. 85–103. DOI: 10.1080/1369118X.2011.637572.

[9] Lauber-Rönsberg A. Data protection laws, research ethics and social sciences. Research ethics in the digital age: ethics for the social sciences and humanities in times of mediatization and digitization. 2018. p. 29–44. DOI: 10.1007/978-3-658-12909-5_4.

[10] Department of Health, Education, and Welfare, National Commission for the Protection of Human Subjects of Biomedical and Behavioral Research. The Belmont report: Ethical principles and guidelines for the protection of human subjects of research. Editor. 1979.
[11] Pascale, J., Lineback, J.F., Bates, N., Beatty, P. Protecting the Identity of Participants. Qualitative Research, Journal of Survey Statistics and Methodology. 2022. 10(3): p. 549–567, DOI: 10.1093/jssam/smab048.
[12] Krumholz HM. Big data and new knowledge in medicine: the thinking, training, and tools needed for a learning health system. Health Affairs (Project Hope). 2014. 33(7): p. 1163–1170. DOI: 10.1377/hlthaff.2014.0053.
[13] Bennett J, Lanning S. The Netflix Prize, in KDDCup '07. San Jose, California, USA. 2007.
[14] O'Neil C. Weapons of math destruction: how big data increases inequality and threatens democracy. New York, NY: Crown. 2016.
[15] Cheney-Lippold J. We are data: algorithms and the making of our digital selves. New York, NY: New York University Press. 2017.
[16] Belle A, *et al.* Big data analytics in healthcare. BioMed Research International. 2015: p. 1–16.
[17] Kankanhalli A, *et al.* Big data and analytics in healthcare: introduction to the special section. Information Systems Frontiers. 2016. 18(2): p. 233–235.
[18] Bellazzi R. Big data and biomedical informatics: a challenging opportunity. Yearbook of Medical Informatics. 2014. 23(01): p. 8–13.
[19] Amnesty International, AccessNow. The Toronto Declaration: protecting the right to equality and non-discrimination in machine learning systems. 2018.
[20] European Commission. Ethics guidelines for trustworthy AI. 2019. Available from: https://ec.europa.eu/digital-single-market/en/news/ethics-guidelines-trustworthy-ai.
[21] UK Government. A guide to good practice for digital and data-driven health technologies, Department of Health & Social Care, Editor. 2021.
[22] UK Government, Data Ethics Framework, Government Digital Services, Editor. 2020.
[23] Pupillo L, Ferreira A, Fantin S. Task Force Evaluation of the HLEG Trustworthy AI Assessment List (Pilot Version). 2020.
[24] Jobin A, Ienca M, Vayena E. The global landscape of AI ethics guidelines. Nature Machine Intelligence. 2019. 1(9): p. 389–399.
[25] Sula CA. Research ethics in an age of big data. Bulletin of the Association for Information Science and Technology. 2016. 42(2): p. 17–21.
[26] Carroll SR, *et al.* The CARE principles for indigenous data governance. Data Science Journal. 2020. 19(43): p. 1–12.

[27] Leslie D. Understanding artificial intelligence ethics and safety: a guide for the responsible design and implementation of AI systems in the public sector. 2019.
[28] Hand DJ. Aspects of data ethics in a changing world: where are we now? Big Data. 2018. 6(3): p. 176–190.
[29] Cresswell KM, Worth A, Sheikh A. Actor-Network Theory and its role in understanding the implementation of information technology developments in healthcare. BMC Medical Informatics and Decision Making. 2010. 10(1): p. 67.
[30] Wehrli S, *et al.* Bias, awareness, and ignorance in deep-learning-based face recognition. AI and Ethics. 2022. 2(3): p. 509–522.
[31] Muirhead W. When four principles are too many: bloodgate, integrity and an action-guiding model of ethical decision making in clinical practice. Clinical Ethics. 2011. 38: p. 195–196.
[32] Herschel R, Miori VM. Ethics & big data. Technology in Society. 2017. 49: p. 31–36.
[33] Parsons TD. Ethical challenges in digital psychology and cyberpsychology. Cambridge, UK: Cambridge University Press. 2019.
[34] Boyd KM. Autonomy, patients' preferences, and leaving decisions to doctors. Journal of the Royal College of Physicians, Edinburgh. 2013. 43: p. 136.
[35] Greenhalgh T, *et al.* Beyond adoption: a new framework for theorizing and evaluating nonadoption, abandonment, and challenges to the scale-up, spread, and sustainability of health and care technologies. Journal of Medical Internet Research. 2017. 19(11): p. e367.
[36] European Commission, Regulation (EU) 2016/679 of the European Parliament and of the Council of 27 April 2016. 2016.
[37] Wiles R, *et al.* Informed consent and the research process: following rules or striking balances? Sociological Research Online. 2007. 12. DOI: 10.5153/sro.1208.
[38] Klare BF, *et al.* Face recognition performance: role of demographic information. IEEE Transactions on Information Forensics and Security. 2012. 7(6): p. 1789–1801.
[39] Rohlfing KJ, *et al.* Explanation as a social practice: toward a conceptual framework for the social design of AI systems. IEEE Transactions on Cognitive and Developmental Systems. 2020. p. 1–1.
[40] Pickering B. Trust, but verify: informed consent, AI technologies, and public health emergencies. Future Internet. 2021. 13(5).
[41] Wang Y, *et al.* Big data analytics: Understanding its capabilities and potential benefits for healthcare organizations. Technological Forecasting and Social Change. 126. p. 3–13. DOI: 10.1016/j.techfore.2015.12.019.

DOI: 10.1561/9781638282372.ch6

Chapter 6

Health Platform Businesses – From Investigations to Platforms

By Anca Mihalache and Marcin Detyniecki

Healthcare is a sector struggling to reduce the cost of care while improving health outcomes, improving providers' productivity, and meeting patients' expectations. This quadruple aim has been relevant for many years and remains unattainable. The consequences of COVID-19, plus the politically, socially, and economically complex environment in Europe, are putting additional pressure on already fragile health systems.

Platform business models have gained significant traction in recent years, bringing scale, affordability, and other advantages that could benefit the healthcare sector as well. However, these new models are present more frequently in certain industries such as e-commerce (e.g., eBay, Craigslist, and Alibaba), travel (e.g., Airbnb and Uber), and communication (e.g., Zoom), to name but a few. They have shaped consumer expectations (e.g., same-day delivery) and triggered traditional businesses to rethink their operating model (e.g., production is done outside of the company via a platform business model). However, platform businesses have had limited traction in healthcare, and it is difficult to identify flagship examples as they exist in other industries.

In this chapter, we will first define what a platform business in healthcare is. We explore how the current state of the art in platform business theory applies to healthcare, including aspects such as open architecture, rules of governance, and core interactions. Subsequently, we test this theory with field observation done around the 12 BigMedilytics study projects (the pilots), leading to a set of requirements to successfully move from a set of innovative products to platform businesses. Finally, considering the theory presented and practical observations, we discuss the potential for a health platform business to be a solution for the quadruple aim in healthcare, namely (1) to reduce the cost of care while (2) improving health outcomes, (3) increasing provider productivity, and (4) meeting patient expectations.

6.1 Brief Overview of Platform Theory and Main Concepts

Platform business models have gained significant traction in recent years, bringing scale, affordability, and other advantages that the healthcare sector has yet to benefit from. In Europe, there are more than 200 companies operating as platforms across 28 countries [1], mostly from France and the UK, and competing against more well-known and established US players. They facilitate transportation (goods and people), offline and online services; employ all skill levels; range from non-profit to for profit (commissioning model, membership fee, flat rate, etc.); vary in size – as small as under €1 million turnover and 10,000 clients and service providers, to as large as €100 million or more, respectively, 1 million clients and service providers. These platforms have shaped consumer expectations (e.g., same-day delivery) and triggered traditional businesses to rethink their operating models. These models are more prevalent in certain industries such as e-commerce (e.g., eBay, Craigslist, and Alibaba), travel (e.g., Airbnb and Uber), and communication (e.g., Zoom), and less so in healthcare, which remains yet to be disrupted by platform models, with fewer representative examples limited geographically and in scope.

Let us first see what a platform is and then focus on health. There is extensive research available on platform models, and in general terms, a platform is an (1) open architecture, [2] with a (2) governance model (that sets the rules of the game – for participation, monetization, sanctions, etc.), facilitating (3) core interactions between parties.

6.1.1 Core Interactions

Platforms are typically designed around a core interaction, where participants are put in contact by a matching algorithm to exchange a value unit, [3] the equivalent of a product (be it tangible or intangible) for a traditional business. Typically, a product is the result of a pre-defined set of ingredients, combined by a company's processes (often its intellectual property), before it reaches the end client for consumption. The value unit of a platform is the result of interactions between producers and consumers enabled by the platform.

6.1.2 Open Architecture

With the core interaction clearly defined, the platform owner designs what is called an open architecture. This is a technical piece of work that is proprietary to the platform owner. Built in-house or with partners, the architecture enables the exchange of information, goods, services, or currency. The platform has built-in functions to pull in both sides of the platform (value producers and value consumers), to match them at the right time with the right value, and to facilitate such exchange. It is modular, meaning it is made of independent parts designed to function as a whole, with visible design rules and hidden design parameters [4]. It has a stable core and highly customizable and diverse features, allowing for personalization and matching in many more ways than a traditional business can [5]. This is also possible thanks to data and advanced analytics, which cannot be dissociated from the platform, being fully embedded in the way it operates. For example, real-time voting, ranking, and feedback loops give information about the performance of current products and inform decisions about future ones, creating an intrinsic value for the platform itself.

6.1.3 Governance Model

A platform would not be complete if, in addition to the open architecture and the core interactions, there were no governance models. These are the laws (European, national, platform-specific, and so forth), norms, architecture, and markets that ensure the appropriate distribution of value between producers, [3] consumers, and platform owner and incentivize future interactions. These are also meant to discourage or penalize misbehavior and create a general environment of trust, as a platform creates value with resources it does not typically own or control. This phenomenon was phrased as the inverted firm, [3] where production does not happen in the company but outside through the company's partners. For example, Uber does not own the cars, but the drivers (producers of value) do. Through the governance rules, the platform locks in value exchange, making it more attractive to do business on the platform than outside.

6.1.4 Health Platforms

After this succinct review of platform definition and its three components, we move on to understand its application in a domain such as healthcare, considering that such an industry that relies on information, generates massive amounts of data, and is highly fragmented is said to be ready to be disrupted by platform models [3]. Despite extensive research, [6] it is complex to apply it to healthcare given the variety of stakeholders involved with misaligned incentives, the sensitive nature of health data, the regulatory framework, unequal technological adoption, etc. The adoption speed of a platform model has been slow in healthcare, yet it is believed to become the "new normal" [7].

To start with, there are multiple interpretations of what a health platform is. For example, there are platform-enabled ecosystems that leverage technology to connect an existing portfolio of partners and their respective goods and services [8]. Building such an asset is seen to be a strategic choice comparable with Mergers and Acquisitions, yet less risky because it is less capital intensive, but it requires pre-existing core operations, a mature customer base, and enough partners available. There are with health information exchange system where parties exchange services, information, and other resources to create smart and sustainable healthcare ecosystems [9]. For the purpose of our analysis, we have simply considered the platform definition presented previously as an open architecture with rules of governance designed to drive interactions within the health domain.

First, as platforms are designed around a core interaction, should this be related to health delivery, health financing, health enablement, or something else? The first is provided by medical professionals with various degrees of specialization (e.g., medical assistants, doctors, nurses, nutritionists, etc.) engaging with patients in different care settings (e.g., primary care office, ambulatory care clinic, digitally, etc.). The second is delivered by the government, insurers, employers, or individuals themselves, who pay fully or partially for the care delivered. Related to the first and second are numerous adjacent interactions for the enablement of care, such as appointment booking, drug delivery, data sharing, etc.

Second, the architecture designed to be open in platform terms to facilitate interaction is generally closed in healthcare (except perhaps for research purposes). This is driven by the national and international regulatory framework from the General Data Protection Regulation (GDPR) and is a consequence of technological planned or unplanned obsolescence, causing significant interoperability issues. For example, a hospital cannot share data with another hospital about a patient because they are using different providers or versions of electronic medical record (EMR) systems. The Social Security institutions of European countries hold the largest volume of health data, and legitimately so. They receive data from medical providers responsible for care and dispatch it to other players for payment purposes, research, etc. Medical providers, be they a solo practice or hospital group, have a view limited to their own patient interactions, which can be limiting, particularly when working with patients with multiple or complex conditions.

Last but not least, governance is mandatory in health and for health platform models, for example, to define the roles and responsibilities of all parties, the operating terms and conditions, the rules of funding, the alignment of incentives, and to penalize in case of misbehavior, malfunctioning, etc. In a traditional health setting, the doctor has the responsibility of ensuring the right diagnosis and treatment. The payment of care is done based on value, or most frequently, on a fee for service defined by local governments and funded by taxes in most European countries. In health platform models, the rules of governance for care delivery and care funding ought to be given the highest attention, building on current best practices and innovating to overcome challenges regarding inefficiency, [10] workforce shortage, health inequalities, [11] or reimbursement, [12] to name but a few.

6.2 Focus on BigMedilytics Studies and Parallels to Platform Theory and Concepts

The BigMedilytics initiative encompassed 12 study projects spread across three themes – Population Health & Chronic Disease Management, Oncology, and the Industrialization of Healthcare Services – with a common goal to prove the positive impact of data analytics on healthcare systems in Europe [13].

The five studies in the Population Health & Chronic Disease Management section aim at demonstrating that big data analytics can reduce the burden on the secondary care institutions through a better triage and orientation of patients to the most appropriate place of care. These studies focus on specific conditions that drive mortality and morbidity in Europe – kidney, diabetes, chronic obstructive pulmonary disease, asthma, and heart failure – and on populations with comorbidities. The three oncology studies aimed at demonstrating how analytics can enable better and personalized treatment with lower complication rates for patients and higher productivity rates for the medical practitioners. With the focus on breast, prostate, and lung cancers, they represent the most frequent cancer types and involve the highest burden in Europe. The four healthcare service industrialization studies aimed at leveraging analytics to improve hospital workflows, critical for productivity (radiology; asset management), and quality of care (sepsis management; stroke

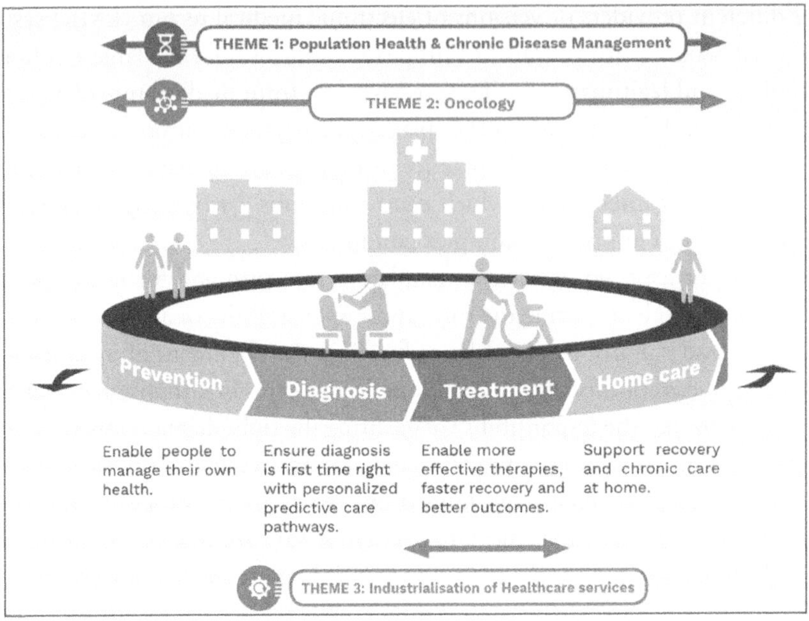

Figure 6.1. Representation of the three themes covered by BigMedilytics studies along the continuum of care.

management). Studies targeted specific customers, had different value propositions, and required tailored activities, resources, or partners. The geographical coverage, clinical focus, or maturity stage of the big data innovation differed as well, with some being in the minimum product development phase while others were preparing a product for commercialization.

To understand the potential of becoming health platforms, the following analysis was carried out on the core components of a platform: architecture, participants, core interaction, and governance.

6.2.1 BigMedilytics: Who Could Become a Health Platform?

First, it is important to identify who the participants are who have the potential to become platform owners? In the BigMedilytics studies, participants were representative of the healthcare sector: medical professionals, medical institutions, health techs, patients, etc. Each study had a lead organization in charge of the overall coordination between study partners and who closely managed the timeline, scope, and budget for its own organization. It brought key capabilities, such as data, technology, or clinical operations, necessary for the study to achieve its goals. In platform theory, this lead organization might be a platform owner, value producer, or consumer of value. This central role in the BigMedilytics initiative does not automatically imply that it is best suited for platform owners.

Research and medical institutions (Incliva VLC Biomedical Research Institute; Charité Medical University; University of Southampton; Erasmus MC Medical University; Karolinska University Hospital; National Centre of Scientific Research Demokritos; ETZ Elisabeth-TweeSteden Ziekenhuis Medical Center) come with the advantage of innovative, modular technology, applicable to diverse sectors, and a commercially driven strategy. They are by nature institutions operating at the intersection of science and healthcare, relying to some degree on legacy technology, and trying to balance research with the delivery of care.

More often than not, the platform owner comes with the technology that enables interactions. In the case of BigMedilytics, although all partners have some degree of technology, yet best equipped to be platform owners would be pure technology companies (e.g., Huawei, IBM, Contextflow, Philips).

This being said, more complex set-ups, including dedicated spin-offs, could overcome some of the above-mentioned challenges. In the end, the purpose of a health platform model – for public good, commercial good, or both – will strongly influence, in the case of healthcare, who the platform owner, producer, and consumers are.

6.2.2 BigMedilytics: Identifying the Core Interaction

Second, can there be a single unifying core interaction for all BigMedilytics studies that could justify the convergence of all studies, leading to a greater impact? Or can an individual study evolve the product around a core interaction? By analyzing the studies, we have identified three main interactions:

- Patients and medical providers exchange information for the purpose of managing the individual's health and ensuring a high quality of care.
- Hospitals' mobile asset providers (or a dedicated service) share data that medical providers use to find and manage assets more efficiently.
- Algorithms generate insights that medical providers consume to help reduce or improve diagnosis and treatment.

Hence, an all-encompassing core interaction could be framed as an exchange of information between people and physical assets in quasi real time for the purpose of faster and better diagnosis and treatment and the remote management of people's health and assets.

6.2.3 BigMedilytics: Open Architecture in Healthcare

Third, what does an open architecture mean in healthcare? The fact that healthcare is highly regulated can seem to be in contradiction with having an open architecture, like the Apple Store has for app developers, Airbnb for house owners, or Craigslist for anyone. Appointment booking solutions have platform characteristics, where medical professionals create an account, pay a monthly fee, and manage their appointments online, while patients search for medical professionals in many specialties nationwide for in-person and online consultations. The more practitioners on the platform, the more patients will use it, and in turn, this will attract more practitioners, generating what is known in platform businesses as the network effect [14].

Interestingly, those BigMedilytics studies focused on location characteristics that might readily evolve into a platform. In fact, the underlying architecture is open enough to include new and more interactions. For instance, if patients or medical professionals are connected in addition to mobile assets, this could provide an opportunity for interactions, both medical and non-medical. For example, a patient in the hospital can see doctors' schedules for meetings during the day; similarly, the patient can be visible in real time to doctors while moving between examination rooms. If the platform is available across hospitals, it could also help to keep track of patients transferred from one to the other easily. For these examples to materialize, data privacy and security measures need to be built into the architecture to evolve and adapt in tandem.

The BigMedilytics studies focusing on a particular disease could further explore the possibility of being the go-to platform for that particular disease for patients, medical providers, funders, and others. For example, a solution for patients with a chronic condition is to interact with all the relevant medical personnel (e.g., doctor, nurse, midwife, etc.) and non-medical experts (e.g., nutritionist, physical exercise trainer) to help better manage the condition. This could have higher relevance for patients with comorbidities, who are often left to navigate between different doctors and miss a coordinated approach. In these examples, in addition to data privacy considerations, the incentivization mechanism and the staffing model ought to be analyzed, so the solution is an integral part of care delivery, enhancing it rather than operating alongside it.

6.2.4 BigMedilytics: Rules of Governance in a Healthcare

Fourth, what are the rules of governance to be used in a health platform model? Laws, norms, architecture, and markets are meant to ensure transparency and instill trust in the platform, reward the good, disincentivize the bad, enable feedback, etc. The purpose of a platform – for example, commercial, public interest, and so forth – is a determining factor for the nature of the rules of governance. In addition to the architecture, the rules of governance dictate how open or closed (and for what) a platform is. The roles and responsibilities of participants – owner, value producer, and consumer – will be covered by these rules both for business as usual as well as for unexpected situations (e.g., platform is down, unable to provide a service, malfunction, and misbehavior). For the 12 studies, the foundation for governance was represented by the consortium's partnership agreement, where roles and responsibilities were clearly defined for each partner. Additionally, European and national data privacy regulations on the management of health data were referenced through study implementation.

6.3 Platform Models as a Potential Solution for the Quadruple Aim in Health

The BigMedilytics studies began before the COVID-19 pandemic. This unprecedented event made the quadruple aim even more challenging to attain. The cost of care increased considerably across Europe, by 6.3% in Germany, 3.9% in France, and 15.7% in the UK, mainly due to the acquisition costs of masks and tests and bonuses for the health workforce [15]. Accelerated development of mental health issues, in particular among the young and the poor, deferred diagnosis and treatment, and waiting times as long as 3 months for an appointment impacted the health outcome [16, 17]. The productivity of the health workforce has been negatively impacted by the shortage of skilled personnel, who were unevenly distributed around territories and whose mental health suffered as well because of the COVID-19 pandemic. Does a health platform model have the potential to attain the quadruple healthcare aim: (1) to reduce cost of care, while (2) improving health outcomes, (3) increasing provider productivity, and (4) meeting patient expectations under these circumstances?

6.3.1 Reducing Cost of Care

First, as per the cost of care across all European countries, hospital services, followed by outpatient services, represent the largest government expenditure on health as a percentage of gross domestic product [18]. In-patient services – those that require the patient to stay in the facility – are expensive and promise a higher success rate though disruptive to the patient's daily life. Outpatient services – those which can be provided at home or in non-hospital settings – are less expensive and less intrusive to the patient's everyday life. Thus, to address the first quadruple aim – reduce cost of care – and have a large addressable market, a platform would best tackle these two service areas.

6.3.2 Improving Health Outcomes

Second, health outcomes are changes in physical and mental health that result from measures of specific healthcare investments or interventions [19]. Standard

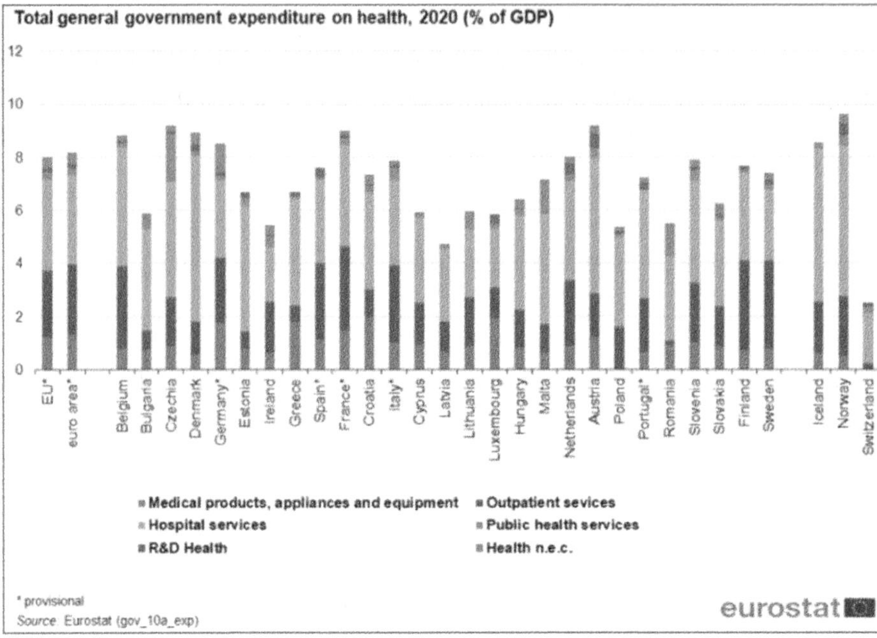

Figure 6.2. Government expenditure on health 2020 (source: Eurostat).

measures are usually general mortality, infant mortality, and life expectancy, but they can be health-related quality of life, functional status, symptoms and symptom burden, health behaviors, or patient experience of care [20]. There are direct and indirect investments and interventions, medical and non-medical, that impact health outcomes, which makes the spectrum of possibilities for a platform very broad. For example, appointment booking solutions that enable quick access to care can count indirectly towards a positive health outcome just like a doctor's intervention, yet the nature (i.e., frequency and magnitude) of the impact is significantly different.

6.3.3 Provider Productivity

Third, the productivity of the medical workforce has been part of the quadruple aim in healthcare for some time now, with more and more demands on a shrinking workforce (15 million more health workers needed by 2030 [21]), which was also highlighted during the COVID-19 pandemic. Technology aimed to automate manual processes to reduce the burden on highly skilled medical providers so they can spend more time with the patients, to remotely monitor patients with severe conditions at home, AI-enabled tools that predict people at risk for a specific condition, to name but a few examples, has yet to prove a positive impact on productivity. Healthcare workforce concerns are related to the ability to meet demand [22], adapt to new operating models, support workforce wellness, and recruit and retain new talent. Health workers and patients are directly impacted by the lack of interoperability among IT systems, so a platform would be expected to communicate with legacy systems with modern technology to reduce the barriers to usage as much as possible and positively amplify the workforce's impact.

6.3.4 Meeting Patient Expectations

Lastly, meeting patient expectations is possibly the most challenging objective in healthcare. People have different experiences and degrees of health literacy, which impact how empowered they feel to take care of their own health versus being taken care of. For example, the Patient Activation Measurement is a survey that assesses an individual's knowledge, skills, and confidence in managing their own health and healthcare [23]. The Patient Activation Measurement shows that a person with a level 1 score feels disengaged and overwhelmed, transferring full control to the medical professional to make decisions about their health. At the other end of the scale, a person with a level 4 is actively pushing further to adopt better behaviors, keeps informed, and discusses treatment with medical professionals. Moreover, patients expect to have access to care when they need it within a reasonable amount of time. For example, waiting times for common surgeries vary from less than a month to more than 8 months [17]. In the UK, in August 2022, 7 million people were waiting for treatment, and around 390,000 had been waiting for over a year (which is 375 times the pre-pandemic data in July 2019) [24]. Patients expect doctors to communicate well, to be empathic and make them feel cared for and regarded, [25] and to be trustworthy, knowledgeable, and loyal [26]. Lastly, patients expect better digital experiences when scheduling and interacting with medical professionals [27].

6.4 Conclusion

The quadruple aim in health, namely (1) to reduce the cost of care, while (2) improving health outcomes, (3) increasing provider productivity, and (4) meeting patient expectations, is more relevant today than ever before. The gaps in cost, outcomes, productivity, and patient expectations have deepened with the COVID-19 pandemic, and new and more efficient ways of delivering and paying for healthcare are expected to emerge.

In this context, the 12 BigMedilytics studies and associated innovations are very promising. Transforming them into business, and more largely to the extent of having an impact across Europe, requires – as observed in the field – significant investments and time.

From business theory, we know that platform models have the potential to alleviate some of the challenges, in particular when scaling the business. Moreover, healthcare platforms can bring a positive contribution by enabling a large number of interactions for a diverse group of people and assets in a timely, efficient, and productive manner.

This is why in this chapter, we not only explored, based on business theory, what it would take to have a successful platform in a healthcare environment, but also analyzed what it would take to evolve BigMedilytics' studies, or as a whole, into a platform business. Beyond our study, there are considerations we did not address since we believe that they require a more intense use-case-specific analysis. The so-called network effect is most notable, but there are also regulatory, technological, cultural, and financial barriers. In any case, what has proven essential to the success of BigMedilytics and will be necessary for any healthcare platform, in particular in Europe, is and will be the cooperation between cross-sector and cross-border parties.

References

[1] European Commission, Joint Research Centre, Beblavý M, Lenaerts K, Fabo B, Kilhoffer, Z. An overview of European platforms: scope and business models. Publications Office. 2018. https://data.europa.eu/doi/10.2760/762447.

[2] Partner Insight. Platform strategy explained with Marshall Van Alstyne, co-author of Platform Revolution. 2020. Available at: https://www.partnerinsight.io/post/platform-strategy-explained-w-marshall-van-alstyne-coauthor-of-platform-revolution.

[3] Parker G, van Alstyne M, Choudary S. Platform revolution: making networked markets work for you. WW Norton & Company. 2016.

[4] Baldwin CY, Clark KB. Design rules: the power of modularity. The MIT Press. Cambridge, MA. USA. 2000.

[5] Baldwin CY, Woodard CJ. The architecture of platforms: a unified view. Harvard Business School Finance Working Paper No. 09-034. 2008. Available at: https://www.hbs.edu/ris/Publication%20Files/09-034_149607b7-2b95-4316-b4b6-1df66dd34e83.pdf.

[6] Eastwood B. The 4 trends driving platform adoption in healthcare. 2022. Available at: https://mitsloan.mit.edu/ideas-made-to-matter/4-trends-driving-platform-adoption-health-care.

[7] Berger R. Future of health – the rise of healthcare platforms. 2020. Available at: https://www.rolandberger.com/en/Insights/Publications/Future-of-Health-The-rise-of-healthcare-platforms.html.

[8] Deloitte Insights. New business models in health care: building platform-enabled ecosystems. 2022. Available at: https://www2.deloitte.com/content/dam/insights/articles/us165009_chs-health-care-ecosystem/DI_CHS-Health-care-ecosystem.pdf.

[9] HealthIT.gov (2020) What is HIE? Available at: https://www.healthit.gov/topic/health-it-and-health-information-exchange-basics/what-hie.

[10] European Federation of Pharmaceutical Industries and Associations. In a world of finite resources, we cannot afford an inefficient use of health spending. 2019. Available at: https://www.efpia.eu/news-events/the-efpia-view/blog-articles/in-a-world-of-finite-resources-we-cannot-afford-an-inefficient-use-of-health-spending/.

[11] EuroHealthNet. Health Inequalities in Europe. 2019. Available at: https://eurohealthnet.eu/wp-content/uploads/documents/2019/191023_Factsheet_HealthEquityEU_WebLayout.pdf.

[12] Baker McKenzie. France: delay in the generalization of the reimbursement of remote medical monitoring. 2022. Available at: https://insightplus.bakermckenzie.com/bm/healthcare-life-sciences/france-delay-in-the-generalization-of-the-reimbursment-of-remote-medical-monitoring.

[13] BigMedilytics. The largest initiative to transform healthcare sector. 2018. Available at: https://www.bigmedilytics.eu/big-data-project/#project-overview.

[14] Hagiu A, Rothman S. Network effects aren't enough. The hidden traps in building an online marketplace. Harvard Business Review. 2016. Available at: https://hbr.org/2016/04/network-effects-arent-enough.

[15] Chardon-Boucaud S. Dépense de santé en Europe: une forte hausse en 2020 sous l'effet de la pandémie de COVID-19. DREES Études et Résultats. 2020. Number 1238. Available at: https://drees.solidarites-sante.gouv.fr/publications-communique-de-presse/etudes-et-resultats/depense-de-sante-en-europe-une-forte-hausse#:~{}:text=Sous%20l%27effet%20de%20la%20pand%C3%A9mie%20de%20COVID%2D19%2C,3%2C9%20%25%20en%20France.

[16] Blay JY, Boucher S, Le Vu B, Cropet C, Chabaud S, Perol D, Barranger E, Campone M, Conroy T, Coutant C, De Crevoisier R, Debreuve-Theresette A, Delord JP, Fumoleau P, Gentil J, Gomez F, Guerin O, Jaffré A, Lartigau E, Lemoine C, Mahe MA, Mahon FX, Mathieu-Daude H, Merrouche Y, Penault-Llorca F, Pivot X, Soria JC, Thomas G, Vera P, Vermeulin T, Viens P, Ychou M, Beaupere S. Delayed care for patients with newly diagnosed cancer due to COVID-19 and estimated impact on cancer mortality in France. ESMO Open. June 2021. 6(3):100134. DOI: 10.1016/j.esmoop.2021.100134.

[17] OECD. Waiting times for health services: next in line. OECD Health Policy Studies. 2020. Available at: https://www.oecd.org/health/waiting-times-for-health-services-242e3c8c-en.htm.

[18] EUROSTAT. Government expenditure on health. 2020. Available at: https://ec.europa.eu/eurostat/statistics-explained/index.php?title=Government_expenditure_on_health#:~{}:text=General%20government%20expenditure%20in%20the,8.0%20%25%20of%20GDP%20in%202020.

[19] Canadian Institute for Health Information. Health outcomes. Available at: https://www.cihi.ca/en/topics/outcomes#:~:text=Health%20outcomes%20are%20changes%20in,attack%20through%20in%2Dhospital%20care.

[20] Cella D, Hahn EA, Jensen SE, Butt Z, Nowinski CJ, Rothrock N, Lohr KN. Patient-reported outcomes in performance measurement. RTI Press. NC. USA. 2015.

[21] World Health Organization. Health workforce. 2023. Available at: https://www.who.int/health-topics/health-workforce#tab=tab_1.

[22] KPMG. Healthcare workforce worries won't go away. 2023. Available at: https://kpmg.com/xx/en/home/insights/2021/06/healthcare-workforce-worries-wont-go-away.html.

[23] Insignia Health. Patient activation measurement. 2022. Available at: https://www.insigniahealth.com/products/pam#:~{}:text=The%20Patient%20Activation%20Measure%C2%AE,versions%20and%20over%2035%20languages.

[24] British Medical Association. NHS backlog data analysis. 2023. Available at: https://www.bma.org.uk/advice-and-support/nhs-delivery-and-workforce/pressures/nhs-backlog-data-analysis.

[25] St George's University, School of Medicine. What makes a good doctor? 7 Surprisingly useful skills for physicians. 2021. Available at: https://www.sgu.edu/blog/medical/what-makes-a-good-doctor/.

[26] Chipidza FE, Wallwork RS, Stern TA. Impact of the doctor-patient relationship. Prim Care Companion CNS Disord. October 2015. 17(5): 10.4088/PCC.15f01840. DOI: 10.4088/PCC.15f01840.

[27] United Health Group. Consumers want better digital tools for finding healthcare: Survey. 2022. Available at: https://www.unitedhealthgroup.com/newsroom/2022/2022-07-20-optum-consumer-survey-better-tools-for-finding-care.html.

Section II

Use Cases in Technology – Population Health

DOI: 10.1561/9781638282372.ch7

Chapter 7

Introduction to Section II: Integration of and Bringing Big Data to Practical Usability

By Igor Paulussen, Alyssa Venema and Gerrit J. Noordergraaf

7.1 Introduction

This Section II on use cases in technology brings you to the operability aspects of data, focusing on user (i.e., patient) interaction with interfaces that bring their data into clinical usability. Data sharing and the digital applications on smart phones and wearable technology have the potential for supporting actual care needs. But, while all of us use apps in one form or another, how much do we know about who is on the receiving end and what they are doing with our data? And inversely, how good are we at inputting data and judging our health and quality of life?

The BigMedilytics (BML) project focused on bringing technology into use. Section II offers a series of four approaches, with divergent points of focus and models. Each chapter brings its own insights and lessons.

7.2 The Use of Health Records for Choices in 'Acute on Chronic' Care Decisions

In a herculean effort and with access to circa four million integral health records over a 5-year period, Navarro-Cerdán and coworkers (Chapter 8: Effects of comorbidities (chronic illness) on hospitalization and mortality risks) developed models for 19 chronic illnesses and how care decisions and all-cause 5-year mortality could be assessed in cohorts and potentially for a single patient. An example might be a middle-aged male with COPD gold 3, poor cardiac function, and now peripheral vascular disease with acute ischemia in the toes of a foot: Would hospital admission, peripheral bypass surgery, or limited amputation support him and his residual, small 'action radius', as well as his 5-year life expectancy? How would you approach such a discussion with a patient? You will find the tools they describe interesting and relevant in terms of user interfaces.

7.3 Monitoring and Risk Management for the Prevention of Transplanted Kidney Failure

Kidney failure and dialysis have a major impact on quality of life, the ability to travel, and life expectancy. Receiving a donor kidney offers a new lease on life. You would expect that the recipient would be totally compliant with everything they could do to support and maintain the donor kidney. However, this does not seem to be true, with poor therapy compliance being a relevant factor in transplantation failure. Duettmann and colleagues (Chapter 9: eHealth and telemedicine for risk prediction and monitoring in kidney transplantation recipients) took a telemedicine and eHealth approach to empowering the patient and reducing failure rates by improving recipient support (and compliance) by self-registration monitoring, leading to input in risk prediction models that could be used as decision support.

The authors, working in Germany, describe the difficulties of data sharing in a federal state and in setting up and using a system in a multidisciplinary setting. They developed a robust dashboard that could then be integrated into the Electronic Medical Record (EMR). The mobile phone app created interesting logistics and responsibility queries: response time, accuracy, access, and the ability for ready and early decision-making.

Since non-adherence to the use of the app could be seen as a risk in and of itself, the study spent time searching for and overcoming resistance to app use and interface issues. You will find a focused narrative offering a framework suitable for many organ-specific approaches.

7.4 Remote Monitoring in Gestational Diabetes

In this chapter, Grossi (Chapter 10: Remote monitoring to improve gestational diabetes care) describes the user case for eHealth in the form of a mobile phone-based interactive real-time app for use by pregnant women who have developed diabetes during their pregnancy. Gestational Diabetes Mellitus (GDM) has an extensive range of complications, both in the immediate future and in the more extended future, as well as for the unborn child. Careful management and tight control of blood sugar levels and ready supportive access to healthcare professionals support good outcomes and were implemented using a self-reporting system.

Grossi offers extensive insights into the developmental aspects of the app and into the choices made to gain valid information. Key needs for success are described, as are the data offered to show the reader that the system works.

In this study, a prognostic model was also developed and implemented. The study was able to show a reduction in the need to visit the outpatient department, reduce overhead costs, and improve blood glucose level stability.

A great example of a user case is where data management, different cohorts, and data sharing using self-reporting can show benefit.

7.5 Quality of Life and COPD Exacerbation (Prognostication)

Chronic Obstructive Pulmonary Disease (COPD) is an international chronic epidemic, reaching all layers of society and not only causing a major disruption in the quality of life, but also creating a serious load on healthcare. Particularly in countries with larger rural areas, the burden of this disease is increased by the large investments needed to reach and be seen by a healthcare professional.

In this chapter, Pickering (Chapter 11: Monitoring wellness in chronic obstructive pulmonary disease using the myCOPD app) approaches a new aspect of the use of self-reporting and big data: the ability to use subjective measures. Different from reporting objective numbers, reporting perception introduces new complexities. Where in Chapter 9, Duettmann and colleagues want to use telemedicine and eHealth to mitigate the decline in self-care, in this chapter aspects such as external influence, the individual's – and potentially changing – self-assessment of wellness, even as a function of seasons (i.e., it is fall and chilly, my COPD should be/will give me more trouble) is taken into account.

The chapter describes and analyzes two substudies to offer the reader insights into the clinically relevant and useful model of bringing data to clinicians and its potential to alter an illness's natural course and thus improve quality of life.

7.6 Privacy-Preserving Techniques Allowing Analysis of Medical Data

Privacy regulations, of which GDPR is only one, have been developed to protect individual. One can imagine that having access to medical data could allow the industry to tune, revise, or innovate more accurately. Being able to gain such insights is, however, complex, as (corporate) interests may not be parallel with the (individual) data holder.

In this chapter, Spini and coworkers (Chapter 12: Privacy-preserving techniques for analysis of medical data: secure multi-party computation), working from TNO (the Dutch Organization for applied scientific research, and thus as a neutral external party) describe a project involving a University Hospital and a large insurance company. They used the real-life scenario of heart failure patients, a chronic illness potentially requiring both admission and technological intensive care. One can imagine that an insurance company well versed in an epidemiologic approach to reimbursement strategies would be more than happy to have detailed insights into such a cohort. A dataset of Achmea and Erasmus MC, once intersected and combined, could, for example, be used to train a prediction model that would identify high-impact lifestyle factors for heart failure and thus, in turn, recognize high-risk heart failure patients.

The authors offer insight into their modeling, a number of algorithmic approaches, extensive references, and explain at some length how such a solution can be reached. For example, a third party can hold the database(s) and perform the calculations – such that the party supplying the data is not actually giving it to the interested other party.

Where privacy regulations have been seen as major hindrances to big data analytics, Spini and coworkers offer a safe and robust strategy to resolve this in a pragmatic fashion.

7.7 Conclusion: What Reading It Can Bring You

Section II describes a range of situations in which (big) data, self-reported or user-driven data generation, can be used to improve, strengthen, and intensify healthcare. While three of the chapters use a telemedicine/eHealth app-based approach, the concepts are generalizable. The different foci, from monitoring and prediction to early intervention to quality-of-life support, potentially offer other interested parties handholds in further development within their niche. Each chapter has its own learnings and is self-supporting.

Healthcare professionals, managers, the industry, and primarily the individual (patient) will recognize them as only partially tapped resources and methodologies described in Section II. It should stimulate and challenge all the stakeholders to continue and intensify their efforts to bring these technologies into practical, safe use.

DOI: 10.1561/9781638282372.ch8

Chapter 8

Effects of Comorbidities (Chronic Illness) on Hospitalization and Mortality Risks: Available to Clinicians Through an App

By José-Ramón Navarro-Cerdán, Manuel Sánchez-Gomis, Patricia Pons, Santiago Galvez-Settier, Francisco Valverde, Ana Ferrer-Albero, Inmaculada Sauri, Antonio Fernández and Josep Redon

8.1 Introduction

Chronic diseases are a major cause of mortality and morbidity, accounting for more than 75% of the healthcare burden in Europe and costing several hundred billion euros each year [1]. Treatment and care for these patients require coordinated input from a wide range of healthcare professionals over a period of many years. Assessing potential risks and benefits are a relevant issue for planning tailored decisions in an 'acute on chronic' setting. Comorbidity, the co-occurrence of two or more chronic diseases, usually produces an incremental increase in the need for hospitalization and in all-cause, 5-year mortality. These risks depend not only on the potentially new reason for admission, i.e., a new health concern, but also on which co-occurrence takes place and impacts the current reason for admission [2].

Efforts have been directed at identifying clinical risk groups in terms of costs, and several approaches have objectified scaling measures to this end. Examples are the CIRS (Cumulative Illness Rating Scale), [3] ICED (Index of Coexisting Disease), [4] and Clinical Risk Groups [5]. Other aggregated scales include gender and age in the disease clusters, e.g., ACGs (Adjusted Clinical Groups), [6] DRGs (Diagnosis-Related Groups), [7] and HRGs (Healthcare Resource Groups) [8]. Each creation procedure is different depending on the objectives pursued and the type of algorithm used. However, the usefulness of these approaches has been questioned because they are purely descriptive and thus not appropriate for making clinical decisions.

The scales described above use agglomerative hierarchical clustering methods dependent on the similarity of patient characteristics with different selection procedures, regardless of whether the procedures are supervised or unsupervised, and use mathematical inferences. Comorbidity clustering, however, allows the reallocation of a patient into comorbidity groups. This so-called divisive hierarchical risk clustering can provide relevant information on risks and can drive information for tuning the relevance and desirability of clinical interventions.

Likewise, the potential impact of a newly developed disease becomes visible as the clinician searches for the impact of a specific comorbidity.

In the present study, a divisive hierarchical risk clustering of circa four million adults observed during a period of five years was performed. Big data technologies were applied to prepare the data for modeling. A mobile app and a dashboard were developed to facilitate clinical use.

8.2 Challenges and Focus

The challenges described in this manuscript are the development of an application and a dashboard to allow the exploitation of the models for clinical risk stratification in such a way as to be useful for the clinician and to allow tailoring for an individual patient. The obtained information for a given patient is useful for intensifying the treatment in order to reallocate the patient into a better risk subset in the corresponding comorbidity group.

This led to the following two tangible goals:

(1) A smart phone app

This app was to be the interface between modeling and clinical needs. It allows a rapid, real-time calculation of risk for an individual subject, visible via the smartphone app. A physician should be able to enter the gender, the age range, the diseases as the basis for the comorbidity group, and finally the values available, such as a lab or functional status, for the relevant clinical features. The application should then generate a report with both general and specific risks for the cohort of patients with a similar profile, including the risk for hospitalization itself or for 5-year mortality for the group and that individual patient. Furthermore, the physician should be able to obtain the impact of each comorbid disease on hospitalization and mortality risk. Designed with input from a multi-disciplinary group, the process was to meet or exceed robust data and privacy protection legislation.

(2) Dashboard

The aim of the dashboard was to provide an easy and intuitive way of exploring the data, such as how hospitalization and all-cause 5-year mortality change across different comorbidity groups or clusters. A further aim is to explore how the need for hospitalization and the projected mortality risk change across different comorbidity groups and differences within the comorbidity group or clusters. The dashboard should have a panel for each outcome measure. Each panel should offer data in multiple forms, including charts displaying information per selected comorbidity group.

8.2.1 Design, Privacy, Study Population, and Data Collection

Data from the universal healthcare system of the Valencian Community (Spain) were used. There is one unique electronic centralized clinical record per patient in this community. This database included 3,799,885 individuals older than 18 years in 2012. Total population data were extracted for the period from 1 January 2012 to 31 December 2016.

The registry includes patient demographics, medications, vital status, medical history, and laboratory data. Patient data underwent a two-step process for privacy purposes. The 1st step was the pseudo-anonymization of all data in the record, and in the 2nd step, automated and manual reviews were performed by masking or deleting variables that could lead to the re-identification of patients. Spanish Law 3/2018 for Data Protection and Guaranty of Digital Rights and corresponding European norms were followed [9]. The Committee for Ethics and Clinical Trials of the Hospital Clinico of Valencia approved the study prior to data extraction with registration number F-CE-Geva-15.

Diseases are listed using the ICD-9 coding system. Aggregate data in the system had been collected by the database system on multiple occasions and from different locations, i.e., wherever the patients had received care. This could mean that not all the baseline variables that were required to adjust for potential confounding were available at the time of inclusion. A 6-month window was therefore defined around the time of data extraction in order to gather the most complete information on lab values and control variables (e.g., body mass index (BMI), blood pressure, serum cholesterol fractions, creatinine, and diabetes marker HbA1c).

For each patient, the set of clinical features was brought into the study database as ordinal values with several levels for each clinical variable. Health-related features measured for each individual were paired with the discrete values assigned to the different intervals. Table 8.1 shows the list of clinical measures included in the modeling.

8.3 Data Management Methods

The architectural layers and the specific technologies deployed in the study are summarized in Figure 8.1. The technological stack was mainly inspired by the Cloudera distribution Hadoop Search for reference. A distributed Cloudera cluster was created using two servers: Operating System, Ubuntu Server 18.04; CPU, Intel(R) Xeon(R) Gold 5118 CPU @ 2.30 GHz with 12 cores; RAM, 1536 GB RAM DDR2 ECC (24 modules, 64 GB, 2666 MHz); and HDD, 5.24TB SSD RAID5 & 32.74TB HDD SATA RAID5. This stack enforced distributed data processing to maximize the use of computing resources.

The data flow in this architecture could be summarized as follows: First, the original data were extracted and processed into a set of files suitable for analysis. This set of files was stored in the Hadoop Distributed File System (HDFS). Next, queries were executed with Hive or SparkSQL and generated a data set with the relevant features. Afterward, this second data set was used to train the different models using Spark and Skitlearn Search as references. Finally, models were stored on an external server and accessed with the Representational State Transfer Application Programming Interface (REST API).

8.3.1 Mathematical Modeling

The mathematical modeling consisted of two different stages: First, the hierarchical clustering identified the distinct comorbidity groups that produce an increment in hospitalization and/or all-cause mortality, taken from a total of 19 diseases and with up to four co-morbid diseases per group (Table 8.1). In the second stage, the patient model aimed to offer a detailed report on each cluster of comorbidities. Previously determined, the risks studied were gender- and age-dependent, and a prior manual stratification of these factors was established. For this, each gender population was divided into five different age groups.

8.4 Results

Data learning and computations were robust, and the translation from descriptive to clinically relevant with respect to privacy legislation was achieved. Output aspects, such that the clinician could assess and use the data, are described below. A digital system displaying the stratification of risks for hospitalization and

Table 8.1. Information about the different data available to work with in the distinct stages of the project. The table shows five main groups of information: gender and age-ranges that help in handily dividing the population into ten different sub-populations, creating one group for each Cartesian combination of gender and age-range; the 19 diseases used to establish the different comorbidity groups with a hierarchical and statistical outlook; the clinical features, another group of ordinal variables used as explanatory variables for the patient models in each comorbidity group; and the two objective variables (risks) of the modularizations.

Gender (number of individuals)	
Man	(1,689,036)
Woman	(1,828,192)
Age-ranges (number of individuals)	
25+ (433,394)	[25–39]
40+ (1,125,338)	[40–54]
55+ (896,373)	[55–69]
70+ (640,417)	[70–84]
85+ (421,706)	[85–∞]
List of diseases selected (number of individuals)	
1. Anemia (632,229)	**11.** Dislipidemia (1,330,191)
2. Anxiety (1,119,416)	**12.** Hypertension (1,134,860)
3. Asthma (155,172)	**13.** Heart Failure (135,323)
4. Atrial Fibrillation (180,232)	**14.** Hypothyroidism (256,199)
5. Cardiomiopathy (29,673)	**15.** NAFLD (65,189)
6. Cirrhosis (112,602)	**16.** Osteoarthritis (270,860)
7. COPD (332,735)	**17.** Stroke (182,743)
8. Chronic Kidney Disease (144,444)	**18.** Vascular Dementia (31,404)
9. Dementia (187,546)	**19.** Venous Thromboembilism (49,752)
10. Diabetes (489,547)	
Clinical features levels (number of records)	
1. Smoker:	**0:** No Smoker, **1:** Smoker
2. TAS: (mmHg) (2,140,114)	**0:** < 100, **1:** $100 - 139$, **2:** > 139
3. TAD: (mmHg) (2,143,090)	**0:** < 80, **1:** $80 - 89$, **2:** > 89
4. Glucose: (mg/dL) (2,404,397)	**0:** $0 - 125$, **1:** > 125
5. HbA1c: (%) (1,031,080)	**0:** $0 - 7$, **1:** > 7
6. Creatinine: (mg/dL) (2,401,173)	**0:** $0 - 1.5$, **1:** > 1.5
7. LDL Cholesterol: (mg/dL) (2,221,718)	**0:** $0 - 100$, **1:** > 100
8. HDL Cholesterol: (mg/dL) (2,235,509)	**0:** $0 - 44$, **1:** > 44

(Continued)

Table 8.1. Continued

Risk (Hospitalization and mortality) of interest (number of records)	
1. Exitus:	**0:** non-dead, **1:** dead. (355,021 subjects)
2. Hospitalization:	**0:** the cause of hospitalization is none of the diseases of the comorbidity group, **1:** the cause of hospitalization is one or more of the diseases that forms the comorbidity group. (3,966,827 admissions) (1,646,059 subjects).

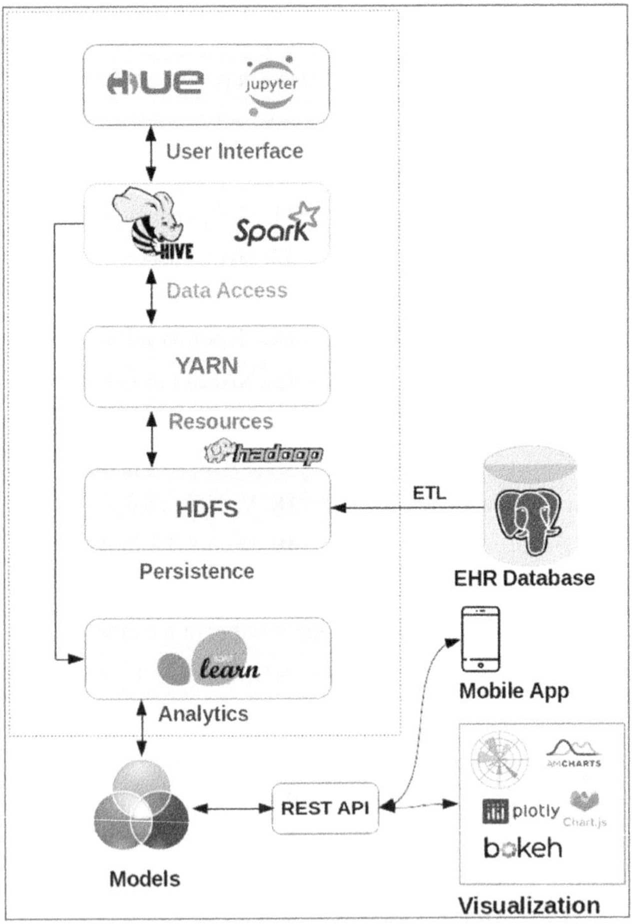

Figure 8.1. Software architecture. Cluster software employed to create the distributed cluster for computation. All brands shown can be trademarks or registered trademarks with their respective owners.

mortality in chronic disease clusters has been developed, which includes 19 chronic diseases, 5 age groups, and gender.

8.4.1 Smartphone App

The pictures shown in Figure 8.2 represent screens of the smart phone application. The first step consists of gender selection, then the physician selects the age range, and then the set of comorbid diseases. This organizes the patients into groups. The

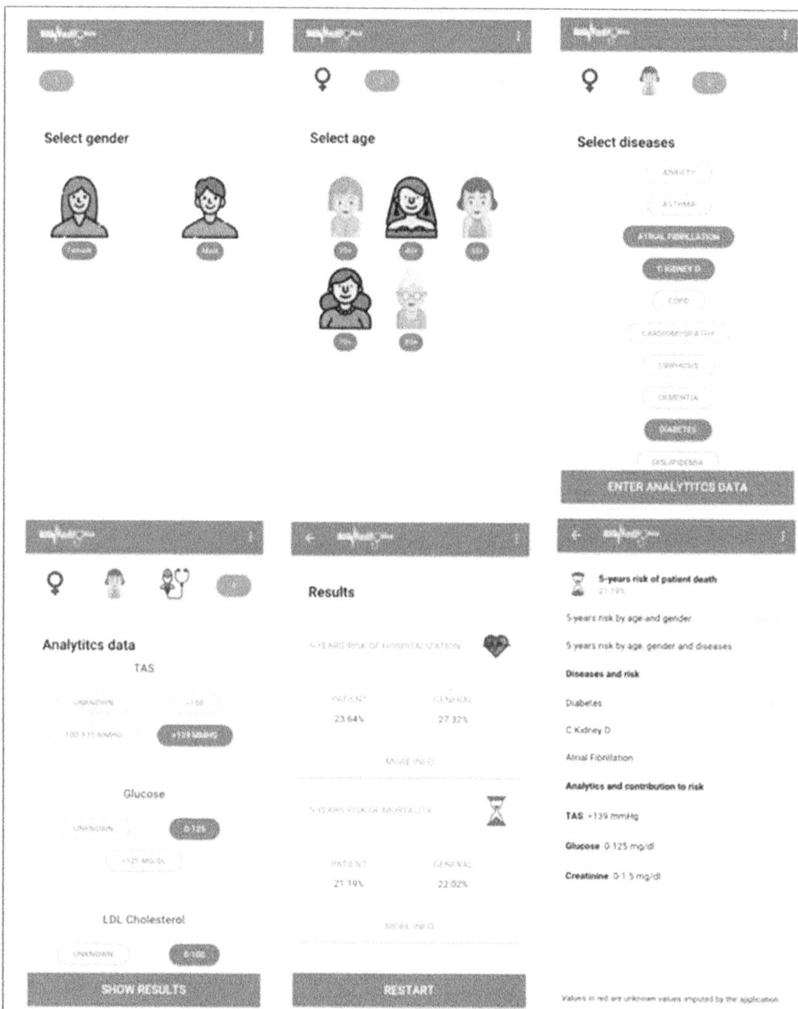

Figure 8.2. Smartphone app. Screens to introduce the different data: category, age range, diseases, clinical features, and finally obtain the distinct risk endpoints or factors and the detailed report about the distinct risk information and the relevance of the clinical variables for the patient risk prediction.

physician can then enter values for relevant clinical features to enable the two risk assessments (hospitalization and 5-year mortality risks). The application shows a report with general and specific endpoints for the group and the patient. Finally, the physician can select more information about each of the risks and receive more details for each one via a new screen.

8.4.2 Dashboard

In order to provide an easy and intuitive way of exploring the huge volume of data analyzed, a reporting web dashboard has been designed and developed. The dashboard is organized with one panel for each of these two risks being analyzed. Each panel shows charts that display information related to the selected comorbidity group. Figures 8.3, 8.4, and 8.5 show the different data charts displaying aspects of mortality risk as a function of comorbidities.

In Figure 8.3, two bar charts display information on the category and age distributions of the specific comorbidity cluster that the user has selected, showing the mortality risk and the number of affected patients.

For a more general overview of the data of interest, a scatter plot can be generated (Figure 8.4). This chart displays each cluster as a different data point, with the number of patients on the Y-axis and the relevant factor on the X-axis. Once the user selects a set of up to four diseases, the chart updates to show the comorbidity

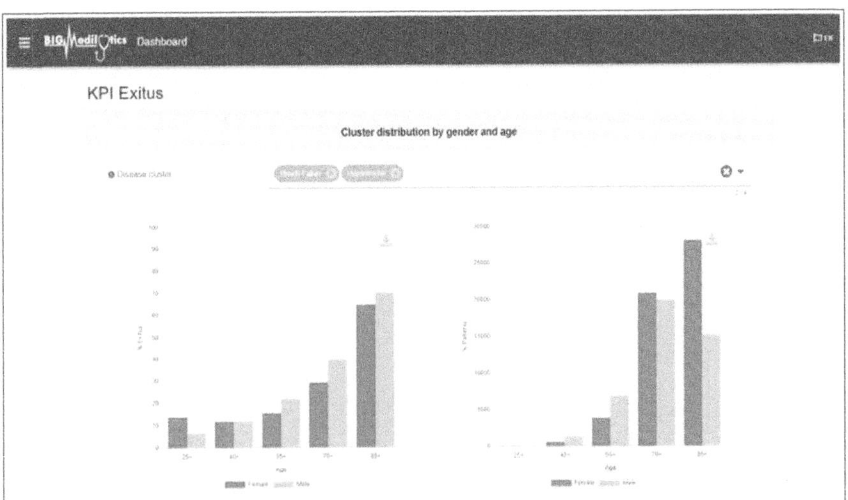

Figure 8.3. Univariate descriptive analysis. Category and age distribution for a chosen comorbidity cluster. On the left, the mortality over time is shown for patients with heart failure and hypertension, distributed in age and gender categories. On the right, the distribution of patients and gender categories with heart failure and hypertension is shown.

Figure 8.4. Number of patients versus the mortality risk over time (presented as a percentage). The picture shows aggregated information for each comorbidity group for a given category and age, focusing on the clusters' mortality risk.

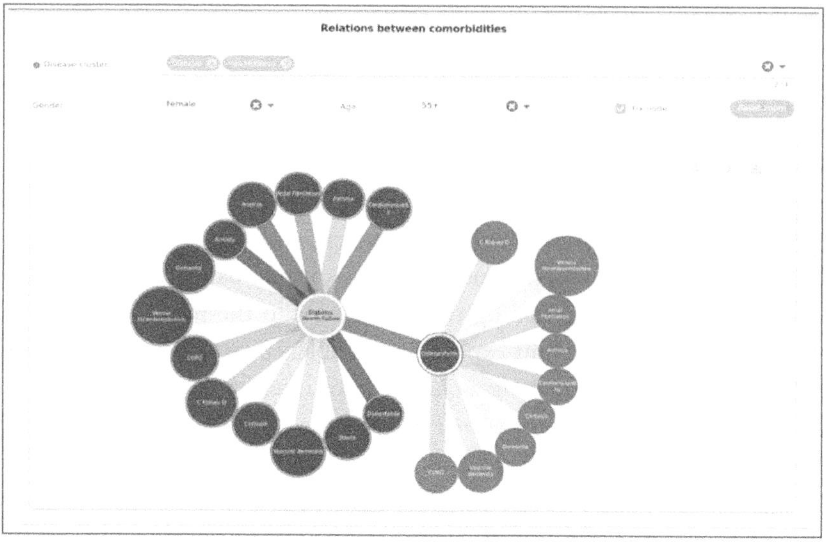

Figure 8.5. Diseases conditional graph. It shows conditioned relations between different comorbidity clusters. The darker the hue between the related paths, the greater the probability of the conditioned transition. The larger the node, the greater the corresponding risk for that comorbidity group.

cluster of the selected diseases, as well as all the clusters that contain them. The user can also filter by age group and/or category in order to see more specific data; he/she can zoom in/out, hover over the elements to see the information of a specific cluster, and download the images.

A graph chart shows the relations between different comorbidity clusters (Figure 8.5). The corresponding risk for each comorbidity group or disease has been previously computed by counting the individuals that show the risk versus the number of individuals in the corresponding group. To this end, each dot in the graph represents a different comorbidity cluster. The initial dot is the comorbidity cluster selected by the user, comprised of N diseases. For each dot, further dots represent the impacts of N + 1 comorbidities on the risks for hospitalization and mortality.

When a user selects a specific age group and category, information regarding the risks and number of patients affected by each comorbidity can be displayed in two ways. On the one hand, an additional information pop-up appears when the user hovers over a specific dot. On the other hand, the size of the dot represents the incidence of that risk in the specific case. The total number of patients involved in the analysis is used to gradually change the color between the overall outcome dot and the dot the user is hovering over.

8.5 Learnings and Outcomes

This chapter describes the process and outcomes of this study, which used big data strategies to translate comorbidity and risks into a clinically useful set of platforms. It developed a divisive hierarchical tree strategy to stratify the risk of hospitalization and mortality for an assortment of comorbidities and comorbidity bundles into clusters of chronic diseases and their corresponding relevant clinical features. This methodology allows better insight into a specific patient group or even an individual patient by conditioning the estimations to the pertinent comorbidity group and the selected relevant explicative variable values. The information for a given patient is useful for making a choice about intensifying treatment to reallocate the patient into a better risk subset in the corresponding comorbidity group or seeing that this effect is unlikely. The potential impact of a newly acquired disease is observable. Furthermore, the software created can be launched over a big data cluster in a transparent way, thus increasing the computational power transparently and dynamically.

8.6 Discussion

In the study described in this chapter, a digital system displaying the stratification of risks for hospitalization and mortality in chronic disease clusters has been developed, which includes 19 chronic diseases, 5 age groups, and gender. The user interface is implemented in two ways: the first identifies the different significant comorbidity clusters for each gender, the age ranges, up to four comorbidities, and their respective hospitalization and mortality risks. The second identifies the most relevant general clinical features for each cluster from a set of eight features and introduces prediction. The system provides information on the risk of each cluster, the contribution of each disease, and the clinical features associated with each, thereby allowing the physicians to make individually tailored decisions for treatment.

The study was conducted using data from the unique Electronic Health Record (EHR) of the general population in a Mediterranean population (Valencian Community, Spain). An interesting observation about this EHR is that the level of quality of life and the diagnosis reported seem to underreport chronic disease and focus on incidental health issues without comorbid context. However, in two recent reviews, the prevalence of chronic health conditions was higher in medical records than in other data sources such as administrative data or even health surveys, [10, 11] while the more symptomatic chronic diseases are more poorly recorded [12, 13].

Previously, the different machine learning approaches used to obtain clinical risk groups focused mainly on stratifying the severity of comorbid diseases or getting information on potential costs, regardless of gender or age. Examples of the former were CIRS, ICED, and the Kaplan Index, while of the latter, ACGs, DRGs, and HRGs. The procedure for group creation differed depending on the pursued objectives and the kind of algorithm used. One approach has used an agglomerative hierarchical clustering method, [14] similar to the approach used in the present study, while other ACGs (Adjusted Clinical Groups), [6] DRGs (Diagnosis-Related Groups), [7] and HRGs (Healthcare Resource Groups), [8] automatically establish the groups of comorbidities by searching for similarities in the clinical measures of patients [15]. An unsupervised disease clustering technique based on a multidimensional nonlineal projection (UMAP) has also been described [16, 17].

The divisive hierarchical risk clustering used in the present study uses a two-step approach to achieve the desired outputs. In comparison, the more general modularizations consider all the information in one step of modeling. The two-step method permits creating specific models for each of the comorbidity groups, which also include only the clinical features required by the group. This method can save time because it evaluates only the clinical features needed for the corresponding group. Our results show that the accuracy of the different models depends on gender, age range, the impact of the group, and the relevant features specific to the group. Note that in our approach, even within the same cluster, clinical features will result in different outcomes for the two risks of hospitalization and all-cause 5-year mortality.

The creation of divisive hierarchical groups permits an individual that belongs to a specific group to pertain as well to another of the more general relevant groups from which an individual comes. Moreover, the use of interpretable models, like decision trees, [18] also allows for their use as recommender systems. With these models, it is possible to obtain a specific location for a patient in the tree and know the clinical variables to enhance in order for a patient to improve their risk position within the group. Furthermore, it can help to forecast the other diseases that are likely to occur in a patient in order to improve the patient's allocation into a more specific group. In addition, this methodology permits the discovery of conditioned knowledge in a natural way, something that could help physicians discard other relevant diseases that might alter the considered factor. Notwithstanding that, it allows different predictions for a patient that is in a sparsely populated group for which it has not been possible to obtain models.

8.6.1 Perspectives

This project focused on the data management and data presentation forms and included choices for models implemented within the data analysis. Its ultimate purpose is to support the clinician in forming policy for an individual patient based on the extensive database information. Validation and implementation were not parts of the study. A clinical and field discussion still needs to be done, potentially driven by specific medical specialties, as well as case/control studies to assess performance in terms of treatment selection and risk reduction.

In identifying the different clusters and the impact of the two risks within the cluster, the methodology used in the current study has limitations. The divisive hierarchical approach, used to obtain the different comorbidity groups, has a higher impact when the number of patients in that group is smaller. This can result in a smaller number of samples for model estimation if there are a larger number of different groups. Consequently, we excluded groups with less than 51 subjects. By increasing the number of individuals by including data from other EHRs, we increased the precision of the comorbidity groups. Collecting more data will increase the capacity to study more complex groups with more cohorts and, in the future, expand the number of diseases included in the research.

The number of clinical parameters is sparse in the EHR, although they are typically relevant for prognosis and risk calculations. However, a more diverse set of clinical variables would improve the results of the models, providing higher accuracy.

Along with the number of clinical features, another relevant point is the conceptual (temporal) frame. Assigning a value to a parameter does not take into consideration the variability of each parameter, potentially introducing bias into the assignment of variables with higher variability. A way to improve this could be to consist of the establishment of a dynamical time interval related to the natural variability of the clinical variable. The methodology used in the current study allows a further approach to a specific patient model by conditioning the risk estimations to the pertinent comorbidity group and selecting relevant and explicative variable values for that group. Furthermore, the created software can be launched over a big data cluster in a transparent way, thus increasing the computational power transparently and dynamically. In the near future, a case/control study will evaluate performance in terms of treatment selection and risk reduction.

8.7 Conclusion

The study described in this chapter goes to the heart of big data use for clinical medicine. By creating user interfaces that allow the clinician to use real data to support choices for a group or even an individual patient with an app or dashboard. The study lays the groundwork for procedures and technologies that others can follow and extend.

With 19 chronic conditions and millions of patient health records to work from, this concept will resonate as the need for objective strategies for consumption in healthcare and quality of life gains traction.

Source Indentification

Icons of the app made by author from www.flaticon.com

- FreePik. Gender identity pack. Woman. Retrieved from https://www.flaticon.com/freeicon/woman_1864518.
- FreePik. Gender identity pack. Man. Retrieved from https://www.flaticon.com/freeicon/man_1864509.
- FreePik. World Pride pack. Female symbol. Retrieved from https://www.flaticon.com/freeicon/femenine_949792.
- FreePik. Family-7 pack. Girl. Retrieved from https://www.flaticon.com/freeicon/girl_375304.
- itim2101. Avatar pack. Business Woman. Retrieved from https://www.flaticon.com/freeicon/business-woman_1439675.
- FreePik. Family-7 pack. Mother. Retrieved from https://www.flaticon.com/freeicon/mother_375257.
- itim2101. Avatar pack. Worker. Retrieved from https://www.flaticon.com/freeicon/worker_1439706.

- FreePik. Family-7 pack. Grandmother. Retrieved from https://www.flaticon.com/freeicon/grandmother_375303.
- Eucalyp. Medical pack. Medical check. Retrieved from https://www.flaticon.com/freeicon/medical-check_946299.
- icon8. Green sandglass icon. Retrieved from https://www.iconsdb.com/greenicons/sandglass-icon.html.
- Vectors Market. Medical. Cardiogram. Retrieved from https://www.flaticon.com/freeicon/cardiogram_607580.

Dashboard graphics created by using the libraries https://www.chartjs.org and https://www.amcharts.com (https://www.amcharts.com/docs/v4/chart-types/forcedirected/).

References

[1] Palmer K, Marengoni A, Forjaz MJ, Jureviciene E, Laatikainen T, Mammarella F, Muth C, Navickas R, Prados-Torres A, Rijken M. Multimorbidity care model: Recommendations from the consensus meeting of the Joint Action on Chronic Diseases and Promoting Healthy Ageing across the Life Cycle (JA-CHRODIS). Health Policy. 2018. 122(1), 4–11. https://doi.org/10.1016/j.healthpol.2017.09.006.

[2] Valderas JM, Starfield B, Sibbald B, Salisbury C, Roland M. Defining comorbidity: Implications for understanding health and health services. The Annals of Family Medicine. July 2009. 7(4), 357–363. https://doi.org/10.1370/afm.983.

[3] Linn BS, Linn MW, Gurel L. Cumulative illness rating scale. Journal of the American Geriatrics Society. 1968. 16(5), 622–626. https://doi.org/10.1111/j.1532-5415.1968.tb02103.x.

[4] Greenfield S, Aronow H, Elashoff R, Watanabe D. Flaws in mortality data. The hazards of ignoring comorbid disease. JAMA. 1988. 260 15, 2253–2255.

[5] Hughes J, Averill R, Eisenhandler J, Goldfield N, Muldoon J, Neff J, Gay J. Clinical risk groups (CRGs): A classification system for risk-adjusted capitation based payment and health care management. Medical Care. 2004. 42, 81–90.

[6] Seow H, Sibley L. Developing a dashboard to help measure and achieve the triple aim: a population-based cohort study. BMC Health Services Research. 2014. https://doi.org/10.1186/1472-6963-14-363.

[7] Cheng SH, Chen CC, Tsai SL. The impacts of DRG-based payments on health care provider behaviors under a universal coverage system:

A population-based study. Health Policy. 2012. 107(2), 202–208. https://doi.org/10.1016/j.healthpol.2012.03.021, https://ideas.repec.org/a/eee/hepoli/v107y2012i2p202-208.html.

[8] Bojke C, Grašič K, Street A. How should hospital reimbursement be refined to support concentration of complex care services? Health Economics. January 2018. 27(1), 26–38. https://doi.org/10.1002/hec.3525, https://ideas.repec.org/a/wly/hlthec/v27y2018i1pe26-e38.html.

[9] The EU General Data Protections GDPR, https://gdpr-info.eu/.

[10] Fortin M, Stewart M, Poitras ME, Almirall J, Maddocks H. A systematic review of prevalence studies on multimorbidity: Toward a more uniform methodology. Annals of Family Medicine. 2012. 10(2), 142–151.

[11] Huntley A, Johnson R, Purdy S, Valderas J, Salisbury C. Measures of multimorbidity and morbidity burden for use in primary care and community settings: A systematic review and guide. Annals of Family Medicine. March 2012. 10(2), 134–141. https://doi.org/10.1370/afm.1363.

[12] Thiru K. Systematic review of scope and quality of electronic patient record data in primary care. BMJ. May 2003. 326(7398), 1070. https://doi.org/10.1136/bmj.326.7398.1070.

[13] Violán C, Foguet-Boreu Q, Hermosilla-Pérez E, Valderas J, Bolíbar B, Fàbregas-Escurriola M, Brugulat-Guiteras P, Muñoz-Pérez M. Comparison of the information provided by electronic health records data and a population health survey to estimate prevalence of selected health conditions and multimorbidity. BMC Public Health. March 2013. 13(1). https://doi.org/10.1186/1471-2458-13-251.

[14] Singh S, Karkare S, Baswan S, Singh V. Unsupervised machine learning forco/multimorbidity analysis. International Journal of Statistics and Probability. September 2018. 7, 23. https://doi.org/10.5539/ijsp.v7n6p23.

[15] Newcomer SR, Steiner JF, Bayliss EA. Identifying subgroups of complex patients with cluster analysis. The American Journal of Managed Care. 2011. 17(8), e324—e332. http://europepmc.org/abstract/MED/21851140.

[16] McInnes L, Healy J, Melville J. Umap: Uniform manifold approximation and projection for dimension reduction. 2018. http://arxiv.org/abs/1802.03426, cite arxiv:1802.03426. Comment: Reference implementation available at: http://github.com/lmcinnes/umap.

[17] Sánchez-Rico M, Alvarado JM. A machine learning approach for studying the comorbidities of complex diagnoses. Behavioral Sciences. 2019. 9(12). https://doi.org/10.3390/bs9120122, https://www.mdpi.com/2076-328X/9/12/122.

[18] Breiman L, Friedman J, Olshen R, Stone C. Classification and regression trees. Wadsworth and Brooks, Monterey, CA. 1984.

DOI: 10.1561/9781638282372.ch9

Chapter 9

eHealth and Telemedicine for Risk Prediction and Monitoring in Kidney Transplantation Recipients

By Wiebke Duettmann, Roland Roller, Bilgin Osmanodja, Verena Graf, Matthias Pfefferkorn, Danilo Schmidt, Anne Schwerk, Marcel G. Naik and Klemens Budde

9.1 Introduction

Patients with end-stage chronic kidney disease need dialysis or kidney transplantation for survival. Many trials confirm that transplantation is the favored option for many patients because of better survival, better quality of life, and lower costs [1–6]. However, many Kidney Transplant Recipients (KTRs) suffer from multiple complications such as rejection, infection, underlying diseases, and side effects of their medication [7, 8]. To detect complications or even avoid them through early interventions, patients must comply with the strict aftercare program, including regular visits to the transplant center, the timely intake of immunosuppressants, the regular measurement of vital signs (to control cardiovascular risks), and a special sensitivity for changes in their health status [9]. Hence, the contributions of the patient, adherence, and patient empowerment are key to successful long-term outcomes [10].

However, some studies showed low adherence to instructions by KTRs and that non-adherence frequently contributes to graft loss [11]. While most KTRs tightly follow the aftercare schedule directly after transplantation, adherence progressively drops over the years. Interestingly, adherence in the first month after transplantation has been shown to be predictive of the long-term organ outcome [11]. Humans can be distinguished into various adherence types with typical patterns, which can be supported by different methods [12, 13]. Therefore, it is important to identify the fewer adherent patients and support them with advice and education and provide a structure which enables these patients to follow their instructions [11]. This process is called empowerment and is crucial for adherence. This empowerment, education, and support must be lifelong. Consequently, adherent or partially adherent patients should also be rewarded with constant support, praise, and sympathy for further motivation.

eHealth products such as mobile phone applications (apps) may have the potential to improve adherence in chronically ill patients and in acute or special medical circumstances such as pregnancy. Apps are permanently available on smartphones and thereby may provide constant support or support upon demand. However, such mobile phone apps improve adherence only if the patients consider the app useful [14]. Ideally, the support system includes some additional human support, typically from friends and family members by healthcare professionals [6].

To integrate this knowledge, we designed a telemedicine service with a mobile phone app, where a telemedicine team in the transplant center supports the KTRs to better empower the patient and increase patient adherence. The integration of this support system into the workflow to ease the working processes of the medical staff was another key aspect. In close interaction with patients, nurses, medical doctors, and computer scientists, we developed this telemedical module, including an app for patients, interfaces, and a front-end for telemedicine staff (a dashboard). The key component of the telemedicine concept was to empower patients to better take care of their health and improve medical and therapeutic adherence. Better adherence should lead to a lower complication rate, e.g., better blood pressure control and a lower frequency of Donor-Specific Antibodies (DSA), which may cause rejections and are an important cause of graft loss. The timely detection of complications such as infections, rejections, or side effects of immunosuppressants is crucial for a better response to treatment and the avoidance of serious, life-threatening clinical courses.

The main goal of our study was to detect critical patients early in order to reduce complications and thereby reduce hospitalizations, which will reduce costs and improve the quality of life of patients. To select and detect critical patients, a telemedicine team was established to regularly evaluate incoming data and take medical action if needed. To support the telemedicine team, which may be overwhelmed with large numbers of constantly incoming data, we developed risk prediction models to better forecast critical endpoints such as rejection, graft loss, and infection [15].

9.2 Challenges

To set up a telemedicine system in the nephrology department at Charité, various challenges had to be addressed, including organizational issues, hospital bureaucracy, and, most importantly, data protection. The Charité has its IT hierarchy and working structure highly protected with a firewall. Thus, applications for the use of specific plug-ins for accessing the internet and the usage of external hardware were necessary. Bureaucracy about different application forms was time-consuming. External hardware might contain computer viruses or spyware; therefore, it had to be evaluated before connecting to the network. In addition, an extensive evaluation of data protection regulations was required. The hospital and each federal state regulate data protection aspects and are different as well as strict. An external lawyer, who is specialized in patient rights and General Data Protection and Regulations (GDPR), evaluated the data protection concept of the telemedicine module. In cases of cooperation with other institutes, guest science contracts must be confirmed. The organizational aspects included a discussion of the necessity and safety of such a new telemedicine project and the need for personnel, equipment, and rooms. For a sustainable solution, negotiations with health insurance companies were necessary, and finally, a contract for financial support was signed and discussions on the potential use of telemedicine services in the future were formalized.

From a technical point of view, no blueprint or standard solution for a telemedicine approach existed. Particularly, integration into the existing hospital infrastructure was not trivial. Because good integration of any telemedicine solution into the workflow is essential for success, we aimed to integrate the dashboard into our patient documentation system, TBase [16]. A telemedicine module has fundamentally new requirements on safety and data protection such that certain safety and privacy aspects had to be evaluated again (privacy impact assessment, etc.).

Unlike the telemedicine system, automatic risk prediction was planned as a proof-of-concept analysis. Therefore, it was not meant to be integrated directly into the telemedicine system or used in direct clinical care for patients since this would require a preemptive and thorough risk-benefit assessment according to the new medical device regulations. The application of risk prediction in a research setting still induces many challenges from the legal side. From a technical point of view, various other problems also had to be addressed. This included access for external researchers, as data had to be processed on Charité premises with limited hardware resources to train machine-learning models. Moreover, as (real-world) clinical data are noisy, they require a great deal of expert and clinical knowledge for adequate processing. For instance, data fields in the database changed over time.

In addition, working on data in a closed "ecosystem" (which cannot be shared) reduces the possibility of comparability (of machine learning models). In this way, it is difficult to learn from existing work, generate similar cohorts, and reproduce systems and results. Other challenges were the interdisciplinary aspects and multilingualism of the teams.

Finally, personnel for a telemedicine team had to be recruited without an existing job description for this new field of medicine. We, therefore, decided to look for experienced healthcare workers with an expressed interest in eHealth. The next step was to create a new working process for telemedicine aftercare with standard operating procedures and to integrate this process into the routine transplant aftercare in outpatient clinics without interfering with the current medical staff [9]. Finally, yet importantly, patients had to be convinced, and after signing a newly developed informed consent form, the formal onboarding process had to be started. Not surprisingly, many time-consuming issues around the download and installation of the app on the patient's mobile phone had to be resolved.

9.3 Methods

The study addresses the following two goals:

- Establishing a telemedicine system
- Development of a risk prediction system

9.3.1 Telemedicine

The telemedicine system includes a telemedicine team, which evaluates incoming data from patients on a daily basis and can react to problematic data with advice and support. The digital infrastructure of the telemedicine system includes a patient app and a telemedicine dashboard. The dashboard is integrated within an approved Electronic Medical Record (EMR) called TBase, which is used for routine documentation of patients with kidney diseases at Charité. TBase is also a research database, which allows scientists to work on the data without having access to the personal data of the patients [16]. The patient app was designed by an interdisciplinary team consisting of nurses, patients, medical doctors, and computer scientists and implemented by an industry partner. The app sends data to TBase via an interoperable Health Level 7 (HL7) Fast Healthcare Interoperability Resources (FHIR) Application Programming Interface (API) [9].

A free (of charge) mobile phone app enables patients to document their medication intake, vital signs (weight, blood pressure, pulse, temperature, blood sugar value, and blood oxygen saturation), as well as their sense of well-being. Moreover,

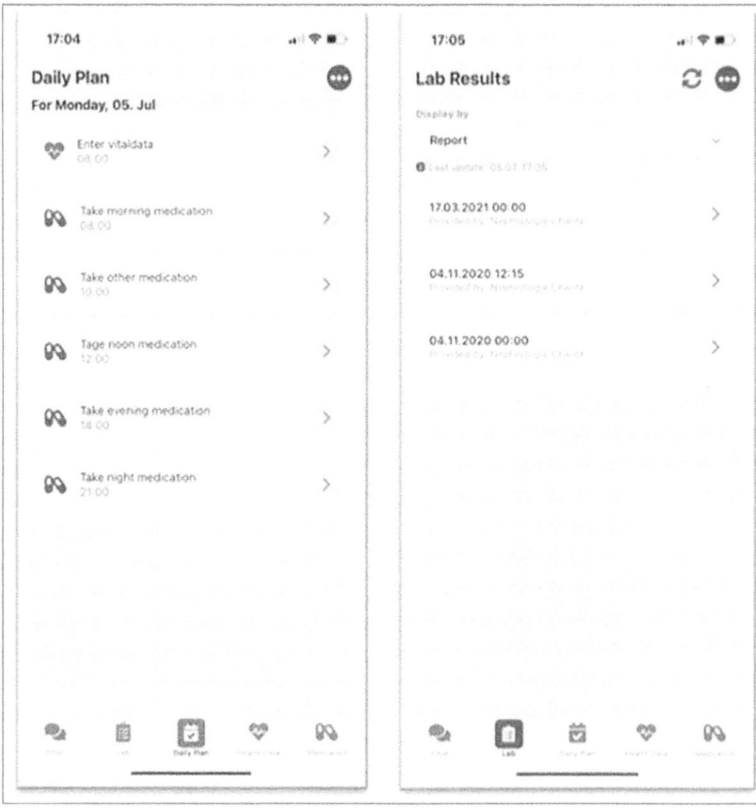

Figure 9.1. Examples of patient app.

the app includes a medication alert and direct contact options for the telemedicine team, which include chat functionality and potentially a video option. Our telemedicine team is available on working days between 7 am and 4 pm. In addition, the app allows for the exchange of documents, laboratory values, and medication plans (Figure 9.1). This means the patient is enabled to have all relevant information 'in his/her hands' ('empowerment') and has access to an easy personal exchange with the telemedicine team ('support').

An FHIR server distributes the data between the patient app, TBase at the transplant center, and other users (such as the data system of home nephrologists). A telemedicine dashboard within TBase displays the data in the transplant center for the physician and telemedicine team (Figure 9.2).

The dashboard was also developed in cooperation between nurses, medical doctors, and computer scientists. The dashboard is constantly adapted to the needs of the telemedicine team and patients. An underlying alert system allows an easy evaluation of adherence (e.g., how often do patients share vital signs with the telemedicine team?). Based on the standard operating procedures and the incoming

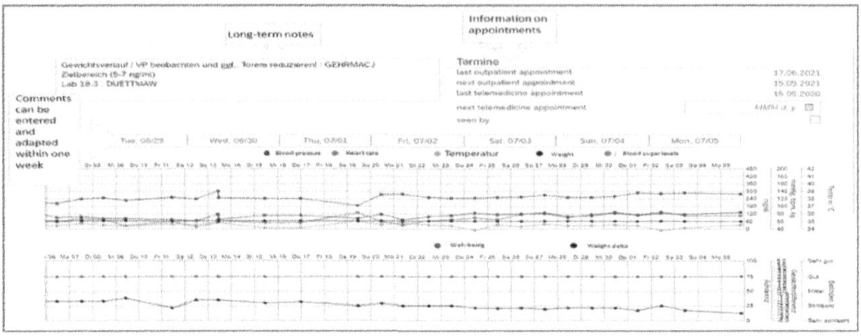

Figure 9.2. TBase dashboard.

	Critical	Suspicious	Normal	Suspicious	Critical
Systolic blood pressure	<90mmHg	90 - 99mmHg	100 - 129mmHg	130 - 180mmHg	>180mmHg
Diastolic blood pressure	<50mmHg	50 - 59mmHg	60 - 89mmHg	90 - 100mmHg	>100mmHg
Heart rate	<50bpm	50 - 59bpm	60 - 89bpm	90 - 120bpm	>120bpm
Temperature	<33.5°C	33.5 - 36.2°C	36.3 - 37.4°C	37.5 - 38.0°C	>38.0°C
Change in weight 1 day	>(-1.5)kg	(-1.5) - (-0.5)kg	+/-0.5kg	0.5 - 1.5kg	>1.5kg
Change in weight 3 days	>(-2.5)kg	(-2.5) - (-1.0)kg	+/-1.0kg	1.0 - 2.5kg	>2.5kg
Change in weight 8 days	>(-3.0)kg	(-3.0) - (-1.5)kg	+/-1.5kg	1.5 - 3.0kg	>3.0kg
Well-being	Very good (5) - green	Good (4) - light green	Medium (3) - yellow	Bad (2) - orange	Very bad (1) - red
Medication adherence	<70%	70 - 89%	>=90%	/	/
Therapy adherence	<70%	70 - 89%	>=90%	/	/

Figure 9.3. Vital signs and medical interpretation with suggestions for actions.

data, the telemedicine team decides when and how to contact the patient or the home nephrologist. The standard operating procedures contain a range of critical vital signs that will cause an immediate or intermediate reaction (Figure 9.3). For instance, if a patient shows raised blood pressure values for a month, the patient is flagged, and the telemedicine team potentially intervenes with different measures, such as intensified antihypertensive therapy. If patients are not adherent to the project (sending no data) and the dialogue with the patient confirms non-adherence (sending no values and do not measure vital signs), the telemedicine team aims to find out the individual resistance to adherence and to help the patient improve their adherence.

A key component of the telemedicine concept is strict compliance with GDPR. As mentioned above, we first designed the concept, let the concept be evaluated by an independent specialized law firm and the data protection units, and then started with the implementation. Key elements are the firewall at Charité, the FHIR authentication server system, the HL7 FHIR APIs, and the data encryption system. TBase is protected by the Charité firewall. The HL7 FHIR API receives and distributes data from external sources to internal sources and vice versa. Patients

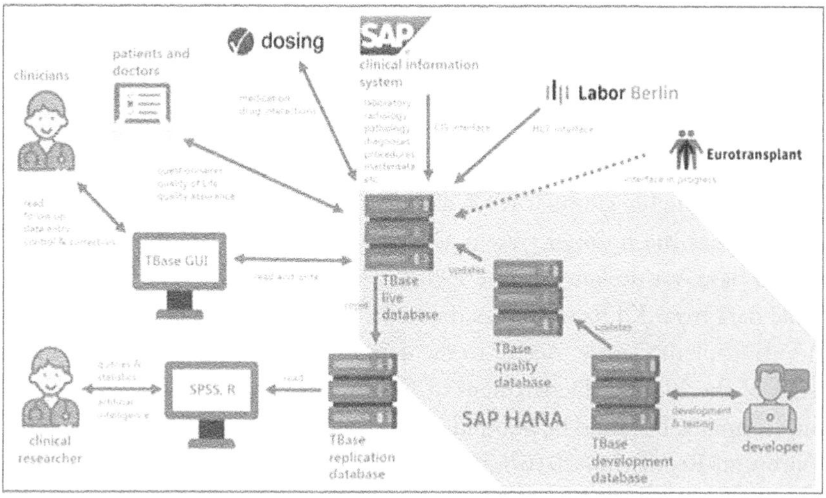

Figure 9.4. Overview of the architecture of TBase within Charité.

have a TBase ID, a telemedicine ID, and the system ID of the home practitioner. The telemedicine module has an FHIR server that receives incoming data, encrypts and decrypts them, and distributes them. This server is located externally on a protected server within Germany. The key to the encryption code lies with the third party that developed the app. The digital infrastructure in which the TBase is embedded is presented in Figure 9.4.

To include a patient in the system, a sophisticated multi-step onboarding system is necessary. First, the medical doctor verifies the patient's identity and the inclusion documents. Then the telemedicine team activates the onboarding process in TBase. This causes an FHIR request to the FHIR server for an empty onboarding sheet. TBase fills in the patient ID and sends it back with self-chosen login data. Now, the patient can open the app with the login data. The patient must change the login data so that these are individualized and private. If a general practitioner is to be included for a specific patient, the same process can be used.

9.3.2 Risk Prediction Models

The risk prediction model targeted the identification of patients at risk of infection, rejection, and/or graft failure. The aim is to identify patients before a critical situation appears, thus preventing that critical event as well as offering support to a physician with appropriate information. This, in turn, should reduce hospitalizations, the duration of the stay, and the intensity of diagnostics and therapy. Fewer hospitalizations will reduce costs and improve the patient's quality of life. The risk prediction model is based on de-identified (removal of names, addresses, etc.) data in TBase. The endpoints of interest were developed in close collaboration between computer scientists and physicians, which are the detection of transplant loss, rejection, and infections within the next 90 days. After extensive data cleansing steps to deal with missing, noisy, and false information, different cohorts (data subsets) were generated.

The primary data source of our risk prediction models is TBase, an EHR system containing highly granular KTR data spanning the last 20 years from different sources, such as the hospital system as well as pathology, laboratories, and other systems. TBase was designed in the 1990s, when prospective data collection of all available data from KTRs started as the main documentation system of the Berlin Kidney Transplant Centre. Access to the data is granted to the scientific and medical staff of the Medical Department of Nephrology and Medical Intensive Care, Berlin, Germany. It should be pointed out that all partners in this study underwrote the European Regulation 2016/679. TBase includes structured and unstructured data and is stored in a relational database. In 2019, TBase was fundamentally re-engineered, and a general telemedicine dashboard was introduced.

As data could not leave the hospital, the model development was conducted within the given infrastructure: first physically within the hospital and then later, during the coronavirus disease 2019 (COVID-19) pandemic, using a Virtual Private Network (VPN) access. The model was trained on a Linux cluster, which had been purchased for this project and was located in a secure space inside the hospital.

We relied on Python and the scikit-learn library for data processing and model development. Instead of starting with a complex model, we decided to start with a simple and robust baseline system that can integrate suggestions by the physicians (expert knowledge). More precisely, we relied on Gradient Boosted Regression Trees (GBRT). To train our model, we use retrospective data from TBase from Charité Mitte and Virchow Klinikum from 2008 to 2020. The data includes more than 4,500 patients with several million Data Points (DPs). A DP describes a moment in a patient's life, or more specifically, a moment when new data about a patient is inserted into TBase. Each of those DPs is used to make new predictions.

Following the suggestions of the physicians, various patients' DPs have been filtered out beforehand to exclude:

- DPs of patients below 18 (at that point in time),
- DPs with target endpoint currently not active,
- DPs within a time frame of fewer than a week after an infection or a rejection,
- DPs within a time frame of fewer than 2 weeks after a transplant, and
- DPs of patients who do not have a follow-up DP in the next 15–180 days.

The model integrates semi-structured data, including:

- Socio-demographics (e.g., gender, age, smoking status)

- Vitals (e.g., blood pressure, weight)
- Primary disease
- Medications
- Laboratory values
- Transplant/donor information
- Previous diagnoses
- Admissions to the hospital

Information comes at different intervals, is updated infrequently at different times depending on the current situation change of the patient, and comes in different formats. Some data, like socio-demographics or transplant information, are relatively static. The models consist of 300 trees and integrate about 300 features using about 100,000 DPs from about 1,400 patients. However, during its development, it turned out that our GBRT 'baseline' already provided promising results (see next paragraph). Thus, instead of integrating a more complex model, we wanted to find out how well physicians can solve the task and if the current system is good enough to support physicians in their daily routine.

9.4 Results

9.4.1 Telemedicine

After signing a contract (according to § 140 German Social Law) with two major health insurance companies in Germany and after the implementation of the telemedicine unit, the telemedicine team started to sign up KTRs in February 2020. Since then, more than 450 KTRs have been treated up to October 2022. The overall acceptance rate was high; only a few dropouts occurred, and patient satisfaction was high. Since the beginning, 95 KTRs dropped out (8.53%), and 38 (3.2%) were excluded by the telemedicine team due to persistent non-participation despite contacts with the team. Other reasons for dropping out or exclusion were technical issues with the app, a lack of satisfaction with the app (usability), and a lack of interest in the project.

The average age of participants is 52 years, and 63.4% of patients are male. The KTRs are mostly transplanted for the first time (85.5%; N = 384). Only 104 KTRs (12.12%) received a second transplant, and 20 KTRs (1.43%) even received a third one. In 39 cases (3.93%), combined transplantation of the kidney and pancreas occurred. Initially, the transplant had been in situ for six years before inclusion in the project. Later, the telemedicine team included almost all newly transplanted patients.

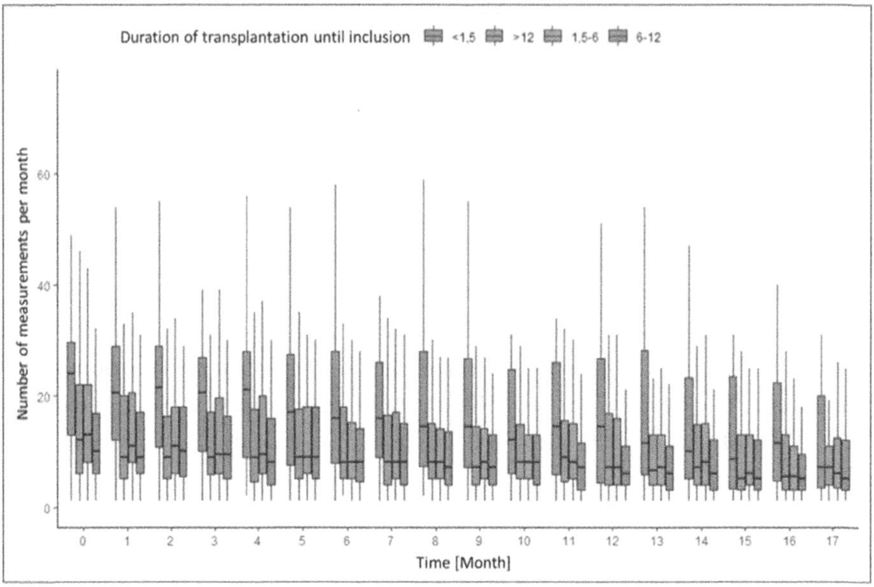

Figure 9.5. Frequency of incoming data distributed to the months since transplantation. X-axis: Time points of measurement in months. Y-axis: Numbers of measurements per month. Legend: Duration of transplantation until inclusion into the project <1.5 months, >12 months, 1.5–6 years, and 6–12 years.

Out of 84,130 incoming blood pressure data, 1,285 were critical (1.5%; Figure 9.3) and led to a contact by a member of the telemedicine team. The same was true for 84,127 heart frequency data, of which 3.337 (4%) were critical (Figure 9.3). Out of 68,564 temperature data, 458 (0.7%) were critical (Figure 9.3). Moreover, of 14.631 blood sugar values, 104 (0.7%) were critical (60–140 mg/dl or 3.3–7.8 mmol/l) and led to contact by the telemedicine team. The incoming data distribution since the start of the project is shown in Figure 9.5. Patients used the telephone, email, and chat to get in touch with the telemedicine team during working days and between 7 am and 4 pm. These frequencies have not been evaluated yet.

The other pillar of telemedicine care is acute consultation in cases of symptoms, prescriptions, appointment service, laboratory tests, and other medical or psychosocial problems. During the COVID-19 pandemic, a major task was COVID-19 counselling in case of positive COVID-19 polymerase chain reaction (COVID-19-PCR) swabs, treatment, and monitoring of KTRs with mild and moderate COVID-19 infection.

To round up the telemedicine care, nine nephrologists in private practice were included in the system for data exchange (laboratory values, medical data, vital signs, and soon the progress note of the attending doctor).

9.4.2 Risk Prediction Models

The risk prediction has been evaluated in two different setups: first, as a retrospective internal study and evaluated within cross-validation (70% training, 15% development, 15% test), and second, within a small reader study, the performance of the machine-learning model was compared to that of physicians with and without automatic decision support.

The first results from the retrospective data predicting the three different endpoints for the next 90 days (endpoints: rejection, graft loss, or infection) were overall promising in terms of high Area Under the Curve (AUC) and Receiver Operating Characteristic (ROC) scores (between 80 and 95 regarding the different aims). However, as medical data can typically not leave the hospital, there was no comparison to other, similar approaches. Feature engineering partially led to minor system improvements.

For the reader study, an ad hoc convenience sample of 120 patients was selected. The random selection was conducted so that we could ensure that a minimum of 20 patients would be within the risk scope of each endpoint. Eight medical doctors in different stages of education and years of work experience (four junior physicians and four senior physicians) were recruited to participate. The reader study was conducted in two parts: first, each physician received 15 patients to examine and had to estimate the likelihood that (at least one of) our endpoints would occur within the next 90 days. Each physician could take up to 30 minutes to examine the medical history of each patient. In the second part, each physician was assigned to 15 different patients, and this time they also received the risk estimation of our Clinical Decision Support System (CDSS; Figure 9.6) in order to reach their decision.

The study showed that (1) the risk prediction system tends to outperform medical doctors according to AUC-ROC, (2) senior medical doctors did not necessarily improve their AUC-ROC performance when offered the risk prediction system in addition to their own analysis of the data, only junior physicians did, (and

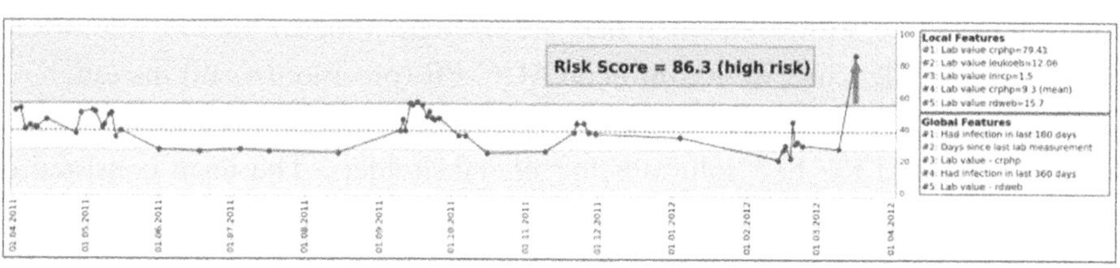

Figure 9.6. This dashboard has been used in the second part of the study. It shows the current risk for a given endpoint (see red arrow) as well as the previous risk scores over time, mapped to a kind of traffic light system. The color red for instance indicates that there is a higher risk that the endpoint might occur within the next 90 days. On the right side, relevant local (relevant for this decision) and global (relevant for the task in general) features are presented, which had an influence on the model's estimation [17].

3) medical doctors and risk prediction partially found different patients at risk. More details about the models, experiments, results, and learnings can be found in [15, 17].

9.5 Learnings

First of all, if one intends to work with sensitive patient data, the data protection unit should be contacted as early as possible, and the concept should be presented in every detail. The data streams should be sketched and evaluated by data protection experts from the beginning. When the security architecture is approved, interfaces can be activated. The data should be stored in the European Union (EU) and cannot leave it. No services from Non-EU providers can be used, e.g., to monitor health activities via an app. Another important issue is to rely on standardized software (e.g., HL7 FHIR standard, FHIR server, Systematized Nomenclature of Medicine – Clinical Terms (SNOMED CT), Logical Observation Identifier Names and Codes (LOINC), Patient Related Outcome Measurements (PROM)).

Another important aspect to consider is that medical data are noisy, incomplete, without context information, and contain unstructured information. If values are missing, for example, it does not automatically mean that the dataset is incomplete and must be deleted for the greater good. Extensive cooperation of data scientists with medical doctors is key for understanding, and time-consuming data cleansing is needed in most cases before the processing of large and unstructured data can start. Imputation of missing data (e.g., using the average or the value of the previous occurrence) did not lead to performance improvements of the prediction model. One reason for that could be that there is a reason why fields are empty, e.g., a certain test was not necessary or the patient was non-adherent.

The development of publicly available datasets/cohorts, such as Medical Information Mart for Intensive Care (MIMIC-III), may improve the comparability of prediction models in the future and may allow better comparisons of AUC-ROC with the literature. However, when data are strongly unbalanced and AUC-ROC is a very unreliable score, we recommend AUC-PR (precision/recall) instead.

The interdisciplinary nature of the team is a critical factor in success and is highly important to find the best solutions for all stakeholders. The team consisted of nurses, physicians in various positions, computer scientists, and medical informatics. In addition, health insurance companies and patients were involved from the beginning. An independent expert for data protection issues is expensive but a good way to find the best solution for various privacy issues.

In the future, the risk prediction model should lead to CDSS and ultimately to Automated Decision Support Systems (ADSS). However, to reach these goals, trustworthy Artificial Intelligence (AI) is necessary, for which the prediction models need to be evaluated and validated within clinical studies to fully assess their utility and benefit. Such studies should ideally be planned and executed by medical experts in close collaboration with computer scientists. Only medical doctors can assess unmet medical needs and design and perform medical trials. Medical experts should rigorously examine the usefulness and explainability of prediction models, and even inexperienced physicians need to understand the consequences and limitations of a model. Moreover, further studies are necessary to explore how such a system could be integrated into the working environment and into the existing processes to achieve the best benefit, as well as how model explanations need to be presented to further increase trust.

9.6 Discussion

We set up routine telemedicine care for adult patients after kidney and/or pancreas transplantation, including an app and telemedicine dashboard, within GDPR guidelines. The telemedicine service relies on an interoperable and standardized software architecture, which allows further modular additions in the future. The telemedicine unit aims to monitor KTRs for early detection of complications and to interact in cases of critical changes. In addition, we aim to support adherence and empower patients to improve their own healthcare [9]. We also developed risk prediction models for rejection, graft failure, and infection in adult KTRs and evaluated the models on retrospective data and within a small experimental study with medical doctors [15].

The key findings are the challenges and learnings from the implementation of a self-financed telemedicine care unit that adheres to the GDPR. At all stages of development, several new challenges had to be addressed. The main hurdles were data protection and long-term funding. Other aspects, which slowed the progress, were bureaucracy, the need for a different mindset, and the need for the same language between computer scientists and healthcare workers. However, the results of the project demonstrate the feasibility of such an interdisciplinary approach and that a human-centric approach is needed in medical informatics and its translation to clinical usefulness. For a successful telemedicine implementation, the human factor is key not only for the design of the software and dashboard but also for the user experience, the integration into the workflow, and the acceptance by the patients [6]. Finally, experienced healthcare workers have a higher impact on patient care and improve the surveillance and treatment of KTRs.

Currently, many new telemedicine approaches for medical care are under development, but with different subgroups or different endpoints, so the final proof of concept still lacks. The first question is how to determine adherence – or non-adherence – in the frame of an app-based telemedicine project. We interpret the rate of participation as adherence, thus the frequency of forwarded vital signs per week, knowing that patients, of course, measure their vital signs but forget to forward them via the app. In the second step, an algorithm was developed to calculate the actual participation and develop a tool to make the comparison easier and more reliable as a pure impression of the telemedicine team.

In the course of our work, two more projects with the aim of improving the care of KTRs in Germany should be mentioned: the project ktx360° ("KidneyTx360") and a Randomized Controlled Trial (RCT) by Schmid and by Kayer *et al.* [18, 19]. Both trials showed a positive impact of the novel treatment approaches on KTRs. ktx360° showed its ability to improve the adherence of patients as well as cardiovascular fitness (which was the aim of the study) [20]. In addition, hospitalization rates due to cardiovascular events were significantly lower compared to the control group, and the loss of graft function with the return to dialysis was significantly lower. Schmid and Kayer showed that telemedicine could reduce costs due to unplanned hospitalization and improve adherence within the first year after transplantation [18, 19]. In addition, KTRs selected for the intervention group described a better quality of life and were more ready to return to employment. Another telemedicine project with KTRs from Australia demonstrated better adherence in the telemedicine group compared to the standard of care [21]. Here, patients were supported for 3 months and followed for 12 months. Other trials describe other telemedicine approaches [21].

During our project, it became clear that for any sustainable telemedicine solution, a clear benefit has to be demonstrated in order to convince the payer to finance such a system. Consequently, a business canvas was developed during the project, and currently we are working on a rigorous large randomized multicenter trial in Germany to demonstrate better outcomes, such as fewer hospitalizations, fewer DSA, better adherence, treatment satisfaction, and better renal function and blood pressure control.

One of the strengths of the telemedicine project is the interdisciplinary app's design, which considers the User eXperience (UX) and the interoperable HL7 FHIR standard with an FHIR server. Another important aspect is the safe and approved digital infrastructure formally evaluated for data safety and protection. Finally, yet importantly, a contract with insurance companies allowed for continued telemedical service with a refund of expenditures (personnel, development of concepts). The weaknesses are the slow development of new features and the bugfixing process.

Over the years, the number of participants and incoming data increased; currently, three nurses and one doctor work in the telemedicine unit as opposed to one nurse and one doctor at the beginning. In addition, more tasks were implemented into the telemedicine unit, for instance, the care of KTRs with mild COVID-19 infection. However, the intense personal contacts with members of the telemedicine team aiming to support the KTRs are the driving factor behind the project. Especially since KTRs can chat via the app and can ask questions or seek help without any hurdles.

The main hurdles for the development of the prediction models were inconsistent, noisy, and imbalanced data with many missing values, which required extensive data cleansing before the model could be developed. Another problem was the lack of external, independent data sets, which limited thorough cross-validation. While better system performance might be of interest, the more interesting question to us was, how good physicians can solve the task, and is the current system already good enough to support physicians? This has been explored in the second evaluation to find out if the tool is useful and if automatic predictions are similar to those made by physicians [15].

Regarding the prediction models, motivation in the form of local and global features on why the prediction models came to a specific solution is provided along with the result of the prediction model, e.g., which laboratory values or signs and symptoms contributed to flagging a patient as critical. Before prediction models are used, their usefulness must be evaluated in the frame of studies. The first study compares the assessments of physicians and the prediction models themselves with each other. In the second step, the prediction models should be implemented into TBase, which is kept for future work. If a patient is flagged with a particular risk, the model explains why, and the telemedicine team watches the scenario develop (i.e., an observational study design). In the end, the sensitivity, specificity, and positive and negative predictive values can be assessed, making statements on the prediction models' usefulness.

In a long-lasting process, the data were cleansed and standardized. In the primary process, where the computer scientist provides an overview of the type of data, interdisciplinary discussions were led so that the computer scientist gained a deep understanding. Transparency was ensured at all times.

As humans play an important role in evaluating the prediction models and the explainability of decisions (telemedicine team), vulnerable and marginalized groups are protected at any time.

Currently, AI prediction models make no therapeutic decisions. As explained above in detail in the first step, they must be evaluated in the frame of clinical studies before being implemented into a life system.

9.7 Conclusion

Building up a telemedicine care unit requires – independent of the subgroup – many preconditions, summarized as funding, an easy-to-modify EMR, an app, and dedicated personnel open to interaction with different disciplines. The participants need to be patient because new features need time to be released and support such digital approaches with feedback. Ultimately, however, it became obvious that the human factor is key to the successful implementation of a highly sophisticated digital platform in medicine, as this needs to be integrated into daily life for patients and into the workflow for caregivers.

References

[1] Wolfe RA, Ashby VB, Milford EL, Ojo AO, Ettenger RE, Agodoa LY, Held PJ, Port FK. Comparison of mortality in all patients on dialysis, patients on dialysis awaiting transplantation, and recipients of a first cadaveric transplant. N Engl J Med. 1999. 341(23): p. 1725–1730.

[2] Suthanthiran M, Strom TB. Renal transplantation. N Engl J Med. 1994. 331(6): p. 365–376.

[3] Schnuelle P, Lorenz D, Trede M, Woude F J Van Der. Impact of renal cadaveric transplantation on survival in end-stage renal failure: evidence for reduced mortality risk compared with hemodialysis during long-term follow-up. J Am Soc Nephrol. 1998. 9(11): p. 2135–2141.

[4] Oniscu GC, Brown H, Forsythe JL. Impact of cadaveric renal transplantation on survival in patients listed for transplantation. J Am Soc Nephrol. 2005. 16(6): p. 1859–1865.

[5] Valderrabano F, Jofre R, Lopez-Gomez JM. Quality of life in end-stage renal disease patients. Am J Kidney Dis. 2001. 38(3): p. 443–464.

[6] Duettmann W, *et al.* eHealth in transplantation. Transpl Int. 2021. 34(1): p. 16–26.

[7] Bamoulid J, *et al.* The need for minimization strategies: current problems of immunosuppression. Transpl Int. 2015. 28(8): p. 891–900.

[8] Liefeldt L, Budde K. Risk factors for cardiovascular disease in renal transplant recipients and strategies to minimize risk. Transpl Int. 2010. 23(12): p. 1191–1204.

[9] Duettmann W, *et al.* Digital home-monitoring of patients after kidney transplantation: The MACCS platform. J Vis Exp. 2021(170).

[10] Russell CL, *et al.* Health facts medication adherence in transplantation (H-MAT) study: a secondary analysis of determinants and outcomes of medication nonadherence in adult kidney transplant recipients. Int J Nephrol. 2022. p. 9653847.

[11] Villeneuve C, *et al.* Adherence profiles in kidney transplant patients: causes and consequences. Patient Educ Couns. 2020. 103(1): p. 189–198.

[12] Adams AJ, Stolpe SF. Defining and measuring primary medication nonadherence: development of a quality measure. J Manag Care Spec Pharm. 2016. 22(5): p. 516–523.
[13] Molloy GJ, *et al.* Intentional and unintentional non-adherence to medications following an acute coronary syndrome: a longitudinal study. J Psychosom Res. 2014. 76(5): p. 430–432.
[14] Wang W, *et al.* Renal transplant patient acceptance of a self-management support system. BMC Med Inform Decis Mak. 2017. 17(1): p. 58.
[15] Roller R, *et al.* Evaluation of a clinical decision support system for detection of patients at risk after kidney transplantation. Front Public Health. 2022. 10: p. 979448.
[16] Schmidt D, *et al.* TBase – an integrated electronic health record and research Database for kidney transplant recipients. J Vis Exp. 2021(170).
[17] Roller R, Burchardt A, Samhammer D, Ronicke S, Duettmann W, Schmeier S, Möller S, Dabrock P, Budde K, Mayrdorfer M, Osmanodja B. When performance is not enough – a multidisciplinary view on clinical decision support. PLoS One. 2023. DOI: 10.1371/journal.pone.0282619.
[18] Schmid A, *et al.* Telemedically supported case management of living-donor renal transplant recipients to optimize routine evidence-based aftercare: a single-center randomized controlled trial. Am J Transplant. 2017. 17(6): p. 1594–1605.
[19] Kaier K, *et al.* Results of a randomized controlled trial analyzing telemedically supported case management in the first year after living donor kidney transplantation – a budget impact analysis from the healthcare perspective. Health Econ Rev. 2017. 7(1): p. 1.
[20] Pape L, Kliem V, Nolting H, Wolff J, Tegtbur U, Schiffer M. Coordinated, multimodal care after kidney transplantation improves graft survival and cardiovascular risks – results of the kidney transplantation 360°-study (ktx360°). American Transplant Congress. 2022. Abstract number: 759.
[21] Duettmann W, *et al.* Digital home-monitoring of patients after kidney transplantation: the MACCS platform. J Vis Exp. 2021(170). DOI: 10.3791/61899.

DOI: 10.1561/9781638282372.ch10

Chapter 10

Remote Monitoring to Improve Gestational Diabetes Care

By Margherita Grossi and Brian Pickering

10.1 Introduction

Rates of Gestational Diabetes Mellitus (GDM) have been rising worldwide over the past number of decades, and Ireland is no exception to this trend. The rising prevalence is a reflection of higher rates of obesity and advancing maternal age in pregnancy.

Epidemiologic studies quote rates of GDM in Ireland and the UK as 8%–24%, varying with study populations and diagnostic criteria used [1]. In our own unit, annual rates of GDM in 2015, 2016, and 2017 were 775, 975, and 974, respectively. This represents a significant increase in 10 years when compared with 2005, 2006, and 2007, when annual rates of GDM were 157, 133, and 153, respectively. The introduction of The International Association of Diabetes and Pregnancy Study Groups (IADPSG) thresholds for diagnosis of GDM in our unit in 2014 has contributed to this significant rise. However, other large contributors are most notably, advancing maternal age and rising rates of obesity in an increasingly more complex obstetric population.

The association between GDM, poor glycemic control, and adverse perinatal outcomes has been established many years ago [2]. Babies born to diabetic mothers have a higher incidence of macrosomia, [3] increased operative delivery rates, [4] increased rates of birth complications, and higher admission rates to the NICU to correct metabolic imbalances [5]. The rising prevalence of GDM also represents a major public health concern as affected mothers are at increased risk of type 2 diabetes in later life [6]. In this chapter, we introduce a novel remote management pathway for diet-controlled gestational diabetes. The concept of an app-assisted lifestyle and blood sugar level monitoring program fosters patient-centered care. This surveillance approach has potential health and economic benefits for both the patient and the overall hospital infrastructure through a reduction in clinic waiting times, hospital attendances, administrative duties, and staff requirements. Ultimately, our aim is to move forward with a patient-oriented model of care for women with GDM. Patients who require prompt intervention beyond dietary and lifestyle changes to optimize their Blood Sugar Level (BSL) can be easily identified. Another anticipated benefit of this strategy in the long term will be reduced healthcare burden and cost. The application of technology in healthcare is a rapidly growing field that can be exploited to achieve and maintain positive healthcare behaviors.

10.2 Methods

10.2.1 Ethics and Privacy Procedures

Prior to the initiation of the study reported here, all necessary documentation to ensure full compliance with both EU and National Irish regulations in terms of data privacy and ethical aspects was fulfilled and met. There was particular attention paid to the GDPR requirements and security measures to avoid any ethical issues or data breaches. Ethical approval to proceed with the study was obtained from the Rotunda Hospital Research Ethics Committee.

As to the classification of the app, the Health Products Regulatory Authority (HPRA) oversees the regulation of medicines and devices used by the public in Ireland. We approached the HPRA for guidance on the classification of our proposed app and portal system to ensure compliance with national guidelines. Inclusion of certain functionalities within the system would have resulted in a requirement for the app to be classified as a medical device.

In our app development phase, we were mindful not to include any functionalities that would change the classification of the app to that of a medical device, as this would have resulted in lengthy delays in the project. The red flag monitoring system we developed within the hospital portal is buttressed by a safety mechanism in that all app-users are also required to report their actual glycemic indices during their scheduled virtual clinic reviews.

As to the consent procedure in the clinical phase, all GDM patients from Rotunda Hospital willing to participate in the study were asked to read our patient information leaflet pertaining to the background and main objectives of the study, the expected benefits of participating, the right to withdraw at any time, the study's methodology, and our assurance of confidentiality. Following review of this document, interested parties were asked to sign our informed consent form.

Other related documents produced were a Data Protection Impact Assessment (DPIA), an internal validation document and risk assessment to evaluate the security by design approach adopted for the whole architecture and data flows, a data privacy policy for the app, the application for the clinical investigation (not needed in the final stage), and all the necessary GDPR agreements between the study participants.

Relevant standards/regulation of reference are:

- EU 93/42/EEC regulation on medical devices
- EN/IEC 62304: Medical device software – software life cycle processes
- ISO 14971: Application of risk management to medical devices
- ISO 13485:2016 "Medical devices – Quality management systems – Requirements for regulatory purposes"

10.2.2 Diagnostic Model

Remote monitoring of women with GDM holds the potential for decreasing pregnancy complications, improving patient quality of life, enhancing the efficiency of healthcare delivery, and reducing healthcare costs. In this paragraph, we present a simple, fast, and flexible method based on a fuzzy inference system for assessing risk levels given glucose readings from patients.

Modern machine learning and artificial intelligence algorithms are used as a core element of Decision Support Systems (DSS), which are typically designed to integrate a medical knowledge base, patient data, and an inference engine to extract insights and generate personalized recommendations. Current DSS exploit embedded expert knowledge through expert system instantiations that eliminate the uncertainty and imprecision associated with the diagnosis of gestational diabetes, e.g., using fuzzy modeling and fuzzy inference [7, 8]. Typical implementations of such systems suffer from the lack of explainability and the long training time that is triggered whenever new patient data become available. Our approach, on the other hand, addresses real-time continuous glucose monitoring in gestational diabetes with a lightweight inference system (no training) that offers timely and interpretable output.

The fuzzy inference system consists of four generic parts (Figure 10.1): the fuzzification interface, which converts the input data into the internal format; the knowledge- and decision-based unit with rule evaluation; and, symmetrically, the defuzzification interface, which provides the estimated risks. In order to develop

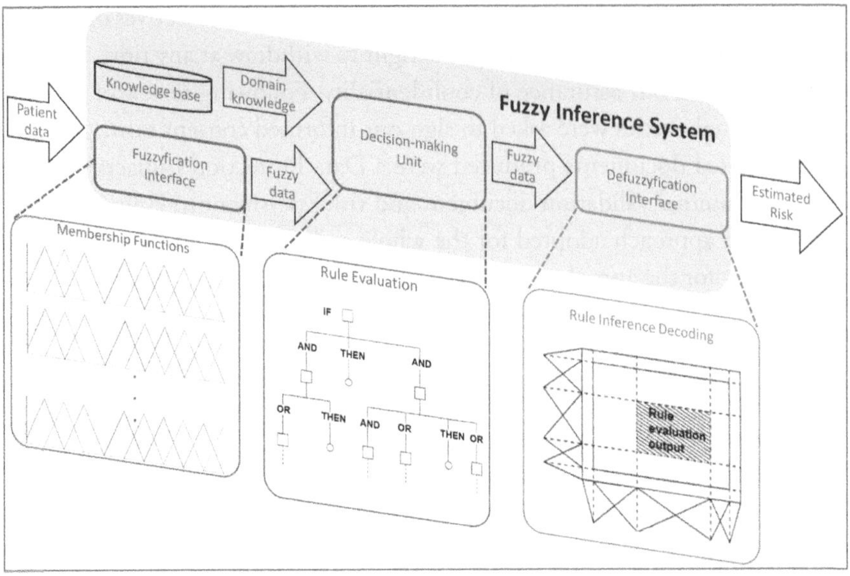

Figure 10.1. Generic architecture and processing of the fuzzy inference system.

and validate the model, input data collected in a preliminary study of the Rotunda Hospital in Dublin were used.

These include fully anonymized data from 50 GDM patients in the 28th pregnancy week. The participants were asked to collect four glucose level measurements per day (one fasting and three postprandial) until delivery, but different levels of adherence to the schedule of measurements were observed (ranging from 10 to 700 measurements in total per patient). Data augmentation was used in order to generate 4,000 synthetic time series of glucose measurements, which closely match the distribution of the historical data. In the diagnostic phase, the system takes as input one week of rolling window measurements, including 7 preprandial and 21 postprandial glucose readings, and is able to assign a risk level between 1 and 100 for each patient based on the weekly measurements. Please notice that results are easy to interpret on a linear and intuitive scale, and a ranking between patients can be done in order to decide which one needs more attention.

Similar to the fuzzy inference systems, in order to monitor GDM, hospitals analyze one week of data and call in the patients with more than 30% of the values above a certain threshold. Following the protocols currently adopted in Ireland, we take the most frequently used values (5 mmol/L for fasting measurements and 7 mmol/L for postprandial ones) in order to define the membership function for fuzzification and add some variability (var = 0.3) to capture interhospital differences. Finally, a set of rules was defined that assigns the output membership value to intervals of measurements that are above the thresholds. This mapping is equivalent to the clinician assessment, which focuses on the percentage of values above thresholds (for more information, please refer to [9]).

10.3 Results

10.3.1 Initial Evaluation

To prove the capability of the system, an evaluation was performed by simulating the model assessment for a larger artificially generated data set (obtained through data augmentation) and comparing the risk levels obtained by the medical criteria. The algorithm was able to achieve 94.68% accuracy compared to current monitoring methods, which rely on periodic face-to-face physician reviews. In particular, it was observed that the system indeed assigns higher risk values to patients having groups of weekly measurements with a very high glucose mean and standard deviation and, conversely, lower risk values to patients with a very low glucose mean. For the border cases, however, our algorithm is able to more accurately evaluate risks compared to hard thresholds. The risk system adapts better to each observation, giving, for example, a greater risk to patients with higher glucose levels on average, even if the number of values above threshold is below 30%, and vice-versa, a lower risk to patients with glucose levels only marginally above threshold.

To summarize, the advantages of using simple fuzzy thresholds include:

- simplicity: the system can be deployed without waiting for the collection of a larger amount of data, it does not require training, and the inference is very fast;
- interpretability: the system is explainable by design since the rules are evaluated and can be easily understood and trusted by the clinicians; and
- accuracy and personalization: the usage of fuzzy logic releases the necessity to have a fixed threshold for risk (different hospitals have slightly different thresholds) and mimics the real assessment of a clinician, which would assign different levels of risk whether the glucose measurement of a patient is slightly above the threshold or extremely high (different membership values in the fuzzy system). The system obtains comparable results in risk assessment for extreme cases (low and high) and can achieve personalized diagnosis in border cases.

10.3.2 Prognostic Model

Besides assisting healthcare professionals with a novel diagnostic model, in the last phases of the study, a new prognostic model was developed with the scope of predicting the risk of abnormal fasting and postprandial glucose levels in the upcoming period of time. Since the analysis is mainly focused on the long-term monitoring of the patients, similar to what has been done for the fuzzy system, patients who show more than 30% of measurements above a given threshold (5.1 mmol/L for preprandial and 7.8 mmol/L for postprandial) within the next 7 days are classified as having a high risk.

Instead of using only the glucose levels like the previous fuzzy inference model, the prognostic model evaluates the risks taking into account personalized patient information, including features such as Body Mass Index (BMI), age, glucose tolerance test measurements, and parity, among others. One key challenge was to interpret, standardize, and then clean some of the values with the help of the medical team. Median imputation is used under the assumption that missing data were random, while features that presented too low variance in their distribution (e.g., ethnicity) were discarded since they would introduce a bias in the results and mislead some of the conclusions. Moreover, a major source of concern was the large number of unknown meal types in the glucose time series collected from the app (up to 40% of the total number of measurements). Since the normal glucose level ranges depend strongly on whether the values represent outcomes from a pre- or postprandial measurement, a correct assignment of those values is essential for the classification of risk.

After agreement with the medical experts, a pre-processing of the data was introduced, allowing the medical personnel to distinguish the patients who had overly high fasting levels and should be monitored further. With this data imputation, the total number of measurements above the normal threshold increased by about 16%, compatibly with the preference for higher recall values for this application. Finally, the quality of the data collected from the app is strongly affected by patient compliance. Sparse reporting or short time series should not be used for the model training and testing (at least 7 days of available measurements).

Before developing the classification model, a survival function for the time to the risk event was built from the data collected by the app up to August 2021 and from the historical data collected in 2019 using a Kaplan-Meier estimator. Comparing the two curves showed that the differences between the two populations were not significant (p-value of log-rank test[i]: 0.46). Based on this analysis, the two data sets were merged in order to increase the number of available patients. Moreover, instead of considering each patient time series as a single training data point, a rolling window approach was adopted. Shifting a cut-out window over the data to create smaller time series from each user (from the beginning until a given

i. The log-rank is a non-parametric hypothesis test to compare the survival distributions of two samples.

point in time), it was possible to create a training data set of 16,900 data points. The rolling mechanism emulates the streaming of data coming from the app and was also applied to derive further features by aggregating the glucose measurements from these smaller time series and to investigate whether they could be good indicators of risk (e.g., in [10], the complexity of the time series is related to the risk of developing type 2 diabetes). The Python package "tsfresh" was used to extract the most descriptive characteristics of the glucose time series [11].

A grid search over a number of tree-based machine learning classifiers was performed to select the best model and its hyperparameters. In order to avoid overfitting, we used a k-fold cross validation (k = 4) on the training data, while the test data were obtained via stratified splitting of the users. Finally, a decision tree classifier was chosen as a predictive model because, while having performance comparable with other most sophisticated algorithms, it is easy to explain (the so called white box model) and robust against missing data and heterogeneous feature types. With respect to the model performance, we set the F1 score as the optimization metric and obtained a total accuracy of 97%, with 78% recall and 90% precision on the test data with the default probabilities threshold.

In order to analyze the reliability of the model, besides looking at its overall performance, different methods to interpret the results were applied, from a simple Pearson correlation coefficient to the more sophisticated Shapley Additive Explanation. As expected, it was found that a higher BMI has a very negative impact on the gestational diabetes risk, as well as a very high mean or median glucose value. The prognostic model results, together with the explanation of the risk factors contributing to the single measurement predictions, have been summarized in a dashboard for internal usage (Figure 10.2).

10.3.3 Evaluation Within the Clinical Setting

A virtual GDM clinic service was established to reduce the footfall in our outpatient departments as a measure of reducing the transmission and acquisition of COVID-19. The virtual clinic facilitated the provision of clinical care through telephonic review while simultaneously reducing the requirement for hospital attendance in a cohort of women with gestational diabetes by 90%. This had a positive impact on the "did not attend" rate and has resulted in a reduction of costs for the patient (absenteeism from work, transport and parking costs, and childcare costs).

While the hospital supplies 6 weeks' worth of testing strips for all GDM patients, cost savings are envisaged with our new remote model through reduction of unit costs for all administrative staff, for the canteen where complimentary breakfast was previously provided, and for phlebotomy and laboratory staff who previously

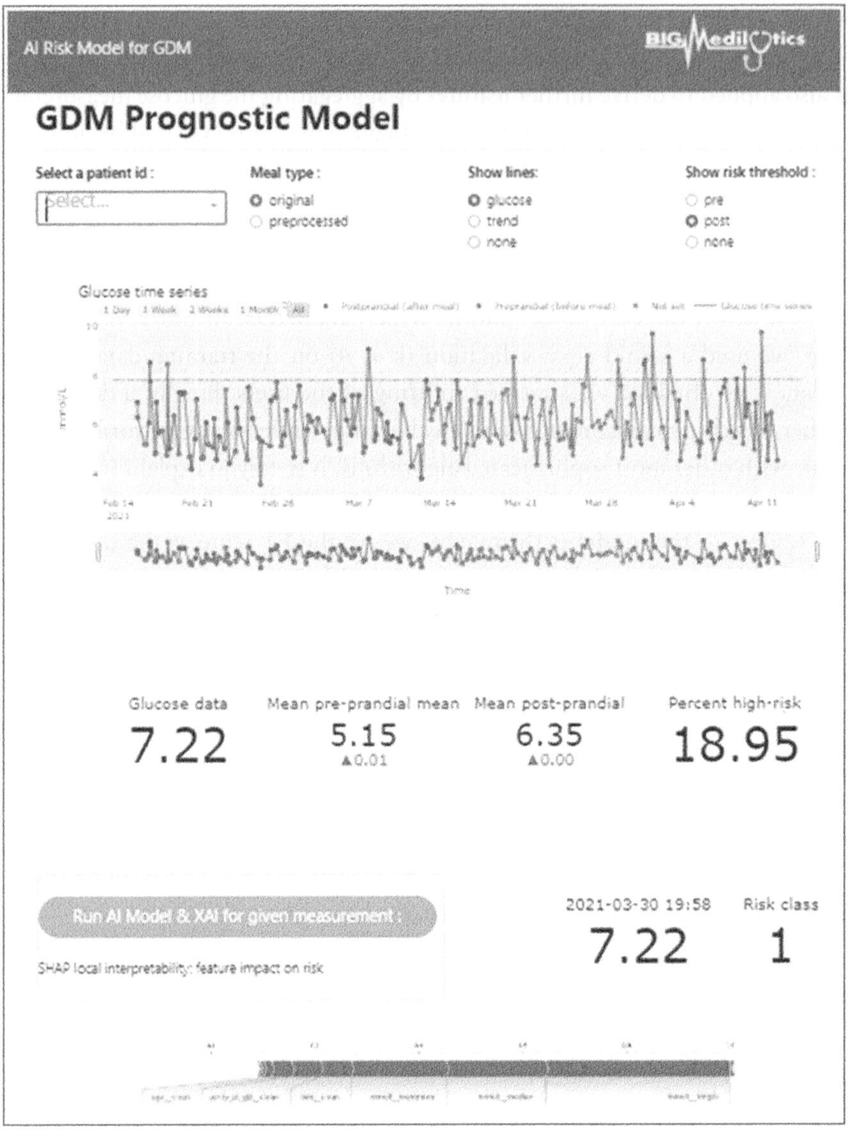

Figure 10.2. Dashboard illustrating the original glucose time series and the prognostic model results. SHAP explanation force plots for the individual predictions can be generated to show the factors contributing to the risk.

provided the service for the acquisition and analysis of two serum glucose samples for each patient every two weeks.

A retrospective cohort study of women with a first-time diagnosis of gestational diabetes was performed from April 2020 through April 2021 following the establishment of the telemedical clinic. Four treatment groups were examined: diet and

Table 10.1. Characteristics of GDM patients based on treatment type (n ± SD).

Characteristic	Diet + Exercise (N = 180)	Metformin (N = 34)	Insulin (N = 67)	P-value
Maternal age (years)	32.0 ± 5.0	34.0 ± 6.0	33.0 ± 5.0	0.282
Maternal weight at booking (kg)	82.0 ± 17.0	86.0 ± 20.0	90.0 ± 22.0	0.015
GA at 3rd trimester scan	33.9 ± 1.7	33.9 ± 1.6	33.1 ± 1.6	0.002
AC centile	58 [30,81]	59 [32,87]	72 [39,95]	0.040
EFW centile	52 [33,74]	54 [39,73]	62 [45,84]	0.051
Gestational weight gain (kg)	6.2 ± 5.0	5.6 ± 4.7	6.2 ± 6.3	0.841
Gestational age at delivery (week)	39.1 ± 2.2	38.9 ± 1.0	38.5 ± 1.3	0.115
Birthweight (g)	3423 ± 603	3389 ± 435	3579 ± 588	0.136
Neonatal hypoglycemia	43 (24%)	18 (30%)	5 (15%)	0.271
NICU admission	28 (16%)	14 (23%)	2 (6%)	0.001

lifestyle, metformin monotherapy, insulin monotherapy, and combined insulin and metformin therapy. Baseline maternal characteristics and an Oral Glucose Tolerance Test (OGTT) glycemia indices at 0, 60, and 120 min were examined. Analysis of variance was used to compare groups and sensitivity to normality was assessed with non-parametric analysis. The latter was reported with the medians and the InterQuartile Range (IQR). Chi-square tests were used to compare categorical outcomes. Statistical significance was assumed for p-values <0.05. No adjustments for multiple teste were performed. A total of 197 women met the criteria for inclusion in the study. Appropriate glycemia control was attained by 73% (n = 144) of those managed with diet and lifestyle interventions alone. Insulin monotherapy was required in 13.7% (n = 27), metformin monotherapy was required in 10.15% (n = 20), and 6 (3.04%) required combined treatment with metformin and insulin. Maternal characteristics between the treatment groups are outlined in Table 10.1. Fasting glucose levels at OGTT were significantly associated with the subsequent requirement for insulin, either as a single agent or in combination with metformin (Table 10.2). Comparing the diet to the insulin group, a ROC analysis using the maximum Youden index suggests the optimal cut-off for fasting OGTT to be 97.2 g/dL (5.4 mmol/L), corresponding to a sensitivity of 81% and a specificity of 57% for insulin use. Elevated fasting glucose is a useful predictor of pregnancy in the GDM population, where insulin supplementation may subsequently be warranted and therefore considered at an earlier gestation.

Table 10.2. Comparison of GGT1, GTT2, and GTT3 between groups, Note: Mean ± SD or median [IQR] are presented for number characteristics. P-value is for any difference between the three groups using the chi-square test or Wilcoxon rank-sum test.

		OGTT1 Time: 0 (fasting)		OGTT2 Time: after 60 min		OGTT3 Time: after 120 min	
Group	Comparison Group	Difference (95% CI)	p	Difference (95% CI)	p	Difference (95% CI)	p
Diet + Exercise	Insulin	−0.40 (−0.57, −0.24)	<0.001	−0.76 (−1.39, −0.14)	0.017	−1.29 (−2.78, 0.20)	0.089
Diet + Exercise	Metformin	0.20 (−0.40, 0.01)	0.064	−0.20 (−0.97, 0.58)	0.619	−0.48 (−1.27, 0.31)	0.236
Insulin	Metformin	0.21 (−0.04, 0.45)	0.097	0.57 (−0.35, 1.49)	0.224	0.82 (−0.81, 2.45)	0.324

The patient outcomes examined cover antenatal, delivery and postnatal areas of maternal and neonatal wellbeing. Mode of labor onset, subsequent mode of delivery, and gestational age at delivery were also collected. The birth weight was collected, and from this rate of macrosomia, a known complication of uncontrolled GDM, it could be calculated. Other surrogate markers of suboptimal glycemia control are neonatal hypoglycemia and hyperbilirubinemia (represented by jaundice), and these were also assessed. Any admission to the Neonatal Intensive Care Unit (NICU) was also documented to allow calculation of the overall NICU admission rate.

These parameters were then compared to historical data to demonstrate the non-inferiority of app-assisted care delivery compared with hospital-based care. We previously compared a telemedical approach to GDM follow-up with in-person hospital attendance through the analysis of 34,399 data points obtained from 283 patients attending either Hospital-based Clinics (HC) or Virtual Clinics (VC). The overall distribution of glucose levels was similar in both groups. The VC appeared to have greater sensitivity for detecting high blood glucose levels at lower thresholds. However, at a Fasting threshold (F) of 95 mg/dL and a PostPrandial threshold (PP) of 140 mg/dL, the results in both clinics were equivalent – 80% (F) and 96% (PP). The median birthweights were 3,350 g and 3,452 g for HC and VC, respectively, a difference that did not reach statistical significance (p=0.241). Birthweights >4 kg were more frequent in the VC group (15%) than the group receiving hospital-based GDM surveillance (10%), but this trend did not reach statistical significance (p = 0.322). An abnormal fasting glucose was associated with Operative Vaginal Delivery (OVD) (p = 0.032) in the VC group, but not in the HC group. Aberrations in postprandial control were less likely to be associated with macrosomia (body weight >4 kg) and OVD or C-section than aberrations in fasting control.

Admissions to the NICU were higher in the HC group (20%) compared to the VC group (14%), but this trend did not reach statistical significance ($p = 0.288$).

We also devised a patient satisfaction survey exploring feasibility, functionality, and utility of the remote monitoring solution – GDMapp – that has been developed in collaboration with all three project partners. While the responses to this survey will not be analyzed until all participants have had the opportunity to complete it, a general overview of the user experience from weekly phone calls with recruited participants has been positive. In general, we have a 90% recruitment rate with most eligible candidates motivated to trial this new eHealth initiative. Out of 115 recruited participants, only two (1.7%) have withdrawn from the study – both due to self-reported increased stress levels attributable to the diagnosis of GDM.

10.4 Discussion

This project created a clinical decision support tool that enables self-management and remote monitoring of GDM, in the form of a patient-facing smartphone application (GDMapp) linked to a medical web portal for use by the obstetric diabetes team. In addition, a diagnostic model based on fuzzy inference systems was developed in the initial stage of the study to support healthcare personnel in monitoring GDM by assigning risk scores based on the glucose levels collected from the app. In the last stage of the project, the model evolved into a prognostic model based on a variety of data, enabling the prediction of those patients whose likelihood of having levels above the established threshold is high.

By study completion, 150 women had contributed to the design of the portal in the pre-study stages of the study, with a further 200 enrolling in app-assisted care using GDMapp, giving scope for validation of the product.

The outcomes of the study on GDM may be summarized as follows:

- Enhancement of patient engagement and education of GDM.
- Promotion of patient-centered care.
- Optimization of compliance with GDM management strategies.
- Elimination of the need for the majority of women with GDM to attend additional hospital appointments.
- Establishment of a telemedical service and incorporation of information and communication technology to complement care provision for obstetric patients with GDM.
- Glycemic data generated from this study will facilitate scalability of the risk assessment algorithm created by Huawei leading to the generation of a clinical

decision-making tool, further enhancing the remote capabilities of this AI solution for gestational diabetes care.
- The introduction of a fully functional solution in the standard GDM care has a positive impact compared to previous practices in terms of: accuracy and quality of data, reduction in the number of admin duties, and staff hours at the hospital.
- Overall, there is a positive tendency in patients in using the mobile app rather than continuous visits to the hospital, particularly in during the COVID-19 epidemic.

At the same time, there were various challenges in collecting and exploiting the data during the study.

- Cleaning, formatting, interpreting, and analyzing real medical data sets from historical data were shown to be a difficult task, due to inconsistencies in the information provided, missing information in some relevant parameters and data privacy issues due to personal information.
- Depending on the granularity and the information contained in the historical data, pre-processing was necessary for integrating those information with the one provided from the app and using them in the training of the machine learning model. This issue was encountered in other studies as well.
- The reliability of the user data collected from the app strongly depends on the correct usage of the device from the end user.
    - In particular, the meal type/timing information, which should have been provided by the patients when taking each measurement, was not done in 40% of the cases (less than 10% of the patients always set the meal type).
    - Postprocessing of the data retrieved from the app in order to impute the missing information has been necessary in order to evaluate the risk, since the threshold is different for post and preprandial glucose measurements.
- Other common challenges for using the app data include:
    - Syntax analysis of unstructured or not standardized input data (especially from the user personalized record) and sparse time series (only 60 patients had at least 1 week of glucose measurements).
    - In a consistent number of cases, moreover, the measurements were regularly repeated twice, so that the frequency of daily measurements increased from 4 to 8.
- Unfortunately, AI applications require many medical sensor datasets that are rarely available and lack diversity. It was not possible to use some of the more complex machine learning models because of the patient statistics and some

of the features (e.g., ethnicity) since they lacked the diversity necessary for generalization.

- It required large data sets to develop robust analytical/prediction model to obtain relevant and accurate outcomes to support the medical staff in their decision-making process.
- Challenges in acquiring a relevant volume of data via the app due to both technical and legal aspects:
    - Extremely lengthy process in obtaining the approval from the Apple Store caused a significant delay in facilitating the last version of the mobile app, as most of the users used an iPhone.
    - Moreover, it was required to put additional efforts to provide a mobile app iOS version fully compliant with Apple requirements, which resulted in additional efforts to change the code in the Android version to obtain an exact mirror of the iOS version.
    - Lack of data from recruited patients due to pairing/connectivity problems caused by a number of unexpected events: a cyber-attack at the hospital that caused failure of critical IT systems at the hospital and network disruptions, making data unavailable.
    - Challenges in collecting a larger amount of personal data from wearable sensors due to some constraints introduced by used protocols (Bluetooth), the main instable connection. In addition, the transfer of data from the edge (e.g., a mobile phone) to the server can be disturbed, requiring flexible methods for checking the consistency of the data transfer.

10.5 Conclusion

In this chapter, we presented the results of exploiting the use of data from patient self-monitoring at home for the prevention and treatment of GDM and its complications. Although the initial aim was purely to demonstrate the feasibility in facilitating appropriate care for this cohort (mothers with a diagnosis of diabetes during pregnancy), which might help relieve the burden on existing hospital provision, the COVID-19 pandemic created an unexpected benefit. Not only is it possible to develop and deploy a monitoring-based patient care process, but this can also support unexpected challenges such as the need for patients to avoid hospital visits unless absolutely necessary. Given the increased incidence of GDM, we believe that our experience can be extended to other facilities to enable and support the effective remote treatment of GDM mothers during pregnancy.

References

[1] Farrar D, Simmonds M, Bryant M, Sheldon TA, Tuffnell D, Golder S, Dunne F, Lawlor DA. Hyperglycaemia and risk of adverse perinatal outcomes: systematic review and meta-analysis. BMJ. 2016. 354.

[2] Billionnet C, Mitanchez D, Weill A, *et al.* Gestational diabetes and adverse perinatal outcomes from 716,152 births in France in 2012. Diabetologia. 2017. 60: 636–644. https://doi.org/10.1007/s00125-017-4206-6.

[3] Kamana KC, Shakya S, Zhang H. Gestational diabetes mellitus and macrosomia: a literature review. Annals of Nutrition and Metabolism. 2015. 66 Suppl 2: 14–20. DOI: 10.1159/000371628.

[4] Zeki R, Wang AY, Lui K, Li Z, Oats JJN, Homer CSE, Sullivan EA. Neonatal outcomes of live-born term singletons in vertex presentation born to mothers with diabetes during pregnancy by mode of birth: a New South Wales population-based retrospective cohort study. BMJ Paediatr Open. January 2018. 30;2(1): e000224. DOI: 10.1136/bmjpo-2017-000224.

[5] Al-Khalifah R, Al-Subaihin A, Al-Kharfi T, Al-Alaiyan S, Al-Faleh KM. Neonatal short-term outcomes of gestational diabetes mellituse in Saudi mothers: a retrospective cohort study. Journal of Clinical Neonatalogy. 2012. 1(1): 29.

[6] Bellamy L, Casas J-P, Hingorani AD, Williams D. Type 2 diabetes mellitus after gestational diabetes: a systematic review and meta-analysis. The Lancet. 2009. 373(9677): 1773–1779.

[7] Okpor MD. Prognostic diagnosis of gestational diabetes utilizing fuzzy classifier. International Journal of Computer Science and Network Security. 2015. 15.6: 44–48.

[8] Übeyli ED. Automatic diagnosis of diabetes using adaptive neuro-fuzzy inference systems. Expert Systems. 2010. 27.4: 259–266. DOI: 10.1111/j.1468-0394.2010.00527.x.

[9] Sánchez CS, *et al.* Fuzzy inference system for risk evaluation in gestational diabetes mellitus. IEEE 19th International Conference on Bioinformatics and Bioengineering (BIBE). 2019.

[10] Rodriguez de Castro C, *et al.* Glucose time series complexity as a predictor of type 2 diabetes. Diabetes/metabolism research and reviews. 2017. 33.2: e2831.

[11] Christ M, Braun N, Neuffer J, Kempa-Liehr AW. Time series FeatuRe extraction on basis of scalable hypothesis tests (tsfresh A Python package). Neurocomputing. 2018. 307: 72–77.

DOI: 10.1561/9781638282372.ch11

Chapter 11

Monitoring Wellness in Chronic Obstructive Pulmonary Disease Using the myCOPD App

By Brian Pickering, Chris Duckworth, Michael Boniface, Alison Blythin and Tom Wilkinson

11.1 Introduction

According to the World Health Organization, Chronic Obstructive Pulmonary Disease (COPD) is the third leading cause of death worldwide. Risks include environmental factors, especially pollution, and behaviours such as smoking. It is persistent and progressive, with an early diagnosis and treatment benefit in controlling the progression of the disease and reducing flare-ups, known as exacerbations. Self-reporting digital apps provide a methodology for remote monitoring and management of patients with chronic conditions in the community. However, the accuracy of what is being reported has been questioned [1]. Both under- and overestimations have been reported [2]. Underestimation may depend on the mode of collection, that is, whether remotely reported or in the presence of a clinician [3]. Other factors include the health condition itself or the perceived sensitivity (e.g., personal invasiveness) of the data being requested [4, 5]. Nevertheless, although self-reported data may not reflect the status of an individual, such data, when aggregated, may be useful to characterize a whole cohort [6].

The myCOPD app used in this study is a digital therapeutic web application designed by respiratory specialists and patients and is available on multiple Internet-connected devices. Using user-friendly multi-channel input to support a broad range of educational and literacy levels, it provides digital support for people with Chronic Obstructive Pulmonary Disease (COPD) and helps them to understand their condition and to effectively self-manage by recognizing their symptoms, thus supporting medication adherence and techniques. Education on healthy behaviours and self-management skills, including exacerbation management, is provided via the app through a 6-week Pulmonary Rehabilitation (PR) programme that has been approved by the National Health Service (NHS). In addition to the patient-facing app, myCOPD supports a connected clinician dashboard, which allows NHS services to monitor COPD patients' health status and interact with them remotely to support medication optimization, PR, and exacerbation management.

For system-generated information (such as time on the app, and how often instructional videos are accessed) and demographic data (age of the user and their (smoking) history), there are two self-reports that we focus on in particular:

1. the *COPD* Assessment Test or CAT Score: an eight-item checklist intended to be an objective indication of the app users' COPD health status [7].
2. the Symptom Score: a four-item, subjective indicator of health status equivalent to the perceived normal state or a mild, moderate, or severe deterioration [8].

Leveraging such data into prognostic models could provide increased personalization of care and reduce the burden of care for people who live with chronic conditions. This study evaluated the predictive ability of prognostic models to predict acute exacerbation events in people with chronic obstructive pulmonary disease based on data self-reported to a digital health app.

The assessments of the two scoring systems will be discussed one after the other.

11.2 Challenges Substudy 1: Prediction and Integration

The main focuses for this study are as follows:

- Can we predict COPD exacerbations from the data provided by the my*COPD* app?
- Can we integrate environmental data sources to inform those predictions?
- Can we identify patterns of behaviour associated with self-reported well-being?

It is also important to remember that the definition of exacerbation can cause problems and is subjective in nature. It is therefore dependent on the patient's own perceptions of their normal state and on what they perceive as an acceptable deviation. But it may also rely on the judgement of a third party, such as a caregiver [9]. COPD sufferers reported using a divergent number of terms, such as a rapid deterioration in breathing (worsening breathlessness), coughing, greater production of sputum, and a change in the colour of sputum.[i]

We should also consider the ethics of using (special category) personal data from equipment that has not been provided by the relevant healthcare provider for study purposes, in this case the NHS in the United Kingdom (UK).

This work received ethics approval from the University of Southampton's Faculty of Engineering and Physical Science Research Ethics Committee (ERGO/FEPS/52137) and was reviewed by the University of Southampton Data Protection Impact Assessment (DPIA 0045) panel, with the decision that the research protocol was of low risk.

11.2.1 Data in Substudy 1 (Exacerbations)

A total dataset from 5,170 app users, providing 94,882 reports, was available over the period from 1 January 2017 through 31 December 2019. These were self-reported, including the objective COPD Assessment Test (CAT) score and a subjective, four-choice *Symptom Score* of general well-being: i.e., I feel normal, I feel worse than normal, and so forth. The reports were cleaned, as has been summarized in [8].

The data controller for these data is My mHealth Ltd., which is responsible for the myCOPD app. Their privacy notice makes it clear that the data provided to the app may be used for ethically approved research, unless the app user opts out. The data subject (e.g., the app user) is free to choose whether they are happy for their data to be used for research or not.

No data held by the NHS were used at this stage. Thus, these are personal data and in most cases special-category (i.e., hyphenate) personal data, since they relate to health. However, since the data are presented to the app by the data subject with the knowledge that they may be used for research if they do not opt out, there was no requirement to seek ethics review or approval from the relevant NHS Research Ethics Committee. Although the app users for this study are receiving treatment under the NHS for their diagnosed COPD, the data they input to the myCOPD app is not curated or governed by the NHS. This would also hold for special-category personal data – health data – from other non-healthcare provider apps.

---

i. See https://www.nice.org.uk/guidance/ng114/chapter/terms-used-in-the-guideline.

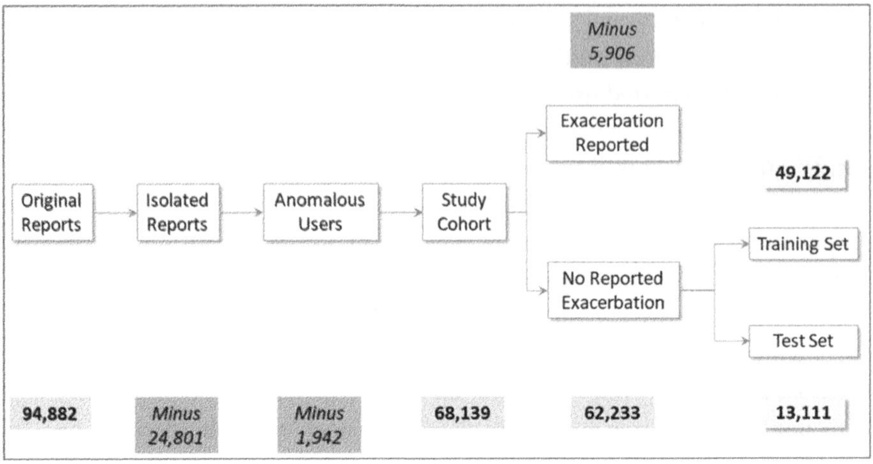

Figure 11.1. Selection of self-reported data in our study cohort, finally containing 2,374 patients. Number of retained self-reports after each filtering criteria given in box. In this study, some of the reports were cleaned and retrospectively analysed to train prognostic models. To this end, only those reports in which the patient did not report an exacerbation event were used (n = 49,122).[ii] We then randomly assigned reports from 19.2% (13,111/68,139) of the patients to a holdout test set.

From the dataset provided by the myCOPD app, 24,801 isolated reports were removed, namely those that were not part of a set with at least three consecutive reports (Figure 11.1). Then, all reports submitted by 1,942 so-called anomalous users were removed. These were internal test users or those submitting reports without being registered. This led to a study cohort of 68,139 reports. Of these, 5,906 reported a severe flare-up (exacerbation). The remaining 62,233, which therefore contained no self-reports of exacerbation events, were divided into a test set (13,111 reports) and a training set (49,122); the test set represented approximately 21% of the circa 62,000 reports (not reporting an exacerbation) registered with the app in the final dataset.

11.2.2 Predicting Exacerbations

A goal of the machine learning in this study was to investigate whether exacerbation events in the near future could be predicted from the data input to the my*COPD* app. If so, this would allow an alert to be raised as part of the care regime for the patient. Furthermore, demonstrating reliable prediction of this sort could then

ii. Note: At this stage, we do not have access to other data, such as hospitalizations.

open up the discussion about who should receive such alerts (the patient, the clinician, or both) and therefore what regulatory approval is needed.[iii]

Briefly, predictions sent to the clinician would allow them, seen as a decision-support prompt, to make an informed decision about how to alter the treatment of the patient. This respects the human-in-the-loop recommendations for AI-based technologies.[iv] Furthermore, this allows the clinician to bring to bear their own experience and knowledge of the patient in making the decision to intervene.

11.3 Methods of Substudy 1

Clinicians with the relevant experience and training recommended a 3-day analysis window. This would be close enough to a future exacerbation event to affect the course of the potential exacerbation and, thus, what goes into the reports. That is, the patient would be expected to be aware of changes (or returning stability) to their well-being. But at the same time, 3 days would be sufficiently far from the projected event to allow time for a range of pre-emptive actions for the patient and clinician. The clinician, for instance, might consult with the patient to develop an appropriate plan of action, which could include changes to medication or (brief, pre-emptive) hospitalization. This could lead to significant savings in resources. For the patient, this would demonstrate that their data are being used for their benefit (making their use of the app more transparent – see also Chapter 26 (Technology acceptance in healthcare)) and perhaps leading to increased awareness of their own health status.

To understand the added value of machine learning, we created a baseline heuristic model based only on a user's most recently reported subjective Symptom Score. The model assigns users to two risk groups:

- Users reporting a Symptom Score of 1 are predicted to be at low risk (1.7% risk) of exacerbation within 3 days.
- Users reporting a Symptom Score of 2 are predicted to be at heightened risk (7.2% risk) of exacerbation within 3 days.

Percentages in brackets correspond to the mean 3-day exacerbation rate for all reports in the training set with Symptom Scores of 1 or 2, respectively. A score of "1" indicates no exacerbation prediction, and "2" indicates the prediction of an exacerbation in the near future. This heuristic model is equivalent to a decision

iii. For a more detailed description of the procedure and results presented in this paragraph, see [8].

iv. See https://digital-strategy.ec.europa.eu/en/library/ethics-guidelines-trustworthy-ai.

Table 11.1. Variables used for modelling.

Variable	Description
Age	User age at time of registration
Gender	User gender
Symptom Score	User-reported Symptom Score
CAT Score	User-reported CAT Score
Smoking Status	One of: smoker, ex-smoker, non-smoker
Smoking Years	How many years smoked
Time from Last Report	Time (in days) since the user last reported
Last Symptom Score	Last user-reported Symptom Score
Last CAT Score	Last user-reported CAT Score
Mean 7-Day Symptom Score	Mean Symptom Score for user over last 7 days
Mean 7-Day CAT Score	Mean CAT Score for user over last 7 days
7-Day Exacerbation Count	Number of days on which user reported an exacerbation event over the last 7 days
Mean 14-Day Symptom Score	Mean Symptom Score for user over last 14 days
Mean 14-Day CAT Score	Mean CAT Score for user over last 14 days
14-Day Exacerbation Count	Number of days on which user reported an exacerbation event over the last 14 days

tree with a depth of 1. Supervised machine learning models make use of patient demographics, lifestyle information, self-reported information, and aggregate features that summarize a patient's (recent) self-reporting history. The variables we used to generate our models are presented in Table 11.1. We built both logistic regression and random forest classifiers to predict exacerbations. Each model was trained using 5-fold cross-validation (grouped by user), which means that reports from individual users appear exclusively in either the training or the test set.

Missing CAT Scores were imputed through forward-filling at the user level where possible. All other missing values were filled using mean imputation within that fold. Either target or ordinal encoding was used for all categorical variables (Table 11.1).

Model hyperparameters were optimized on the out-of-fold validation samples by Bayesian optimization via the Tree Parzen Estimator algorithm as implemented in the HyperOpt Python library [10, 11]. Model performance was evaluated on the holdout test set, and 95% Confidence Intervals (CIs) were estimated by bootstrapping. To create a binary decision about exacerbation risk, model predictions were dichotomized with thresholds chosen to yield either a fixed specificity or the maximum Youden's J statistic on the test set [12].

11.4 Results of Substudy 1

On the holdout test set, the baseline heuristic model obtained an Area Under the Receiver Operating Characteristic (AUROC) of 0.655 (95% CI 0.676–0.689). The logistic regression model yielded an AUROC of 0.697 (95% CI 0.689–0.711) and the random forest model 0.727 (95% CI 0.720–0.735) on the holdout test (Table 11.2).[v] The significantly higher performance of the random forest model ($p < 0.001$) suggests either interactions between variables are important in discriminating between reports associated with exacerbation within 3 days or nonlinear relations are present.

In Table 11.2, we show the sensitivity and specificity of the baseline model and the machine learning models evaluated on the holdout test set. Although the baseline model is already dichotomized, a threshold must be chosen to binarize the continuous exacerbation risks it produces for the machine learning models. The baseline model obtained a sensitivity of 0.551 (95% CI 0.508–0.596) with specificity of 0.759 (95% CI 0.752–0.767), as shown in the table. Although neither machine learning model significantly outperforms the baseline model at the same specificity (e.g., compare models A and E in Table 11.2), the tuning of the threshold used to dichotomize the machine learning model predictions can lead to a range of sensitivities and specificities (compare models C, D, and E in Table 11.2) on the holdout test, which could be tuned to match different escalation policies and interventional strategies. For example, the random forest model can be tuned to yield a sensitivity of 0.921 (95% CI 0.907–0.935) or 0.576 (95% CI 0.553–0.594) with respective specificities of 0.250 (95% CI 0.246–0.254) or 0.750 (95% CI 0.749–0.751).

Table 11.2. Model performances evaluated on the holdout test set.

Name	Model	Area under the receiver operating characteristic curve	Threshold	Sensitivity	Specificity
A	Baseline model	0.655	N/A	0.551	0.759
B	Logistic regression	0.697	Youden's J statistic	0.708	0.644
C	Random forest	0.727	Youden's J statistic	0.755	0.629
D	Random forest	0.727	Specificity = 0.25	0.921	0.250
E	Random forest	0.727	Specificity = 0.75	0.562	0.750

v. The 95% CIs are given in [11].

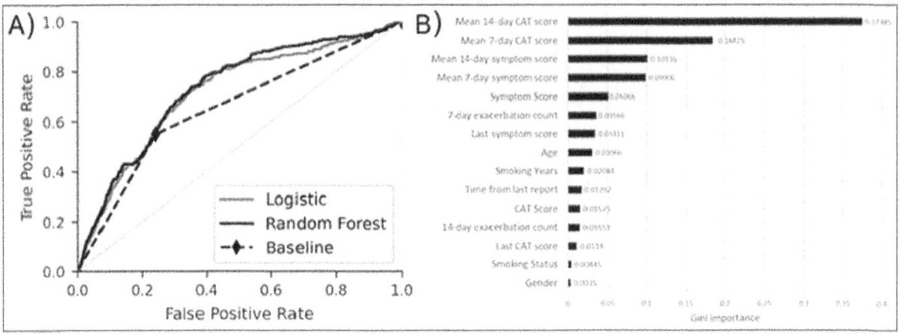

Figure 11.2. Model performance evaluated on the patient holdout test set.

Figure 11.2 shows the Receiver Operating Characteristic (ROC) curve comparing a set of prognostic models to predict exacerbation in the left-hand panel. This includes a baseline model alongside the two machine learning models – a logistic regression model (the continuous grey line) that does not consider variable interactions and a random forest classifier that does (the continuous black line). The baseline prognostic model captures the key features about exacerbation events observed in our data: people reporting a deterioration of symptoms are significantly more likely to experience an exacerbation event in the next 3 days compared to those reporting normal symptoms ($p < 0.001$), with a relative risk of 4.16 (95% CI 3.8–4.5).

In the right panel of Figure 11.2, we present the Gini importance of the features used in our random forest model.[vi] The most important features include the patients' recent CAT Scores (mean 14-day CAT Score and mean 7-day CAT Score). The importance of the CAT Score per se is to be expected since the 8-item instrument has been separately validated [7]. It is also consistent with research identifying CAT Scores as an effective way to quantify the severity of a patient's COPD, which is linked in turn to their exacerbation risk [13]. The next most important features are those quantifying recently reported Symptom Scores. Symptom Scores reflect the symptoms a patient is (or was recently) experiencing, and Figure 11.3(e) shows that people reporting higher Symptom Scores are more likely to report an exacerbation event within 3 days after having reported the step-up in score compared to those reporting lower Symptom Scores. It follows that this information would be helpful in developing a machine learning model.

vi. It is worth noting at this stage that CAT scores are typically provided monthly, whilst Symptom Scores are provided each time the app user accesses the app.

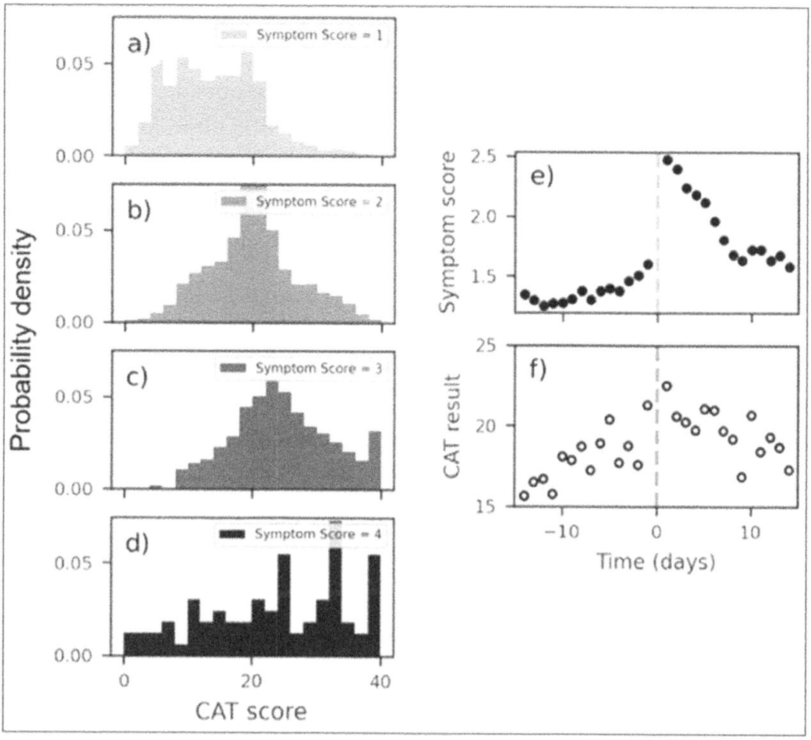

Figure 11.3. Self-reported Symptom Scores and results of Chronic Obstructive Pulmonary Disease Assessment Test (CAT) for reports in our overall 2,374 patient cohort.

11.5 Learnings from Substudy 1

There are three main areas to highlight here. First, our results suggest that self-reported data submitted to a digital health app, designed for the management of people with COPD, can be used to identify users at risk of exacerbation within 3 days after a step-up in scores, with moderate discriminative ability (AUROC 0.727, 95% CI 0.720–0.735). Further research utilizing additional linked data (particularly from medical devices such as smart inhalers, physiological monitoring sensors, and environmental sensors) is expected to increase the accuracy of these models.

We also investigated the potential to include environmental factors in building our models. We found that linking environmental data to improve prediction might be expected to be non-trivial. Referring to the traditional 'V's for big data:

- Velocity: pollution data, for instance, is delivered at regular intervals that are difficult to synchronise with the self-reported frequencies;
- Volume: pollution and weather data may not be available at the level of granularity relevant to many app users; for instance, sensor stations are typically

available across multiple streets, not close enough for an individual to track their movements between locations;
- Variety: pollutants are different in the home versus outside. Without knowing where an app user is at any given time makes it difficult to match data sources and the specific environment they would be exposed to; and
- Veracity: it is still not clear which pollutants, for instance, are more or less relevant (see [14, 15]).

The status of the data should be carefully considered. If the data to be used for modelling are clearly curated and owned by a healthcare provider, then there should be a requirement to seek ethical review and approval from an external body to avoid double jeopardy for the patient.

However, there needs to be a broader debate about the status of personal data submitted to a self-reporting app. In this study, we did not use NHS data, even though the data we accessed were special-category personal data relating to health. Although the ethical responsibilities remain the same when exploiting such data, institutional ethics review is sufficient.

11.6 Substudy 2: Behaviours Around App Usage

Although our primary focus was to examine the predictability of exacerbation events from the data reported in the my*COPD* app, the self-reported data might also show changes in behavioural patterns over time. For example, Symptom and CAT Scores may both deteriorate (i.e., become higher) moving from autumn into winter, as a function of worsening weather. Subsequently, they may improve (i.e., become lower) as the weather gets better again in the spring. In addition, the scores reported by the app users are based on their own perceptions of their 'normal state' and therefore on how they evaluate any deviation from that state. Furthermore, app users may be prone to anxiety about changing weather conditions, which may intrinsically affect their subjective evaluation of their COPD status. It is important, therefore, to consider what we might infer from reporting behaviours, in particular as the seasons change.

In addition, though, and as highlighted in the right panel of Figure 11.2, permutations of the CAT and the Symptom Scores contributed significantly to the model reported in the first part of this chapter. Indeed, the Gini importance in the figure suggests greater significance for these scores than smoking status and gender. Although the CAT Score has been separately validated, [7] the Symptom Scores are low-dimensional (there are only four options). Furthermore, COPD status in general has been associated, in the most severe of cases, with a subjective response from the patient but is also potentially influenced by their carer [9]. Therefore, it is important to consider the reliability of the scores or, in big data terms, their veracity.

11.7 Methods of Substudy 2: Behaviours Around App Usage

An extract was created of the mean CAT and Symptom Scores for the periods autumn 2018 (September through November), winter (December through February), and spring 2019 (March through May). We used the data from those who reported three or more CAT Scores during a period, which resulted in 128 app users. From the 128 app users, the mean CAT Score and corresponding mean Symptom Score were calculated for each of the three periods, resulting in six scores per app user.

This study was approved by the Faculty of Engineering and Physical Sciences research ethics committee at the University of Southampton, reference ERGO/FEPS/56580.

11.8 Results of Substudy 2: Behaviours Around App Usage

For the periods from 2018 going into 2019, the mean temperature was 9.77°C, 5.17°C, and 8.40°C for autumn, winter, and spring, respectively.[vii] There was little difference in the mean CAT or Symptom Scores across the same period: the average CAT Scores for autumn, winter, and spring were 16.75, 16.89, and 17.53, respectively. The average Symptom Scores for autumn, winter, and spring were 1.44, 1.46, and 1.48, respectively. The differences were not significant (Wilcoxon test).

This suggests that neither objective CAT nor subjective Symptom Score changes over the three seasons; there does not appear to be any seasonal effect with these changes in terms of temperature. In addition, Figure 11.4 shows the fraction of self-reported exacerbations (i.e., >2) of all registered Symptom Scores on a given day. Days with a higher fraction of reported exacerbations have a darker shade. Visually, we see little discernible systematic seasonality in the daily exacerbation rate, although there are some indications that winter may be worse. At any rate, it is difficult to identify consistent trends at this time.

To investigate this further, we analysed the scores to establish if responses could be clustered in any meaningful way. For this, the six scores for each of the 128

vii. https://www.metoffice.gov.uk/research/climate/maps-and-data/summaries/index.

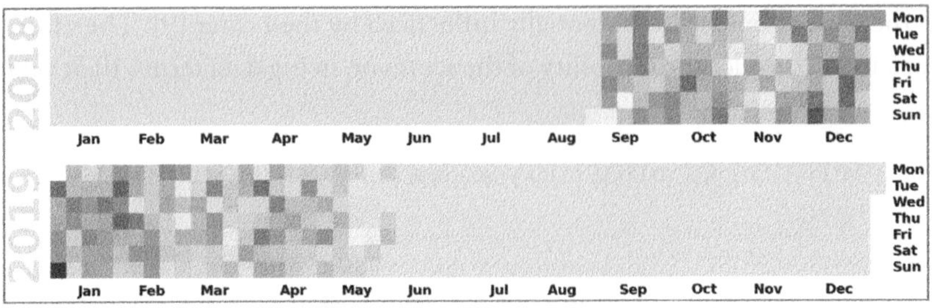

Figure 11.4. Calendar plot of exacerbation rate for study period. Each individual day shows the fraction of users reporting an exacerbation (3 or 4) out of all users reporting Symptom Scores on that day.

app users were converted to normalized (z) scores and clustered as follows: first, the amount of variance accounted for by the number of clusters was plotted for each season.[viii] For all four seasons, a four-cluster solution consistently showed good separation between the clusters. Figure 11.5 shows all 128 combinations of CAT and Symptom Scores for winter (left panel), along with the mean value for the assumed four clusters for each of the three time periods (right panel). The four clusters may be summarized as follows:

- Cluster 1: both CAT and Symptom Scores are low.
- Cluster 2: CAT Score is high; Symptom Score is low. The app user seems to be underestimating their symptoms.
- Cluster 3: both CAT and Symptom Scores are high.
- Cluster 4: CAT Scores are low, Symptom Scores are high. The app user seems to be overestimating their symptoms.

We would expect CAT and Symptom Scores to correlate: the objective CAT would be reflected by a corresponding subjective Symptom Score. Clusters 1 and *3* represent the ideal situation.

Table 11.3 shows how many individuals were assigned to a given cluster across the three seasons of autumn, winter, and spring.[ix] The average temperature (Deg C in the table) came from the UK Met Office as referenced. The final column shows the number of app users who were clustered into Cluster 1 or Cluster 3, where CAT and Symptom Scores correspond, namely those whose objective and subjective self-reports are in line.

The left panel of Figure 11.6 shows a schematic representation of the clusters from Figure 11.5. Clusters 1 and 3 are shown in blue in the figure. These two clusters are expected because CAT and Symptom Scores correspond, as stated, to

---

viii. That is, the difference between the sum of squares and the total sum of squares (using R-Studio).

ix. K-means clustering using IBM SPSS Ver 28.

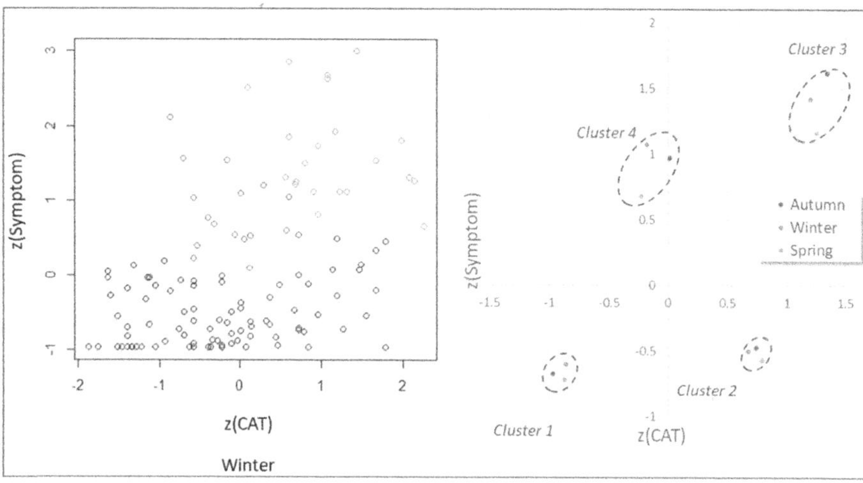

Figure 11.5. Clusters of CAT and Symptom Scores over the seasons (with k = 4).

Table 11.3. Cluster membership by season (total N = 128).

		Cluster				
Season	**Deg C**	**1**	**2**	**3**	**4**	**1+3**
Autumn	9.77	50	36	16	26	66
Winter	5.17	57	32	25	14	82
Spring	8.40	52	28	23	25	75

52%, 64%, and 59% of the 128 app users in autumn, winter, and spring, respectively. 48% for the autumn, 36% for winter, and 41% for spring therefore did not report their expected status. These individuals cluster either in Cluster 2, where they underestimate on the Symptom Score, or Cluster 4, where the CAT Score is lower than expected.

Looking at the clusters over the three seasons, 85 app users (66.4% of 128) stayed within the same cluster, either the expected ones (57% or 67% of the 85 in Clusters 1 and 3, respectively) or not (28% or 33% in Clusters 2 and 4, respectively). Staying in the same cluster suggests they noticed no seasonal effects: the differences in temperature reported by the UK Met Office did not provoke any changes in reported COPD status. Note that seasonal changes may involve dampness and other factors as well as temperature.

Around one-third (128 − 85 = 43, or 33.6%) did change clusters. The arrows on the right panel in Figure 11.6 show possible changes: the blue arrow between Clusters 1 and 3 represents situations where reports remain consistent in that both CAT and Symptom Scores vary together. An app user's condition might have been

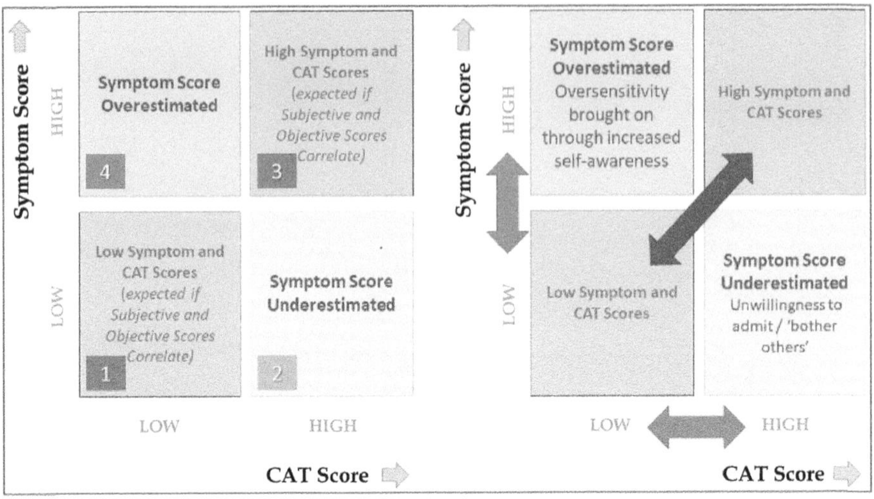

Figure 11.6. Schematic of the clustering of CAT and Symptom Scores.

expected to deteriorate (move from 1 to 3), for example, from one season to the next, and then either return to what it was or remain unchanged.

The central aspect was: which clusters did individuals move to, and can we account for any such moves? In the right panel of Figure 11.6, the arrows suggest expected changes in cluster. For instance, the blue arrow (labelled a) would represent the following scenario: an app user reporting low CAT and Symptom Scores (Cluster 1) might start to feel worse as the weather deteriorates. This would most obviously involve a move to Cluster 3. As the weather improves, this would either result in a return to Cluster 1: the app user feels better, and hence the arrow is double-ended. Alternatively, the app user may stay in Cluster 3, because their condition has genuinely worsened, and thus the assessment persists despite the better weather.

Table 11.4 summarizes which clusters those who move clusters (43 of the total 128 app users) are in for which season. There appears to be an order effect, if not a seasonal one. In autumn, there are less users reporting in Clusters 1 and 3 – the expected clusters where CAT and Symptom Scores correlate highly and follow the blue areas in Figure 11.6. The majority of reports fall in Clusters *2* and *4*, with 17 reports in each. By winter, they are at least more consistent across the clusters, with 13, 13, and 12 in Clusters 1, 2, and 3, respectively. By spring, Symptom Scores seem to be exaggerated (Cluster 4), perhaps by an oversensitivity to changeable conditions in a British spring.

Table 11.5 summarizes which clusters app users start in and where they move to in the following season. Note that the movement expressed in this table could be from autumn to winter or from winter to spring. As can be seen from the principal diagonal (numbers in **bold** in the table), 23 (or 30%) of the 79 entries in this table

Table 11.4. Cluster membership by season for the population changing cluster (total N = 43).

	Cluster			
Season	**1**	**2**	**3**	**4**
Autumn	6	17	3	17
Winter	13	13	12	5
Spring	8	9	10	16

Table 11.5. Cluster membership changes by season (total N = 43).

	To Cluster			
From Cluster	**1**	**2**	**3**	**4**
1	**8**	3	0	8
2	6	**6**	11	5
3	0	8	**4**	3
4	5	0	7	**5**

show no season-to-season movements; they remain for at least two seasons in the same cluster. Furthermore, as mentioned previously and shown by the blue areas in Figure 11.6, there are no cases from one season to the next where app users move from Cluster 1, where both CAT and Symptom Scores are low to Cluster 3 where both are high. This would be expected as an indication of a worsening condition. The same progression in reverse (from Cluster 3 back to 1), where the condition settles down again, is also not found. What is shown, however, is that 56 out of the 79 movements (70% of the movements) shift from one cluster to a different one.

Returning to the right panel of Figure 11.6, the changes in cluster across seasons suggest instability in reporting rather than specific effects of the changing seasons. In the figure, we suggest that movement to Cluster 4 (high Symptom Score, low CAT score), which represents 16 (29%) of the 56 movements in the table, reflects increased awareness by the app users of their condition: app-users are perhaps oversensitive to minor changes in their overall well-being and therefore exaggerate symptoms. Movements to Cluster 2, 11 (20%) of the 56 movements, perhaps reflect denial: their condition is deteriorating (as evidenced by the higher CAT score), but they are unwilling to admit it by underestimating the Symptom Score.

Although we have not looked specifically at three-stage reporting across autumn, winter, and spring here, movement from Cluster 4 or Cluster 2 into either Cluster 1 or Cluster 3 (29% or 52% of the 56 movements) could represent increasing awareness of health status and thereby increasing confidence about reporting in that the Symptom Scores would reflect the independently validated CAT Scores. Alternatively, their health status as measured by the CAT Score changes, and yet their subjective view as shown by the Symptom Score does not. The suggested explanations for the changing behaviours here, although finding some support in the literature, require further investigation in follow-on work.

The reliability of self-reporting has been examined in many different studies (for instance, [1]). In healthcare specifically, this may result in characteristics of the cohort reporting status that potentially influence their condition or the context in which reporting is done and an unwillingness to be seen as a burden on health professionals [16–18]. For COPD, Stelmach and colleagues suggested deliberate misreporting under some conditions, [19] whilst Sigurgeirsdottir and colleagues found evidence that the complex interaction between different factors, including anxiety and feelings of isolation, might influence how patients are willing to engage [20]. Similarly, in a series of studies with COPD patients in the Netherlands, Korpershoek and colleagues found that not everyone is suited for self-management [21]. Patient engagement with self-reporting may be influenced by whether they feel they can affect the outcome of their treatment or are dependent on (other) external factors [22]. In all, COPD patients are subject to denial, inexperience, their support system, underplaying their health status, and their trust in the healthcare ecosystem [23].

11.9 Learnings From Substudy 2: Behaviours Around App Usage

Examining the two data types – *CAT* Score and Symptom Score and which have been shown to contribute significantly to the machine-learning models (see the right panel of Figure 11.2) – does not show any clear seasonal effects: scores did not worsen as the weather deteriorated going into winter or improve going into spring.

This could, of course, be the result of app users staying indoors more during the winter or even that the temperature changes were not sufficient to affect their perceptions of their well-being. However, deviation from expected behaviours – Clusters 1 and 3 in the figures of this paragraph, where CAT and Symptom Scores correlate – may either reflect fluctuating sensitivity by the app users to their condition, a required period of adaptation to changing perceptions, or even an unwillingness to acknowledge the seriousness of their condition. Those using self-reporting apps that take subjective responses as input may need time to develop user trust in how the healthcare app fits into their existing healthcare regime. At all events, the Veracity of the data needs to be seen in the context of reporting behaviours.

11.10 Discussion and Conclusion Both Substudies

In this chapter, we have reported on the initial findings of two approaches to the use of apps and data analysis for clinical effects. Both the substudies sought to investigate whether data coming from self-reporting apps could support the development of a machine-learning model that could then be able to predict exacerbation events. In the first sub-study, we show promising results based on a relatively small set of data. This was encouraging, not least because we did have to deal with the challenges involved in integrating environmental factors (i.e., COVID-19) directly into the models. In the second substudy, we examined behavioural aspects which could be inferred from the data. Using simple *k*-means clustering, we identified four intuitively plausible clusters. Looking at how these changed across reporting periods suggested that instability in self-reports (changes in reporting or movement between clusters) probably reflects app-user perceptions and adaptations to the app as part of their healthcare rather than external, seasonal changes.

Taken together, this study has demonstrated the potential and value of machine learning in exacerbation prediction whilst also highlighting the need to investigate behavioural aspects of app usage. In this respect, our study differs from some of the other studies where self-reporting is based on more objective measures (e.g., blood sugar levels in an app supporting gestational diabetes). It therefore contributes to big data healthcare research based on subjective self-reports.

Acknowledgements

We would like to acknowledge our former colleagues, Dr. Francis Chmiel, who finalized some of the machine learning results reported in this study, and Dr. Banafshe Arbab-Zavar, who contributed to earlier modelling work.

References

[1] Newell SA, Girgis A, Sanson-Fisher RW, Savolainen NJ. The accuracy of self-reported health behaviors and risk factors relating to cancer and cardiovascular disease in the general population: a critical review. American Journal of Preventive Medicine. 1999. 17(3), 211–229. https://doi.org/10.1016/S0749-3797(99)00069-0.

[2] Prince SA, Cardilli L, Reed JL, Saunders TJ, Kite C, Douillette K, Fournier K, Buckley JP. A comparison of self-reported and device measured sedentary behaviour in adults: a systematic review and meta-analysis. International Journal of Behavioral Nutrition and Physical Activity. 2020. 17(1), 31. https://doi.org/10.1186/s12966-020-00938-3.

[3] Scribani M, Shelton J, Chapel D, Krupa N, Wyckoff L, Jenkins P. Comparison of bias resulting from two methods of self-reporting height and weight: a validation study. JRSM Open. 2014. 5(6), 2042533313514048. https://doi.org/10.1177/2042533313514048.

[4] Wu SC, Li CY, Ke DS. The agreement between self-reporting and clinical diagnosis for selected medical conditions among the elderly in Taiwan. Public Health. 2000. 114(2), 137–142. https://doi.org/10.1016/s0033-3506(00)00323-1.

[5] Barrett EM, Maddox R, Thandrayen J, Banks E, Lovett R, Heris C, Thurber KA. Clearing the air: underestimation of youth smoking prevalence associated with proxy-reporting compared to youth self-report. BMC Medical Research Methodology. 2022. 22(1), 108. https://doi.org/10.1186/s12874-022-01594-w.

[6] Sandmo SB, Gooijers J, Seer C, Kaufmann D, Bahr R, Pasternak O, Lipton ML, Tripodis Y, Koerte IK. Evaluating the validity of self-report as a method for quantifying heading exposure in male youth soccer. Research in Sports Medicine. 2021. 29(5), 427–439. https://doi.org/10.1080/15438627.2020.1853541.

[7] Jones P, Harding G, Berry P, Wiklund I, Chen W, Leidy NK. Development and first validation of the COPD assessment test. European Respiratory Journal. 2009. 34(3):648–654. https://doi.org/10.1183/09031936.00102509.

[8] Chmiel FP, Burns DK, Pickering JB, Blythin A, Wilkinson TM, Boniface MJ. Prediction of chronic obstructive pulmonary disease exacerbation events by using patient self-reported data in a digital health app: statistical evaluation and machine learning approach. JMIR Medical Informatics. 2022. 10(3):e26499. https://doi.org/10.2196/26499.

[9] Rodriguez-Roisin R. Toward a consensus definition for COPD exacerbations. Chest. 2000. 117(5):398S–401S. https://doi.org/10.1378/chest.117.5_suppl_2.398S.

[10] Bergstra J, Bardenet R, Bengio Y, Kegl B. Algorithms for hyper-parameter optimization. Advances in Neural Information Processing Systems. 2011. 24.

[11] Bergstra J, Yamins D, Cox D. Making a science of model search: hyperparameter optimization in hundreds of dimensions for vision architectures. In International Conference on Machine Learning. 2013. Pages 115–123. PMLR.

[12] Youden WJ. Index for rating diagnostic tests. Cancer. 1950. 3(1):32–35. https://doi.org/10.1002/1097-0142(1950)3%3A1<32%3A%3AAID-CNCR28 20030106>3.0.CO%3B2-3.

[13] Mackay AJ, Donaldson GC, Patel AR, Jones PW, Hurst JR, Wedzicha JA. Usefulness of the chronic obstructive pulmonary disease assessment test to evaluate severity of COPD exacerbations. American Journal of Respiratory and Critical Care Medicine. 2012. 185(11):1218–1224. https://doi.org/10.1164/rccm.201110-1843OC.

[14] Hansel NN, McCormack MC, Kim V. The effects of air pollution and temperature on COPD. COPD: Journal of Chronic Obstructive Pulmonary Disease. 2016. 13(3):372–379. https://doi.org/10.3109/15412555.2015.1089846.

[15] Schikowski T, Mills IC, Anderson HR, Cohen A, Hansell A, Kauffmann F, Kramer U, Marcon A, Perez L, Sunyer J, *et al.* Ambient air pollution: a cause of COPD? European Respiratory Journal. 2014. 43(1):250–263. https://doi.org/10.1183/09031936.00100112.

[16] Kriegsman DMW, Penninx BWJH, van Eijk JTM, Boeke AJP, Deeg DJH. Self-reports and general practitioner information on the presence of chronic diseases in community dwelling elderly: a study on the accuracy of patients' self-reports and on determinants of inaccuracy. Journal of Clinical Epidemiology. 1996. 49(12), 1407–1417. https://doi.org/10.1016/S0895-4356(96)00274-0.

[17] Sallis JF, Saelens BE. Assessment of physical activity by self-report: status, limitations, and future directions. Research Quarterly for Exercise and Sport. 2000. 71(sup2), 1–14. https://doi.org/10.1080/02701367.2000.11082780.

[18] Johnsen H, Clausen JA, Hvidtjørn D, Juhl M, Hegaard HK. Women's experiences of self-reporting health online prior to their first midwifery visit: a qualitative study. Women and Birth. 2018. 31(2), e105–e114. https://doi.org/10.1016/j.wombi.2017.07.013.

[19] Stelmach R, Fernandes FLA, Carvalho-Pinto RM, Athanazio RA, Rached SZ, Prado GF, Cukier A. Comparison between objective measures of smoking and self-reported smoking status in patients with asthma or COPD: are our patients telling us the truth? Jornal Brasileiro de Pneumologia. 2015. 41, 124–132. https://doi.org/10.1590/S1806-37132015000004526.

[20] Sigurgeirsdottir J, Halldorsdottir S, Arnardottir RH, Gudmundsson G, Bjornsson EH. COPD patients' experiences, self-reported needs, and needs-driven strategies to cope with self-management. International Journal of Chronic Obstructive Pulmonary Disease. 2019. 14, 1033. https://doi.org/10.2147/COPD.S201068.

[21] Korpershoek YJ, Bos-Touwen I, de Man-van Ginkel J, Lammers J-W, Schuurmans MJ, Trappenburg J. Determinants of activation for self-management

in patients with COPD. International Journal of Chronic Obstructive Pulmonary Disease. 2016. 11, 1757. https://doi.org/10.2147/COPD.S109016.

[22] Korpershoek Y, Vervoort SC, Nijssen LI, Trappenburg JC, Schuurmans MJ. Factors influencing exacerbation-related self-management in patients with COPD: a qualitative study. International Journal of Chronic Obstructive Pulmonary Disease. 2016. 11, 2977. https://doi.org/10.2147/COPD.S116196.

[23] Korpershoek Y, Vervoort SC, Trappenburg JC, Schuurmans M. Perceptions of patients with chronic obstructive pulmonary disease and their health care providers towards using mHealth for self-management of exacerbations: a qualitative study. BMC Health Services Research. 2018. 18(1), 1–13. https://doi.org/10.1186/s12913-018-3545-4.

DOI: 10.1561/9781638282372.ch12

Chapter 12

Privacy-Preserving Techniques for Analysis of Medical Data: Secure Multi-Party Computation

By Gabriele Spini, Marie Beth van Egmond, Thijs Veugen and Alex Sangers

12.1 Introduction

Modern machine-learning techniques require large-scale and well-characterized datasets to achieve their full potential. In the medical domain, this requirement translates to a need to store medical patient data and to combine information from different institutions; the COVID-19 outbreak is an example of a situation where this is deemed crucial [1, 2].

However, the collection, processing, and exchange of personal data are a sensitive matter, and the risks of privacy violations are especially high for medical data. This has led to legal frameworks that regulate and restrict the usage of personal (medical) data, with the General Data Protection Regulation[i] (GDPR) and the Health Insurance Portability and Accountability Act[ii] (HIPAA) being two prominent examples. These regulations mandate informed consent from patients in order

i. https://gdpr-info.eu/.

ii. https://www.govinfo.gov/content/pkg/PLAW-104publ191/pdf/PLAW-104publ191.pdf.

to use the corresponding medical data; however, asking for consent for machine-learning purposes is often impractical, since it is a time-consuming process and since contact with patients may have been lost since the moment of data collection.

This conflict between, on the one hand, the need to gather, combine, and process large amounts of data for better machine-learning techniques and, on the other hand, the need to minimize personal data usage for privacy protection has led to the development of several solutions for privacy-preserving data analysis. In particular, a collection of cryptographic techniques known as Secure Multi-Party Computation, or MPC for short, is being applied more and more in the medical domain. Intuitively, the goal of MPC is to allow several parties to compute the output of a certain function or computation, depending on the private inputs of each party, without actually disclosing information on their inputs to each other.

Within the BigMedilytics project, The Netherlands Organization for Applied Scientific Research (TNO), together with university medical center Erasmus MC and health insurance company Achmea, developed a secure algorithm to predict the number of hospitalization days for heart failure patients. Although the project does not use real patient data in its current phase, the MPC solution that we present is based on the following real-life use case, which serves as a motivating example. In Rotterdam, a group of individuals took part in the 'Rotterdam study', [3] a program in the Epidemiology department of Erasmus MC. Erasmus MC collected data on the lifestyle of patients, for example, their exercising, smoking, and drinking behaviors. Achmea, on the other hand, has claims data from its customers (including several participants in the Rotterdam study), which encompass different aspects, such as hospitalization days and healthcare usage outside of the hospital. Recent work has shown that using machine-learning models on medical data has the potential to predict the survival of heart failure patients [4]. The datasets of Achmea and Erasmus MC, once intersected and combined, could be used to train a prediction model that identifies high-impact lifestyle factors for heart failure and thus, in turn, to recognize high-risk heart failure patients.

However, privacy concerns mean that Erasmus MC and Achmea cannot simply share their data with each other to allow for a straightforward analysis. TNO has therefore developed and implemented the MPC-based Proof of Concept described in this article, which allows Erasmus MC and Achmea to securely train a prediction model without disclosing any personal medical information.

Before we present the details of our solution, we offer an overview of the current landscape of privacy-preserving data analysis techniques, focusing on the medical domain and on solutions that bear resemblance to ours. We will then discuss how our solution compares to these existing techniques. The contents of this chapter are largely based on a scientific article and two blog posts describing the experiment and solution [5–7].

12.1.1 Previous and Related Work

A straightforward approach for privacy-preserving data analytics consists of data anonymization and pseudonymization. These methods ensure that only feature data are revealed, instead of identifiers. However, feature data can often uniquely identify an individual, especially if other related data are acquired through public sources, as shown in several studies [8, 9]. Thus, in practice, data anonymization and pseudonymization offer little guarantee for the protection of the identities of individuals involved in collaborative data analysis.

A more sophisticated and popular approach consists of federated learning, where algorithms are trained on decentralized devices or servers, each possessing its own data, by only exchanging intermediate model coefficients with each other. Federated learning shows great potential to facilitate big data usage for medical applications, in particular for international consortia [10]. Federated learning works fairly straightforward for horizontally partitioned data (where institutions hold the same type of data on different individuals), while vertically partitioned data remain a challenge to be tackled.

Cryptographic solutions such as MPC typically overcome these limitations, but with an inherent overhead in terms of computation time and communication volume compared to non-cryptographic solutions. Specific applications in the medical domain cover a wide range, including, for instance, disclosure of case counts, while preserving the confidentiality of healthcare providers [11]; sharing insights on the effectiveness of HIV treatments, while preserving both the privacy of involved patients and the confidentiality of practitioners' treatment choices [12, 13]; patient risk stratification [14]; privacy-preserving analysis of hospital workflows [15]; secure genome study and secure distributed logistic regression for medical data [16, 17]. Compliance of MPC techniques with the GDPR has been discussed in [18].

With regard to concerns related to working with MPC techniques, a challenge in secure distributed data analysis lies in the combination of different datasets: namely, different institutions hold, in general, data on different individuals, and a first challenge consists of determining which individuals are present in both datasets, and retrieving their relevant features. Various works have been done on 'secure set intersection' (also referred to as 'private set intersection'), [19–22] where the different parties learn which individuals are present in all datasets, but it is guaranteed that no information on individuals outside the intersection will be revealed. To the best of our knowledge, however, no previous work has been published that describes a secure inner join solution where individuals in the intersection are determined but not revealed and where the corresponding feature values are associated with each individual.

Concerning the secure training of a linear regression model on distributed data, a lot of work has been done on a variant of linear regression known as Ridge regression, e.g., [23–32]. Privacy is often preserved by using homomorphic encryption techniques, [24–27] yet there are also implementations that make use of secret sharing, [23] or garbled circuits [28].

The solution that we present here focuses on another linear regression method called Lasso, which has the advantage that once the model has been (securely) trained, less data are needed to evaluate the model. This is a very desirable property for a healthcare-prediction scenario, and in particular for the identification of high-impact factors for heart failure, as described at the beginning of this paragraph: gathering and using only the data that is strictly necessary to apply the model is important to comply with privacy regulations and their data-minimization requirements. In [4], it is even shown that for the prediction of the survival of heart failure patients, training a model on two features alone can yield more accurate predictions than those made using all available features.

12.1.2 The Contributions of the BigMedilytics Project

Within the BigMedilytics project, a solution was developed for (1) computing a secure inner join of two datasets and (2) securely training a Lasso regression model on the obtained (encrypted) data.

Our solution is tailored to the heart failure use-case described above and involves Achmea and Eramus MC as data parties and healthcare information intermediation company ZorgTTP as helper party. The solution has been installed on a test infrastructure by the three involved parties, generated artificial data, and been tested for performance in terms of the quality of the obtained model and efficiency. We elaborate on the benefits and lessons learned from this experiment at the end of this chapter.

12.2 Applications

12.2.1 Description of the Desired Functionality

We first discuss the details of the functionality that we aim to realize. Privacy and security aspects are not considered here and will instead be discussed in paragraph 2.2, following the same structure as the current paragraph.

Table 12.1. AC dataset.

Identifier	Feature $\alpha^{(1)}$	...	Feature $\alpha^{(\ell)}$
a_1	$\alpha_1^{(1)}$	...	$\alpha_1^{(\ell)}$
a_2	$\alpha_2^{(1)}$	...	$\alpha_2^{(\ell)}$
$\vdots$	$\vdots$	$\vdots$	$\vdots$

Table 12.2. EMC dataset.

Identifier	Feature $\beta^{(1)}$	...	Feature $\beta^{(m)}$
b_1	$\beta_1^{(1)}$	...	$\beta_1^{(m)}$
b_2	$\beta_2^{(1)}$	...	$\beta_2^{(m)}$
$\vdots$	$\vdots$	$\vdots$	$\vdots$

12.2.1.1 Description of the setting and data formatting

We begin with the general setup and a description of the format of the input data. In our setting, two data-providing parties are involved: a healthcare insurance company, Achmea (AC), and a university hospital, Erasmus MC (EMC). We assume that each party owns a dataset where several features of various customers/patients are contained. Each row in the dataset corresponds to a customer or patient, and we refer to it as a record. Specifically, we denote the dataset of Achmea, and its element, as in Table 12.1, and we denote by A its set of identifiers $\{a_1, a_2, \dots\}$.

The dataset of Erasmus MC, on the other hand, is depicted in Table 12.2, and we denote by B the set of identifiers $\{b_1, b_2, \dots\}$.

Before discussing the properties of identifiers and features, we stress the fact that the research described in this article did not use any actual identifiers or features corresponding to existing individuals. For the running time, accuracy, and performance experiments, synthetic data were created or existing public data sets were used.

It was assumed that identifiers in A and B are of the same type; for simplicity, one may think of them as the social security number of a customer/patient. In particular, it is assumed that if a_i and b_j refer to the same person, then $a_i = b_j$. Notice that we are actually interested in the intersection of A and B, as we want to train a regression algorithm on all features.

For what concerns the features, both $\alpha^{(i)}$ and $\beta^{(j)}$ are assumed to be numerical or Boolean. One of the features serves as a target; intuitively, we aim to predict its value as a function of the other feature values. We formalize this intuitive goal in the following sub-paragraphs.

Table 12.3. AC and EMC example datasets, respectively.

Identifier	Hospitalization days
000000	10
111111	5
555555	8
777777	9

Identifier	Hours of exercise per week
000000	0
111111	2
777777	1
999999	3

Table 12.4. Inner join example.

Identifier	Hospitalization days	Hours of exercise per week
000000	10	0
111111	5	2
777777	9	1

Table 12.5. Inner join dataset.

Identifier	Feature $\alpha^{(1)}$	...	Feature $\alpha^{(\ell)}$	Feature $\beta^{(1)}$	...	Feature $\beta^{(m)}$
$a_{i_1} = b_{j_1}$	$\alpha_{i_1}^{(1)}$	...	$\alpha_{i_1}^{(\ell)}$	$\beta_{j1}^{(1)}$	...	$\beta_{j1}^{(m)}$
$a_{i_2} = b_{j_2}$	$\alpha_{i_2}^{(1)}$	...	$\alpha_{i_2}^{(\ell)}$	$\beta_{j2}^{(1)}$	...	$\beta_{j2}^{(m)}$
⋮	⋮	⋮	⋮	⋮	⋮	⋮

12.2.1.2 Inner join of the data

In order to find a correlation among different features, the first necessary step is to identify which features belong to the same customer/patient. Namely, not every person in Achmea is necessarily present in the database of Erasmus MC (as not all customers of AC took part in the social and behavioral study of EMC), and vice versa.

Therefore, the two parties need to (i) compute the intersection of A and B (i.e., identify which persons are represented in both databases) and (ii) ensure that the feature values $\alpha_i^{(\cdot)}$ and $\beta_j^{(\cdot)}$ are identified for all i and j such that the identifiers a_i and b_j coincide and belong to the intersection of A and B (i.e., assign to each identifier in the intersection the corresponding features). In Tables 12.3 and 12.4, an example of the aimed result of this intersection is shown, inspired by the heart failure use-case presented in the introduction paragraph.

More abstractly, Table 12.5 would therefore be obtained, using the notation of Tables 12.1 and 12.2.

This type of operation is commonly referred to as Inner join in the field of database management [33].

The next step is to train a regression algorithm on the data contained in Table 12.5. We remark that, at this point, the identifier column is no longer necessary and will indeed play no role in the regression step.

12.2.1.3 Lasso regression algorithm

Given Table 12.5, we are now interested in finding a way of expressing a given feature (the number of hospitalization days) as a linear combination of the other features or as an approximation of such a linear combination. This is accomplished by training a linear regression model on Table 12.5. In this sub-paragraph, we give some information on this process; for a more complete explanation, the reader can refer to the scientific article describing this experiment [5].

A linear regression problem can be informally expressed by the following question: for a known matrix $\mathbf{X} \in \mathbb{R}^{n \times m}$, where n is the number of records and m is the number of features, and a target vector $\mathbf{y} \in \mathbb{R}^{n \times 1}$, can we find a weight vector $\mathbf{w}$ such that the equality $\mathbf{Xw} = \mathbf{y}$ is satisfied? In general, the system is overdetermined, and there exists no solution. Instead, one aims to find $\mathbf{w}$ such that some function of the approximation error vector $\mathbf{Xw} - \mathbf{y}$ (and possibly some other arguments) is minimized.

We focus on a variant of this problem known as Least Absolute Shrinkage and Selection Operator (*Lasso*), [34, 35] which automatically discards features with little impact on the target vector.

12.2.1.4 Gradient descent approach

Gradient Descent (GD) is a general optimization algorithm that finds a local minimum of an objective function. The algorithm takes repeated steps in the opposite direction of the (approximate) gradient of the objective function at the current point. In that way, it moves to the direction of the steepest descent. GD is a building block for many different models, including Ridge regression and support vector machine.

12.2.2 Description of the Secure Solution

12.2.2.1 Aim and assumptions

The goal of this sub-paragraph is to show how the functionality described in paragraph 2.1 can be realized in a secure way. This means that while both parties will learn the output of the Lasso regression (i.e., the model coefficients) trained on the inner join of their datasets,[iii] no other information on the datasets of each party will be disclosed to any other party.

---

iii. To be completely precise, we also reveal the size of the intersection of the two datasets to the involved parties.

Our secure solution involves a third party, which does not supply any input and does not receive any output (except for the size of the intersection of the two datasets). For our Proof of Concept, this third-party role is taken by ZorgTTP, a company that offers consultancy and practical solutions on the topic of privacy-preserving data analysis in the healthcare sector. The addition of such a party has two benefits, relating to the two steps of our solution: secure inner join and secure Lasso regression. For the first step, the presence of a third party allows us to design a custom, highly efficient protocol; for the second step, we are able to use the MPyC library, [36] which provides useful building blocks but requires at least three parties to guarantee security.

Before discussing the details of our solution, we give a brief introduction to Secure Multi-Party Computation. Notice that we chose to present cryptographic concepts with a focus on intuition so as not to burden the reader with an unnecessary level of formalism. The reader can refer to [37, 38] for a more formal discussion of general cryptographic concepts (including cryptographic hash functions, homomorphic encryption, and secret sharing) and to [39, 40] for an in-depth discussion of MPC and secret sharing.

12.2.2.2 Secure inner join

As outlined in paragraph 2.1, in order to realize a protocol that securely implements our desired functionality, the first step to be performed is to compute the so-called inner join of the datasets of Achmea and Erasmus MC. Namely, we need to obtain a database with the identifiers that are present in both the datasets of Achmea and Erasmus MC, and with the corresponding features coming from both datasets. Notice that we do not wish to reveal the dataset obtained in this way to any party, as it would still contain highly sensitive personal data (in the case of an application involving real data). The inner-join database will thus remain secret, yet computing the coefficients of a Lasso regression model on this secret dataset will be possible.

Our solution makes use of three core components: (keyed) cryptographic hash functions, (additively) homomorphic encryption, and 2-out-of-2 secret sharing.

- Hash functions. A cryptographic hash function is a deterministic function H: $\mathcal{D} \to \mathcal{C}$, that maps any alphanumeric string $s \in \mathcal{D}$ to another alphanumeric string $H(s) = z \in \mathcal{C}$, called *digest*, of fixed length. Such a function enjoys the property that given a digest $z \in \mathcal{C}$, it is unfeasible to compute a string s such that $H(s) = z$.
- Homomorphic encryption. An (additively) homomorphic encryption scheme is a public-key encryption scheme such that there exists a special operations on ciphertexts $\boxplus$ with $\mathrm{Dec}(\mathrm{Enc}(m_1) \boxplus \mathrm{Enc}(m_2)) = m_1 + m_2$, and similarly for the “minus” operation.

Table 12.6. Encrypted data sent to ZorgTTP by AC and EMC, respectively.

Hashed identifier	Encrypted feature α
$H(a_1 \| r)$	$[\alpha_1]_{AC}$
$H(a_2 \| r)$	$[\alpha_2]_{AC}$
⋮	⋮

Hashed identifier	Encrypted feature β
$H(b_1 \| r)$	$[\beta_1]_{AC}$
$H(b_2 \| r)$	$[\beta_2]_{AC}$
⋮	⋮

Table 12.7. Encrypted data obtained and intersected by ZorgTTP.

Matching identifiers	Feature α	Feature β	Value AC	Value EMC
$H(a_i \| r) = H(b_j \| r)$	$[\alpha]_{AC}$	$[\beta]_{EMC}$	$[\alpha - z]_{AC}$	$[\beta - s]_{EMC}$

Table 12.8. Final tables of secret-shares obtained by AC and EMC, respectively.

α-share	β-share
$\alpha - z$	s

α-share	β-share
z	$\beta - s$

- 2-out-of-2 secret sharing. This building block can be seen as a form of keyless encryption, distributed among two parties, and works as follows: given a secret (numerical) value s, two elements s_1 and s_2 called shares are randomly sampled, but subject to the condition that $s_1 + s_2 = s$. Then, s_1 is assigned to a party and s_2 to another party; in this way, each party has individually no knowledge of s (since the share s_i that they have is a random number), but the original secret value s can be reconstructed when the two parties cooperate and communicate their shares to each other.

The presence of a third party (ZorgTTP) allows us to design a novel, highly efficient protocol for secure inner join, which we believe to be of independent interest. The goal is for AC and EMC to obtain a secret-shared version of the features from Table 12.5. Our secure inner join protocol between AC, EMC, and ZorgTTP uses cryptographic hash functions, and both AC and EMC have an (additively) homomorphic encryption key pair; we used SHA-256 as a hash function and the Paillier homomorphic encryption scheme in our implementation [41, 42].

We did not discuss how the secure inner join was realized; the reader can refer to the article [5] for a detailed discussion.

12.2.2.3 Secure lasso regression

Once the steps of paragraph 2.2 have been performed, we obtain a '2-out-of-2 secret-shared' version of Table 12.5: namely, Achmea and Erasmus MC each have a table filled with apparently random numbers, but if they were to add up the corresponding numbers, they would obtain exactly Table 12.5.

Recall that our purpose is to train a linear regression model – specifically Lasso – on this table. Now letting Achmea and Erasmus MC communicate their datasets to each other in order to reconstruct Table 12.5, and then train the regression model, is clearly not an option: the information that they would obtain consists of personal data, the exchange of which has to be prevented.

Instead, we present a solution that is able to compute the regression coefficients from the two datasets without leaking information on their content.

The fundamental building block that allows us to design and implement this solution is Shamir Secret Sharing, which can be seen as a form of key-less distributed encryption (just like 2-out-of-2 secret sharing), but with different privacy and reconstruction guarantees; in particular, Shamir Secret Sharing can ensure that shares are distributed among three parties instead of two. We make use of the software platform MPyC, [36] which implements this form of secret sharing and other useful communication and computation tools.

Such a secret-sharing scheme can be used to construct MPC protocols; assume that the three involved parties (Achmea, Erasmus MC, and ZorgTTP) have access to a Shamir Secret Sharing scheme. Let us assume that parties wish to perform some computation on a value α (held by Achmea) and β (held by Erasmus MC). The three parties can then proceed as follows: first, Achmea secretshares α, i.e., computes $(\alpha_1, \alpha_2, \alpha_3) = \mathit{Share}(\alpha)$, such that Achmea, Erasmus MC, and ZorgTTP will receive α_1, α_2, and α_3, respectively. Notice that by the privacy property of the scheme, no information on α is leaked at this point. Erasmus MC then similarly secret-shares β, i.e., computes and distributes $(\beta_1, \beta_2, \beta_3) = \mathit{Share}(\beta)$.

The key property now is that for any operation that the parties wish to perform on the values α and β, there exists a corresponding operation that can be performed *on the shares* α_i, β_i, resulting in some other sharing s_1, s_2, s_3, in such a way that no information at all is leaked on α, or β.

It then becomes possible to evaluate a complex algorithm such as Lasso regression on several features of Achmea and Erasmus MC: parties can secret-share their features, then decompose the Lasso regression into basic operations, and perform the corresponding operations on the shares. Eventually, they will obtain shares of the regression coefficients; Achmea and Erasmus MC at this point simply need to exchange their shares with each other in order to reconstruct the coefficients.

12.3 Results

In this paragraph, we first present the security results of our solution. We only give a brief overview and once again refer to [5] for a detailed discussion.

12.3.1 Security Results

The security of our solution is guaranteed under the following assumptions: First of all, we assume that any two parties are connected by secure channels. We assume that parties do follow the instructions of the protocol; in the cryptographic lexicon, they are thus assumed to be semi-honest. We assume that no party will collude with any other party and exchange information with them.

Under the above conditions, it is guaranteed that the only information that will be revealed are regression coefficients and the size of the intersection between the datasets of Achmea and Erasmus MC.

12.3.2 Running Time

We implemented our solution in Python. In order to test the efficiency of our implementation, we ran several experiments on three machines, under the control of Achmea, Erasmus MC, and ZorgTTP, respectively, and geographically separated.

The experiments include the secure inner-join computation and the protocol to securely train a Lasso regression algorithm as described in paragraph 2.2. For the same reason, no test data are extracted from these artificial datasets.

In order to test the efficiency of our solution, we sampled artificial datasets with an increasing number of records and features, and ran several instances of our solution. We vertically split the dataset into two datasets with an equal number of features (up to one difference) and a complete overlap in record IDs, i.e., the identifiers in the Achmea dataset were identical to those of the Erasmus MC dataset for each iteration.

The total running time (thus encompassing both secure inner join and secure Lasso regression) is shown in Figures 12.1 and 12.2. Our solution thus takes roughly 3500 seconds, slightly less than 1 hour, to process two datasets with 5000 records each and a total of 30 features. Moreover, the running time of our solution scales linearly with the number of records and features.

12.3.3 Performance and Accuracy Results

To test the performance and accuracy of our secure model, we use the 'Medical Costs' dataset by Brett Lantz [43]. This public dataset contains 1338 records of patients with 12 features each (including age, BMI, children, gender, and medical costs), of which four are numerical and eight are Boolean. We centered and scaled the data in advance, such that the feature values are between 0 and 1. We also split them into a train and a test set (10% of the data, randomly selected).

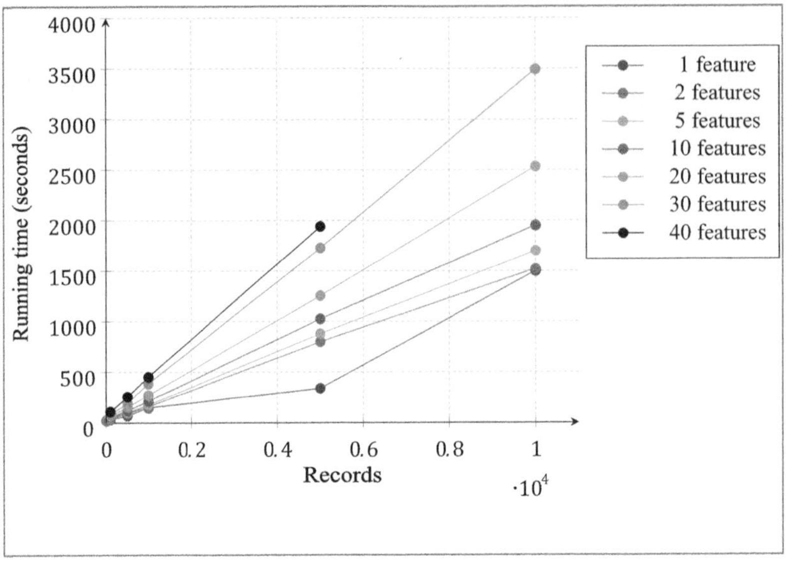

Figure 12.1. Total running time of the experiments as a function of the number of records (median values).

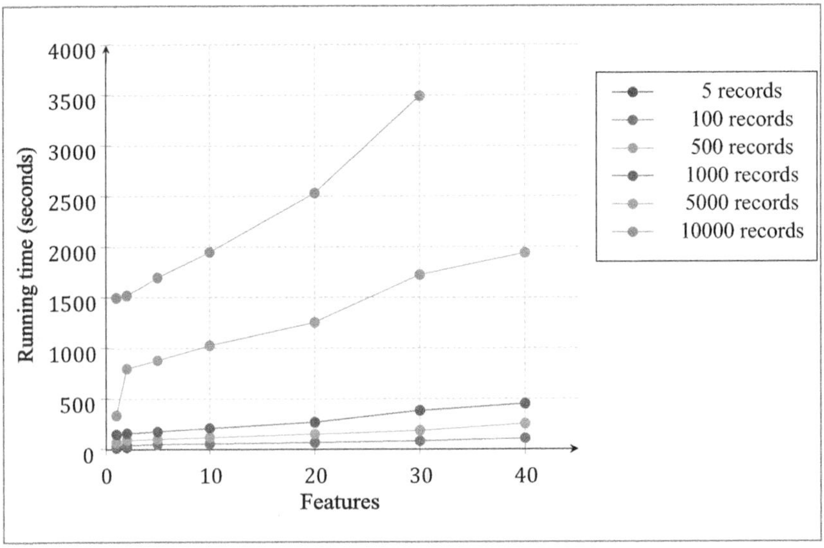

Figure 12.2. Total running time of the experiments as a function of the number of features (median values).

12.3.4 Performance of Lasso Regression

To test the performance of our solution, we compare the results of our secure model with the non-secure scikit-learn Lasso model [44]. Note that the secure inner join has no influence on the performance of the Lasso regression. Therefore,

Table 12.9. Comparison plaintext model and Sklearn Lasso: objective, R^2, mean squared error, and mean absolute error.

Model	Obj	R^2	MSE	MAE	Intercept
scikit-learn	0.009	0.66	0.012	0.082	0.39
our secure model	0.013	0.74	0.008	0.062	0.18
Abs. diff.	0.004	0.08	0.004	0.020	0.21

Table 12.10. Comparison plaintext model and Sklearn Lasso: coefficients.

Model	c1	c2	c3	c4	c5	c6	c7	c8	c9	c10	c11
scikit-learn	0.08	0.01	0	0	0	−0.03	0	0	0	0	0
our secure model	0.17	0.10	0.001	0	0	−0.19	0.18	0	0	0	0
Abs. diff.	0.09	0.09	0.001	0	0	0.11	0.18	0	0	0	0

as input into our secure model, the data is secretly shared between the three parties.

We trained our secure model on 11 features of the train set for predicting the (numerical) target feature of medical costs by varying λ and tolerance. We found the optimal choice, leading to a good fit (R^2, mean squared error) and enough coefficients set to zero to be $\lambda = 0.001$ and tolerance $= 0.0001$. Applying the trained model to our test set, we achieve an R^2 of 0.70, a mean squared error of 0.0086, a mean absolute error of 0.062, and an objective of 0.013. As a validation of the solving method that we used, we compare these results with the (highly optimized) Lasso model of scikit-learn, [44] using the same parameters. After the model was trained on the train set, on the test set, we found an R^2 value of 0.66, a mean squared error of 0.012, a mean absolute error of 0.082, and an objective of 0.0090. Although the goodness-of-fit measures of our secure model are better than those of the scikit-learn model, it has a larger objective value. In Tables 12.9 and 12.10, one can see that in the scikit-learn model, two more coefficients are set to zero, which is one of the aims of Lasso. Therefore, we can conclude that our secure model has good performance, although the (highly optimized) scikit-learn model performs slightly better.

12.4 Benefits

In light of the results shown in paragraph 3, we conclude that our solution does provide a viable way of securely training a Lasso regression model on distributed patient data in a privacy-preserving way. In particular, the good quality of the obtained model, together with its satisfying efficiency in a fairly realistic setup, makes our solution a promising tool for privacy-preserving analysis of distributed patient data.

On a more general level, the use of MPC can help organizations to comply with privacy regulations when analyzing medical data. In particular, MPC can be seen as a strong form of pseudonymization, and the outcome itself (the only data being revealed) is typically anonymous. Moreover, since all parties are required to participate in the MPC process, they can ensure that the data are only being used for a purpose they have vetted; this is in contrast with more classical solutions, where data owners need to rely on the bona fide of data processors for what concerns the type of analysis that is run on the data.

12.5 Learnings

A number of lessons can be extracted from the process of devising and implementing the solution described in the previous paragraphs.

- MPC is a powerful tool that has reached a high level of maturity. In particular, even relatively complex functionalities like training machine-learning models can be realized with it.
- Using MPC does incur a large computational and communication overhead, like for many other privacy-enhancing technologies; in particular, this means that training a machine-learning model with MPC is significantly slower than on plaintext data. However, the efficiency guarantees for this type of computation are not very stringent, and a running time of around an hour is generally deemed acceptable.
- While conclusions from this and other projects indicate that MPC can help organizations in reconciling data analysis with privacy regulations, there are no explicit national or international regulations that concern MPC. One of the consequences of this is that the digital privacy impact assessment of MPC solutions may take more time to be reviewed by the relevant parties.
- According to Achmea and Erasmus MC, the process was technically and organizationally complex to implement in a corporate environment. MPC is a complex technology on both conceptual and technical levels, and more familiarity with it is needed in order to speed up its adoption in production environments.
- In more general terms, moving a to higher level of technology readiness requires a bigger focus on non-technical challenges, such as compliance and legal aspects, and to ensure that employees and management are properly involved in the process and get acquainted with the used techniques, which constitutes a time-consuming process.

Additional Funding

The authors of this Chapter were supported in part by the Future PET project, financed by the Ministry of Justice and Security of the Netherlands. Further funding was provided by TNO.

References

[1] Dwivedi YK, Hughes DL, Coombs C, Constantiou I, Duan Y, Edwards JS, Gupta B, Lal B, Misra S, Prashant P, *et al.* Impact of COVID-19 pandemic on information management research and practice: Transforming education, work and life. International Journal of Information Management. 2020. p. 102211.

[2] Raisaro JL, Marino F, Troncoso-Pastoriza J, Beau-Lejdstrom R, Bellazzi R, Murphy R, Bernstam EV, Wang H, Bucalo M, Chen Y, Gottlieb A, Harmanci A, Kim M, Kim Y, Klann J, Klersy C, Malin BA, Méan M, Prasser F, Scudeller L, Torkamani A, Vaucher J, Puppala M, Wong STC, Frenkel-Morgenstern M, Xu H, Musa BM, Habib AG, Cohen T, Wilcox A, Salihu HM, Sofia H, Jiang X, Hubaux JP. SCOR: A secure international informatics infrastructure to investigate COVID-19. Journal of the American Medical Informatics Association. July 2020. 27(11), 1721–1726. https://doi.org/10.1093/jamia/ocaa172.

[3] Ikram MA, Brusselle GG, Murad SD, van Duijn CM, Franco OH, Goedegebure A, Klaver CC, Nijsten TE, Peeters RP, Stricker BH, *et al.* The Rotterdam study: 2018 update on objectives, design and main results. European Journal of Epidemiology. 2017. 32(9), 807–850.

[4] Chicco D, Jurman G. Machine learning can predict survival of patients with heart failure from serum creatinine and ejection fraction alone. BMC Medical Informatics and Decision Making. 2020. 20(1), 16.

[5] van Egmond MB, Spini G, van der Galien O, IJpma A, Veugen T, Kraaij W, Sangers A, Rooijakkers T, Langenkamp P, Kamphorst B, *et al.* Privacypreserving dataset combination and lasso regression for healthcare predictions. BMC Medical Informatics and Decision Making. 2021. 21(1), 1–16.

[6] van Egmond MB. Identifying heart failure patients at high risk using MPC. https://medium.com/applied-mpc/identifying-heart-failure-patients-at-high-risk-using-mpc-ab8900e75295, accessed: 2022-11-25.

[7] van Egmond MB. Identifying high-risk factors for diseases while preserving privacy. https://www.tno.nl/en/newsroom/insights/2021/09/identifying-high-risk-factors-diseases/, accessed: 2022-11-25.

[8] Narayanan A, Shmatikov V. Robust de-anonymization of large sparse datasets. IEEE Symposium on Security and Privacy. 2008. pp. 111–125.

[9] Sweeney L. Weaving technology and policy together to maintain confidentiality. The Journal of Law, Medicine & Ethics. 1997. 25(2–3), 98–110.

[10] Zerka F, Barakat S, Walsh S, Bogowicz M, Leijenaar RT, Jochems A, Miraglio B, Townend D, Lambin P. Systematic review of privacy-preserving distributed machine learning from federated databases in health care. JCO Clinical Cancer Informatics. 2020. 4, 184–200.

[11] Emam KE, Hu J, Mercer J, Peyton L, Kantarcioglu M, Malin BA, Buckeridge DL, Samet S, Earle C. A secure protocol for protecting the identity of providers when disclosing data for disease surveillance. Journal of the American Medical Informatics Association. 2011. 18(3), 212–217. https://doi.org/10.1136/amiajnl-2011-000100.

[12] De optimale HIV behandeling vinden met MPC, https://www.tno.nl/nl/tno-insights/artikelen/de-optimale-hiv-behandeling-vinden-met-mpc/, accessed: 2020-10-26.

[13] Spini G, Mancini E, Attema T, Abspoel M, de Gier J, Fehr S, Veugen T, van Heesch M, Worm D, De Luca A, *et al.* New approach to privacypreserving clinical decision support systems for HIV treatment. Journal of Medical Systems. 2022. 46(12), 1–11.

[14] Dong X, Randolph DA, Weng C, Kho AN, Rogers JM, Wang X. Developing high performance secure multi-party computation protocols in healthcare: A case study of patient risk stratification. AMIA Summits on Translational Science Proceedings. 2021. 200.

[15] Spini G, van Heesch M, Veugen T, Chatterjea S. Private hospital workflow optimization via secure k-means clustering. Journal of Medical Systems. 2020. 44(1), 8:1–8:12. https://doi.org/10.1007/s10916-019-1473-4.

[16] Zhang Y, Dai W, Jiang X, Xiong H, Wang S. Foresee: Fully outsourced secure genome study based on homomorphic encryption. BMC Medical Informatics and Decision Making. 2015. Vol. 15, p. S5. Springer.

[17] Shi H, Jiang C, Dai W, Jiang X, Tang Y, Ohno-Machado L, Wang S. Secure multi-party computation grid logistic regression (SMAC-GLORE). BMC Medical Informatics and Decision Making. 2016. 16(S–3), 89. https://doi.org/10.1186/s12911-016-0316-1.

[18] van Haaften W, Sangers A, van Engers T, Djafari S. Coping with the general data protection regulation; anonymization through multi-party computation technology. 2020.

[19] Cristofaro ED, Tsudik G. Practical private set intersection protocols with linear complexity. In: Sion, R. (ed.) Financial Cryptography and Data Security, 14th International Conference, FC 2010, Tenerife, Canary Islands, Spain,

January 25–28, 2010, Revised Selected Papers. Lecture Notes in Computer Science. 2010. Vol. 6052, pp. 143–159. Springer. https://doi.org/10.1007/978-3-642-14577-3_13.

[20] Freedman MJ, Nissim K, Pinkas B. Efficient private matching and set intersection. Eurocrypt. Lecture Notes on Computer Science. 2004. Vol. 3027, pp. 1–19.

[21] Pinkas B, Rosulek M, Trieu N, Yanai A. Spot-light: Lightweight private set intersection from sparse OT extension. Cryptology ePrint Archive. 2019.

[22] Pinkas B, Schneider T, Tkachenko O, Yanai A. Efficient circuit-based PSI with linear communication. Advances in Cryptology – EUROCRYPT. 2019. pp. 122–153. https://doi.org/10.1007/978-3-030-17659-4_5.

[23] Bogdanov D, Kamm L, Laur S, Sokk V. Rmind: A tool for cryptographically secure statistical analysis. IEEE Transactions on Dependable and Secure Computing. 2008. 15(3), 481–495.

[24] Dankar FK, Brien R, Adams C, Matwin S. Secure multi-party linear regression. EDBT/ICDT Workshops. 2014. pp. 406–414. Citeseer.

[25] de Cock M. Dowsley R, Nascimento AC, Newman SC. Fast, privacy preserving linear regression over distributed datasets based on pre-distributed data. Proceedings of the 8th ACM Workshop on Artificial Intelligence and Security. 2015. pp. 3–14. ACM.

[26] Hall R, Fienberg SE, Nardi Y. Secure multiple linear regression based on homomorphic encryption. Journal of Official Statistics. 2011. 27(4), 669.

[27] Hu S, Wang Q, Wang J, Chow SSM, Zou Q. Securing fast learning! ridge regression over encrypted big data. IEEE Trustcom/BigDataSE/ISPA. Augustus 2016. pp. 19–26. https://doi.org/10.1109/TrustCom.2016.0041.

[28] Nikolaenko V, Weinsberg U, Ioannidis S, Joye M, Boneh D, Taft N. Privacypreserving ridge regression on hundreds of millions of records. Security and Privacy, IEEE Symposium on. pp. 334–348. 2013.

[29] Chen YR, Rezapour A, Tzeng WG. Privacy-preserving ridge regression on distributed data. Information Sciences. 2018. 451–452, 34–49. https://doi.org/10.1016/j.ins.2018.03.061.

[30] Blom F, Bouman NJ, Schoenmakers B, de Vreede N. Efficient secure ridge regression from randomized Gaussian elimination. IACR Cryptol. ePrint Arch. 2019. 773.

[31] Gascón A, Schoppmann P, Balle B, Raykova M, Doerner J, Zahur S, Evans D. Privacy-preserving distributed linear regression on high-dimensional data. Proceedings on Privacy Enhancing Technologies. 2017. 4, 345–364.

[32] Giacomelli I, Jha S, Page CD, Yoon K. Privacy-preserving ridge regression on distributed data. IACR Cryptology ePrint Archive. 2017. 707.

[33] Join Clause (SQL). https://en.wikipedia.org/wiki/Join_(SQL)#Inner_join, accessed: 2020-10-06.

[34] Santosa F, Symes WW. Linear inversion of band-limited reflection seismograms. SIAM Journal on Scientific and Statistical Computing. 1986. 7(4), 1307–1330.

[35] Tibshirani R. Regression shrinkage and selection via the lasso. Journal of the Royal Statistical Society: Series B (Methodological). 1996. 58(1), 267–288.

[36] Schoenmakers B. MPyC – secure multiparty computation in python, https://github.com/lschoe/mpyc.

[37] Katz J, Lindell Y. Introduction to Modern Cryptography, Second Edition. CRC Press. 2014. https://www.crcpress.com/Introduction-to-Modern-Cryptography-Second-Edition/Katz-Lindell/p/book/ 9781466570269.

[38] Menezes A, van Oorschot PC, Vanstone SA. Handbook of Applied Cryptography. CRC Press. 1996. https://doi.org/10.1201/9781439821916.

[39] Cramer R, Damgård I, Nielsen JB. Secure Multiparty Computation and Secret Sharing. Cambridge University Press. 2015. http://www.cambridge.org/de/academic/subjects/computer-science/cryptography-cryptology-and-coding/secure-multiparty-computation-and-secret-sharing?format=HB&isbn=9781107043053.

[40] Lindell Y. Secure multiparty computation. Communications of the ACM. 2021. 64(1), 86–96. https://doi.org/10.1145/3387108.

[41] FIPS 180-4. Secure Hash Standard. National Institute of Standards and Technology. 2005. p. 36.

[42] Paillier, P.: Public-key cryptosystems based on composite degree residuosity classes. In: Stern, J. (ed.) Advances in Cryptology – EUROCRYPT '99, International Conference on the Theory and Application of Cryptographic Techniques, Prague, Czech Republic, May 2–6, 1999, Proceeding. Lecture Notes in Computer Science, vol. 1592, pp. 223–238. Springer (1999). https://doi.org/10.1007/3-540-48910-X_16.

[43] Medical Costs Dataset, Brett Lantz, https://www.kaggle.com/mirichoi0218/insurance. Accessed: 2020-10-26.

[44] Pedregosa, F., Varoquaux, G., Gramfort, A., Michel, V., Thirion, B., Grisel, O., Blondel, M., Prettenhofer, P., Weiss, R., Dubourg, V., Vanderplas, J., Passos, A., Cournapeau, D., Brucher, M., Perrot, M., Duchesnay, E.: Scikit-learn: Machine learning in Python. Journal of Machine Learning Research 12, 2825–2830 (2011).

Section III

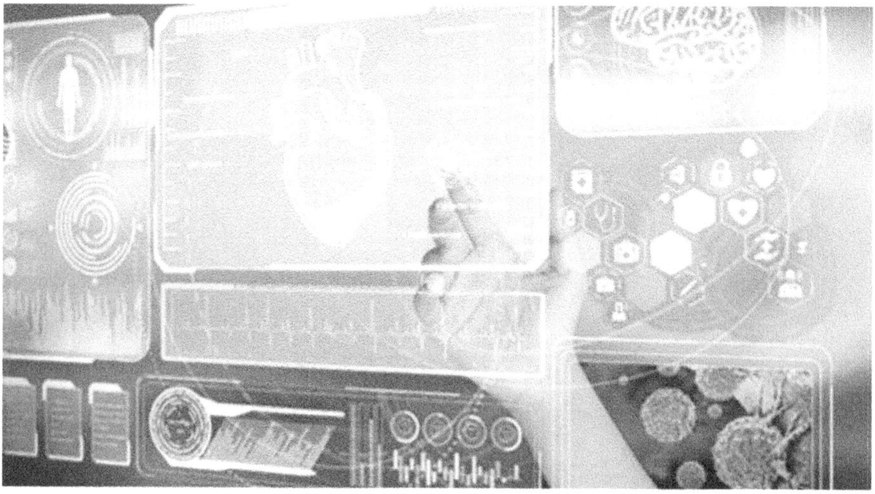

Use Cases in Technology – Oncology

DOI: 10.1561/9781638282372.ch13

Chapter 13

Introduction to Section III: Bringing Big Data to Oncology

By Brian Pickering

According to the World Health Organization (WHO), cancer was one of the most widespread causes of death worldwide in 2020[i] along with cardiovascular disease (ischemic heart disease and stroke). That year, it accounted for 10 million or one in six deaths. There were 2.6 million cases of breast cancer, 2.21 million of lung cancer, and 1.41 million of prostate cancer. Mortality rates are reduced with early detection and treatment, with investment for detection devoted on the one hand to appropriate and timely diagnosis and to preventative screening on the other. The rationale is simple: when cancers are identified early, they are more likely to respond favorably to treatment. This in turn has two major outcomes: first, for the patient, this increases the probability that they will survive; and second, for health services, the effective and early treatment reduces the associated care costs. Coupled with screening, especially of at-risk groups, and changes in lifestyle, the message here is clear: get in early, make an appropriate diagnosis, or take preventative action, and all will be well.

That is not the whole story, though. Notwithstanding cultural and global differences in access to healthcare, as WHO acknowledges, each cancer requires treatment via a different regimen. More importantly, though, an appropriate regimen must take into account not only the disease but also the individual patient being

i. https://www.who.int/news-room/fact-sheets/detail/cancer.

treated. Looking back at some of the most common cancers, breast cancer involving either partial (lumpectomy) or total mastectomy can have psychological consequences for gender identity. Similarly, treatments for prostate cancer which do not preserve the function of adjacent structures affect the quality of life for male patients and potentially their partners. In the following three chapters, the focus is on breast cancer (Chapter 16) and prostate cancer (Chapter 14)—one specific to women and the other to men—and the third, lung cancer (Chapter 15), affecting all genders as well as smokers and non-smokers.

Bringing together partners from industry, healthcare, and research, the breast cancer study reported here faced a very specific problem that it sought to resolve using large datasets including multimodal data routinely collected during screening. Where advanced breast cancer has developed locally, patients are often given NeoAdjuvant Chemotherapy (NAC) prior to surgery, involving chemotherapy alongside other targeted treatments. To date, clinicians have struggled to predict the outcome of NAC even where patients share similar prognostic factors. Using both clinical data (essentially the medical health record) and image data (such as MRI scans and so forth), the study reported here was able to predict four different outcomes accurately: pathologic complete response (the patient recovered) or one of three relapse states (including local reoccurrence and metastasis). The results were similar to a retrospective study using historical patient records as well as in a well-known external competitive study. At the same time, of course, this study faced all the common challenges for big data in healthcare: the sensitivity of the data as well as missing and inaccurate data. Overcoming these, however, and achieving a more encouraging prediction of outcomes for this cohort, demonstrates what can be achieved through appropriate governance and data linkage. This is big data revealing patterns in existing health records for the benefit of both service users (the women suffering a local, advanced breast cancer) and service providers (the clinicians trying to predict NAC benefit).

A naive approach to a tumor would be to remove or reduce it via chemo- or radiotherapy, surgery, or a combination thereof. Apart from the assumption that the tumor is discrete, it also fails to take into account the patient: whether they are physically or psychologically able to undergo such treatment. In the case of prostate cancer, there is a distinct danger that treatment could affect both the gender and sexual identity of the patient. Too much of the neighboring tissue is cut out, for instance, and the patient may lose sexual function or bladder control. Further, the diagnosis and surgical treatment alone calls for a MultiDisciplinary Team (MDT) to deal with oncology, urology, and radiology. It is not just the sensitivity of the medical records which is the issue here but also supporting all the required disciplines to interact and collaborate.

Led by the Karolinska Institute, one of the leading tertiary cancer care centers in Sweden, together with Philips in the Netherlands, the prostate cancer study adopted a mixed methods approach to evaluate the effects of introducing advanced technology into the clinical setting (i.e., prediction based on big data) as well as patient and clinician responses to that technology. Across both retrospective and prospective cohorts, the team looked at the quality of the MDT conferences and patient satisfaction with the introduction of the predictions into the decision-support environment. Predictions were generated by modeling the big datasets and integrating them into Philips's visualization environment. Positive outcomes were reported, especially for the clinicians. Of course, they too faced the common issue of data quality—including setting themselves a particular challenge in attempting to integrate an analysis of freeform text generated across many different hospitals—and the de facto sensitivity of the data. What they have demonstrated though is the potential for predictive modeling in the delivery of effective cancer treatment which by its nature requires collaboration between colleagues from different specializations to deliver the maximum benefit to the patient.

Despite obvious advances, lung cancer treatments are still not personalized and can be associated with adverse effects in consequence. One particular challenge is identifying how long to engage with chemotherapy. By its very nature, chemotherapy is toxic, and identifying outcomes, especially for atypical patient groups, is difficult. Yet, as with many areas of medicine and clinical care, there is not only a significant amount of historical as well as current patient data such as electronic health records but also a substantial research literature. If treatment planning is based only on the specific health records of the patient, though, it would be difficult to identify broader trends that may help patient care going forward. More importantly, perhaps, it would also mean that what appears an exceptional or rare case in one hospital is not seen against the context of potentially many others reported in the literature. Given enough time and resources, clinicians may well be able to consult the literature or other experts. Chapter 19 (Implementation and Impact of AI for the Interpretation of Lung Diseases in Chest CTs), for instance, explores one way of searching for relevant image data to support radiologists. In the lung cancer study, the scope is broadened out to help the clinician visualize what is in the literature and to exploit such knowledge in the service of not only diagnosis but also preventative screening.

The study demonstrates the integration of multiple and disparate data sources into a single knowledge base (in this case, a knowledge graph) representing an ontology of one and a half million triplets associated with lung cancer incidence, potential indicators via emergency room visits, and adverse, oncologically related drug interactions. Data sources include not only traditionally sensitive healthcare records but also open-source reports from the academic literature. Exploiting the latter, of course, required Natural Language Processing (NLP) capabilities. In the prostate cancer study, the effectiveness of NLP was compromised by the variability in freeform text from different teams in different institutions. Here though, the NLP has been shown to provide real benefit in the more constrained, though more verbose text of academic literature. As a result, clinicians can then query the knowledge graph—even via freeform text queries—in support of their own treatment planning as well as screening activities.

The three studies in this section deal with some of the most frequent cancers affecting women, and men as well as both. Despite the obvious challenges of data sensitivity and the consequent governance structures that must be respected (Chapter 4—Lessons Learned in the Application of the General Data Protection Regulation to the BigMedilytics Project) and the common problems of data quality (Chapter 25—Data Processing in Healthcare Using CRISP), the three studies have demonstrated the real practical potential for big data in the fight against cancer. Integrating data from different sources, in different formats, and providing different types of information relevant to the specific case, these studies show what can be done with big data in the provision of healthcare services at various stages of the healthcare lifecycle. Perhaps, more importantly, in supporting the patient and optimizing their outcomes, but also for the clinicians, the use of big data here facilitates cross-disciplinary collaboration and consulting multiple sources. Like the other chapters in this volume, these oncology studies have moved beyond the assumed problems with big data exploitation in healthcare to demonstrate real potential across the sector.

DOI: 10.1561/9781638282372.ch14

Chapter 14

Usability of Enhanced Decision Support and Predictive Modelling in Prostate Cancer

By Per Henrik Vincent, Pieter C. Vos, Erik Rönmark, Olof Akre and Ralf Hoffmann

14.1 Introduction

Prostate cancer accounts for some 7.8% of all cancers worldwide and 15.1% of all male cancers [10]. It ranked as the most common cancer among men in the European Union (EU) in 2012 and among the top four most costly cancers in the EU. Furthermore, its incidence is predicted to rise, with major differences between countries [1]. This represents a significant burden on healthcare services. Beyond the generic challenges of cancer treatment – namely, early diagnosis increasing successful outcomes and attempting to predict the longer-term prognosis for the patient – prostate cancer poses specific problems for both patient and clinician. Since the case fatality rate for prostate cancer is low and disease progression is slow, there is a low tolerance for side effects of treatment. Furthermore, tumour location is problematic, and the cancer implicates multiple disciplines beyond pathology, including urology, radiology, and of course oncology, among others. Its diagnosis and associated treatment plan therefore require collaboration across departments. Successful care is dependent on multiple factors, though feedback is sparse and unstructured, with patient-generated data particularly underdeveloped. The latter is particularly relevant. Treatment is ultimately about patient satisfaction and post-operative quality of life. But these are dependent on oncological outcomes (residual cancer) as well as functional outcomes (potential incontinence and sexual dysfunction).

For some time now and before the advent of big data technologies, researchers have been aware that the introduction of new technologies as part of a clinical intervention requires careful management, specific to the complexity of a clinical or healthcare setting; it is not simply a question of robust and effective technology, for example [2–4]. To begin with and beyond the innovative technology, communication and decision-making strategies, as well as the social context for the innovation, need to be considered [4]. Subsequently, the focus has been on encouraging the engagement of appropriate stakeholders (known as 'cognitive participation'), [3] or the stages and stakeholder discussions required to not only accept the new technology-based intervention but also ensure its long-term adoption [2]. Although not specifically intended as a critical evaluation of these different perspectives, the work reported in this chapter offers an opportunity to explore some of the diverse factors involved in introducing a technology-enhanced innovation into standard clinical practise. We concentrate here on the combination of predictive modelling in decision-making for prostate cancer, whilst also gaining some insight into the main stakeholder attitudes (patients and clinicians) towards an enhanced Clinical Decision Support (CDS) system, within the context of prostate cancer care in a nationally recognised center for tertiary care.

Led by the Karolinska University Hospital (KAR) in Stockholm, Sweden, this prostate cancer exploratory study, therefore, set out to enhance patient outcomes and increase productivity in the health sector through the application of big data technologies for predictive modelling and the integration of advanced visualisation techniques applied to complex datasets to support and encourage cross-disciplinary consultation. At the same time, of course, health data are almost exclusively special-category personal data irrespective of their provenance, including several medical and non-medical disciplines: urology, oncology, pathology, radiology, nursing, health economics, and patients themselves. In consequence, the security of these data and guaranteed privacy for patients are of paramount importance not only to ensure regulatory compliance but also to enhance patient trust.

The research study reported in this chapter was based on the design of an updated CDS system based on the IntelliSpace Precision Medicine (ISPM) Prostate from Philips,[i] implemented at KAR. Since the appropriate treatment plan is typically the result of a MultiDisciplinary Therapy conference (MDT), the CDS was intended

---

i. https://www.philips.co.uk/healthcare/medical-specialties/oncology.

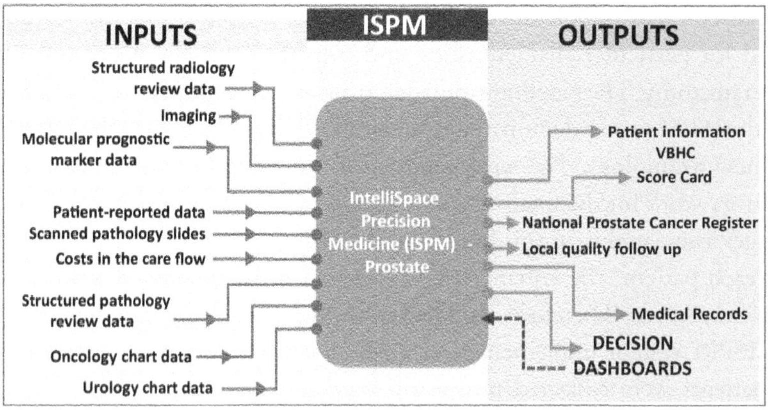

Figure 14.1. A schematic representation of the IntelliSpace Precision Medicine System from Philips.

to support primary treatment decisions in a pre-prostatectomy MDT setting at KAR. A schematic diagram is shown in Figure 14.1, where the decision dashboards represent the clinicians' perspective. In addition, any captured big data were used to create decision models to improve oncological and functional outcome predictions after primary intervention. Results associated specifically with the introduction of the updated CDS have been reported elsewhere [5]. It is worth noting, finally, that during the lifetime of the project, the COVID-19 pandemic introduced significant and unforeseen consequences for healthcare services and the social context within which those services are delivered. Although the strategy in Sweden involved social responsibility, including social distancing, there was no imposed lockdown as in other countries. This is important because it affected working practices for clinicians dealing with coronavirus patients without the socially isolating context for other patients.

14.2 Methods

In order to evaluate the potential for the enhanced CDS and for big data prediction modelling, a comparative study was carried out at KAR comparing two cohorts and their data:

- Baseline: a group of 924 patients at the hospital between Q1 2017 and Q3 2019
- ISPM: a group of 498 patients[ii] at the hospital between Q4 2019 and Q1 2021

ii. In total, there were 689 patients; 498 were collected prospectively and 191 retrospectively (thereby not part of the clinical study but used for modelling).

These represent opportunity samples from the hospital, were not at this time screened for particular characteristics, and consisted entirely of patients planned for prostatectomy. The baseline group demonstrates current practice at the hospital, whilst the ISPM group demonstrates the proposed approach with the introduction of the new technology. The work reported in this chapter represents some of the preparatory work for the final version reported in [5], and it highlights some of the challenges associated with this kind of evaluation.

For each patient, the enhanced CDS needed to be populated with data from the patient records. Therefore, data had to be imported in the first instance as part of the ISPM system implemented at KAR. Each week, patient data for around 5–15 patients were collected prospectively to populate the ISPM Prostate CDS system. A proof-of-concept for this integration was demonstrated by importing basic patient data (e.g., patient name, Swedish personal identification number – uniquely identifying the patient, date of birth, patient age, and Prostate-Specific Antigen (PSA) data) to ISPM Prostate from KarDa (the KAR datalake). At the same time, well-structured data, for instance, including surgery planning systems, financial records, and the Electronic Medical Records (EMR), were exported to KarDa. Semi-structured data, such as pathology biopsy reports, were also accessible via the same route. Figure 14.2 shows a schematic of the data architecture, including the various data import and export pipelines that have been implemented.

KarDa is the Microsoft SQL server at KAR. The following tables were imported to KarDa:

- Patient contains basic demographic information such as age, name, etc.;
- PSA contains one or more PSA test results;
- BiopsyReport contains any pathology reports for the patient as the result of any biopsies. As such, it contains semi-structured data on tissue samples and therefore the aggressiveness of the cancer;
- HealthDeclaration contains patient responses to the initial health screening questionnaire;

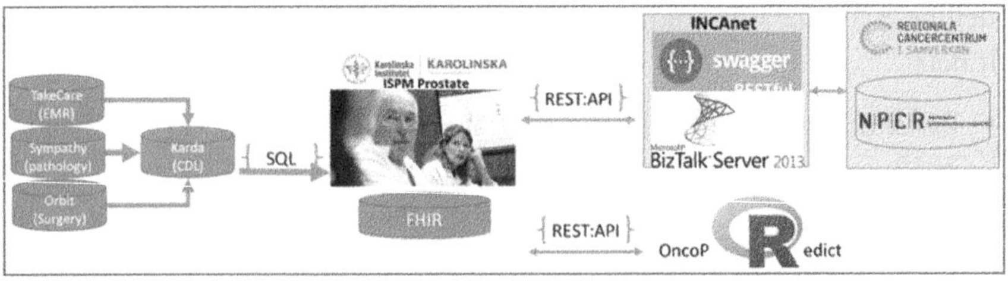

Figure 14.2. Architectural overview of data systems used and the interactions involved to fetch and load different data elements to a structured format in the ISPM Prostate dashboard.

- SurgeryReport, a detailed report on any surgeries, scheduling, those attending, etc., from the surgery planning system Orbit;
- PathologyReport, a detailed report from any prostatectomy carried out at KAR, including detail on the primary tumour and any metastases.

From left to right in the figure, three data sources are shown: TakeCare contains the patients' EMR, Sympathy the pathology reports, and Orbit the surgery schedule. These data sources are queried by scheduled tasks for extraction and import into the KarDa. The ISPM Prostate system collects data from KarDa into a prostate data model and stores the result in the Fast Healthcare Interoperability Resources (FHIR) database.

The ISPM Prostate system scheduler has the capability to automatically send data to the INCAnet server using a RESTful API. INCAnet serves as a proxy to validate the patient data before sending it on to the National Prostate Cancer Register (NPCR) in Sweden. OncoPredict is an R-based Shiny application supporting population analytics directly on the FHIR database via a token-secured RESTful API. OncoPredict was therefore used to monitor real-time completeness and validation of the data, deploy risk models, monitor discriminating performance of risk models, and calculate real-time risk for the patients who would be discussed at the MDT meeting.

14.2.1 Data Collection

In total, 689 patients were collected in the ISPM software for patients that were scheduled for prostatectomy. For those patients, clinical diagnostic information such as PSA, DRE, MRI data (e.g., PI-RADS scoring and ADC values), and biopsy information were collected. Similarly, post-surgical outcomes for the subset of patients who had undergone surgical treatment were collected to enable predictive analytics. The completeness of relevant information is shown in Figures 14.3 and 14.4.

For our study, data on patients being prepared for radical prostatectomy were organised as follows:

- Procedure: the patient had undergone prostate biopsy, in a systematic and/or targeted way.
- Descriptors: completeness of data was analysed for PSA, clinical stage assessed during DRE, PI-RADS v2 score from MRI (PI-RADS), median ADC value measured in the index lesion, systematic biopsy performed (Systematic Bx), Gleason Grade Group from systematic biopsy obtained tissue (sys Bx GGG), image guided biopsy performed (image guided Bx), and Gleason Grade Group from image guided biopsy obtained tissue (Img Bx GGG) (see Figure 14.3).

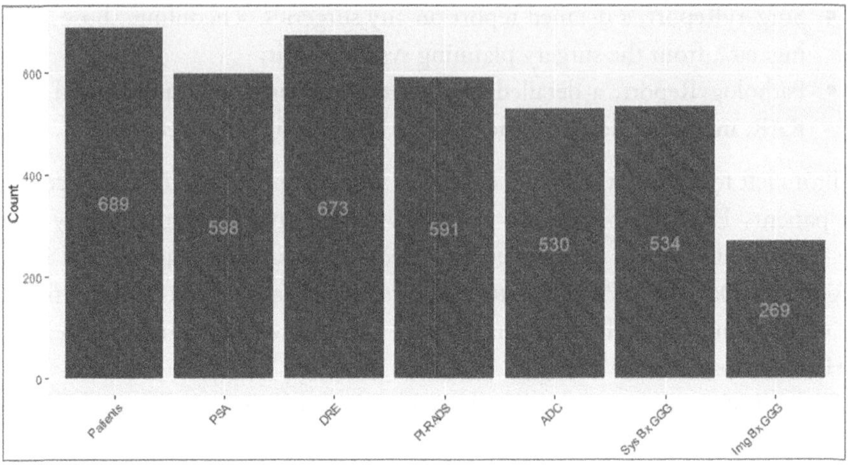

Figure 14.3. Completeness of data for some of the clinical, biopsy, and MRI variables, from left to right: Number of patients; PSA; clinical stage assessed during Digital Rectal Exam (DRE); PI-RADS v2 score from MRI (PI-RADS), median ADC, Gleason Grade Group (GGG) obtained with systematic biopsy, and GGG obtained with image guided biopsy.

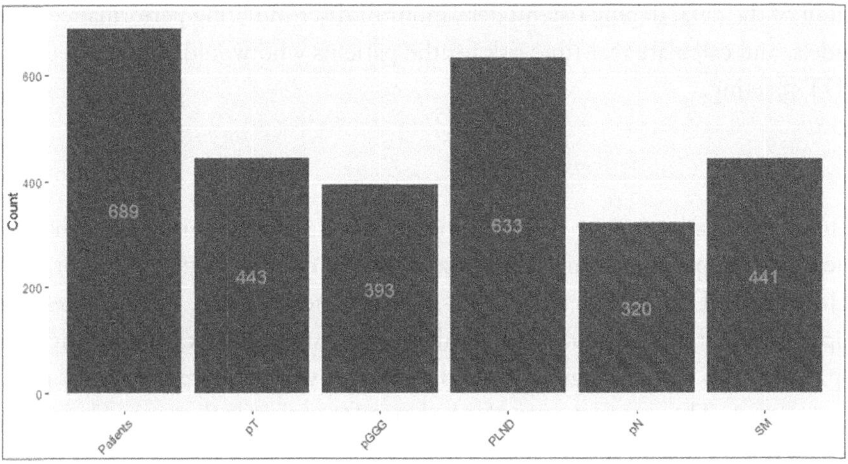

Figure 14.4. Completeness for most relevant outcome parameters from left to right: Number of patients included (Patients); pathologic T stage (pT); pathologic Gleason Grade Group (pGGG); and Information on whether Pelvic Lymph Node Dissection (PLND) was performed or not.

- Outcome: pathologic Gleason Grade Group (pGGG), pathologic T stage (pT), Pelvic Lymph Node Dissection (PLND), pathologic lymph Node involvement (pN), and Surgical resection Margin (SM); see Figure 14.4 for completeness of data. Note that for all patients, there is a record if they had a PLND, but for those without PLND, no follow-up date of Lymph Node Involvement (LNI) is known.

14.3 Challenges

As with other studies in this volume, data cleaning, imputation, and the synchronisation of data from different sources were required on occasion. The implemented solution relies on manual entry of radiology data in ISPM, whereby structured radiology reports are automatically rendered for further use, e.g., automatic writing to the EMR or transfer to registries. In the present research setting, the radiology data generated in ISPM are being used for visualisation at pre-treatment conferences and upon treatment execution as well as for predictive analytics. Automating manual data entry has continued beyond the end of the project to improve the CDS system's usability.

To date, there have been many predictive models proposed within prostate cancer research, though very few are in clinical use. The lack of clinical adoption is attributable to three main reasons:

(1) Generalisability: Models generated for one population often perform poorly on another, and so they need to be validated and adapted to the local patient population.
(2) Data Heterogeneity: Diagnostic and outcome data are exceedingly heterogeneous and rarely conform to a (structured) format suited to predictive modelling.
(3) Process Integration: ICT systems delivering the data and predictive modelling to the point of treatment decision and execution are lacking, sometimes hampered by local governance and control procedures.

Thus, an automated system to capture, compile, and visualise structured diagnostic and outcome data combined with predictive modelling capabilities constitutes a prerequisite for daily use in a clinical setting. In our prostate cancer study, a selection of pre-existing predictive models was chosen as proof-of-concept. With that in mind, the framework used in our study can be employed to adapt any existing models or generate entirely new models using a variety of techniques from classic mathematical modelling up to unsupervised AI methods. For instance, the prediction of prostate cancer LNI as devised by Briganti *et al.* was adapted to the local patient population at KAR as described below in the results Section [6].

Beyond specific big data issues, there are always challenges when assessing technologies and potential process changes in a clinical setting. Patient outcomes remain the most significant focus: there must be tangible benefit to the patient as identified not only through clinical outcomes but also regarding patient perceptions. One of the challenges here, of course, was that the ISPM timeframe includes the onset of the COVID-19 pandemic. This affected healthcare services in general, but also patient confidence. At the very least, this may be a confounding factor in any patient-reported survey. Second, taking consecutive time periods may coincidentally include changes and improvements to clinical practice independent of any planned benefit of technology.

Other factors that must be addressed include the financial cost or savings associated with the introduction of the change. In Sweden, for example, healthcare is primarily funded through taxation. Justifying costs is therefore a significant issue. But in addition, and as discussed in [2–4] and in Chapter 26 (Technology acceptance in healthcare), any change to a clinical care process may be disruptive, affecting not only patients and clinicians in the first instance but also other stakeholders.

To address these issues, a combination of quantitative and qualitative methods was used to provide some indication of the success of the exploratory work as implemented in the clinical setting at KAR.

14.4 Results

In this section, we present some preliminary results in relation to the big data approaches to the data imported into the enhanced CDS system, as represented in Figure 14.2. This is followed by a summary of the quantitative and qualitative surveys carried out during the evaluation period.

14.4.1 Big Data for Predictive Modelling

Here, we detail some of the data selection used for the study and some of the analyses carried out with these data. First, we consider the recommendation for extending surgery to include a PLND, following official guidance. We then show some of the predictive analyses associated with metastasis prediction. Both illustrate the types of big data analyses used to pre-process the data feeding the enhanced CDS.

14.4.2 Selection Strategy for Pelvic Lymph Node Dissection (PLND)

The first example of pre-processing involved the prediction of additional surgery to be performed for some patients; in this case, it appears that other structures outside the prostrate are involved. The European Association of Urologists (EAU) recommends prostatectomy surgery be extended with a PLND when the Briganti nomogram predicts a positive LNI above 5%. Out of the total selected data, 248 patients had a PLND, information on LNI was available, and the input variables to calculate the Briganti risk score were complete. The KAR strategy therefore involved a

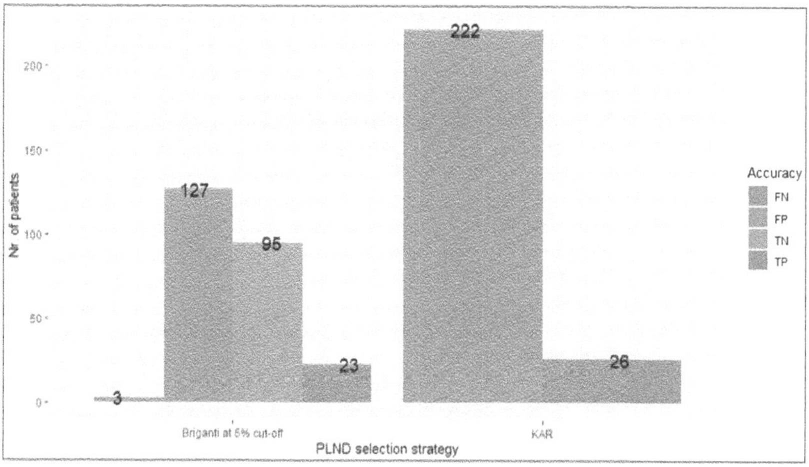

Figure 14.5. Accuracy of two PLND selection criteria.

selection based on MRI information, the Briganti LNI risk score, and patient preference. Some men actually prefer to undergo a PLND, although the risk of LNI is low, while others decline PLND despite the high risk because of the potential side effects of the procedure. The results are summarised in Figure 14.5. This resulted in 26 patients who indeed had True Positive lymph nodes (TP) and in 222 men to whom False Positive lymph nodes (FP) were found. The EAU guidelines recommend use of the Briganti nomogram at a cut-off value of 5% (selection criteria Briganti at 5% cut-off) and results in 3 False Negatives (FN) and 95 True Negatives (TN), meaning that 95 men could have been spared a PLND at the cost of missing three patients with positive lymph nodes.

Ultimately, the MDT will decide if the PLND will be recommended. However, providing this analysis to the team should increase the richness of the data they have available to make those decisions in a timely manner.

14.4.3 Experiment Predicting Lymph Node Invasion

As mentioned previously, the OncoPredict module includes risk prediction. With this in mind, the 2012 Briganti nomogram needed to be adapted for the current dataset [6]. First, an external validation of the 2012 Briganti nomogram was performed using the area under the Receiver Operating Curve (ROC) (labelled AUC in the figure) as a performance indicator. The external validation included 248 complete patient cases where the input parameters PSA, clinical T-stage, biopsy primary and secondary Gleason scores, number of biopsies, number of positive biopsies, and the MRI PI-RADS scoring were known. Figure 14.6 shows that the Briganti nomogram was able to predict LNI with an AUC of 0.73. A calibration plot showing the predicted probability of LNI in patients compared to the actual

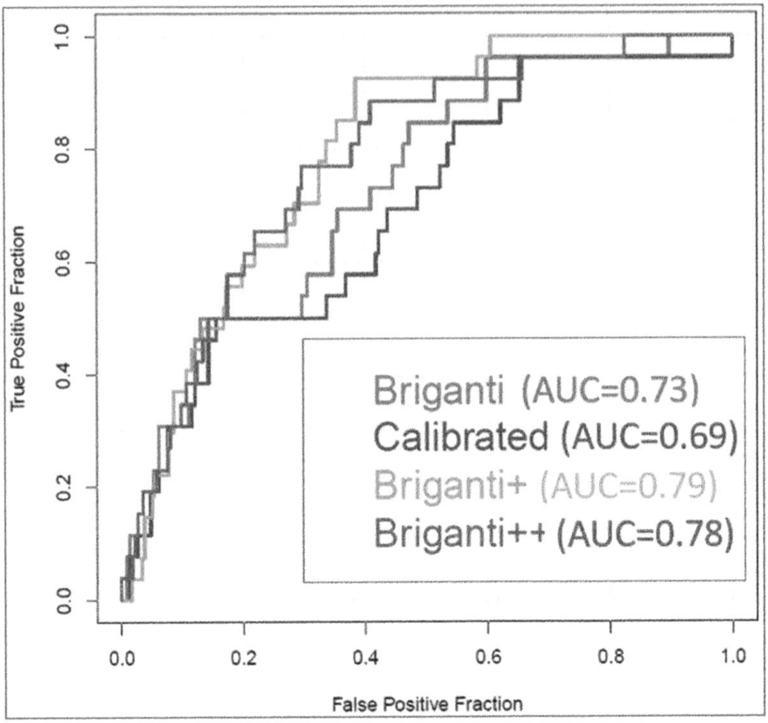

Figure 14.6. Receiver Operating Curves (ROC) showing the discriminating performance of four risk models. The first risk model (Briganti) is the nomogram published online and recommended in the EAU guidelines. The second risk model is a calibrated logistic regression model (Calibrated). The third risk model (Briganti+) is a Random forest classifier that was trained using the same set of input variables as the Briganti risk model by means of a leave-on-patient-out training and testing scheme. The fourth risk model (Briganti++) is a similar Random forest classifier using additional input information from MRI (PI-RADS scores). The Area Under the Curve (AUC) was calculated for each risk model.

percentage of patients with LNI is shown in Figure 14.7. Figure 14.8 shows the decision curve that demonstrates the net benefit associated with the use of the Briganti 2012 nomogram.

Second, the Briganti probabilities were calibrated by training a logistic regression model to predict the true class of a sample as a function of the uncalibrated class probability. Figure 14.6 shows that calibration does not improve the discriminating performance, most likely because at higher probabilities the model is poorly calibrated.

Next, a Random forest classifier was trained with the same input variables as the Briganti nomogram, and the discriminating performance was estimated by means of a leave-one-patient-out cross-validation [8]. Figure 14.6 shows that the Random forest classifier can predict LNI with an AUC of 0.79.

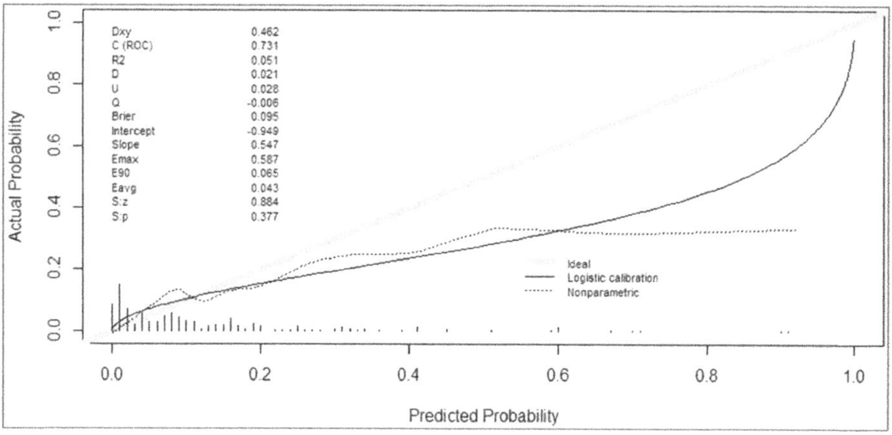

Figure 14.7. Calibration plot showing the predicted probability of LNI in patients on the x-axis compared to the actual percentage of patients with LNI (y-axis). Perfect calibration would fall on the black diagonal line where predicted risks equal observed rates of LNI [7]. Note that at higher probabilities, the model is poorly calibrated.

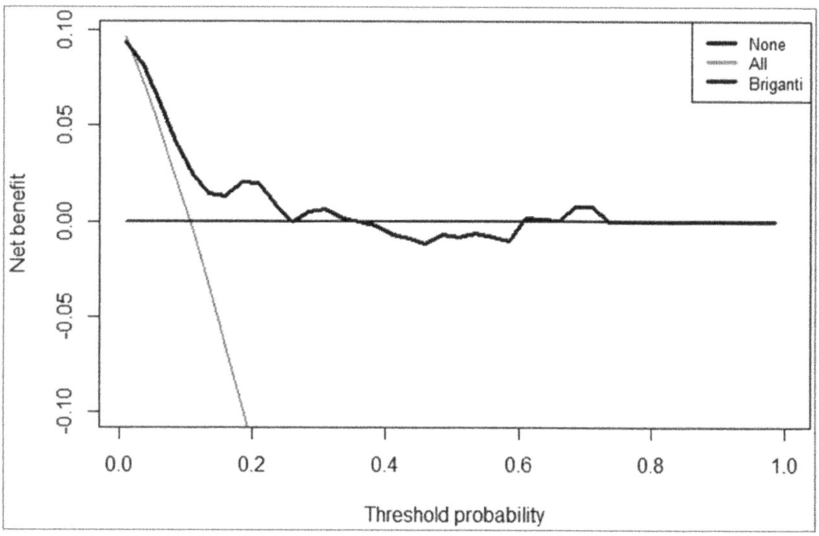

Figure 14.8. Decision curve analyses demonstrating the net benefit associated with the use of the Briganti 2012 nomogram for 248 patients [6]. The net benefit can be interpreted as the proportion of all patients who have lymph node metastases and are recommended for surgical excision of pelvic lymph nodes.

Finally, the same Random forest classifier was trained but now included the PI-RADS scoring as an additional input variable. The discriminating performance was estimated by means of a leave-one-patient-out cross-validation. Figure 14.6 shows that the Random forest classifier can predict LNI with an AUC of 0.78, indicating that PI-RADS scoring did not improve the discriminating performance.

14.4.4 Generation of Prediction Models

A Random forest classifier was trained using a preselected clinically relevant set of 24 variables to predict

(1) LNI and
(2) ExtraProstatic Extension (EPE).

Although the Random forest classifier has an internal ranking of feature importance, low-ranking features can still have a negative effect on the overall discriminating performance of the model. Therefore, an automatic iterative exclusion of low-ranking features was used to collect the optimal set of features using the area under the receiver operating characteristic curve as an optimisation strategy.[iii]

The outcome classes of LNI and EPE are imbalanced as a limited amount of prostate cancer patients have EPE and only a small proportion have LNI. Therefore, the Random forest was trained by balanced bootstrapped undersampling of the minority class, see also [5]. The difference is that the complete Random forest is trained on a bootstrap sample, and the data are bootstrapped until all patients from the majority class have been selected. The resulting set of Random forests is then combined into a single one. The prospective performance of the Random forests was estimated by means of leave-one-patient-out cross-validation. A bootstrap resampling approach with 10,000 iterations was used for estimating the bootstrap mean AUCs and 95% confidence intervals.

14.4.5 Natural Language Processing

We applied Natural Language Processing (NLP) technology to cater for the various freeform reports included in patient records. NLP algorithms were specifically developed for this purpose and tested against two test sets of pathology biopsy reports from patients previously treated at KAR. The success rate of these algorithms was limited and very much dependent on both the content and language quality of the reports.[iv] Some variables (like Gleason score) were detected with a high recall rate (i.e., high sensitivity) and with high precision (i.e., high positive

iii. Patent WO US 16/648797 (Vos, Hoffmann & Schuurkamp).

iv. See, by contrast, the results reported in Chapter 9 (eHealth and telemedicine for risk prediction and monitoring in kidney transplantation recipients).

Table 14.1. Objective clinical outcomes for the patient.

Patient Outcomes			
Metric	**Baseline**	**ISPM**	**Delta**[1]
Frequency of Post-Surgical tumour-positive resection Margins (PSM)	29%	26%	−10%
Frequency of urine incontinence pad use after prostatectomy	28%	25%	−8%
Frequency of sexual dysfunction after prostatectomy	74%	72%	−3%

[1]That is: (1-Baseline/ISPM)*100.

Table 14.2. Patient perceptions.

Patient Satisfaction			
Metric	**Baseline**	**ISPM**	**Delta**
Urinary function satisfaction	47%	52%	+10%
Sexual function satisfaction	17%	16%	−6%

predictive value), typically above 80%–90%. Others (like tumour stage) were frequently overlooked (i.e., lower sensitivity) or interpreted incorrectly (i.e., lower positive predictive value). The main reason for these outcomes was the significant variability in reporting and almost complete lack of structure in a large proportion of the reports. KAR is primarily a treating hospital, not a diagnosing hospital. In consequence, most biopsy reports are created in outpatient clinics, and therefore, KAR has very limited opportunity to dictate the rules for pathology reporting.

Implementing these techniques and validating them in this way allowed for appropriate analysis of the data available prior to ISPM implementation. In the next paragraphs, we consider the response to including the big data-driven enhanced CDS into the MDT for prostate cancer patients at KAR.

14.4.6 Quantitative Assessment of the Utility of the Enhanced CDS

Table 14.1 summarises the observed outcome measures for prostate cancer patients at KAR. Although not statistically significant, there is a reduction in incidence of these complications in outcomes after prostatectomy (as shown in the final column in the table labelled 'Delta').

In addition to the objective measures summarised in Table 14.1, patient perceptions were investigated. Table 14.2 summarises patient perceptions on two particularly important dimensions: the ability to hold back urine and to achieve and maintain an erection, specifically how much the patient is bothered by sequelae related to these functions. Again, the final column is illustrative only. Recognising that such results reflect only one perspective on the technology-enhanced intervention, it is important to consider the subjective patient perceptions of the clinical outcomes as they affect them.

The other major stakeholder group, beyond the patients themselves, are the clinicians. By definition, the MDT comprises experts from different disciplines. Facilitating discussion between them in terms of the information they receive as well as the process of moderating and engaging in MDT discussions are both relevant. The efficiency of the MDT was measured as Time spent at the MDT (seconds). The quality of the MDT was evaluated by external viewers using a modified version of the validated MDT-MODe metric on a *3-step* Likert scale as follows:

1. No knowledge was available (*1p*)
2. Vague first-hand or strong second-hand knowledge was available (*3p*)
3. Comprehensive first-hand knowledge was available (*5p*)

Table 14.3 summarises the findings.

For Patient's view, a score of 5, for example, would mean that there was comprehensive first-hand knowledge of what the patient wanted and felt was available in the MDT. Conversely, a score of 1 would mean no such information was available. With these scores, a Mann–Whitney U statistic was calculated (not shown) as an indicator of the significance of the difference between the baseline and ISPM cohorts.

Metric labels that have been italicised do not show a significant change. For all other metrics, there was a significant improvement with the introduction of the enhanced CDS. This is an encouraging result, though further investigation is required, firstly to establish the significance of individual factors and secondly to determine their effect on MDT members and their decision-making.

The reduction in time spent per patient can be assigned a rough monetary value with the assumptions that ~10 clinicians discuss ~10 patients in each MDT, and there are 60 similar weekly conferences in the Theme Cancer at KAR.

14.4.7 Qualitative Assessment of the Utility of the Enhanced CDS

As a consequence of the COVID-19 pandemic, the availability of staff to provide feedback on the enhanced CDS was restricted. Nevertheless, a small representative cohort of nine urology consultants and one radiology consultant responded to a brief survey designed to capture their experiences of the CDS as part of the MDT. In Table 14.4, responses had been recorded originally on a 5-point Likert scale, labelled as shown in the table. For simplicity, results were reduced to three values summarised as positive (+), neutral (0), and negative (−). Positive summed

Table 14.3. Process and financial outcomes.

Patient Outcomes				
Metric	**Description**	**Baseline**	**ISPM**	**Delta**[1]
Time spent at MDT		300 s	240 s	−20%***
Patient's view	What the patient wants or perceives about their treatment	1.86	2.15	+16%
Psychosocial	The patient's social and psychological situation	2.08	2.63	+26%**
Co-morbidity	Patient medical history	2.69	3.32	+23%***
Pathology	Histopathological information	2.88	2.99	+4%*
Imaging	Radiological information	4.95	4.96	0
History	Case history	3.96	3.99	+1%
Decision	Whether any relevant decisions were taken at the current MDT	4.68	4.71	+1%
Members	Did members contribute to the discussion	3.94	4.65	+18%***
Chair	How did the leader affect the running of the MDT	3.10	4.44	+13%***
Participation in discussion	Proportion of staff making a contribution to the discussion	36.4%	40.8%	+18%*
Financial Outcomes				
Metric		**Baseline**	**ISPM**	**Delta**
Accumulated cost saving per patient		101 kSEK	103 kSEK	+2%

[1] Significance levels for the reported differences are shown as follows: $^{*}p < 0.05$, $^{**}p < 0.01$, $^{***}p < 0.001$.

responses for "Strongly agree" together with "Agree", "Much higher confidence" and "Higher confidence", or "More satisfied" and "Satisfied" respectively; negative correspondingly "Disagree" with "Strongly disagree", "Less confident" and "Much less confident", or "Dissatisfied" and "Very dissatisfied".

Overall, and although the responses came from a small cohort, responses to the qualitative assessment statements regarding the use of the enhanced CDS as part of the MDT were positive: 63 responses out of a total of 89 in Table 14.4. Note, however, that "I could easily perceive the treatment recommendations made within the MDT" did not elicit an unequivocally positive response, suggesting that there may still be work to be done to improve the comprehensibility of outputs.

In addition to the general agreement/satisfaction questions in Table 14.1, when asked: "Compared to the traditional MDT format, the discussion length per patient

Table 14.4. Summary of responses to qualitative assessment of the enhanced CDS as part of the MDT.

	Scale	+	0	–
The information in ISPM helps me build a comprehensive overview of the case for staging	Strongly Agree to Strongly Disagree	8	1	1
The information in ISPM helps me build a comprehensive overview of the case in order to decide on treatment		8	0	2
I could easily perceive the treatment recommendations made within the MDT		4	3	3
The ISPM prototype facilitated me with detailed insights in patient status		6	2	2
The ISPM prototype facilitated me with detailed insights in relevant diagnostics across medical domains		7	2	1
My confidence level regarding the treatment recommendations made within the MDT was	Much Higher to Much Lower	8	1	–
Compared to the traditional way of working, how would you rate your confidence in the decision made with the ISPM dashboard visible during discussion		9	1	–
How satisfied are you with ISPM overall?	More Satisfied to More Dissatisfied	6	2	2
	TOTAL	63	15	11

when using ISPM is..." eight respondents thought discussion length to be shorter, and two that it was a similar length; no one claimed it took longer. Finally, in response to the question: "In order to build a comprehensive overview of the case in your mind for staging and treatment decisions, which of the following would you prefer as a way of working", nine said that they preferred working with the enhanced CDS, one with an unspecified other method, and no one responded that they preferred the traditional way of working.

These results are encouraging. However, there is some scope to investigate further how the response wording has been interpreted. Specifically, comparing

Tables 14.1 and 14.4, it will be important to reflect how the same stakeholders respond to related issues.

14.5 Discussion

In this chapter, we describe the baseline (before use of ISPM) and follow-up measurements (after implementation of ISPM) of pre-prostatectomy MDTs, the prostate-cancer patients discussed at these conferences, and the staff satisfaction in relation to data presentation at the MDTs. While the introduction of ISPM was associated with higher MDT conference quality and efficiency, no statistically significant change in patient outcomes could be seen. Overall, we have observed positive staff feedback on the use of the technology during the MDT.

14.6 Lessons Learned

From our experience in this exploratory study, we would highlight the following:

1. Introduction of CDS technology may save time in the MDT setting, but to achieve an overall efficiency gain in a clinical setting, system integration is an absolute must.
2. NLP may have some benefit. However, there needs to be careful consideration of the format (and variability) of the source data, and the intended use of the NLP-generated structured data set.
3. We recommend that specific resource be devoted to high response frequency for patient-reported data.

The rationale for each of these recommendations is outlined below.

System integration: To achieve efficiency gains from CDS technology, data must be automatically retrieved from source systems, enriched using the CDS at the point of care, and subsequently made available for downstream clinical applications and secondary uses such as research, quality assurance, predictive modelling, and feedback learning. Significant effort should be made to avoid manual transfer of data, which is known to introduce errors, delays, loss of data resolution, reduced staff satisfaction, increased staff turnover, and increased costs. It can also be argued that care quality is all but impossible to assess unless source data are used throughout the care processes.

The full potential of data-driven precision medicine can only be reached when data are truly liberated. We therefore recommend that care providers in conjunction with med-tech providers, structure all data at the source using internationally adopted standards for clinical informatics and interoperability.

Natural Language Processing: Although we did not achieve clinical-grade precision in NLP, the field is rapidly evolving and may soon provide tools capable of doing so even for poorly structured input data, given enough data for training [9]. Nevertheless, NLP will likely play a major role in structuring retrospective medical chart data for, e.g., calibration or the creation of predictive algorithms, where the tolerance for (random) misclassification is higher. From our experience, NLP may have some benefits. However, there needs to be careful consideration of the format (and variability) of the source data and the intended use of the NLP-generated structured data set.

Patient Surveys: A significant part of this exploratory study involved the recording of patient perceptions. Not least, given the literature on intervention adoption in healthcare, we felt it essential to be able to compare how patients felt about their treatment. Survey response rates were significantly higher in the ISPM in comparison to the baseline cohort. This is a direct consequence of our attempts to encourage participation and not a result of the implementation of ISPM. Patient-reported data should be an integral part of clinical decision-making and therefore supported by technology, for patients to enhance patient engagement, at the point of care to enable precision medicine, and for secondary use to ensure appropriate generalisability of findings. We therefore recommend that specific resources be devoted to the integration of patient interaction tools with CDS technology.

General

In this prostate cancer study, we have measured the impact of the ISPM technology from multiple operational, clinical, patient, and staff satisfaction perspectives. In order to be able to achieve study goals, we had to evaluate the potential for exploiting standard big data techniques. For our domain (prostate cancer), standard algorithms seem appropriate for inclusion as input to enhanced CDS. We went further, though. Recognising that multiple stakeholders are affected by the possible inclusion of these technologies – not least because patient-affecting decisions are made within a cross-disciplinary setting (the MDT) – we have investigated through quantitative and qualitative instruments the perceived benefits of including these innovations. Our findings in this respect are very encouraging and will provide benefit to related studies within a clinical setting. Just as significantly, though, we have highlighted some of the challenges and potential issues that need to be considered moving forward.

14.7 Conclusion

In this chapter, we have presented the findings on the introduction of big data technologies into an enhanced decision support system based on the integration of an existing, commercially available software solution. The data suggest that this approach makes MDTs more efficient and improves the process of decision-making.

References

[1] Luengo-Fernandez R, Leal J, Gray A, Sullivan R. Economic burden of cancer across the European Union: A population-based cost analysis. The Lancet Oncology. 2013. 14(12): 1165–1174. DOI: 10.1016/S1470-2045(13)70442-X.

[2] Greenhalgh T, Abimbola S. The NASSS framework – A synthesis of multiple theories of technology implementation: A knowledge base for practitioners. Applied Interdisciplinary Theory in Health Informatics. 2019. 263: 193–204. https://doi.org/10.3233/SHTI190123.

[3] May CR, Mair F, Finch T, MacFarlane A, Dowrick C, Treweek S, Rapley T, Ballini L, Ong BN, Rogers A, Murray E, Elwyn G, Légaré F, Gunn J, Montori VM. Development of a theory of implementation and integration: Normalization Process Theory. Implementation Science. 2009. 4(1): 29. https://doi.org/10.1186/1748-5908-4-29.

[4] Sanson-Fisher RW. Diffusion of innovation theory for clinical change. Medical Journal of Australia. 2004. 180(S6): S55–S56. DOI: 10.5694/j.1326-5377.2004.tb05947.x.

[5] Ronmark E, Hoffmann R, Skokic V, de Klerk-Starmans M, Jaderling F, Vos P, Gayet MCW, Hofstraat H, Janssen M, Akre O, Vincent PH. Effect of digital-enabled multidisciplinary therapy conferences on efficiency and quality of the decision making in prostate cancer care. BMJ Health & Care Informatics. August 2022. 29(1): e100588. DOI: 10.1136/bmjhci-2022-100588.

[6] Briganti A, Larcher A, Abdollah F, Capitanio U, Gallina A, Suardi N, Bianchi M, Sun M, Freschi M, Salonia A, Karakiewicz PI, Rigatti P, Montorsi F. Updated nomogram predicting lymph node invasion in patients with prostate cancer undergoing extended pelvic lymph node dissection: The essential importance of percentage of positive cores. European Urology. March 2012. 61(3):480–487. DOI: 10.1016/j.eururo.2011.10.044.

[7] Steyerberg E. Clinical Prediction Models. New York: Springer. January 2009. DOI: 10.1007/978-0-387-77244-8.

[8] Chen C, Liaw A, Breiman L. Using random forest to learn imbalanced data. Univ. California, Berkeley. 2004. no. 1999, pp. 1–12.
[9] Iroju OG, Olaleke JO. A systematic review of natural language processing in healthcare. International Journal of Information Technology and Computer Science. 2015. 8: 44–50. DOI: 10.5815/ijitcs.2015.08.07
[10] Figures for 2020 from World Cancer Research Fund International https://www.wcrf.org/cancer-trends/worldwide-cancer-data/.

DOI: 10.1561/9781638282372.ch15

Chapter 15

Monitoring and Decision Support in Treatment Modalities for Lung Cancer

By Alejandro Rodriguez Gonzalez, Ernestina Menasalvas, Fotis Aisopos, Dimitrios Vogiatzis, Anastasia Krithara, Georgios Paliouras, Samaneh Jozashoori, Ariam Rivas, Ahmad Sakor, Maria-Esther Vidal, Maria Torrente, Mariano Provencio Pulla, Anna Trinatafyllou and Athanasios Dalianis

15.1 Introduction

In the European Union, the total cost of cancer was €126 billion in 2009, with health care amounting to €51.0 billion (40%). The health care cost reached €102 per citizen. Because of early death, productivity loss costs €42.6 billion, while there were €9.43 billion lost working days. Lung Cancer (LC), in particular, had the highest economic impact (€18.8 billion or 15% of overall cancer costs), followed by breast cancer (€15.0 billion, 12%), colorectal cancer (€13.1 billion, 10%), and prostate cancer (€8.43 billion, 7%) [1]. The current clinical approach to LC is standardized with reference ratios, regardless of the patient. However, the sub-optimal care and management of cancer patients affect the well-being of patients, as well as the healthcare cost [2–4].

In particular, the limitations of the current treatments can be detected at: (1) diagnosis — inter-patient variability preventing personalized treatments [5–7]; (2) therapy and response — determining the optimal duration of chemotherapy,

[8, 9] and more effective therapies are sought with fewer toxic effects; (3) adverse effects — over 5% of hospital admissions are due to the adverse effects of drugs [10]; and (4) comorbidities and side effects. The presence of comorbidities complicates the decisions about treatments. They are often underrepresented in clinical trials, and information regarding treatment effectiveness is often extrapolated from studies of younger patients without comorbidities. Thus, patient management is often sub-optimal and not personalized, affecting survival [11].

We designed and implemented an LC study application based on big data technologies to address the above concerns. First, the study harvests heterogeneous data from open sources and the Electronic Health Records (EHR) of LC patients from the Hospital Universitario Puerta de Hierro Majadahonda (HUPHM). The harvested data are analyzed, and a structure is extracted. Then the data are annotated with concepts from the Unified Medical Language System (UMLS). Next, all the data are integrated into a knowledge graph with semantic web technologies. The knowledge graph contains clinical data, and open data about LC, and can be accessed by oncologists via a web-based dashboard. The oncologists can focus on specific patient cohorts and obtain information about survival curves, toxicities, and drug–drug interactions. The knowledge graph also integrates structured representations of scientific publications; they can be traversed and ranked according to relevance to an input request.

This chapter presents the main outcomes achieved in developing the LC study in the context of BigMedilytics. It is organized as follows: in Section 15.2, we refer to the data analysis requirements for LC and how they are addressed by the study, i.e., the kind of information that can be obtained by an oncologist via a dashboard. In Section 15.3, we refer to data harvesting and analysis from various resources. Next, in Section 15.5, we refer to the data integration process that creates the knowledge graph. This is followed by a description of the software framework in Section 15.6. The results are presented in Section 15.7, and conclusions are drawn in Section 15.8.

15.2 Requirements for the Lung-Cancer Study

High-level requirements for the LC study as posed by the oncologists of HUPHM are concerned with the investigation of the following pieces of information:

- Over-treatment and non-scheduled visits
- Number of visits to the Emergency Room (ER)
- Time to spend searching for related cases in the bibliography
- Observed adverse events due to comorbidities

Figure 15.1. LC dashboard.

How does the study address the requirements: A web-based dashboard enables access to analytics of the clinical data and the LC knowledge graph. Figure 15.1 depicts an exemplary visualization of the clinical data outcomes. This dashboard allows clinicians to perform the following analysis: Patient data segmentation: First, the study can focus on segments of the population based on demographic and behavioral filters, e.g., gender, age, smoking habit, familial antecedents, as well as on the presence of biomarkers. Then there are filters related to the diagnosis of cancer, such as the histology (squamous, non-squamous, other), the stage of cancer at diagnosis (I–IV), performance status, comorbidities, the reception of non-oncological drugs, systemic and local progression, and finally, the existence of brain metastasis.

Hospitalization statistics: Based on the above filters, the dashboard can produce not only survival curves but also information about the length of hospitalization, number of toxicities, time from diagnosis till the first hospitalization, and the 10 most frequent diagnoses before being diagnosed with LC.

The Knowledge Graph Exploration: The open data integrated into the knowledge graph can be explored. These data included scientific publications, drug–drug interactions, and side effects of treatment.

Dashboard question answering: This provides answers and contextual information to questions posed in free text. The question types are as follows:

- Yes/No, e.g., "Is TREM2 associated with Lung Cancer?"—Factoid, e.g., "What type of LC is Afatinib used for?"—List of questions, e.g., "List drugs interacting with Afatinib."

15.3 Data Sources

EHRs: The HUPHM provided information about 8,901 patients diagnosed and treated for LC from 2008 to 2018. After data cleaning to remove corrupted EHRs, or EHRs with many missing values, we ended up with 988 EHRs of patients. Out of the 988 patients, 416 had been hospitalized. The EHRs contained 315,891 notes and 16,550 reports representing clinical variables of LC patients and services consulted by patients before and after diagnosis; each EHR had 320 attributes. The EHR contained both structured and unstructured information in the form of free text in Spanish.

Data anonymization: The study uses confidential information about patients of the HUPHM. Only the oncologists and the IT department have access to it and must conform to the applicable laws and HUPHM policies. The patients included in the project were informed of the project's aims, signed the informed consent form, and could request further information at any time. The patients' data usage was limited to the current investigation.

The EHRs were anonymized by removing entities such as name and address and replacing them with an ID. Only clinical data (e.g., regarding follow-up, treatments, and toxicities) related to the disease were shared with the rest of the study partners. The database with the relation between the anonymized data and the actual patient is stored in a server, which is not connected to the Internet. The transfer of anonymized data between the study partners was done physically or exceptionally via a corporate email of password-protected databases.

The project follows the Organic Law 15/1999 on the Protection of Personal Data and Anonymization of the Data and the EU General Data Protection Regulation 2016/679 (GDPR), regarding lawful data processing. The investigator and the promoter must keep the collected data for at least 25 years after completion. Thus, patients' data will be kept by the HUPHM as the promoter for the patients' benefit and further scientific research.

Open data sources: The following open data sources were used:

- PubMed: Provides access to the MEDLINE database of references and abstracts of scholarly articles for the life sciences. This repository was harvested for LC-related publication abstracts and the MeSH topics and relevant metadata. The PubMed Central (PMC) was also used to provide full-text access to some of the articles found in PubMed.
- DrugBank: An open database of drugs and targets.
- OBO Foundry: A repository of a wide range of interoperable biomedical and chemical ontologies. It is used for hierarchical harvesting relations for genes and diseases from the Gene Ontology and Disease Ontology, respectively.

Open data harvesting: Open data included 163,000 articles, 1.5M drug–drug interactions, 10K drug–target interactions, and OBO LC ontologies.

15.4 Analysis of Harvested Data, Natural Language Processing

NLP on Clinical Data: Natural Language Processing (NLP) is applied to the EHR text in Spanish [12]. The NLP pipeline is also depicted in Figure 15.2:

- Annotation: Rule-based annotators are deployed to extract: LC diagnosis using UMLS Metathesaurus, [13] the cancer stage using the TNM notation3, dates and times expressions, and family members mentions.
- Disambiguation: In the previous step, there can be generated ambiguous annotations due to the presence of negation, speculation, and annotations that do not belong to the patient as a subject. This step filters annotations affected by negation, speculation, and annotations that mention family history but do not refer to the patient. The disambiguation process automatically generates a new data set containing annotations without negation, speculations, or family history.
- Diagnosis Extraction: The cancer diagnosis and the diagnosis date are extracted from disambiguated annotations obtained in the previous step.

NLP on Open Data 163,000 harvested scientific publications (from PubMed and PMC) has been processed with NLP using named entity recognition and relation extraction to create an open graph of 402,020 nodes and 12,256,983 edges (see also Figure 15.3). SemRep was used to extract UMLS-based biomedical information [14]. The output of SemRep is semantic triples of the form subject–predicate object, where the subject and object entities are concepts from the UMLS, and the predicate is the relation between them. SemRep uses MetaMap, an entity extraction tool [15]. MetaMap uses symbolic NLP and computational linguistic techniques to

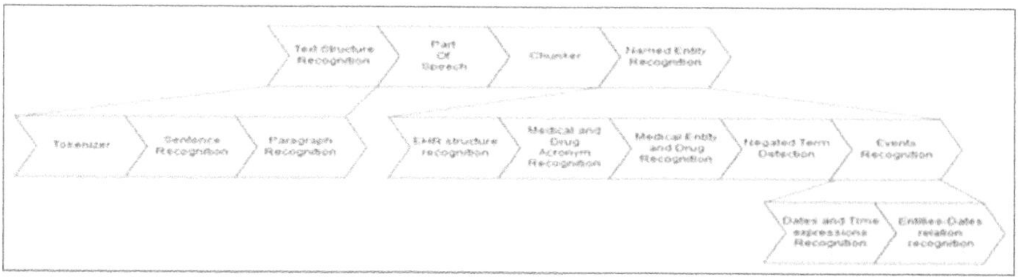

Figure 15.2. Information extraction from EHR.

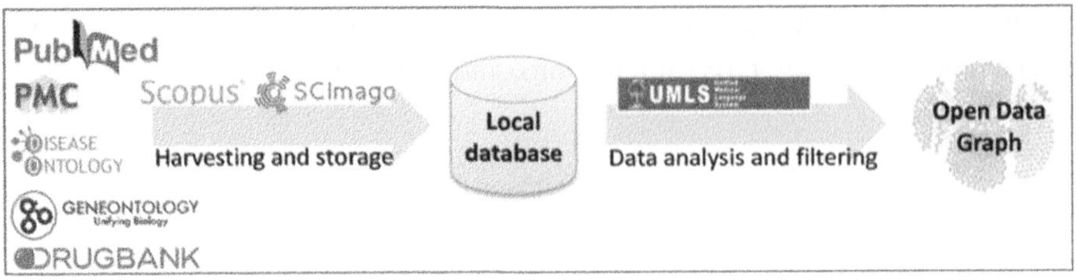

Figure 15.3. Open data harvesting and analysis.

map biomedical text to Metathesaurus concepts. An example of an extracted triplet is: (subject: radiation dose, relation: treats, object: body_tissue_injury).

15.5 The Lung Cancer Knowledge Graph

Knowledge integration is used to create and populate the knowledge graph with data provided by the Open Data graph, the analysis of the EHR, and other data sources. A unified schema allows for describing the integrated data into a knowledge graph. Additionally, NLP techniques are used for extracting relevant knowledge from the short text in available data sets, e.g., indications of contracts are extracted from the drug description in the Drugbank data set. Furthermore, linking techniques enable linking the knowledge graph with existing biomedical, e.g., Bio2RDF,[i] and general domain knowledge graphs, e.g., DBpedia[ii] and Wikidata.[iii] The knowledge graph is accessible via SPARQL endpoints or a federated query engine. Figure 15.4 depicts a portion of the knowledge graph. Pattern discovery is performed on top of the knowledge graph to identify communities or constellations of patterns that are similar. Ontologies express contextual information, and novel similarity measures are defined to decide when two patients are identical in a given context. Community detection algorithms (e.g., semEP [16]) are used for partitioning the knowledge graph into communities that represent meaningful patterns. They are described in terms of contextual information encoded in the knowledge graph.

---

i. https://bio2rdf.org/.

ii. https://www.dbpedia.org/.

iii. https://www.wikidata.org/wiki/Wikidata:Main_Page.

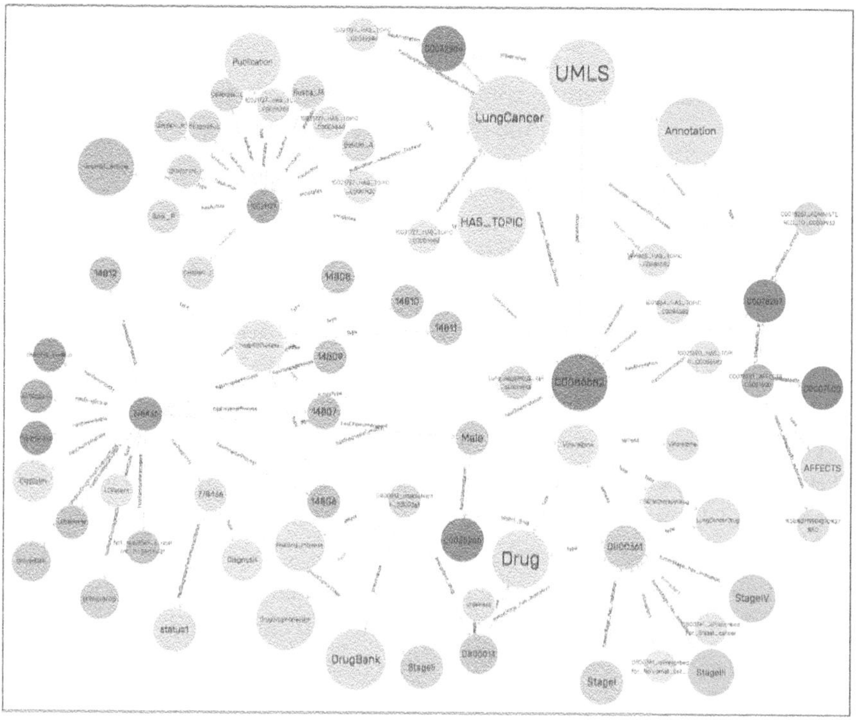

Figure 15.4. The LC knowledge graph.

15.6 Study Software Framework

The high-level software architecture of the LC study follows a layered model, where each layer provides certain functionality. The layers interact in a top-down way, with each layer having access to all layers below; they are as follows:

- Hardware Layer: Docker is used as a packaging and deployment mechanism for the study components.
- Resource Management Layer: Manages docker containers.
- Data Layer: Archive of all heterogeneous data sources.
- Extraction Layer: Information extraction from heterogeneous data sources.
- Platform Layer and Semantic Layer: Contains the big data tools used by the study's components. The Semantic Layer part of the layer semantically integrates all the heterogeneous data sources and the knowledge extracted at the Extraction layer. The result of the semantically integrated heterogeneous data sources is a knowledge graph.
- Analytics Layer: Pattern discovery on the knowledge graph.
- Presentation Layer: Dashboard and visualization modules.
- Support Layer: Offers utilities in multiple layers and components.

- Access Control Layer: Provides a centralized authentication and authorization service so that all components can communicate securely and reliably. Furthermore, some study components are remotely hosted, and they communicate with the rest of the platform over REST APIs.

15.7 The Lung Cancer Study Results

The oncologists, via the use of the dashboard, were able to identify some initial patterns that could have an immediate impact on the well-being of the patients. First, it was researched whether there is evidence before the diagnosis of LC that may lead physicians to clinical suspicion of LC. The risk of developing LC was associated with medical services used before diagnosis. The top-5 medical services used between 4 and 15 months before diagnosis were as follows: *cardiology, pneumology*, and *emergencies* (see Figure 15.5a).

Second, the patients who visit the ER and are discharged from the hospital were analyzed. The aim was to investigate whether this visit corresponds to a predictable, expected, and avoidable event. Whether it was necessary to conduct a proper initial evaluation. In particular, the number of ER admittances was associated with the EHR's features (e.g., age, gender, or comorbidities). For instance, in Figure 15.5b, we depict the number of ER services related to comorbidities.

Third, drug toxicities between non-oncological and oncological drugs and their association with long- and short-term survival were studied. For instance, in Figure 15.6, the survival curve combinations of oncological drugs (e.g., Vinorelbine, Pemetrexed, and Cisplatin) with a non-oncological drug (e.g., Omeprazole) are depicted.

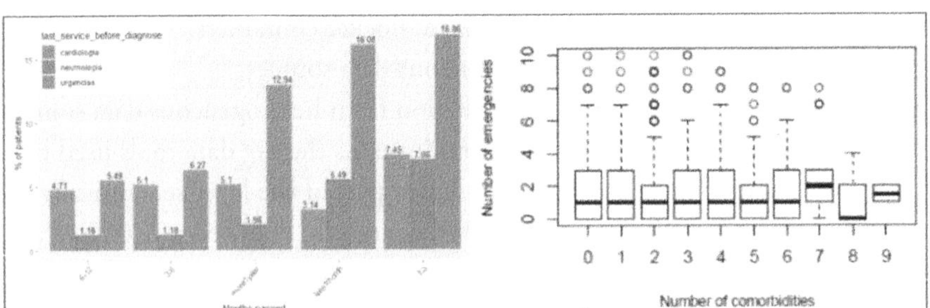

Figure 15.5. Analytical results. (a) Medical services used before diagnosis. (b) Emergency service usage per number with LC of comorbidities.

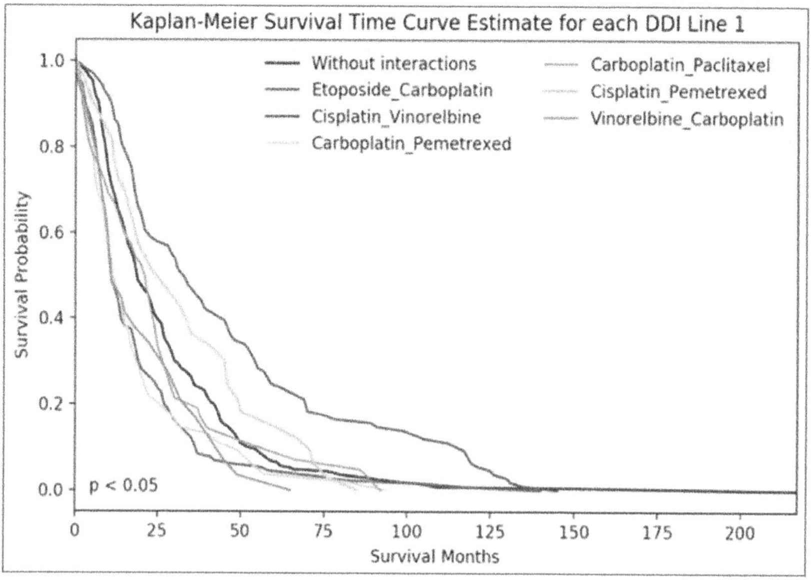

Figure 15.6. Drug interactions and toxicities.

15.8 Conclusion

The LC study has achieved some important results. First is integrating biomedical literature, structured databases (such as Drugbank), and EHR in a knowledge graph comprising 150M triples for the LC. Second, the study offers a web-based dashboard that allows access to the knowledge graph, including the usage of free text questions. Third, we were able to obtain certain associations that will ultimately benefit the patients. In particular, some evidence for the prediction of LC was extracted; then the pattern of the patient characteristics that visit the ER was analyzed; finally, drug interactions and toxicities for combinations of oncological and non-oncological drugs were associated with survival curves. This marks not the end of the investigation, as the information is being periodically updated with new open data, and further investigations are underway to allow oncologists to select the most appropriate treatment according to the patient's profile.

References

[1] Luengo-Fernandez R, Leal J, Gray A, Sullivan R. Economic burden of cancer-across the european union: a population-based cost analysis. The lancet oncology. 2013. 14(12), 1165–1174. DOI: 10.1016/S1470-2045(13)70442-X.

[2] Al-Badriyeh D, Alameri M, Al-Okka R. Cost-effectiveness research in cancer therapy: a systematic review of literature trends, methods and the influence of funding. BMJ open. 2017. 7(1), e012648. DOI: 10.1136/bmjopen-2016-012648.

[3] Gill J, Sullivan R, Taylor D. Overcoming cancer in the 21st century. UCL School of Pharmacy. 2015.

[4] Poonacha TK, Go RS. Level of scientific evidence underlying recommendationsarising from the national comprehensive cancer network clinical practice guidelines. Journal of clinical oncology. 2011. 29(2), 186–191. DOI: 10.1200/JCO.2010.31.6414.

[5] Detterbeck FC, Marom EM, Arenberg DA, Franklin WA, Nicholson AG, Travis WD, Girard N, Mazzone PJ, Donington JS, Tanoue LT, *et al.* The iaslc lung cancer staging project: background data and proposals for the application of tnm staging rules to lung cancer presenting as multiple nodules with ground glass or lepidic features or a pneumonic type of involvement in the forthcoming eighth edition of the tnm classification. Journal of Thoracic Oncology. 2016. 11(5), 666–680. DOI: 10.1016/j.jtho.2015.12.113.

[6] Group NMaC. Preoperative chemotherapy for non-small-cell lung cancer: asystematic review and meta-analysis of individual participant data. The Lancet. 2014. 383(9928), 1561–1571. DOI: 10.1016/S0140-6736(13)62 159-5.

[7] Sculier JP, Berghmans T, Meert AP. Tnm classification and clinicopathological factors: what is helpful for adjuvant chemotherapy decision after lung cancer resection? Journal of thoracic oncology. 2014. 9(3), 266–270. DOI: 10.1097/JTO.0000000000000110.

[8] Carcereny E, Ramirez JL, Sanchez-Ronco M, Isla D, Cobo M, Moran T, de Aguirre I, Okamoto T, Wei J, Provencio M, *et al.* Blood-based chrna3 single nucleotide polymorphism and outcome in advanced non-small-cell lung cancer patients. Lung cancer. 2010. 68(3), 491–497. DOI: 10.1016/j.lungcan.2009.08.004.

[9] Provencio M, Isla D, Sánchez A, Cantos B. Inoperable stage iii non-small celllung cancer: Current treatment and role of vinorelbine. Journal of thoracic disease. 2011. 3(3), 197. DOI: 10.3978/j.issn.2072-1439.2011.01.02.

[10] Garrido P, González-Larriba JL, Insa A, Provencio M, Torres A, Isla D, Sanchez JM, Cardenal F, Domine M, Barcelo JR, *et al.* Long-term survival associated with complete resection after induction chemotherapy in stage iiia (n2) and iiib (t4n0-1) non-small-cell lung cancer patients: the spanish lung cancer group trial 9901. Journal of clinical oncology. 2007. 25(30), 4736–4742. DOI: 10.1200/JCO.2007.12.0014.

[11] Søgaard M, Thomsen RW, Bossen KS, Sørensen HT, Nørgaard M. The impact of comorbidity on cancer survival: a review. Clinical epidemiology. 2013. 5(Suppl 1), 3. DOI: 10.1002/ijc.10882.

[12] Solarte Pabón O, Torrente M, Provencio M, Rodríguez-Gonzalez A, Menasalvas E. Integrating speculation detection and deep learning to extract lung cancer diagnosis from clinical notes. Applied Sciences. 2021. 11(2), 865. DOI: 10.3390/app11020865.

[13] Bodenreider O. The unified medical language system (umls): integrating biomedical terminology. Nucleic acids research. 2004. 32(suppl_1), D267–D270. DOI: 10.1093/nar/gkh061.

[14] Rindflesch TC, Fiszman M. The interaction of domain knowledge and linguisticstructure in natural language processing: interpreting hypernymic propositions in biomedical text. Journal of biomedical informatics. 2003. 36(6), 462–477. DOI: 10.1016/j.jbi.2003.11.003.

[15] Aronson AR. Effective mapping of biomedical text to the umls metathesaurus: the metamap program. Proceedings of the AMIA Symposium. 2001. p. 17. American Medical Informatics Association.

[16] Palma G, Vidal M, Raschid L. Drug-target interaction prediction using semantic similarity and edge partitioning. Proceedings of The Semantic Web – ISWC. 2014. https://doi.org/10.1007/978-3-319-11964-9_9.

DOI: 10.1561/9781638282372.ch16

Chapter 16

Artificial Intelligence to Support Choices in Neoadjuvant Chemotherapy in Breast Cancer Patients

By Simona Rabinovici-Cohen

16.1 Introduction

Breast cancer remains one of the most widespread and deadly cancers among women today [1]. NeoAdjuvant Chemotherapy (NAC), in which chemotherapy and optionally targeted therapy are administered prior to surgical therapy, is one of the approaches used to treat locally advanced breast cancer. Today, the clinical parameters used to select the NAC option are based on breast cancer subtype, tumor size, disease grade, number of malignant nodes, age, and tumor growth, among others [2]. Imaging is being used to evaluate the position of the tumor and its size, but not to predict the outcome of the treatment.

Predicting the outcomes of NAC is an important clinical question. If this future outcome could be predicted based on data available prior to the initiation of NAC treatment, it could impact the treatment selection. However, clinicians have difficulty estimating the outcomes of this treatment prior to its start. In fact, some matching patients have similar prognostic parameters, yet one patient experiences a positive outcome, while the other encounters a negative one. Clinicians' treatment selection and decision-making could be assisted and empowered by Artificial

Intelligence (AI) models that could accurately predict NAC outcomes. These AI models are an important enabler of precision medicine.

The breast cancer study aimed to improve NAC outcomes prediction using AI on multimodal data of different types. We used Deep Learning (DL) and image processing models for medical imaging data, classical Machine Learning (ML) models for clinical data, and ensembles of individual clinical and imaging models. The study was a collaboration among Institut Curie in France, VTT in Finland, and IBM Research in Israel which also led the study. The Institut Curie provided the anonymized dataset and clinical expertise, while VTT developed the image processing models, and IBM developed the AI-based multimodal imaging, clinical and ensemble models.

16.2 Study Design

We created a cohort of 1,738 anonymized patients that included women with breast cancer who have received NAC between 2012 and 2018. To comply with regulations such as GDPR and French laws, the anonymized dataset was made available to the processing collaborators, through a controlled-access connection to access a local server provided by Institut Curie. We used a model-to-data paradigm where all the data remained at Institut Curie infrastructure. All computations were implemented on a strong GPU-enabled server that resided in Institut Curie, and various pipelines of analytics models were transferred to the server and executed there.

In the study, we explored the prediction of several outcomes of the NAC treatment which were deemed important by the clinicians. The NAC treatment includes six months of chemotherapy and optionally targeted therapy, followed by surgical therapy. Figure 16.1 depicts the significant NAC outcomes that we tried to predict prior to the chemotherapy start. It includes (1) pathologic Complete Response (pCR) at the time of surgery, which is achieved for about 30% of the patients,

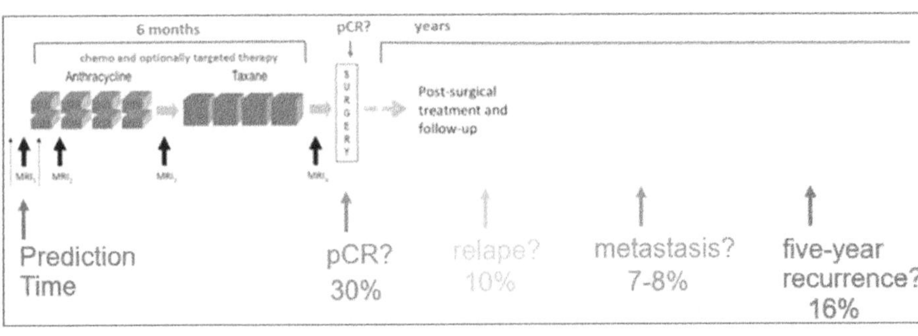

Figure 16.1. Significant outcomes in NAC treatment. Accordingly, the study explored four prediction tasks: pCR, relapse, metastasis, and five-year recurrence.

(2) return of cancer in the same location (relapse), which occurs for about 10% of the patients, (3) return of cancer in a distant location (metastasis), which occurs for about 7–8% of the patients, and (4) cancer recurrence (relapse or metastasis) within five years since disease diagnosis, which occurs for about 16% of the patients. Note that the first outcome, pCR, is a positive outcome, while the other three are negative ones and may suggest treatment reassessment.

16.3 Methods

We worked with a real-world retrospective dataset of patients, composed entirely of women diagnosed with breast cancer who had received NAC. The data of each patient included clinical information such as height, weight, age, histological type of the tumor, progesterone status, and many more features. We consider all these data as a single clinical modality. Some of the patients also had in their record medical imaging acquired prior to NAC initiation, which is considered a second modality. Our dataset had labels for the four treatment outcomes that we tried to predict: pCR, relapse, metastasis, and five-year recurrence. However, not all patients had all four labels, and there were some missing values. Given that we have different sizes of datasets for the different modalities and different tasks, our overall multimodal method for the four prediction tasks was as follows (see Figure 16.2). We divided our model into two branches. One branch was trained using clinical data and images, while the other branch was trained using only clinical data. We then combined the two branches into one final ensemble model. To evaluate the models, we performed cross-validation and computed the Receiver Operating Characteristic (ROC) curve and the Area Under the ROC Curve (AUC) with Confidence Interval (CI), as well as measured sensitivity, specificity, and other metrics.

16.3.1 Clinical Model

The clinical model was similar for all four prediction tasks. We split the cohort with clinical information into five folds with equally distributed positive and negative samples among folds. To select the best classifier for our task, we pre-processed and modeled the data with three known ML algorithms: random forest, logistic regression, and XGBoost. The pre-processing included a scaler that scaled all features to the [0, 1] range and an imputation process to replace missing values with the mean value. Since our data were highly unbalanced, we used sample weighting that is inversely proportional to the class frequencies in the input data for the random forest and logistic regression classifiers. For XGBoost, we used positive scaling that is proportional to the ratio between negative and positive samples.

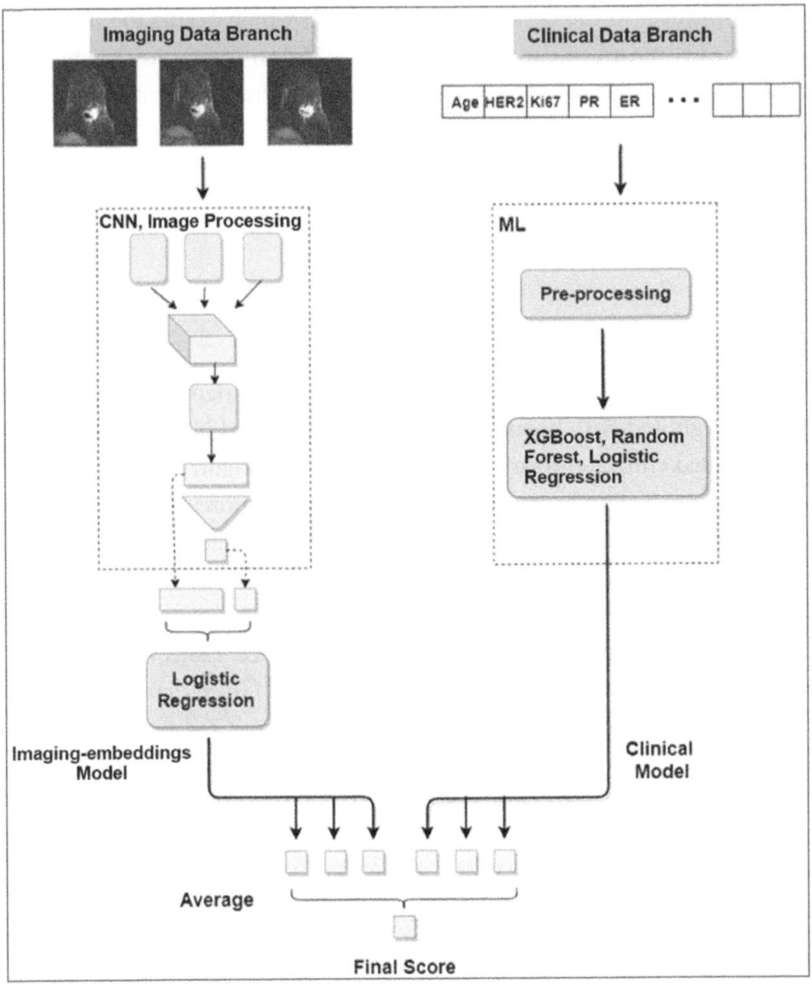

Figure 16.2. Overall multimodal method for the four prediction tasks. The left branch is trained using clinical data and images. The right branch is trained using clinical data only. The two branches are combined into one final ensemble model.

16.3.2 Imaging Model

Interestingly, there was not one imaging algorithm that fits all four prediction tasks, but, instead, each task required a different approach and algorithm to achieve improved performance. For predicting pCR, we used MammoGraphy (MG) imaging. We detected the tumor using a pretrained model and then extracted radiomics features from the tumor area. For predicting relapse, we used Dynamic Contrast-Enhanced Magnetic Resonance Imaging (DCE-MRI). We annotated the most important subtraction volume and the significant slice in which the tumor was the largest and then applied a DL method to train the imaging data. For predicting metastasis, we used both DCE-MRI and MG. Using a DL method, we automatically estimated tumor depth of invasion from the 3D MRI, and using the clinical reports, we extracted tumor size measured in 2D MG. For predicting five-year recurrence, we used multiparametric MRI including DCE, Dixon, and Apparent Diffusion Coefficient (ADC) volumes of MRI. We used both DL and image processing techniques to get improved results, and we also interpreted the features' contribution.

High sensitivity is important in our problem setting as this is the operation point used in clinical practice. It is also important to achieve good specificity at these high-sensitivity operation points. Adding medical imaging to our AI models enabled us to improve the specificity at high-sensitivity operation points. This signifies the importance of using medical imaging in the AI models that are going to be deployed in clinical practice.

16.3.3 Ensemble Model

The ensemble model was similar for all four prediction tasks. It received six scores per patient: three scores based on clinical data and three scores based on the imaging data. To improve generalizability, we created multiple variations of each model, in which a different variation started its training with a different seed. Thus, the three scores for clinical data are produced from three clinical models' variations that differ in their training seed initialization, and the three scores for MRI data are produced from three MRI models' variations. We then examined several strategies for combining and "ensembling" the models. We first tried the stacking classifier in which we trained a meta-model on top of the six models' scores. We also tried several voting strategies, in which some of them consider the threshold of individual models. However, we found that the most effective strategy used the mean value of all available scores per patient, so this became the selected option.

16.4 Results

In this section, we briefly describe the results in each one of the four prediction tasks, as well as in the BMMR2 external competition. The results of each prediction task are also associated with a publication that we reference for a more detailed description.

16.4.1 Predict pCR

A patient achieves pCR if, in the surgery following chemotherapy, an invasive residual tumor in the breast and invasive disease in the axillary nodes are both absent.

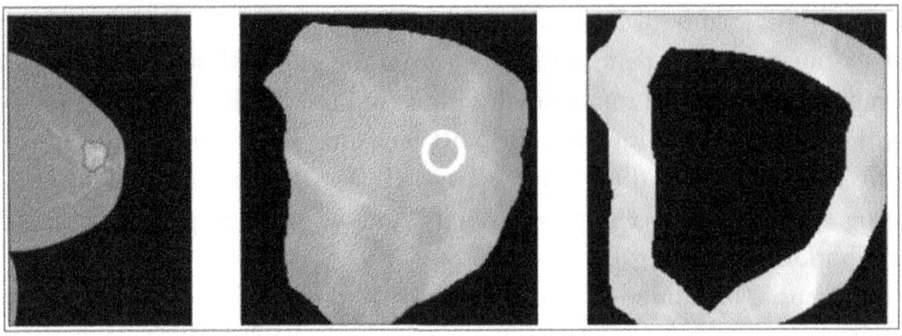

Figure 16.3. Network output predictions of tumor detection. Left: MG image from Curie dataset with a detected contour around tumor area. Middle: Tumor patch extracted from detected area. Right: Tumor margins extracted.

Achieving pCR after NAC is correlated with an improved disease-free state and overall survival compared with those experiencing a partial or no response to NAC. We developed several models for the task of predicting pCR post-NAC treatment and published some of our results in [3]. We created a clinical model, an MG model that is based on MG images, and an ensemble model that combines the clinical and imaging models.

In our dataset, 528 patients had MG scans, and we found that with this limited amount of data, we could not create a robust DL model that directly predicts pCR. We selected instead a different approach. We utilized a DL model that was pretrained on IBM proprietary data, which consists of thousands of annotated mammograms to classify the existence of a tumor. That model extracted a heatmap in Curie MG images which represents the tumor detection. We then extracted radiomics texture features from the tumor area and the peritumoral margin of the tumor. The final step in the imaging model was to apply a random forest classifier on the extracted radiomics features from the MG imaging. Figure 16.3 shows the output of the detection on an MG image and the tumor margins we used for radiomics feature extraction.

The final ensemble model combined six models: three models based on clinical data and three models based on features extracted from the MG images. It achieved an AUC of 0.708 and a sensitivity of 0.954 while maintaining a good specificity of 0.222.

16.4.2 Predict Relapse

A patient encounters relapse if after treatment the breast cancer reoccurs in the same breast. We created multimodal AI models that analyze MRI and clinical data. For the MRI model, expert radiologists annotated the most important subtraction

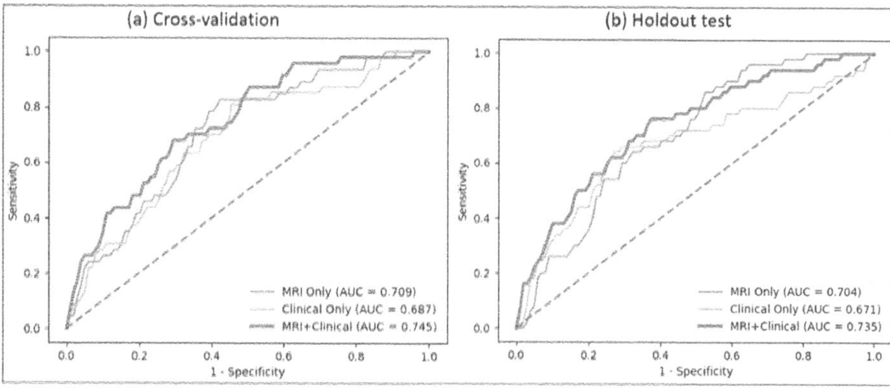

Figure 16.4. Cross-validation and holdout ROC curves. (a) Cross-validation evaluation with MRI+Clinical ensemble model mean AUC of 0.745. (b) Holdout evaluation with MRI+Clinical ensemble model mean AUC of 0.735.

volume in which the tumor appeared to be the brightest in terms of relative illumination. In the selected volume, they also annotated the significant slice in which the tumor was the largest. Our MRI model included a Convolutional Neural Network (CNN) that is a modification of ResNet as a classifier. We specifically used the ResNet18 formulation but reduced the number of filters per layer to speed up training and avoid overfitting.

Figure 16.4 shows the cross-validation and the holdout test ROC curves for the various models. They exhibit similar trends. In both, the MRI model shows promise in predicting relapse after NAC treatment with good specificity for above 0.95 sensitivity. The clinical model shows the ability to predict relapse with higher specificity of around 0.5 sensitivity but lower specificity of around 0.95 sensitivity. The ensemble of MRI and clinical leveraged both modalities and improved the AUC and specificity at various operation points achieving an AUC of 0.735 and a specificity of 0.44 on the holdout dataset. The full description of the models and the results were published in [4].

16.4.3 Predict Metastasis

A patient encounters metastasis if, after treatment, the breast cancer reoccurs in other areas of the body. We explored the use of tumor size explainable features computed from multimodal imaging and combined it with clinical data to predict the risk of post-treatment metastasis. Tumor depth of invasion was automatically estimated from 3D MRI subtraction volumes using a DL method that classifies the range of slices in which the tumor is seen and the significant slice. Tumor size as seen in 2D MG and in clinical examination was extracted from reports. As the patients that have MRI and the patients that have MG only partially overlap, we

Table 16.1. Fivefold cross-validation evaluation of the per-modality models as well as the ensemble model to predict metastasis.

	Cohort Size	AUC	Spec at Sens = 0.95
MRI	551	0.643	0.252
MG	498	0.610	0.166
Clinical	1738	0.649	0.271
Ensemble (MRI Cohort)	551	0.745	0.440

created a separate model per modality and then ensembled the three models. The ensemble model that combined MRI, MG, and clinical data significantly improves the per-modality model as shown in Table 16.1.

Our method to estimate the tumor depth from MRI scans is fully automatic and thus more relevant for clinical practice. Moreover, an important aspect of tumor sizes is that these are explainable features, and thus a model based on these predictive features is more likely to be adopted in clinical practice. The full description of the models and the results were published in [5].

16.4.4 Predict Five-Year Recurrence

We say that a patient encounters five-year recurrence if after treatment the breast cancer recurs either locally in the breast (relapse) or distant in other areas of the body (metastasis) within five years from diagnosis. We explored the use of clinical and multiparametric Magnetic Resonance Imaging (mpMRI) to predict the risk of post-treatment recurrence within five years. The mpMRI model uses multiple volumes of the same study and consists of two components. The first component is based on DL features extracted from DCE subtraction volumes as done for predicting relapse. The second component is based on traditional image processing methods on Dixon and ADC volumes to generate morphological and texture volumetric features. The final ensemble model that combined clinical and mpMRI models achieved in cross-validation 0.750 [0.698, 0.796] AUC and 0.466 specificity at 0.95 sensitivity operation point, while in the holdout test, it achieved 0.734 [0.680, 0.781] AUC and 0.413 specificity.

We also use interpretability methods to explain the model and identify important clinical features for predicting recurrence that when combined can serve as novel candidate composite biomarkers. Figure 16.5 provides an explanation of the clinical model via the SHapley Additive exPlanations (SHAP) algorithm. SHAP considers all possible combinations of features with and without a specific feature to evaluate its contribution to the prediction. It reveals each feature's importance and demonstrates how each feature of each patient affects the predictive model's

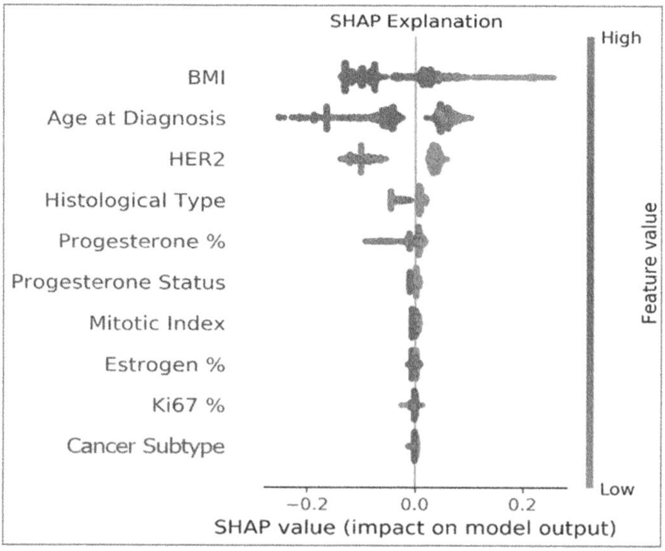

Figure 16.5. Clinical feature contribution. A summary plot of the SHAP values of the top features in the clinical model. Each point represents a single patient.

results. The figure depicts the top 10 clinical features in descending order that had the most influence on the five-year recurrence prediction. A positive SHAP value means a positive impact on the prediction, while a negative value leads the model to predict 'recurrence-free'. The color of each point represents the values that each feature can take, including red for high values, blue for low values, and purple for values that are close to the average value.

The categorical clinical features in the data can take the following values:

> HER2: 0—HER2 negative and 1—HER2 positive; histological type: 1—NST, 2—lobular, 3—medullary, and 4—other; progesterone status: 0—progesterone negative and 1—progesterone positive; mitotic index: number of mitoses; and cancer subtype: 1—TNBC, 2—LuminalA, 3—LuminalB, and 4—HER2+.

Interestingly, Body Mass Index (BMI) and age at diagnosis are ranked highest in terms of association with the outcome. In particular, lower values of BMI as well as younger age at the time of diagnosis tend to be associated with a higher risk of five-year recurrence. The full description of the models and the results including interpretation and sub-group analysis were published in [6].

16.4.5 BMMR2 Challenge

We used technologies developed in the breast cancer study to validate them in an international external challenge, Breast Multiparametric MRI for prediction of

NAC Response (BMMR2), [7] organized by the Breast Imaging Research Program of UCSF.[i] The competition was aimed at predicting pCR based on retrospective analysis of a multicenter clinical trial of cancer patients who completed NAC prior to surgery. In the competition, IBM was placed second (AUC 0.8380) only marginally lower than the value from Penn Medicine (AUC 0.8397). The open-source technology that the team shared, called FuseMedML, [8] a PyTorch-based DL framework for medical data, played a significant role in the team's ability to quickly experiment with multiple different models and variations and select the best performing one.

16.5 Discussion and Conclusion

In this study, we explored the prediction of future outcomes in women with locally advanced breast cancer who are treated with NAC. We introduced multimodal prediction models that are based on clinical data and medical imaging taken prior to NAC treatment. Our results demonstrated the ability to predict outcomes prior to NAC treatment initiation using each modality alone. However, a multimodal, ensemble model offers better results. We used DL and image processing algorithms to analyze our imaging data and classical ML algorithms to analyze the clinical data. Using two branches enabled us to use the best method per modality and utilize the maximum available data for each data type.

Imaging analysis is generally done via deep neural networks with millions of parameters that need to be learned. Training such a network generally requires thousands of image data and some annotations on the images relating to thousands of patients. However, the medical imaging data available for analytics are scarce and confidential, and access to data is protected and limited. Moreover, in medical imaging, the annotations require medical expertise and are expensive, time-consuming, and inconsistent. Finally, in the medical domain, there is a diversity of populations, genetic variations, and environmental differences that may have an impact on the features exhibited in the imaging, and this effect is not quite understood yet. As a result of all these challenges with analyzing medical imaging, the creation of robust AI models needs to consider new advanced approaches. Pre-trained models and transfer learning that reuse models trained on external datasets, and federated learning that trains simultaneously on multiple protected datasets can be beneficial approaches to increase the usable dataset and address the medical imaging AI challenges.

i. https://www.ucsf.edu/

In medical imaging AI, multiple modalities are needed as different features are exposed in different modalities. For example, breast density shows up on MG images but not on ultrasound images, and breast calcifications show up on MG but typically not via ultrasound and never show up on MRI. Thus, multimodal AI models have the potential to provide a better performance, and we need to create frameworks and tools for multimodal analysis, such as the FuseMedML open source, [8] to ease the research of multimodal analytics.

Medical data are complex. It includes different types such as structured data, text data, genomic data, imaging of different modalities (X-ray, MRI, ultrasound, CT, pathology, and so on). Understanding all these modalities and different types of data is complex and requires special expertise. Even within the same modality, different medical centers create different data. For example, MRI has no standardized protocol for scan acquisition and high variance of image resolution, voxel size, and image contrast dynamics. This diversity of modalities increases the data complexity and requires special pre-processing and selection of different methods per modality.

AI models that may affect the treatment selection, have a direct impact on the patient's health, and must be first validated and tested in clinical trials and then approved by regulatory authorities such as the FDA in the United States and the EMA in Europe. This makes the clinical validation long and difficult, and thus only few validation cycles are possible. Additionally, to increase the acceptance of the AI models, the stakeholders need the ability to interpret the models and understand their reasoning. In our study, we provided explanations of our models via the SHAP algorithm as well as via other methods as described. SHAP considers all possible combinations of features with and without that specific feature to evaluate its contribution to the prediction.

Some of our methods were further reused in a following EU Horizon 2020 project, named CAncer PAtients Better Life Experience (CAPABLE). In CAPABLE, we developed AI models to predict three- and five-year overall survival rates for patients with metastatic Renal Cell Carcinoma (mRCC). The proposed predictive model, which was constructed as an ensemble of three individual predictive models, outperformed all well-known mRCC prognostic models to which it was compared [9].

References

[1] Sung H, Ferlay J, Siegel RL, Laversanne M, Soerjomataram I, Jemal A, Bray F. Global Cancer Statistics 2020: GLO-BOCAN Estimates of Incidence and Mortality Worldwide for 36 Cancers in 185 Countries. CA Cancer J. Clin. 2021. 71, 209–249. DOI: 10.3322/caac.21660.

[2] Fitzgibbons PL, Page DL, Weaver D, Thor AD, Craig Allred D, Clark GM, Ruby SG, O'Malley F, Simpson JF, Connolly JL, *et al.* Prognostic factors in breast cancer. Arch. Pathol. Lab. Med. 2000. 124, 966–978.
[3] Rabinovici-Cohen S, Tlusty T, Abutbul A, Antila K, Fernandez X, Grandal Rejo B, Hexter E, Hijano Cubelos O, Khateeb A, Pajula J, Perek S. Radiomics for predicting response to neoadjuvant chemotherapy treatment in breast cancer. Proc. of SPIE 11318, Medical Imaging 2020: Imaging Informatics for Healthcare, Research, and Applications, Vol. 11318. DOI: 10.1117/12.2551374.
[4] Rabinovici-Cohen S, Abutbul A, Fernandez X, Hijano Cubelos O, Perek S, Tlusty T. Multimodal Prediction of Breast Cancer Relapse Prior to Neoadjuvant Chemotherapy Treatment. Proc. of International Workshop on Predictive Intelligence in Medicine (PRIME-MICCAI). 2020. 188–199. DOI: 10.1007/978-3-030-59354-4_18.
[5] Rabinovici-Cohen S, Tlusty T, Fernández XM, Grandal Rejo B. Early prediction of metastasis in women with locally advanced breast cancer. Proc. of SPIE 12033, Medical Imaging 2022: Computer-Aided Diagnosis, Vol. 12033. DOI: 10.1117/12.2613169.
[6] Rabinovici-Cohen S, Fernández XM, Grandal Rejo B, Hexter E, Hijano Cubelos O, Pajula J, Pölönen H, Reyal F, Rosen-Zvi M. Multimodal Prediction of Five-Year Breast Cancer Recurrence in Women Who Receive Neoadjuvant Chemotherapy. Journal of Cancers. 2022. 14(16):3848. DOI: 10.3390/cancers14163848.
[7] Breast Multiparametric MRI for prediction of NAC Response Challenge (BMMR2 Challenge) – The Cancer Imaging Archive (TCIA) Available online: (accessed on 11 March 2023).
[8] Golts A, Raboh M, Shoshan Y, Polaczek S, Rabinovici-Cohen S, Hexter E. FuseMedML: a framework for accelerated discovery in machine learning based biomedicine. Journal of Open Source Software. 2023. 8 (81). DOI: 10.21105/joss.04943.pdf.
[9] Barkan E, Porta C, Rabinovici-Cohen S, Tibollo V, Quaglini S, Rizzo M. Artificial intelligence-based prediction of overall survival in metastatic renal cell carcinoma. Journal of Frontiers in Oncology. 2023. 16;13:1021684. DOI: 10.3389/fonc.2023.1021684.

Section IV

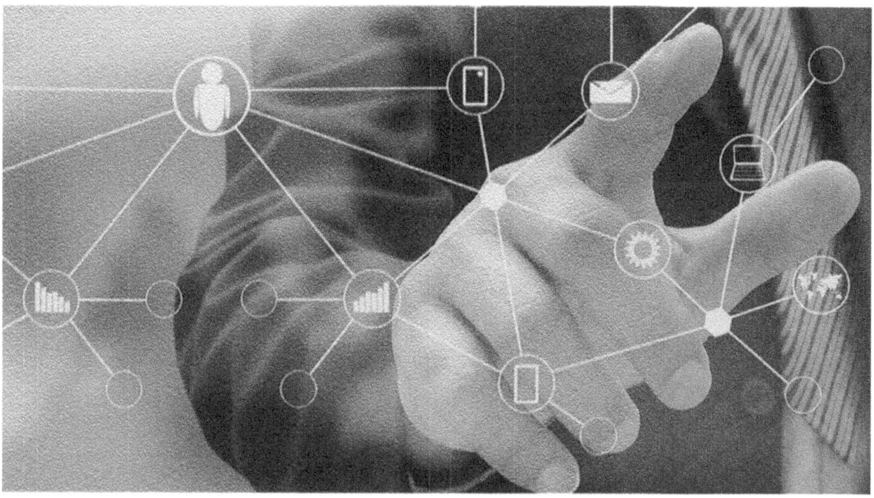

Use Cases in Technology - Industralisation of Healthcare

DOI: 10.1561/9781638282372.ch17

Chapter 17

Introduction to Section IV: Supporting Workflows and Making Workflow Insightful

By Igor Paulussen, Bart Spruijt and Gerrit J. Noordergraaf

17.1 Introduction

This section on use cases in technology brings you to artificial intelligence, decision support, and three different examples of making workflow and care pathways insightful. From aspects of analysis in radiology to helping caregivers and management see how workflow in acute and hyper-acute care is actually going will be described. Making what we think is 'good' even 'better' requires detailed and accurate information and a sound understanding of what the information (may) mean.

The BigMedilytics (BML) project focused on bringing technology into use. This section offers a series of two settings and four different projects, with divergent points of focus and models. Each chapter brings its own insights and learning.

17.1.1 A Technical Description of Real-Time Location Technology (RTLS)

Many, many processes, care pathways, analysis, and diagnostic and therapeutic care in healthcare in general consist of a series of steps. Most of these are serial in nature, but parallel activities may occur. While these steps are often detailed in procedural documents, and some even include timelines, understanding efficiency, effectivity, and movements in caregivers and patients is difficult.

Where healthcare has learned from flight procedures to strengthen safety, we can also learn from logistically focused businesses on process management. An example of this could be the 'just in time' (Toyota motor corporation and its concept of Lean management). However, logistics involves physical motion, and much of healthcare is content driven, with very little outward motion to be detected.

In this chapter (Chapter 18: Real-Time Location System), an evidence-based solution is described. Wearing badges and labeling assets and patients with InfraRed (IR) and Radio-Frequency (RF) technology is combined making it safe for the high-technology density in healthcare. Importantly, the coding of tags and badges can be carefully configured to meet the privacy needs of individual, group, or cohort levels, thus dealing with potential concerns.

As you will see in this chapter and those following (Chapter 20: Innovative Use of Technology for Acute Care Pathway Monitoring and Improvements, Chapter 21: Monitoring Sepsis Patients in the Emergency Department, and Chapter 22: Technological Support for Paramedical Asset Management in a Hospital Setting), careful design is a key to success. Wireless technology makes the system easy to install and remove, as well as allowing it to be moved to other locations as needs occur.

We note as a point of general interest that the RTLS system used in BML allows for coding levels for badges, but is not suitable for data mining based on roosters (i.e., to assess whether an individual badge wearer is serially present and whether this is a confounder in the pathway.

17.2 Using Artificial Intelligence and Decision Support to Buttress Assessment of CT Scans of the Lungs

The amount of information is exploding, but our capabilities to search, assess, and use the stockpile have not improved proportionally. In a recognizable user case, the assessment and reading of CT scans in pulmonary disease were used to analyze its effect on accuracy, put-through time, and professional confidence in junior and senior radiologists (Chapter 19: Implementation and Impact of AI for the Interpretation of Lung Diseases in Chest CTs).

The expert system (Contextflow GmbH) was integrated into the hospital ICT system. When a radiologist had labeled an area of interest in a pulmonary CT investigation, the expert system would look for similar effects, search for descriptions and differential diagnostic options, and offer them to the radiologist for consideration in their specific case. This is all within seconds.

In a neatly worked out prospective study in both junior and senior staff radiologists (as both usability and needs might be influenced by experience on the job), Roehrich and coworkers show that it is safe and effective, as well as acceptable to the professional. They recognize in the lessons learned that cooperative efforts with the IT department and careful management of the use of AI and decision support must be monitored and coached. The 'right answer' remains that determined by the professional – the expert system offers input to be weighed and considered. Important in their study is that not only was put-through time analyzed, but they also looked at the professional aspects.

As using Big Data starts to be integrated into healthcare, this study allows generalizable insights into careful and safe integration. How often are we not aware of how 'the machine' is supporting us?

17.3 RTLS in Hyper-acute Care in the Emergency Department for Patients Suspected of Stroke

In this chapter, Paulussen and coworkers (Chapter 20: Innovative Use of Technology for Acute Care Pathway Monitoring and Improvements) describe a multidisciplinary, multi-location study into a mature time-sensitive workflow. They set out to assess whether this workflow: with only limited physical movement by the patient, but very time and content sensitive: can be analyzed using RTLS with the incorporation of selected data from the Electronic Medical Record (EMR).

Ischemic stroke requires rapid recognition, presentation in an Emergency Department (ED), diagnostics, and potential treatment. Stroke is an important cause of morbidity, chronic decrease in quality of life, and healthcare costs. The Elisabeth-TweeSteden Hospital is strongly organized, formally worked out an 12-step workflow, and offers both intravenous thrombolysis and intra-arterial thrombectomy on a 24/7 basis – therapy to be started within an hour of arrival in the ED.

Paulussen and colleagues use this mature system to assess the RTLS and query whether the use of the EMR time stamps is valid. They use RTLS and EMR data to search for potentially unknown bottlenecks in the workflow.

They argue and show data that EMR timestamps are non-valid and may even be confusing; that with cooperation by healthcare professionals – who need to be aware of how RTLS works, wear badges, and potentially adapt the positioning of the patient – RTLS can be very valuable. Their numbers suggest that the neurology workflow is far faster and the spread is far smaller than that department thought based on EMR data. They also show that analysis of EMR data requires deep mining as well as a user-based understanding of what is done with EMR timestamps.

This study also mentions (see also Chapter 4: Lessons Learned in the Application of the General Data Protection Regulation to the BigMedilytics Project) that while regulations may focus on the protection of the patient and their data, less work has – as yet – been done on the privacy aspects for the professional. Their study stayed well away from individual professional monitoring and focused on cumulative (group fidelity) data. With more than 4.5 million RTLS data points and a large number of EMR items, it is almost self-evident that a Big Data approach is needed.

They were able to find, discuss, and implement remediation as well as analyze the effects of this remediation. The reader should be able to translate their study and its environs to situations and locations they might be interested in.

17.4 RTLS in the Emergency Department for Patients Suspected of Being Septic

In this chapter (Chapter 21: Monitoring Sepsis Patients in the Emergency Department), Redon and coworkers, working in the Incliva Hospital Emergency Department, describe their use of RTLS in patients suspected of being septic. Their focus is on time-to-treatment in their high-volume, physically large ED.

Using a null measurement with retrospective EMR data to understand what the patient journey might look like, they carefully designed an RTLS environment within the ED to capture the important steps in the journey.

Using RTLS and adding selected EMR data points, they performed a prospective follow-up study to assess whether there was an overlap in the times found. As you might expect, they found strongly different times, with as an example a 1-hour time difference between the EMR time of departure compared to the RTLS data. This impacts the workload in the observation unit and may even delay or slow down earlier steps in the patient's journey, delaying treatment with antibiotics and potentially impacting morbidity and mortality. While not a focus in their study, Redon and colleagues report on how ill these patients were.

This group also advocates that the use of RTLS will allow analysis of outliers – in this case in times – and analysis of time spreads using the proprietary dashboard developed by Leitao and coworkers at Philips Research. Even the untrained eye can quickly assimilate information using this technique.

17.5 Finding Assets and to Use of RTLS to Support This

What is more frustrating than being in need of some medical device, be it a stethoscope or/and ECG kart, an anti-decubitus mattress, or something else? Looking where it should be all too often only increases the frustration.

Gutteling and Nelissen (Chapter 22: Technological Support for Paramedical Asset Management in a Hospital Setting), working at the OLVG in the Netherlands, describe an interesting alternative use for RTLS: a search and find tool. They use RTLS in a ward setting to label and monitor the location of a wide range of specific use and general use assets. They start by investigating how much time (nursing) staff need to find assets and using questionnaires how they feel about this. They even add a tool to the nursing Computer On Wheels (COW) and are disappointed when changes in logistics negate some of the expected effects.

In contrast to the other two chapters in this section which describe RTLS use, they use asset location as the principal input, instead of having the focus on patient and staff movement. They avoided the need for EMR data input and had little limitation from privacy aspects.

Using their study, they were able to produce data which suggest that using RTLS and by returning assets to predetermined location – but even if this later is not done – an institution may for the first time have actual insight into how many of a specific asset sort is needed to be able to always have one available, but without overinvesting in purchase and maintenance of assets. In other words, the dilemma of how many do we need to always have one available if we (really) need it, can be resolved using RTLS. They are even able to calculate potential savings.

Interestingly, they also suggest the generalization of use within healthcare and suggest that the department of medical technology might be a good choice as the 'owner' and facilitator of such a system, making it available to interested parties as needs and wants to arise.

17.6 What Reading It Can Bring You

This section describes two different applications of Big Data technologies within healthcare. First, artificial intelligence and decision support via an expert system (context flow) offer focused output from large databases, relevant decisions, and consideration, which can support a medical professional in weighing their perception for the most correct diagnosis or differential diagnosis. Second, real-time localization technology offers insights into a patient journey whether there are bottlenecks, and whether EMR data are in fact true. Tracking and facilitating medical assets and thus potentially reducing the bulk needed can also be done with RTLS.

The reader should have little difficulty – regardless of their work setting – in translating the information and models offered in this section to their own wants and needs. While not a focus, threads running through the chapter reinforce the need for multi-disciplinary approaches, a strong stakeholder, and careful preparation. Another thread the reader will pick up on is that despite RTLS being supportive technology, privacy, training, and careful monitoring require suitable attention.

DOI: 10.1561/9781638282372.ch18

Chapter 18

Real-Time Location System: A Methodology to Gain Insights Into Healthcare Processes

By Igor Paulussen, Frederick Callebaut and Gerrit J. Noordergraaf

18.1 Introduction

Clinical medicine makes extensive use of workflow: a series of steps leading to a desired goal. These steps may involve logistic processes such as the physical movement of caregivers, materials, or patients, which may be time-sensitive. Care pathways have been shown to offer strengthening in the quality of care, the standardization of care, and the reduction of costs [1]. The workflow may also involve the sequential administration of medication or the steps in an invasive procedure. A Real-Time Location System (RTLS) is able to track in real time assets or humans. The system can be used to automate clinical workflows which contributes to more efficient daily operations and improved patient safety and healthcare professionals' work satisfaction. RTLS enhances the coordination of care with visibility into the location and status of patients, staff, and equipment. This visibility can be on a departmental level as well as with more granularity on a single-room level.

Assessing the use and quality of workflow, however, is challenging as placing an observer in or next to the procedures introduces bias, may hinder the procedures themselves, and is time-intensive. Technology has offered solutions, one of which is RTLS, suitable for the limitations of in-hospital use.

The generic term RTLS provides solutions for positioning or localization indoors, where traditional outdoor technologies such as GPS may not work due to signal interruption or not offer the resolution needed. Positioning refers to applications. Well known are the route assistance devices, whereby an app on a smartphone determines its own location, using beacons in contact with a satellite, signal masts, or marker posts along the route. Interaction with location systems in smartphones is routinely used to offer traffic information by measuring the time the smartphone needs to travel between two fixed points and then cumulating these measurements to calculate the information needed.

Localization refers to applications such as tracking, whereby the RTLS system continuously monitors the locations of electronic tags, which can be placed on mobile equipment for asset tracking, on wristbands for patient localization, or provided in the form of electronic badges for staff localization.

There are many different RTLS technologies on the market, and new ones are still emerging. The technology can roughly be divided into two main categories: those using Radio-Frequency (RF) signals transmitted or received by static beacons in the building to estimate an (X,Y) coordinate with respect to the predetermined reference frame of the static beacons (i.e., using Wi-Fi, Bluetooth Low Energy (BLE) and Ultra-WideBand (UWB)), or those using optical or acoustic signals, which do not pass through walls, to directly establish the presence of a marker in individual rooms or zones (InfraRed (IR), ultrasound).

For the purpose of the studies described in Section IV which make use of RTLS technology, as an example of the common use forms in healthcare, room-level accuracy and room-level certainty are not only sufficient but also essential: certainty in whether a patient has entered a specific room or is still waiting just outside the room must be 100% clear. As RF signals pass through walls and ceilings, to date, room-level certainty can typically only be provided by non-RF techniques. In the BigMedilytics (BML) studies, we therefore selected the IR solution provided by CenTrak (https://centrak.com/).

18.2 Technology

In the different BML studies, RTLS was used for a wide variety of purposes; for workflow and patient tracking in a cohort suspected of an ischemic stroke (Chapter 20: Innovative Use of Technology for Acute Care Pathway Monitoring and Improvement), following the movement of critically ill patients in an acute care setting (Chapter 21: Monitoring Sepsis Patients in the Emergency Department) and for asset tracking in a ward setting (Chapter 22: Technological Support for Paramedical Asset Management in a Hospital Setting). In the study settings, the CenTrak RTLS system (http://www.centrak.com) was installed. The placement was limited to the areas of interest for each specific study.

The CenTrak system is a commercially available system designed specifically for hospital environments, FCC and CE certified. It has been installed in over 900 hospitals worldwide for a wide range of purposes. RTLS has also been extensively used in logistic-focused business and warehouse settings, with positive outcomes. Configuration software for the hardware is also provided as part of the standard installation package by CenTrak. Installation of the system was performed by Philips Research.

The CenTrak System (hardware) consists of four main components:

- Wireless beacons (monitors and virtual walls)
- Dedicated routers (stars)
- Data server
- Tags and badges

Cable-free (wireless, battery-operated) IR beacons are placed at the ceiling of rooms or hallway zones, where localization is desired. The beacons emit (invisible) IR light, containing a unique code representative for that zone, which reflects from the walls, floor, and ceiling of the room, thus "filling" the room with the coded IR light signal. A tag or badge entering this area detects this IR code as soon as they enter the room and send this zone code, together with their own unique ID, wirelessly to one of the so-called "Stars." The Stars act like input access points for the system and also transfer the information to the central server that collects and processes all events. Registration can be as often as once per 3 seconds when active (in motion) and as slow as once per 5 minutes when in sleep mode (no motion).

A special type of IR beacon makes it possible to create virtual walls, that is, to virtually separate large rooms into subzones, down to the area of one bed (1 m by 2 m). These virtual wall beacons are also used where walls have large windows or glass doors (because the IR signal will pass through them) or to secure a sharp boundary in, for example, a hallway, i.e., where an open nurse station merges with the hall, or for patient rooms with doors permanently open.

The mobile components are tags or badges. A broad array of tags is available for this system, including patient tags, asset tags, and staff badges with different sizes, different features, and specifications. Some tags and badges have a dual RF and IR function (see below). Versions are also available which can be used in areas covered by IR beacons, and also in areas only covered by a Wi-Fi localization system, for coarse localization where room-level accuracy and certainty are not needed.

The staff badges also have an extra facility in the form of a (3) push-button option. These color code buttons send an extra signal to the star with the identifier of that badge, which can be used to time-label an activity that is not seen in terms of physical movement.

Beacons as well as tags have a battery life of typically 4–5 years. RTLS setup was used in the stroke care workflow (Chapter 20: Innovative Use of Technology for Acute Care Pathway Monitoring and Improvement), initial sepsis management at the ED (Chapter 21: Monitoring Sepsis Patients in the Emergency Department), and monitoring of assets (Chapter 22: Technological Support for Paramedical Asset Management in a Hospital Setting).

There is no risk of interference by the RTLS system with hospital equipment, its networks, or equipment. CenTrak systems are designed specifically for hospital environments.

18.3 Special Requirements for Use

The CenTrak system does have a number of important to realize technical aspects. Tags should be worn as specified to assure proper detection. Patient tags may be worn using a regular patient wristband holding the tag (see Figure 18.1). However, to assure correct location data, the IR detector must remain uncovered by clothing or blankets. Placing the arm tightly against the patient's body, i.e., for CT scanning may also cause loss of data. This is called 'occlusion' as the system is aware that

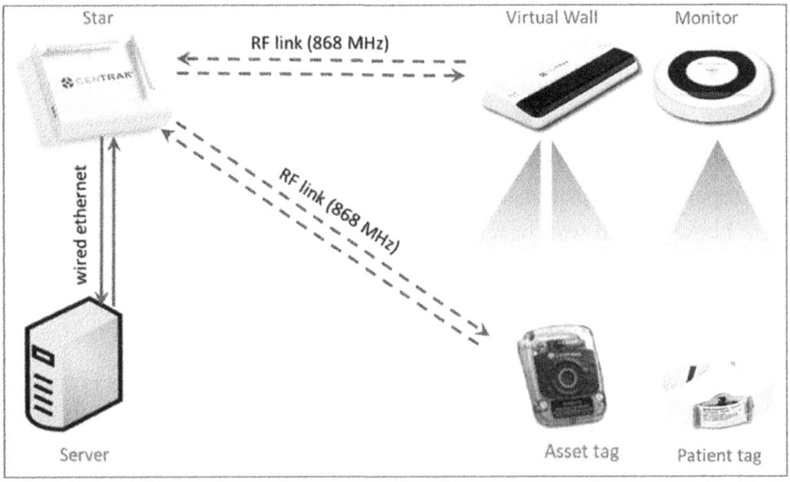

Figure 18.1. The components and communication overview in the CenTrak RTLS system.

the tag is in a general area (RF, active in the RTLS 'world' but is uncertain of its exact location, IR). The potential for this limitation, which makes analysis more difficult, should lead to consideration of an alternative location(s) on the patient, depending on which process is being monitored.

Staff badges should be worn on the chest, outside the clothing, in a fashion similar to existing staff badges. The badges are heavier than IDs and do not fit in regular ID badge holders. The best performance is achieved if the IR sensor is facing out. Naturally, the RTLS badges must be worn outside of radiology protective gear. Asset tags can be affixed to the outside of the asset (e.g., not put in a drawer or box).

Tags and badges contain metallic electronic components and should be removed in case a patient or staff moves to the magnetic field associated with an MRI scan. In one study (Chapter 20: Innovative Use of Technology for Acute Care Pathway Monitoring and Improvement) where MRI scanning was probably done, instructions to remove the tag in case a patient is going for an MRI were provided in the training at the start of the study, MRI staff was notified of this specific risk, as well as printed on the wristband itself. The badges and tags for patients and staff were dealt with as any metallic objects with the MRI protocol of the hospital.

Tags and badges can be programmed as to their identification makers: this can be at an individual level, be a group level (e.g., residents, nursing staff, or technician), or just as a care professional.

18.4 An Example of RTLS Use in a Hyper-acute Workflow Hospital Setting

The stroke workflow study made use of RTLS in the Emergency (ED), RAdiology (RAD), and Operating Room (OR) Departments of a hospital setting and focused on whether RTLS could offer insights into bottlenecks in the care pathway. More specifically, the study aimed to provide the stroke care pathway owners as well as management with high accurate, detailed, information about how efficiently the ED and RAD functioned with respect to the time course management and treatment of patients suffering from stroke and offer input to strive for and achieve improvements [2, 3].

18.4.1 A Brief Introduction to Stroke Care in the Context of RTLS

Stroke (also known as a cerebrovascular accident or CVA) is a major source of morbidity and mortality [2]. It is an illness with both a large short-term and an extremely large long-term component [4, 5]. The short-term aspects involve diagnosis in the briefest possible time to limit morbidity and mortality. This requires that the institution maintains a standing service to provide optimal care 24/7, including the instruments in care, such as expensive catheters or thrombolysis medication. The window of opportunity for treatment is small and expresses itself in (i.e., 4–6 hours) after the onset of complaints. Door-to-Needle (DTN) time is an international quality indicator and indicates that once in the ED a patient should be diagnosed and if applicable treatment started, within 60 minutes. The long-term costs involve loss of work, chronic support, and care, as well as difficulty to objectify loss of quality of life for the patient and their environs [2, 4, 6, 7].

There are two major types of CVAs: ischemic and hemorrhagic. A stroke, which occurs when a cerebral artery is blocked, is referred to as an ischemic stroke, whereas rupturing of an artery is known as a hemorrhagic stroke. The direct cause of the damage is therefore divergent, with ischemic strokes the focus of the study as this can potentially be treated. Establishing whether the stroke is ischemic or not is an important part of the workflow as this determines the potential for any type of treatment. This requires high-acuity, hyper-acute, workflow capabilities.

If the cause of the stroke is ischemic, within a time window of hours after onset (American Heart Association Guidelines), interventions to alleviate the thrombus have been shown to be beneficial [2–4]. The CT-angio (CTa) must show a so-called 'stop' picture within the brain. Then a procedure known as 'thrombectomy' may follow. This is a minimally invasive procedure, often under local anesthesia, where a microcatheter is introduced through the femoral or radial artery allowing access to the clot, which is then removed. If the location is unsuitable for thrombectomy, or if other aspects do not allow or support thrombectomy, a systemic thrombolytic agent, such as tissue Plasminogen Activator (tPA), can be given to attempt to dissolve the clot [8–10]. Local protocols do vary in the 'hard' time limits, as the risk-to-benefit windows are yet, unclear, and continue to change [2, 3]. The study described in Chapter 20 (Innovative Use of Technology for Acute Care Pathway Monitoring and Improvement) has a strong, carefully described, multidisciplinary, workflow, which is described there.

Noteworthy is that the workflow, while involving a series of some (12) steps, in the study setting, with a roll-over CT scanner in the crash room used for the primary survey, the CT scan(s), potentially the start of thrombolysis, could all be performed without physical movement of the patient. The use of room-level accuracy can thus be a limitation.

18.4.2 Potential Benefits of Using RTLS

As described above, the time to treatment after the arrival of a patient at an ED is potentially a critical determinant in mortality and morbidity. Nonetheless, busy

EDs may have challenges in the early recognition of the stroke patient, in the availability of (the right) staff, in the availability of diagnostic measures, and their interpretation [8, 10]. Hospital workflows for treating such hyper-acute patients can often experience small, cumulatively time-relevant, bottlenecks due to a multitude of factors. As most EDs are busy and have no permanent facilities for (objective) workflow observation, collecting insights is difficult. This severely hampers hospitals in monitoring, performing maintenance, or making improvements in their workflows [11].

The stroke study using RTLS provided the hospital with detailed, accurate, and objective, information about how effective and efficient the hospital is with respect to managing patients requiring hyper-acute care in the population suspected of having a stroke. This involved combining selected EMD data with data streaming in from the RTLS [12, 13].

18.4.3 Justification for the RTLS and the Study

The performance of clinical processes is typically based on direct observation of the process by external (non-obstructive) observers. Their focus is determined prior to their placement. After having observed the status quo and provided a report, they might suggest actions that enable workflows to be optimized with respect to time and adherence to, for example, guidelines. There are several drawbacks to this traditional approach: the context within the observation is by necessity incomplete, and the presence of the observer influences their observations by changing workflow (i.e., Hawthorn effect). The number of observations may be limited and case-specific. The whole process is time intensive. A consultant- or observer-driven exercise is useful for highlighting high-level operational limitations that might exist in the care workflows. After implementing recommended changes, it is difficult – if not impossible – to monitor how well the changes are adhered to.

Interviews and surveys may capture the status quo from the perspective of an interviewee. However, a major drawback is that perceptions do not always reflect reality and are often colored by the desire to give the 'correct' answer, the interviewee's perceptivity of rightness, and may be influenced by the most recent events or incidents. Humans are not capable of observing (long-term) trends and may recall only abnormal, infrequent, outliers, which might have a significant, but incidental, detrimental impact on the care workflow.

18.4.3.1 Combining RTLS with selected EMR data

The use of an EMR for time-sensitive monitoring is inferior to an objective RTLS system. Data (time of) entries in EMR are often retrospective or performed through logging procedures. This can result in incorrect times being registered by the system.

As a result, analysis of manually entered data may lead to inaccuracies. Entries lack information about the duration of interactions that might take place among key stakeholders during the decision-making process.

The study using RTLS illustrates how traditional consulting approaches can be greatly enhanced by analyzing a combination of hospital records and data streaming from the real-time locating system, which monitors patients, staff, and devices. This allowed workflow metrics to be studied in an objective fashion. It also helped to analyze the performance of all active workflows accurately and in real time.

The (combined) RTLS and EMR data generated by integrating multiple real-time/non-real-time hospital data sources can be analyzed (e.g., by the use of a performance dashboard) and can make it easier for a hospital to identify inefficiencies/bottlenecks in ED workflows in order to improve the overall delivery of healthcare services.

18.5 RTLS and Hospitals: An Opportunity to Close the Loop

The use of RTLS in healthcare is a potentially strong example of using technology to monitor, maintain, and allow improvements in the many care pathways, processes, and workflows common or even specific to a medical setting. Placement requires care in placement but is wireless and minimally invasive to infrastructure. Close collaboration with ICT and medical technology departments facilitates this process.

The core strength of RTLS is movement in and out of areas or spaces and the ability of RTLS to mark this movement exactly. Each of the chapters in Section IV will describe its specific implementation.

References

[1] Busse R, Klazinga N, Panteli D, *et al.* Improving healthcare quality in Europe: Characteristics, effectiveness and implementation of different strategies. Health Policy Series. 2019. No. 53. Copenhagen (Denmark): European Observatory on Health Systems and Policies.

[2] Powers WJ, *et al.* and on behalf of the American Heart Association Stroke Council. Guidelines for the Early Management of Patients With Acute Ischemic Stroke: A Guideline for Healthcare Professionals From the American Heart Association/American Stroke Association. Stroke. 2018. 49:e46–e99.

[3] Evans MRB, White P, Cowley P, Werring DJ. Revolution in acute ischaemic stroke care: a practical guide to mechanical thrombectomy. Pract Neurol. Augustus 2017. 17(4):252–265. DOI: 10.1136/practneurol-2017-001685.

[4] Lachkhem Y, Rican S, Minvielle É. Understanding delays in acute stroke care: a systematic review of reviews. Eur J Public Health. June 2018. 28(3):426–433. DOI: 10.1093/eurpub/cky066.
[5] McGrath K, Cunningham N, Moloney E, O'Connor M, McManus J, Peters C, Lyons D. Enhancing acute stroke services: a quality improvement project. BMJ Open Qual. July 2018. 7(3):e000258. DOI: 10.1136/bmjoq-2017-000258.
[6] Sørensen KE, Dreyer P, Rasmussen M, Simonsen CZ, Andersen G. Endovascular therapy after acute ischaemic stroke-Experiences and needs of relatives. J Clin Nurs. March 2019. 28(5–6):792–800. DOI: 10.1111/jocn.14664.
[7] Forlivesi S, Cappellari M, Baracchini C, Viaro F, Critelli A, Tamborino C, Tonello S, Guidoni SV, Bruno M, Favaretto S, Burlina A, Turinese E, Ferracci F, Zambito Marsala S, Bazzano S, Orlando F, Turazzini M, Ricci S, Cadaldini M, De Biasia F, Bruno S, Gaudenzi A, Morra M, Danese A, L'Erario R, Russo M, Zanette G, Idone D, Basile AM, Atzori M, Masato M, Menegazzo E, Paladin F, Tonon A, Caneve G, Bozzato G, Campagnaro A, Carella S, Nicolao P, Padoan R, Perini F, De Boni A, Adami A, Bonetti B, Bovi P. Intravenous thrombolysis for ischemic stroke in the Veneto region: the gap between eligibility and reality. J Thromb Thrombolysis. January 2019. 47(1):113–120. DOI: 10.1007/s11239-018-1753-8.
[8] Menichelli D, Ettorre E, Pani A, Violi F, Pignatelli P, Pastori D. Update and Unmet Needs on the Use of Nonvitamin K Oral Anticoagulants for Stroke Prevention in Patients With Atrial Fibrillation. Curr Probl Cardiol. February 2019. pii: S0146-2806(19)30019-2. DOI: 10.1016/j.cpcardiol.2019.02.002.
[9] Price CI, Shaw L, Dodd P, Exley C, Flynn D, Francis R, Islam S, Javanbakht M, Lakey R, Lally J, McClelland G, McMeekin P, Rodgers H, Snooks H, Sutcliffe L, Tyrell P, Vale L, Watkins A, Ford GA. Paramedic Acute Stroke Treatment Assessment (PASTA): study protocol for a randomised controlled trial. Trials. February 2019. 20(1):121. DOI: 10.1186/s13063-018-3144-z.
[10] Sheehan JJ, Tsirka SE. Fibrin-modifying serine proteases thrombin, tPA, and plasmin in ischemic stroke: a review. Glia. June 2005. 50(4):340–50.
[11] Subic A, Cermakova P, Norrving B, Winblad B, von Euler M, Kramberger MG, Eriksdotter M, Garcia-Ptacek S. Management of acute ischaemic stroke in patients with dementia. J Intern Med. April 2017. 281(4):348–364. DOI: 10.1111/joim.12588.
[12] Ismail M, Armoiry X, Tau N, Zhu F, Sadeh-Gonik U, Piotin M, Blanc R, Mazighi M, Bracard S, Anxionnat R, Schmitt E, Mione G, Humbertjean L, Lacour JC, Richard S, Barbier C, Lapergue B, Gory B. Mothership versus drip and ship for thrombectomy in patients who had an acute stroke: a systematic

review and meta-analysis. J Neurointerv Surg. January 2019. 11(1):14–19. DOI: 10.1136/neurintsurg-2018-014249.

[13] Loftus CM, Hoffmann M, Heetderks W, Zheng X, Peña C. Regulation of Neurological Devices and Neurointerventional Endovascular Approaches for Acute Ischemic Stroke. Front Neurol. June 2018. 9:320. DOI: 10.3389/fneur.2018.00320.

DOI: 10.1561/9781638282372.ch19

Chapter 19

Implementation and Impact of AI for the Interpretation of Lung Diseases in Chest CTs

By Sebastian Roehrich, Helmut Prosch, Mia Ilic, Allan Hanbury, Georg Langs and Markus Krenn

19.1 Introduction

This chapter describes the implementation and integration of an Artificial Intelligence (AI)-based Content-Based Image Retrieval (CBIR) system in a clinical setting at the Medical University of Vienna and the Vienna General Hospital between 2019 and 2020. The system enables radiologists to find similar cases during the assessment of lung diseases in chest Computed Tomography (CT) data and was implemented and validated in a radiology department in the course of the BigMedilytics (BML) project.

19.2 Clinical Need and Context

In daily clinical practice, radiologists face a rapidly increasing volume of data or cases. They need to assess more imaging data and, at the same time, deal with a growing complexity of diagnoses and corresponding treatments. This causes a gap between the number of available experts and their capacity. AI solutions that can reduce the time needed to reach a diagnosis and to improve diagnostic accuracy are therefore highly relevant.

On average, radiologists see structures (i.e., pathology) with which they are not familiar in some 20% of CT or Magnetic Resonance (MR) images. While this percentage varies with experience and width of knowledge, it constitutes a substantial part of studies viewed on a daily basis. The process of finding additional information in these cases, in order to write a report, takes up to ±20 minutes (e.g., involving asking colleagues, paging through reference books, performing online searches, or consulting other sources).

When assessed by multiple radiologists, there is a significant variation in the identification of pathologies in the same images, for example, in pneumonia [1]. This suggests that pinpointing a diagnosis is challenging given the information typically available. Errors and discrepancies in practice are uncomfortably common, with an estimated day-to-day rate of 3–5% of studies reported, while even higher rates have been reported in publications [2].

The increasing gap between the volume of medical imaging data and the number of qualified radiologists makes the increase in efficiency a pressing issue. The improvement of quality by leveraging knowledge encoded in more than 1 billion unused CT and MRI scans in Europe is critical to provide fast and high-quality diagnostics to the European population. Prototype search software was developed to tackle this problem by (1) enabling fast and effective access to, and use of large medical imaging databases and (2) enabling clinicians to deliver higher accuracy diagnoses in a smaller amount of time, with the aim that the outcome will have a direct impact on the clinical productivity of radiologists and medical professionals using imaging data.

In the course of the BML project, the contextflow integrated prototype software was used to improve the radiology workflow in a clinical setting. It aimed at reducing the time to diagnosis in radiology departments and at the same time improving the quality of diagnosis by providing an efficient search engine for digitally available comparative radiological data. Using the prototype, radiologists could access comparable cases, connected information, and reference cases useful for a differential diagnosis, based on visual queries in the imaging data they were reading. The increase in diagnosis efficiency and the ability to effectively search in large databases of medical imaging data is critical as about 30% of worldwide storage capacity will be occupied by biomedical imaging data over the next years with more than 125 million CT and MR examinations being performed yearly in the EU alone [3].

Radiologists need rapid access to information and document evidence to back up their initial interpretation of the images before formulating a diagnosis. External resources are being used in about 20% of cases, consuming a significant amount of time. In many cases, radiologists need to ask their colleagues or search for reference literature or web resources, which is time-consuming and prone to errors.

Generally, radiologists follow the same procedure from opening a lung-CT case until the report is finished. As a first step, the predominant pattern in the image(s) needs to be identified. The software and CBIR may already help at this stage by providing an automated estimate of the quantity and location of different disease patterns. Next, the spatial distribution of the patterns needs to be assessed. By providing mapping in the CT image of the distribution of pathologies, a quick estimate of the distribution can be made at a single glance (instead of scrolling through the whole volume and using different views). Then, additional findings have to be taken into consideration to narrow the list of differential diagnoses. Again, the quantification and detection of 19 different patterns by contextflow may help at this stage of the diagnostic process.

Finally, all of the abovementioned imaging findings need to be put together to formulate a main diagnosis and, if necessary, several differential diagnoses. In order to support radiologists during this task, contextflow provides information relevant for interpreting image findings such as lists of relevant diagnoses, tips, and possible pitfalls together with references to external resources such as Radiopaedia or STATdx.

Two quality indicators in radiology workflow are reading time and diagnostic quality. To assess the impact of the prototype on these indicators, the final software version was deployed at the Department of Biomedical Imaging and Image-guided Therapy of the Medical University of Vienna, and a reader study to evaluate the software prototype was conducted at the Medical University of Vienna, with eight radiologists. The design was chosen to resemble clinical routine as much as possible in terms of case variety and the process of reading to further improve comparability and integration into the daily radiological workflow [4].

19.3 The AI Solution

The CBIR system that was implemented in the clinical setting as part of BML consisted of software that analyzes CT data and searches for similar cases based on marked regions of interest. The user assesses a patient's CT and marks a Region Of Interest (ROI) in the volume data. The software extracts features and searches for similar patterns in thousands of reference cases in less than a second. It presents the resulting cases together with suggested descriptions of the findings and relevant information for differential diagnosis (see Figure 19.1).

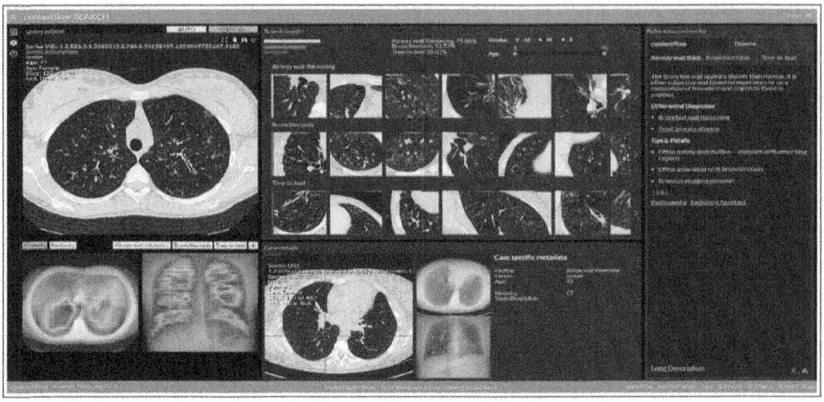

Figure 19.1. The contextflow search prototype, which was used during the intervention phase, is a web application executable from the local PACS. (1) The radiologist initiates the search for similar cases by drawing an ROI in the current CT scan. (2) A "heat-map" in the lower left corner visualizes and quantifies the distribution of one of 19 selectable lung patterns for the current scan. (3) Similar cases to the three most predominant patterns in the ROI are shown arranged according to the highest lung pattern classification probability. Choosing one case leads to (4) more information about the visually similar case (bottom middle). (5) Relevant content to the predominant pattern is presented as a list of differential diagnoses with links to the respective Radiopaedia.org page, tips and pitfalls for the patterns, and additional in-product content for differential diagnoses (right-hand side).

During a typical assessment of radiological imaging data, the radiologist takes into consideration reducing the images to their component part, reports on findings, and, in difficult cases, consults a range of sources, to identify the finding, verify suspected findings, or put the finding in the context of the disease. The software prototype developed for BML supported this by enabling radiologists to trigger searches by marking an ROI in the imaging data. The software then compared the marked patterns with a large database of cases, ranked cases, and showed the most similar cases, together with a summary and scoring of findings, and additional information such as differential diagnosis guidance, or direct links into curated literature optimized for supporting radiologists.

This contextflow search system allows search in radiology image archives containing image examples of a wide variety of diseases with accompanying radiology reports. The focus of the study was lung diseases. It allowed a radiologist to select an ROI in the 3D CT image. The deployment of the contextflow prototype consisted of the integration into the hospital infrastructure and the on-site Picture Archiving and Communication System (PACS) used for managing and viewing medical images. Integrating the contextflow search software directly into the PACS facilitates the integration of the search capability into existing workflows of radiologists easily accessible through an additional search button on their standard image viewing (PACS) interface. The system was deployed at the Medical University of Vienna.

In general, deployment is an important part of enabling effective and efficient use for a system deeply integrated into the daily routine of healthcare workers. In the project, deployments were managed by a single Deployment Master node that coordinated the deployment for all sites and had all deployable packages available. Two kinds of deployment sites were present—first, hosts which are globally accessible and, second, hosts which are located within the protected intranet of a hospital. The Retrieval Backend is generally deployed in the first scenario. The Application Backend is usually deployed inside a protected intranet, but public instances can be deployed as well.

19.3.1 User Interface for Radiologists

The Contextflow platform was used by radiologists reading individual patient cases. They used the platform via their viewer or a browser-based interface to obtain relevant information for the current case. The user interface enabled the radiologists to (1) trigger a search by marking an ROI in the image or volume in front of them and (2) view and explore the search results. The user interface enabled the user to:

- Trigger a search based on a marked ROI
- View search results and their statistical characteristics (e.g., findings)
- Group search results
- Explore search results by providing a detailed view in which the user can inspect all cases in the result list, scrolling through the volume, and visualizing the distribution of areas similar to the query
- Find reference information relevant to the diagnosis and differential diagnosis

19.3.2 Search Model and Engine

During a search, the radiologist inspects an image and marks an ROI to indicate a pattern that should serve as the basis for the search. This information is sent to the search model and engine as a query. Together with the query image, the retrieval engine can receive the image information together with other data such as location or patient-specific information. The search is performed on a local image content level. The index consists of billions of image locations across thousands of reference CT volumes. Triggered by the query ROI, locations with similar appearance are found and ranked across the index, and cases are then ranked corresponding to the found image regions they contain. The retrieval unit ranks the images based on the query and enables further filtering with query information. It provides the results either as an output to the user at the user interface or as an input to further processing. The retrieval unit can perform multiple searches serving different users simultaneously and can also search multiple indices.

19.4 AI Components

The contextflow search platform performs CBIR in the biomedical domain using deep-learning techniques such as Convolutional Neural Networks (CNNs) for data processing. To initiate a search, the user marks an ROI containing the pattern in the case that is being assessed. Based on this query, it ranks indexed examples corresponding to their visual similarity to the query imaging data. These ranked examples form the query result. When receiving the query, the platform can also pseudo-anonymize the query data in the browser.

The AI components solve two problems. First, they have to learn an effective visual similarity function that captures disease-relevant similarity, as a substantial amount of variability exists but is not linked to the diagnosis. Second, the component needs to accelerate the comparison of a query with billions of examples. As the search is performed on a region level, many thousands of regions are indexed for every image volume in the search database. In practice, this amounts to billions of entries, for which the similarity measure has to be evaluated in the time between the user query and the display of the search results. Machine learning algorithms are used to process imaging data, learn which features to extract, and how to compare them, and are active to conduct the search. Machine learning is a crucial part of image processing as appearance differences associated with disease and diagnosis are often subtle compared to the overall variability in the normal population. However, here they have to drive the image search during radiological diagnosis. Deep learning was used to train the models on lung diseases and to compare measures based on imaging data reflecting the disease-specific appearance.

19.4.1 Indexing

The indexing engine is given a dataset and optimized metrics that have been taught during a training phase. It creates a structure holding the data and facilitates finding data similar to a query case. It is optimized to store the information of image features, optionally together with metadata information, and to enable parallel searches. The indexing uses the trained machine learning model that quantifies a metric between image patches. In the resulting representation, simple distances can be used to rank cases reflecting the similarity of visual information. That is, after mapping to the embedding space by the learned representation function, a simple distance such as the Euclidean distance is used for the ranking of similar cases. This yields a representation of the entire dataset. For each representation of a region, it is also known from which volume at which position it comes from so that once a region is identified as a high-ranked match, a user can be presented with the corresponding image.

19.4.2 Retrieval

Given an image, and optionally a user-indicated ROI, retrieval finds the most similar image representations in the index and returns a sorted list of regions and corresponding images. These results can be extended by information (e.g., textual information, specific structured information, or variables) linked to the volumes contained in the list. The retrieval unit can also perform retrieval based on whole images or parts of the images. In either case, the ranking of retrieval results can be presented on the block or volume level.

The retrieval can be performed either as a single retrieval or as a Retrieval Cascade (Figure 19.2), where the result of one retrieval (e.g., a weighted list of textual terms associated with the top-ranked examples) can serve as an enrichment of a subsequent retrieval step that uses both the initial query and the enrichment as input. For example, the retrieval of similar cases can yield statistics about the terms in radiology reports associated with the top-ranked cases. In a second retrieval, the initial ROI and image information together with these candidate terms are used to perform a retrieval in other sources.

19.5 Integration Into Clinical Settings

For a seamless use of the contextflow search system prototype, the software was directly integrated into the local PACS of the Department of Biomedical Imaging and Image-Guided Therapy at the Medical University of Vienna and the General Hospital of Vienna (Austria). This integration allowed the evaluation to be under circumstances that resemble clinical routine. Looking at the early observations in the project study, we identified the need to close the gap between the routine use of the PACS and the image retrieval prototype to minimize the time needed for its use. Using the experience from this integration, the contextflow search system was also integrated into other PACS, enabling a so-called 'deep integration' into the radiology workflow; among them are Philips, Medigration, and Sectra. The framework for deployment and updating of the contextflow search system was created, allowing straightforward deployment and maintenance over installations in multiple hospitals.

The key goals of deep integration were as follows: (1) making the prototype available within the typical working environment and systems of the radiologists (2) testing its usefulness in terms of workflow and assessment support on site.

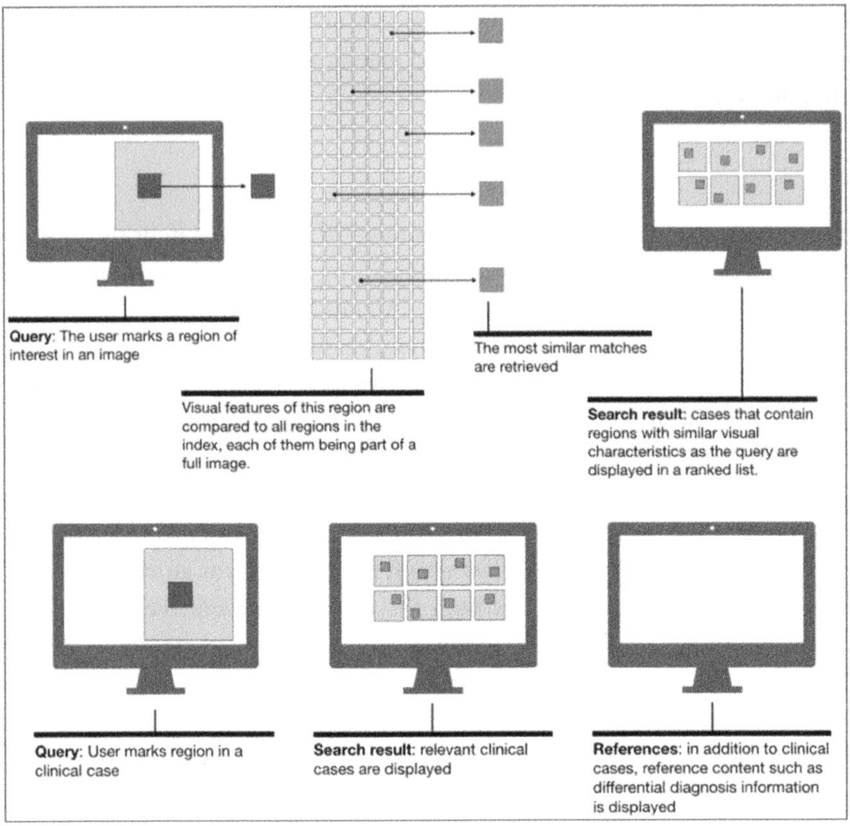

Figure 19.2. User query based on image content, after training and indexing are finished.

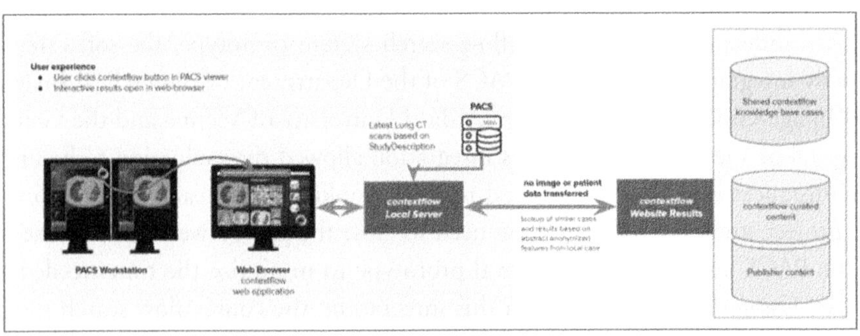

Figure 19.3. Integration of contextflow SEARCH into the PACS workflow.

A context diagram of the system integration is shown in Figure 19.3, illustrating the integration of the system into the clinical routine of the hospital.

A physician interacts with the system via the graphical user interface (application frontend) of the search application component. Here, they select a dataset to examine, execute queries, and explore search results. The system is integrated into the Information Technology (IT) infrastructure (e.g., in a hospital). The PACS system pushes datasets that can be examined into the system. Subsequently, these datasets get selectable by the user. Search results are further linked to additional information such as metadata and reports and other sources such as publications, articles, and curated knowledge bases. The system is implemented with three major components, each of which covers different system requirements:

- The search Application Frontend is the user interface that allows selecting datasets, executing queries, and retrieving and exploring search results.
- The Application Backend is responsible for preparing incoming datasets for examination, managing query execution, combining query results, and presenting this functionality in an API that is used by the Application Frontend.
- The Retrieval Backend performs retrieval queries and serves linked data such as images, meta information, and other sources.

19.6 Clinical Evaluation of the Software

While there is research on technical aspects of medical image processing, including the retrieval of semantic information, there is little research published on user evaluation of the technology and clinical utility. The technology can be useful for tackling diagnostic problems by providing radiologists with similar cases and additional information such as online reference content and thus improving the radiological workflow. In clinical settings, it means potential improvement in reporting on interstitial lung diseases or chronic obstructive pulmonary disease, for example [5].

The goal of the study was to measure the impact of the tool in the clinical settings on the radiologists' workflow of interpreting pulmonary chest CTs by allowing them access to additional, relevant information which they could use at their convenience.

Such evaluation is valuable for proving there is a connection between the CAD tool and an improvement in diagnosis or the workflow turnaround time, which would show the clinical benefit of the CAD tool.

19.6.1 Materials and Methods

For the reader study, the database of query cases held 108 chest CTs obtained from five scanner manufacturers in 2018, of which 100 cases had a confirmed diffuse parenchymal lung disease, and 8 cases without. Each CT had a diagnosis confirmed by a sub-specialized thoracic radiologist with 20 years of experience using

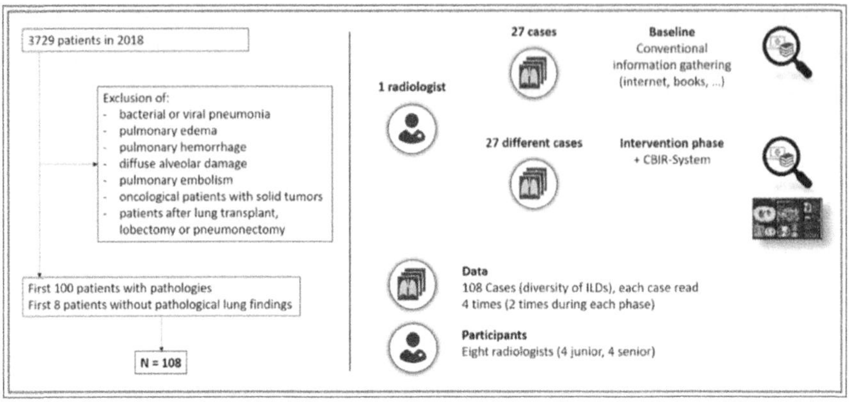

Figure 19.4. Left: Exclusion and inclusion criteria. Right: Distribution of cases [4].

the existing clinical information available in the patient records. Ethical approval was obtained as part of the BigMedylitixs project.

Chest CTs were blinded to eight radiologists, divided into four junior and for senior professionals. They were each given 54 pulmonary CT cases – chosen at random – to read and report in two phases in a setting that resembled the realistic clinical one: each radiologist read 27 CTs without support from the contextflow search prototype as part of the baseline phase and another 27 CTs with the contextflow search prototype as part of the intervention phase. There was a washout period between the reads. In the end, each of the 8 participants had read their 54 unique cases, resulting in a total of 432 readings of cases (Figure 19.4).

During both reads, the participants were allowed access to additional information of their choice such as books or online literature, but not to intercollegiate discussion. In the intervention phase, they also had access to the reference content of the contextflow search prototype. The cases selected were unknown to the participating radiologists, and a 'correct answer' for each was available for comparison purposes.

19.6.2 Study Findings

The system was evaluated in a multireader study with 8 radiologists creating 430 reports. The study showed that time savings of more than 30% were achieved by using the AI system as part of the case assessment. Results were published in 2022 [4].

The overall turnaround time of the radiological workflow per case decreased by 31.25% ($p < 0.001$) when the contextflow prototype was used (Figure 19.5). As the participants had access to reference content in both reads. Additional content was available in the intervention phase in the form of AI, and the results show they

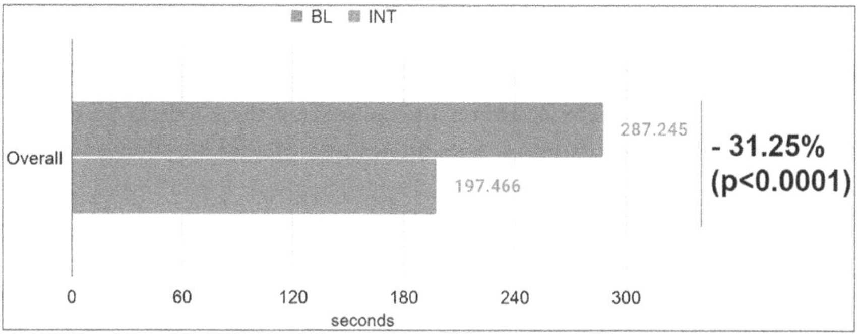

Figure 19.5. Overall average reporting time per chest CT case corrected for other factors such as seniority without the contextflow tool (baseline, BL) and with it (intervention, INT), in seconds [4].

searched more often during the intervention phase (24%) despite the reduction of time investment. Although the results show that the participants searched through more additional information while reading chest CTs, the participants needed less time to complete the cases when they searched for additional information in the contextflow tool (110 vs. 39 seconds used, $p = 0.002$).

Although not statistically significant, there is a tendency toward higher diagnostic correctness in the intervention read ($p = 0.083$).

19.6.3 Conclusion of the Reader Study

The results show that there is an effect of the CAD on the interpretation of chest CTs containing diffuse parenchymal lung disease and an improvement of the radiological workflow by lowering the reading time, in spite of the increased use of the relevant literature during the readings. Due to the use of the contextflow search system, the average time saved per read is 30%. This exceeds the increase in speed of 20% hypothesized at the beginning of the BML project.

It is important to look at this also from the disease diagnosis level. Although the evaluation does not show a significant improvement in diagnostic accuracy when a CAD is used, it shows there is no loss of diagnostic correctness and hence no negative impact on the diagnostics.

The prototype is based on lung patterns and retrieves visually similar cases without diagnosis information. However, in combination with a highly curated dataset, this technical construct has the potential for an upgrade, which would help diagnostic accuracy and correctness. The prototype developed during the project was used to develop a more comprehensive product that shows predominant patterns in chest CTs, gives quantification values for certain lung patterns, and retrieves visually similar cases from an internal database and is commercially available.

19.6.4 Limitations of the Reader Study

The participants were given chest CTs without accompanying clinical data or previous examinations. The study was interrupted by the COVID-19 outbreak, and the participants had a strongly variable washout period between 4 weeks and 15 months, and it may be expected that the participants, especially junior radiologists, gained more experience in the meantime.

19.7 Lessons Learned

This paragraph summarizes practical lessons learned during the implementation and evaluation of the system.

19.7.1 IT Requirements

Often the IT infrastructure in hospitals grows organically over the years, and it is challenging to implement substantial changes necessary for establishing novel technology. Innovations might need considerable effort to be deployed in this environment with complex infrastructure and the necessary framework of regulations of hospitals.

In cases where the hospital does not provide a sufficiently powerful computing environment or access is restricted, it may be necessary to install separate servers, sometimes with graphic processing units (GPUs), and integrate them into the existing IT infrastructure. This might increase the project (capital) expense, and the integration of new hardware might take time and will doubtlessly require approval from a number of departments. Overall, it is important to be flexible and be able to find quick solutions in a collaborative manner to make the system work. Effective and continual communication with the hospital IT departments is a key accelerator in this process.

Moving to a secure cloud infrastructure could help address these points and make innovation move faster. At the moment, the outlook and legislation (see Section I for extensive considerations) environment of hospitals in Europe is very different compared to the United States when it comes to cloud-based propositions. Innovation in healthcare and big data will most likely move faster in countries where the cloud is adopted earlier.

19.7.2 Imaging Data

Training AI models to analyze imaging data requires sufficient data of good quality and high-quality segmentation work by experts. Training AI requires big datasets with images from a large number of patients, from different CT scan vendors with different diseases and technical parameters. However, the imaging data available are scarce, and access to data is limited [6]. It is also tied to various regulatory and ethical approvals that need to be obtained in advance of the model training. This makes the process of data acquisition, preparation, and annotations lengthy and potentially very expensive. Additionally, imaging technology changes continually; thus, the training and adaptation of AI models is a critical and continuous process.

19.7.3 Clinical Validation

New AI solutions that may have an impact on the treatment selection have a direct impact on patients' health and must therefore be approved by regulatory bodies such as the European Medicine Agency (EMA) in Europe and United States Food and Drug Administration (FDA) in order to be sold and used on the market. However, regulatory approval is in some cases not enough and the solutions need further clinical validation to gain the trust of users. In addition, the explainability of AI needs to be addressed as buyers and users need to understand the software and the AI behind it in order to trust it and hence use it effectively.

References

[1] Walsh, Simon L. F., Lucio Calandriello, Nicola Sverzellati, Athol U. Wells, and David M. Hansell. 2016. "Interobserver Agreement for the ATS/ERS/JRS/ALAT Criteria for a UIP Pattern on CT." Thorax. https://doi.org/10.1136/thoraxjnl-2015-207252.

[2] Brady, Adrian P. 2017. "Error and Discrepancy in Radiology: Inevitable or Avoidable?" Insights into Imaging. https://doi.org/10.1007/s13244-016-0534-1.

[3] High Level Expert Group on Scientific Data. 2010. "Riding the Wave, How Europe Can Gain from the Rising Tide of Scientific Data, Final Report of the High Level Expert Group on Scientific Data." European Commission. https://ec.europa.eu/eurostat/cros/system/files/riding%20the%20wave.pdf.

[4] Röhrich, Sebastian, Benedikt H. Heidinger, Florian Prayer, Michael Weber, Markus Krenn, Rui Zhang, Julie Sufana, *et al.* 2022. "Impact of a Content-Based Image Retrieval System on the Interpretation of Chest CTs of Patients with Diffuse Parenchymal Lung Disease." European Radiology, July. https://doi.org/10.1007/s00330-022-08973-3.

[5] Pieler, M. *et al.* Evaluation of automatic volumetry of honeycombing and ground glass opacity patterns in lung CT scans (2022). European Congress of Radiology 2022. https://dx.doi.org/10.26044/ecr2022/C-15193.

[6] Hofmanninger, Johannes, Forian Prayer, Jeanny Pan, Sebastian Röhrich, Helmut Prosch, and Georg Langs. 2020. "Automatic Lung Segmentation in Routine Imaging Is Primarily a Data Diversity Problem, Not a Methodology Problem." European Radiology Experimental. https://doi.org/10.1186/s41747-020-00173-2.

DOI: 10.1561/9781638282372.ch20

Chapter 20

Innovative Use of Technology for Acute Care Pathway Monitoring and Improvements: Workflow Management in Acute Stroke Diagnosis and Care

By Igor Paulussen, Gerrit J. Noordergraaf, Ana Leitão, Julia van Tuijl, Ben P. W. Jansen, Frederick Callebaut and Supriyo Chatterjea

20.1 Introduction, Context, and Background: Care Management

20.1.1 Planned and Unplanned Care

Healthcare can be planned or unplanned. When planned, it is a strongly organized process, often including predictable, plannable actions with the goal of narrowing down the presenting complaints and symptoms, determining the correct diagnosis, weighting, and sharing the decision on an appropriate course of therapy. Each patient requires unique patient-centric care [1]. This makes the process of healthcare so divergent from those in 'lean' or 'just on time' management strategy, as process steps may need to be performed in alternative order to suit the individual case [2].

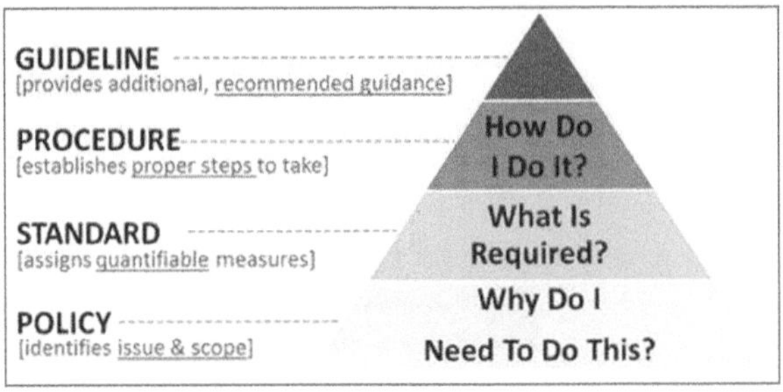

Figure 20.1. Relationships between terms used for care processes [8]. Workflow sits on the top of the pyramid as "overall integration".

On the other hand, unplanned care, typically in an Emergency Department (ED), room setting has the same requirements in terms of quality but has an important time-sensitive time aspect as well as a higher, improvisational, multidisciplinary character.

20.1.2 Care Pathways, Procedure, and Workflow

So-called 'care pathways' have become popular in healthcare and have been shown to have a positive influence on quality, patient acceptance, costs, healthcare provider satisfaction, and even as a methodology for internal process improvability [3, 4]. Introduced in 1985 and attributed to K. Zander and K. Bower, this system for making and documenting steps has been embraced worldwide. Newer iterations of care pathways have integrated patient, medical, and financial aspects in care and may be computer-supported [5, 6]. Similar strategies, such as directed or goal driven care, involve more detailed, feedback-driven strategies for specific aspects of healthcare [7].

Many of the above terms are used interchangeably. Figure 20.1 shows a practical approach to the hierarchy herein. In this hierarchy, the concept of workflow sits at the pinnacle of the pyramid [8]. Great workflow has been described as "working like the Viennese Waltz with the Reverse (Left Cross) Turn": lovely, efficient, and stimulating but requiring compliance of everyone to avoid collisions. In multidisciplinary teams, workflow is the highest attainable level.

20.1.3 Unplanned and Emergent Care

Things change when care becomes unplanned or emergent. Many patients who are admitted to an ED face a lengthy care workflow. Triage is typically applied to determine who needs attention first.

Some subgroups of patients require urgent care with international standards defining time to intervention and time to care (i.e., therapy started within

60 minutes of arrival at the hospital). It has been difficult for hospitals to validate where time is spent during the workflow, particularly in time-sensitive settings with multi-step pathways. These insights could decrease patient morbidity and mortality, increase efficiency, and lower costs including ED overload.

It is noteworthy that even patients with direct life and quality of life-threatening conditions must go through a diagnostic process (i.e., be seen by a nurse and a physician who will, for example, order the requisite ultrasound in order to reach the 'urgent' status needed) [9, 10]. It has been suggested that explicit workflows, and pathways supporting selection, improve care and lower costs [11–13]. Monitoring these pathways and the intended workflow, however, remains challenging [14–16].

Monitoring hyper-acute workflow remains difficult, and physical observation can be a limiting factor. Primarily, the concept of the Hawthorn Bias – that essentially the study of something such as a process has a direct influence on the process and thereby influences the outcome – is applicable [17, 18]. Furthermore, the more complex or acute the workflow is, the more difficult it is to follow its process. Observing (or more accurately analyzing) the effects of content in the process requires a full understanding of the complete pyramid (Figure 20.1) by the observer. In the ED setting, getting a non-obstructive and non-participating expert observer to be on station on time may also be a major logistic difficulty.

20.1.4 Use of Innovative Technology in Workflow Assessment

So-called Big Data, industrialization, and machine learning technologies have been put forward as being able to offer insights into workflow. The most difficult is coupling times to context information. Previous work by our group has shown this to be the case in the healthcare sector [19].

To explore this technology, and more specifically, a Real-Time Locating System (RTLS) in a (hyper-)acute and highly granular, content-rich, setting, we designed a study to track staff and patients presenting at the ED with the working diagnosis of an ischemic, neurologic, stroke.

The death rate and level of disability resulting from strokes could be dramatically reduced by immediate and appropriate medical care: the primary survey, diagnostics, and potential therapy (so-called 'door to needle' time) should all be completed within 1 hour and are described in a step-by-step workflow [20]. Our goals were to validate the usability of RTLS as a monitor of this workflow, RTLS integration of timing integration with the Electronic Medical Record (EMR), develop Big Data feedback allowing insights and potential improvements into the workflow, initiate workflow adaptations, and monitor these effects.

20.2 Methods and Materials in the Study Iteration in ETZ

20.2.1 Setting

The ED at Elisabeth-TweeSteden Hospital (ETZ) is a modern facility including two major intervention rooms (also known as trauma rooms) with a roll-over CT scanner (Siemens^{TM}) servicing both rooms. Workflow patients are admitted directly onto the scan table, and clinical investigation, and therapy (i.e., thrombolysis) can be done immediately.

The ED is manned 24/7, with residents and staff from different disciplines. For the stroke care pathway, a designated consultant neurology staff member is on call 24/7 and on-site within 15 minutes with an on-site neurology resident starting the workflow. Assessment of scans is done in real time, and the hospital has a view-online system that allows neurologic staff to also evaluate a scan on their smartphone and offer advice from anywhere. The Department of Neurology has developed, validated, and implemented a workflow within the setting of the ED – Radiology Department (angio suites) – Stroke Unit to standardize and facilitate the rapid, exact care for these patients (Table 20.1).

20.2.2 RTLS and Its Study Setup in ETZ

RTLSs provide solutions for positioning or localization indoors, where traditional outdoor technologies such as GPS do not work. For the purpose of this study, room-level accuracy was essential (i.e., InfraRed (IR) and Radio-Frequency (RF) solutions by Centrak^{TM}).

Cable-free (wireless, battery-operated) IR beacons were placed on the ceilings. A specific type of IR beacon makes it possible to create virtual walls, that is, to virtually separate large rooms into subzones, down to bed level. The beacons emit invisible IR light containing a unique code representative for that zone, 'filling' that space. The tags detect this IR code when they enter that area, and send this zone code, together with their own unique ID, to a 'Star.' The Stars act as access points and transfer information to the central server. Tags include patient tags, asset tags, and staff badges. Tag location changes were registered continuously, with update rates up to once every second. Data collected include time, tag ID, location ID, motion factor, button press events, and tag type (i.e., function group) [19].

We built the RTLS world within the ED, adjacent halls, Radiology (angio suite), and OR (hybrid operating room). Each professional in a nursing, medical, and logistic discipline involved in the stroke workflow was given an individual badge to wear. A box with reserve badges was made available such that individuals could exchange badges (within their function group) if they so desired to enhance the

Table 20.1. Hyper-acute stroke care pathway for patients who need to be treated by IVT and/or IAT. 1: Ambulance personnel, 2: ED-RN, 3: resident NEU, 4: Tech. RAD, 5: resident RAD, 6: NEU supervisor/staff, 7: RAD supervisor/staff, 8: intervention RAD, 9: anesthesiologist, 10: intensivist, and 11: ANE-RN.

Steps	Time	Events
1	0 min	(2) records exact patient arrival time; (1) hands over to (2, 3); (1,2) transfers patient to CT-table; (2) measures vitals; IV access (2); Blood drawl for lab results (2); PoC Glucose and INR (2); (4) is standby.
2	+5 min	Anamnesis and neurologic examination (3); (3) Orders plain CTC; (3) informs (5); (2) takes away shoes and socks of patient; (4) makes plain CTC.
3	+10 min	(3) evaluates CT-scan, if no intracerebral blood, order CTCa; (3) communicates glucose and INR; (2) makes ECG; (4) makes CTCa; (5) is standby in ED.
4	+15 min	(3) identifies contra-indications for IVT and consults (6); If IVT: (3) gives assignment for thrombolysis preparation to (2); (3) give patient thrombolysis bolus; If CTCa: (5) evaluates CTCa and if necessary consults (7).
5	+20 min	If IVT: (2) starts thrombolysis perfusor; If CTCa: (3) evaluates lab results and contra-indications IAT; (3,5) indicate IAT; If IAT: (3) informs (6) to come; second IV access (2); (3 or 6) informs (8) and asks them to come to angio suite.
6	+25 min	If IAT: (3 or 6) calls (9) and decides necessity for help; (3 or 6) calls (10) if help by (9) is needed but is kept at OR; If help needed by (9 or 10), (11) is sent to angio suite; (3 or 6) asks (4) to arrange two extra colleagues; (3 and/or 6) leave to angio suite.
7	+30 min	If IAT: (3 or 6) organizes admission to SCU for later; (4) opens Angio Suite and informs (2) that patient may come; (11) tests anesthesia station and informs (9 or 10) to come.
8	+35 min	IF IAT: (2) transports patient to angio suite
9	+40 min	IF IAT: (3 or 6) hands over to (4); (2) transfers monitoring to (11); (2) hands over to (11).
10	+45 min	IF IAT: (3 and/or 6) monitor patient and if indicated give medication; (8) arrives at angio suite
11	+50 min	IF IAT: (4) covers patient in sterile drapes for intervention; (9 or 10) gives anesthesia.
12	+55 min	IF IVT only: Thrombolysis ready, (2) transfers patient to SCU. IF IAT: (3 and/or 6, 11) monitor patient; (8) punctures groin and performs IAT; (3) documents IAT procedure in EMR (time arrival ED ("door"), time CT, time start IVT/IAT, NIHSS, delays, etc.)

Abbreviations: CT: Cat Scan; CTCa: Ct scan of the carotid arteries with contrast; ECG: electrocardiogram (12 leads); IVT/IAT: intravenous thrombolysis/intra-arterial thrombectomy; PoC: NIHSS: National Institute of Health Stroke Scale; point-of-Care lab determination such as INR, blood glucose level, hemoglobin level, blood gas, and so on.

feeling of privacy. Upon entry into the ED, each patient received a bracelet with a tag which was removed at the end of the initial care pathway. The senior (coordinating) nurse registered the patient's name, hospital ID number, and wristband number in a dedicated file with a date-time stamp.

20.2.3 Inclusion and Privacy (GDPR)

Management of the General Data Protection Regulation (GDPR) played a major role in the study. Enrolment occurred as a matter of course for all patients suspected of having a stroke. Patients were eligible for inclusion if they were diagnosed as having an ischemic stroke and received an intervention in the form of IntraVenous Thrombolysis (IVT), Intra-Arterial Thrombectomy (IAT), or both. Not fulfilling both these criteria or refusal or inability to achieve informed consent led to exclusion. Informed consent was requested in the days following the stroke pathway. EMR data were only accessed and entered into the database after informed consent was received. The local institutional board and the regional Ethical Committee, the hospital data protection officer, the social committee, the legal counsel, and the Board of Directors approved the study [21].

Professionals were informed about the study via their management structure and asked to participate using blinded badges at a functional level (e.g., 20 similarly coded badges for the cohort of residents in neurology). Individual professionals could opt out of wearing a badge.

EMR data were withdrawn by the Data Warehouse service within the hospital, cleaned of GDPR-sensitive data, and entered in an Excel database. Combining EMR data with RTLS has a specific role in ensuring the privacy and ethics of the study as was defined for this specific study. Because some actions might be performed before and after departure from the RTLS monitoring area, the study team defined ±1 hour for EMR data usage retrieval around admission to the ED.

This database was screened for privacy-sensitive data again before transfer. Raw RTLS data were stored within a dedicated and protected section of the hospital servers. RTLS data were transferred to Philips for further analysis, machine learning, and dashboard composition only after it was reduced to include only data from patients included in the study and who had given informed consent. Subsequently, data are cleaned (e.g., removed if the location is not clear from a process point of view, or manually filled in, from occasional artifacts (i.e., missing detailed location called 'occlusion' in the CenTrak system when a tag is covered by a blanket, the IR signal is blocked but the RF signal works), and formatted for analysis.

20.2.4 Data Analytics Techniques

Once received by Philips, the first step was analytics, which includes a Data Miner, for machine learning-based predictions. Another component was the Data Processor, which aligns the data with different sources, for example, merges two data sources according to timestamp and entity ID. A pattern extractor extracts patterns from the merged data. One level above analytics is the logic and application level, with four components. First is the real-time Machine Learning Scoring Engine. There is an interface between this Scoring Engine with the Data Miner component from the level below. The models produced in the Data Miner were deployed onto the Scoring Engine for real-time scoring. A Rule Engine was responsible for detecting interesting and risky patterns. The Query Engine took queries from the user interface, translated the query into SQL, executed them in the database, and returned data results. The Reporting Engine could run predefined reports given customized parameters.

The top level is the visualization and alert level. This level interacts directly with users and consists of two parts. The first part is the Alert Dispatcher, which dispatches alerts generated by the Rule Engine to specified users. The Visualization Component was implemented by a Java web server as a back-end and an HTML 5-based front-end. It visualized the current status information and analytic results for the users in the dashboard (Figure 20.2).

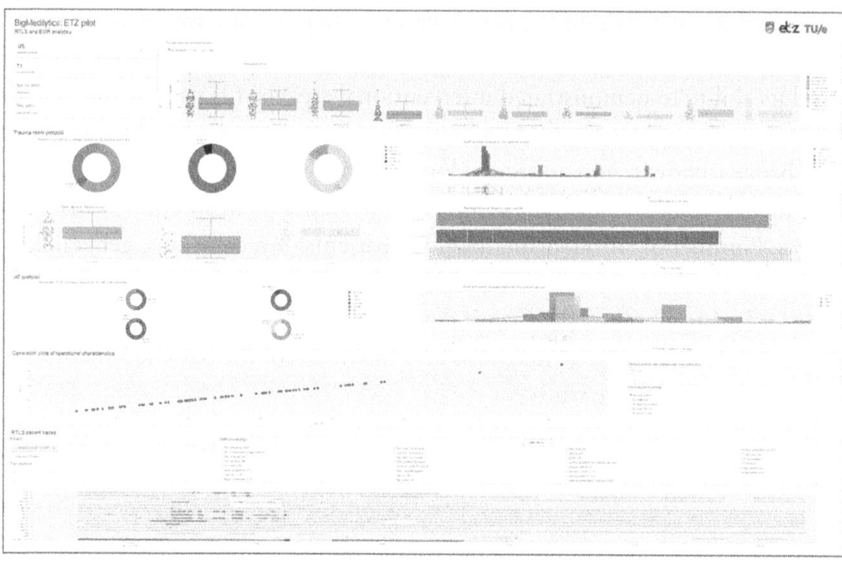

Figure 20.2. An example of Dashboard output, showing the monitoring of specific endpoints and observations. Note, at the lowest level, the report of the (dis)continuous reception of signals from the RTLS.

20.2.5 Combining Context Information with RTLS Output

In many workflows, it is possible to recognize the phase of care using RTLS alone. This is particularly true if the RTLS areas being monitored are carefully defined, the patient is physically moved from room to room, and an association is created between locations, staff members, and the different phases of actions in the workflow. The stroke workflow is highly granular as most of it occurs in one location, with limited staff movement. By integrating staff members with the patient tag, it is possible to define that a step could occur if a particular staff member or group of staff members (i.e., the neurology resident and an ED-RN) were present in the same room as the patient. Nonetheless, in the workflow, there remain contextual steps that are impossible to detect with RTLS. An example is the actual initiation time of thrombolysis. It is defined by the workflow that the start of therapy (an IV bolus of thrombolysis) is done in the intervention room, with the rest of the IV medication given by pump potentially elsewhere in the ED or the angio suite. The preparation of the thrombolysis medication takes time, as does the calculation of the correct dose. While there are timestamps in the EMR and it requires some movement by the ED-RN, it is difficult to pinpoint. EMR timestamps may be pre-, ante-, or post hoc notations.

20.2.6 Primary Endpoints

The primary goals of the study were as follows: (1) Evaluation of the ability of RTLS to offer (useful) insights into the performance of hyper-acute workflow steps, with special regard to the user model of RTLS with EMR data as a high-fidelity monitor, and its ability to demonstrated interventional aspects; (2) patient and caregiver satisfaction and acceptance of RTLS, with special attention to insights into the use of staff badges, patient, and asset tags; logistics involved and scalability; generalization in different use models (anonymity and its consequence); and (3) insights in measures: Number of enrolled and included patients; interventions; general demographics; measurability of time door to CT scan (plain); and times to start treatment (i.e., door-to-thrombolysis (IVT) and door-to-thrombectomy (IAT)).

Note that the neurological diagnosis and treatment of the patient remained outside the parameters of the study.

20.3 Results

Data were collected in the period from September 2020 to August 2021, continuing through the COVID-19 pandemic. A brief pilot (three patients not included in the study) was performed to validate practical and technical aspects.

All consecutively admitted patients via the ED, presenting with signs of stroke (cerebrovascular accident, CVA) were enrolled. In June 2021, interventions into time-sensitive aspects in the workflow were introduced to validate the ability of RTLS to monitor these changes and measure their effects in time.

20.3.1 Primary Outcomes

In total, 829 patients were enrolled. A total of 127 were approached for informed consent of which two patients refused, leaving 125 inclusions (98% inclusion rate), with 32 inclusions in the post-intervention phase of the study. Of the 125 patients, 80 received IVT treatment, 29 patients underwent IAT treatment, and 16 received both IVT and IAT. The mean age of included patients was 70.5 ± 13.2 years. Totally, 62 patients were female (49.6%). There were no patients < 21 years old, or mentally impaired prior to their admission.

One RTLS tag or badge generated approximately 3,600 data points per hour. Per patient, overall, 10 tags and 1 badge were involved and of interest. This leads to 36,000 data points per included patient, or approximately, 4.5 million RTLS data points overall.

An accurate T0 is essential for three of the most important indicators for our pathway. Door time = T0 is the patient arrival time at the ED and the beginning of the DTN time. T0 was documented in 100% of cases in the EMR. However, other senior ED-RNs with other work strategies were shown to impact its actuality [22]. For example, T0 was inaccurate when the senior ED-RN mistook which ambulance had just arrived. An RTLS solution for this issue is described below. Accuracy in data points was diverse. Cross-checking T0 with other data in EMR, as well as with RTLS, confirmed inaccuracies.

20.3.2 Patient and Caregiver Satisfaction and Compliance

Professionals were sensitive to (their) privacy and autonomy. To our knowledge, only two opted out. Compliance (i.e., all RTLS badge data for a professional during one workflow was available) was 67%. Compliance was affected by badges not being seen by the registration points, particularly due to clothing or positioning for CT scanning. This remained an issue despite retraining on the importance of the position. Alternative locations (i.e., on the shoulder) were found to have their own limitations. Some expressed concerns that the data could be used for other purposes such as 'benchmarking' individual workload, speed, or accuracy. Overall practical acceptance of badges was good.

20.3.3 Dashboard Representation

The core analytics were represented in the Dashboard with RTLS, EMR, and combined data point representations. The dashboard could show individual cases or aggregated data over any cohort or time frame selected. Thus, we can use data from a unique source, such as RTLS, the EMR (i.e., the CT scan), or a combination of both. The dashboard was ideal to analyze whether a reduction of some 20% in the workflow (time) aspects could be reached and where or how.

20.3.4 Study Interventions and Their Effect

Interventions with the care pathway, based on big data insights, were initiated in June 2021 and continued until the closure of enrollment. The week prior to the start of inclusion and interventions was used for training purposes.

The interventions in June were as follows: (A) Focusing on accuracy in patient arrival time by using RTLS badges as a push button system at the ED ambulance bay entrance (to be used by the EMS nurse – which worked well), senior nurse workplace, and intervention room entrances; (B) tagging the IVT intervention box and bundling all the medication and materials in it and move it into the intervention room, which removes the need for nurses to leave the intervention room area; and (C) permanently placing an anesthesia cart in the angio suite for IAT.

Additionally, on point B, the medication was previously kept in the central medication room within the ED. This is a locked location, with the medication spread according to the alphabet in drawers and syringes, tubing, etc., kept in their own drawers.

The overall time effect of the interventions was a clinically relevant reduction of more than 20% (as a clinically relevant measure).

20.4 Discussion

To our knowledge, this study is the first to use RTLS and Big Data technology to monitor a fully operational medical hyper-acute workflow with the incorporation of time-sensitive content data from the EMR as a methodology to find improvement points, create interventions, and monitor the effects of the interventions.

We were able to enroll (signed informed consent) 98% of the patients who were eligible and created a database with 125 patients with an ischemic stroke who received treatment. More than 200 different individual professionals wore badges. Millions of data points were collected. We identified, added remediation, and monitored the effects of >3 points in the workflow to good effect.

20.4.1 Brief Learnings

Patient and caregiver satisfaction and acceptance of RTLS: The study was able to show that it is possible to get a large number of professionals to accept and wear the RTLS badges. We note that the study team was fully blinded to which professional (as an individual) was actually wearing a specific badge. However, an overall compliance of 67% is not high. Badges were anonymously handed out to the different functional groups and changing badges within that functional group was encouraged. This did mean that maintenance of badges (i.e., battery state), recognition of non-compliance (i.e., badge inside obstructive pockets), and follow-up of missing data (i.e., furthering understanding of why certain data points were not being registered) were not possible. In many patient cases, one or more staff members were not seen (in the RTLS data) during the workflow. Since the patient was progressing through the workflow, and EMR entries confirmed their presence, they had to have been there. This interfered with machine learning rules, and in some cases required manual assessments [23]. Our study confirms findings from other settings that privacy concerns may remain an active threat to the use of this technology [24]. Good information, an understanding of the technology, and the data it produces are essential for success [2]. Acceptability seems to be strongly associated with personal and professional responsibility and autonomy, as shown by RTLS success in many logistics-oriented sectors. Our study is unique, as it is the largest in the medical setting, involved both professionals and patients and involved a time-sensitive workflow that is used by healthcare authorities as a quality measure. RTLS was shown to be more accurate (shorter times) than EMR data in reporting workflow (run-through) time, supporting the enthusiasm of the responsible professionals in their participation. Future improvements can be made by institutions in adding privacy and monitoring aspects to employment contracts.

All patients enrolled were happy with the wrist tag: it was not annoying, and keeping it uncovered (i.e., outside blankets) was possible. The two patients who refused informed consent did so from privacy concerns.

Evaluation of the ability of RTLS to offer (useful) insights into the performance of hyper-acute workflow steps: Fidelity in the (timing of) tagging the patient with special attention to arrival time was complex and a central aspect in its use [25, 26]. Despite all the patients being presented by EMS and pre-announced, clarity in 'door time' (T0) proved itself a relevant confounder. The EMR allows patients to arrive (digitally) before physically, i.e., to 'block' the room and allow orders to be placed. The study documented one patient in whom the EMR time for CT scan was 20 minutes before their physical arrival. RTLS data were suggested to be highly accurate, as far as ground truth data or verification was possible. These discrepancies make machine learning difficult.

The study investigated the high granularity of data, as gross movement (i.e., from room to room) was limited. The combination of EMR data with RTLS, after choosing ground truth items, such as the time registered in the CT-scan slices themselves, was very valuable and reproducible. Important delay markers in the workflow were able to be found, interventions conceived and implemented, and their effects monitored for validity without much difficulty. Three main interventions were the addition of RTLS badges to verify T0, moving and bundling the thrombolysis medication such that the nurse need not leave the intervention room (and thus would not be distracted by others while walking through the ED on the way to-and-from the medication storage, leading to time loss), and supporting ready-to-start anesthesiology setup in the angio suite. Clinically relevant time (20%) saving was demonstrated and maintained, showing no Hawthorn effect.

We plan an even higher granularity study with EMR and RTLS using the teams involved in trauma admission.

Insights in measures: The results show that RTLS can offer insights into a hyper-acute pathway when combined with EMR data. RTLS can support the process aspects and has allowed for interventions to be introduced. The age (ca. 70 years old), with a relevant spread in pre-existing comorbidity underlines that early and accurate diagnostics and treatment will have a major impact on the rest-of-life healthcare costs, such as healthcare consumption, costs of supportive care, and so on, even though return to the workplace is not a focus.

The industrialization of care pathways via RTLS, thus, requires monitoring and intense care in its analysis. Using time stamps from EMR remains fraught with dangers as time stamps from orders, start investigation and stop investigation as well as its formal report, often had a chronological progression which was physically impossible (i.e., the patient must be present to perform a CT scan).

The RTLS system is readily placed or removed for other purposes and could be used by the institution to achieve similar goals elsewhere. A potentially good choice for the role of "owner/facilitator" would be the medical technology department.

20.5 Conclusion

The integration of EMR data with RTLS data in the proprietary Philips dashboard generated unique insights and interventions that resulted in clinically relevant improvements. Big Data showed strengths and bottlenecks otherwise invisible. Machine learning requires high compliance from users. Our integrated EMR and RTLS data showed that the use of only EMR data may skew analysis not only in statistical but also in (large) clinically relevant ways.

Granularity using workflow to allow sufficiently detailed understanding to be developed, combining selected data from the EMR with the RTLS, in a team approach should also be manageable not only in the ED but also in a wide range of potential locations within healthcare. We showed a >20% reduction in put-through time as a clinically relevant time-saving after monitoring. Compliance needs to be further investigated in the clinical setting.

References

[1] Hunter DJ, Fairfield G. Disease management. BMJ. 1997;315:50–3.

[2] D'Andreamatteo A, Ianni L, Lega F, Sargiacomo M. Lean in healthcare: A comprehensive review. Health Policy. 2015 Sep;119(9):1197–209. PMID: 25737260.

[3] Anonymous. Brave new world: case managers and the future of clinical pathways. Hosp Case Manag. 1998 Apr;6(4):65–9. PMID: 10178912.

[4] Rosique R. 2022 Care Pathways |The basics | Healthcare Management (asianhhm.com).

[5] Glassman KS, Kelly J. Facilitating care management through computerized clinical pathways. Top Health Inf Manage. 1998 Nov;19(2):70–8. PMID: 10338716.

[6] Favor G, Ricks R. Preparing to automate the case management process. Nurs Case Manag. 1996 Jul-Aug;1(3):100–6. PMID: 9197680.

[7] Walsh M, Thomas SG, Howard JC, Evans E, *et al.* Blood component therapy in trauma guided with the utilization of the perfusionist and thromboelastography. J Extra Corpor Technol. 2011 Sep;43(3):162–7. PMID: 22164456.

[8] Bahadur P. 2014. (99+) Difference between Guideline, Procedure, Standard and Policy | LinkedIn.

[9] Wittels K. Aortic emergencies. Emerg Med Clin North Am. 2011 Nov; 29(4):789–800, vii. PMID: 2204070.

[10] Wang LJ, Locham S, Dakour-Aridi H, Lillemoe KD, *et al.* Sex Disparity in Outcomes of Ruptured Abdominal Aortic Aneurysm Repair Driven by In-hospital Treatment Delays. Ann Surg. 2019 Oct;270(4):630–8. PMID: 31356266.

[11] Berntsen G, Strisland F, Malm-Nicolaisen K, Smaradottir B, *et al.* The Evidence Base for an Ideal Care Pathway for Frail Multimorbid Elderly: Combined Scoping and Systematic Intervention Review. J Med Internet Res. 2019 Apr 22;21(4):e12517. PMID: 31008706.

[12] Montejo M, Paniagua N, Saiz-Hernando C, Martínez-Indart L, *et al.* Reducing Unnecessary Treatments for Acute Bronchiolitis Through an Integrated Care Pathway. Pediatrics. 2021 Jun;147(6):e20194021. PMID: 33958438.

[13] Duflos C, Troude P, Strainchamps D, Ségouin C, *et al.* Hospitalization for acute heart failure: the in-hospital care pathway predicts one-year readmission. Sci Rep. 2020 Jun 30;10(1):10644. PMID: 32606326.

[14] Venketasubramanian N. Stroke pathways. Ann Acad Med Singap. 2001 Jul;30(4 Suppl):27–35. PMID: 11721275.

[15] Co JP, Johnson KB, Duggan AK, Casella JF, *et al.* Does a clinical pathway improve the quality of care for sickle cell anemia? Jt Comm J Qual Saf. 2003 Apr;29(4):181–90. PMID: 12698808.

[16] Basch E, Barbera L, Kerrigan CL, Velikova G. Implementation of Patient-Reported Outcomes in Routine Medical Care. Am Soc Clin Oncol Educ Book. 2018 May 23;38:122–34. PMID: 30231381.

[17] Pfungst O, Rahn CL. Clever Hans (the horse of Mr. von Osten) a contribution to experimental animal and human psychology. 1911. New York, H. Holt and company LCCN: 11010970.

[18] Landsberger HA. Management and the worker: its critics, and developments in human relations in industry: Hawthorne revisited. 1958. Cornel Library, Ithaca NY (USA). LCCN: 58063022.

[19] http://www.bigmedilytics.eu/pilot/stroke-management (posters (a-d) @ publication section).

[20] Man S, Xian Y, Holmes DN, Matsouaka RA, *et al.* Association Between Thrombolytic Door-to-Needle Time and 1-Year Mortality and Readmission in Patients With Acute Ischemic Stroke. JAMA. 2020 Jun 2;323(21):2170–84. PMID: 32484532.

[21] Guo H, Huang Z, Yeo JYP, Wang Y, *et al.* Psychosocial determinants of healthcare personnel's willingness to carry real-time locating system tags during daily inpatient care in hospital managing COVID-19 patients: insights from a mixed-methods analysis. JAMIA Open. 2021:5;4(3):ooaa072. PMID: 34505000.

[22] Bowen ME, Wingrave CA, Klancher A. Craighead JD. Tracking technology: Lessons learned in two health care sites. Technology and Health Care. 2013;21:191–7 DOI: 10.3233/THC-130738.

[23] Jones TL, Schlegel C. Can Real Time System Technology (RTLS) Provide Useful Estimated of Time Use by Nursing Personel? Res Nurs Health. 2014 February; 37(1): 75–84. PMID: 24338915.

[24] Griffin JM, Hellmich TR, Pasupathy KS, Funni SA, *et al.* Attitudes and Behavior of Health Care Workers Before, During, and After Implementation of Real-Time Location System Technology. Mayo Clinic Proceedings: Innovations, Quality & Outcomes. 2020 February; 4(1): 90–8. PMID: 32055774.

[25] Overmann KM, Barrick L, Porter SC. Improving Documentation Using a Real-Time Location System in a Pediatric Emergancy Department. Appl. Clin. Inform. 2021; 12:459–68. PMID: 34041733.

[26] Stübig T, Zeckey C, Min W. Citak M. *et al.* Development of a WLAN-based real time localization system for patients tracking in a Level I Trauma center. Technology and Health Care. 2012; 20:317–27. PMID: 23006912.

DOI: 10.1561/9781638282372.ch21

Chapter 21

Monitoring Sepsis Patients in the Emergency Department: The Use of a Real-Time Location System

By Ana Leitão, Pau Redon, José-Ramón Navarro-Cerdán, Santiago Galvez-Settier, Evert van Loenen and Josep Redon

21.1 Introduction

Sepsis is a worldwide condition with high incidence and morbimortality. It is caused by a dysregulated response of the organism to an infection and affects one million people every year [1]. According to the Third International Consensus Definition Task Force (Sepsis-3), sepsis is defined as a suspected or documented infection with a rapid increase of two points on the Sequential Organ Failure Assessment (SOFA) scale [2, 3]. There are several quick diagnostic scales that were designed for the early detection and management of septic patients, although there has been disagreement on the convenience of their use [4–14]. Likewise, contradictions about their prognostic value have been noticed, not only in Community-Acquired Sepsis (CAS) studies but also in studies based on specific groups of patients, such as the critically ill, [15] surgical, [16] cirrhosis, [17] and oncologic [18].

Although actual sepsis incidence remains unknown, according to the data published in Spain in 2014, 333 cases for every 100,000 inhabitants every year is the estimated rate, some of which evolve into septic shock [19]. Among them, CAS is frequently present: in circa 10% of patients affected by infectious diseases that attend the Emergency Departments (EDs). Moreover, 30–40% of septic patients in intensive care units have their origin in CAS. The economic impact is difficult to quantify due to different definitions and ascertainment methods. Nevertheless, an epidemiological study estimated an average cost of £25,000/case with an annual population-based incidence between 40 and 455 per 100,000 [20]. Measurable increases in healthcare costs, mortality, and secondary endpoints adverse effects are associated with every minute of delay in the administration of treatment.

The sepsis care challenges are currently managed through home-based and in-hospital strategies. Home-based strategies are mainly based on educational programs targeting the early recognition of symptoms. In-hospital strategies involve clinical, nursing, and ancillary staff and are based on: (1) the development of specific early screening and response tools, (2) time reduction for complementary tests, and (3) development of more accurate diagnostic tests and extended eligibility for aggressive treatment procedures. However, these approaches cannot address all elements of the complex cascade of patient work-up in the ED but rather aim to improve one specific aspect (e.g., disease recognition by nursing staff). Dynamic bottlenecks in the ED workflows can only be detected when all elements are analyzed systematically and simultaneously.

Early identification and appropriate management in the initial hours after the disease are associated with lower morbidity and mortality as well as a reduction in healthcare costs. However, the current data management systems are not capable of systematically identifying unnecessary time delays, bottlenecks, and other weaknesses in the workflow. The use of additional resources such as monitoring with a Real-Time Location System (RTLS) could provide improved time-to-intervention in sepsis patients arriving at the ED.

Big Data is required to address this problem due to the volume (e.g., data generated from the intervention of multiple healthcare professionals and the use of multiple facilities), velocity (e.g., real-time data will be generated from the RTLS system), variety and veracity (e.g., Electronic Medical Record (EMR), National (Nationwide) Inpatient Sample (NIS) database, RTLS, Machine log, and Lab data), and value (e.g., resource optimization in ED and time reduction for diagnosis and treatment). Secondary outcomes expected by applying a Big Data approach included better asset, installations, and staff management, increased patient safety, and increased patient throughput through the ED. The coupling of all information could be useful for hospital and department management because it will identify weaknesses in the workflow and help develop improved protocols.

21.2 Methods and Materials for Monitoring Sepsis Patients in the Emergency Department

To identify such potential delays in sepsis patients' care, two methods are applied.

First, data analysis was applied to retrospective patient record data, to establish a general baseline of present outcomes and lengths of stay. Current data management systems were found to be unsuited for identifying unnecessary time delays, bottlenecks, and other weaknesses in the existing workflow for sepsis patient management.

Consequently, an RTLS layout was developed and the system was deployed in the ED of Hospital Clínico-INCLIVA in Valencia, Spain. The RTLS system provides accurate timestamps of logical (physical) procedure steps that involve patient location changes, such as transport, period in waiting rooms, and so on. Selected medical record data from this patient cohort were used to add other essential timestamps, such as those of sending blood samples for analysis, receiving lab results, completing diagnosis, starting treatment, and so on.

Depending on potential bottlenecks identified, an intervention will be introduced, and the RTLS system and EMR data will subsequently be used in the next stage to measure the post-intervention improvements quantitatively.

21.2.1 Inclusion and Patient Selection

21.2.1.1 Inclusion criteria for subject selection

The subjects are as follows:

- Regarding the retrospective data, data will be extracted from the EMR of those subjects with clinical data of sepsis identified by the quick SOFA (qSOFA) criteria in the triage room during the 2 years prior to the start of BigMedilytics (BML).
- For the prospective RTLS study: RTLS platform implementation and tracking in a real context of adult patients (older than 18 years at the time of admission to ED), both male and female, which have signed the consent document (within 24 hours of ED admission) and with a sepsis diagnostic identified by the qSOFA (2) criteria in the triage room.

21.2.1.2 Exclusion criteria for subject selection

The exclusion criteria are as follows: un-signed consent form and/or no sepsis diagnosis.

21.2.1.3 Criteria and procedures for subject withdrawal or discontinuation

- Subjects can leave the study at any time for any reason if they wish to do so without any consequences for their treatment or management. The investigator can decide to withdraw a subject from the study for urgent medical reasons.
- Withdrawn participants will be replaced until 200 participants have completed the study or when decided that time is too limited to include more participants and finish the measurements according to the project planning.
- The point of enrollment is the time at which, following recruitment, a subject signs and dates the informed consent form. The first subject is expected to be enrolled in September 2018. The clinical investigation is expected to take 18 months. The duration of the participation of each subject can range from hours up to several days (in case of hospitalization).

21.2.2 Study Design

The study was divided into four stages:

The first stage of the study consisted of joint, multidisciplinary, sessions to get a common and full understanding of the sepsis care paths, patient routing, and staff workflow (Figure 21.1).

In the second stage, an initial design for the system layout was made, focusing on the granularity of the RTLS system (Figure 21.2).

Third stage. In a joint session on-site, a so-called Radio-Frequency (RF) survey was performed. In this survey, a test setup is used to check if the actual RF ranges of the stars (receivers for the patient and asset tags and the staff badge signals) correspond to the nominal ranges. RF ranges may deviate, for example, due to elevators or where walls are much thicker than usual.

Based on the outcomes, a final design was made (Figure 21.3).

In the fourth stage, inclusion was started. Patient tags were placed in the triage room. Transition times were collected by the RTLS and monitored from the hospital's Electronic Medical Records (EMRs) of the patients. The time points collected

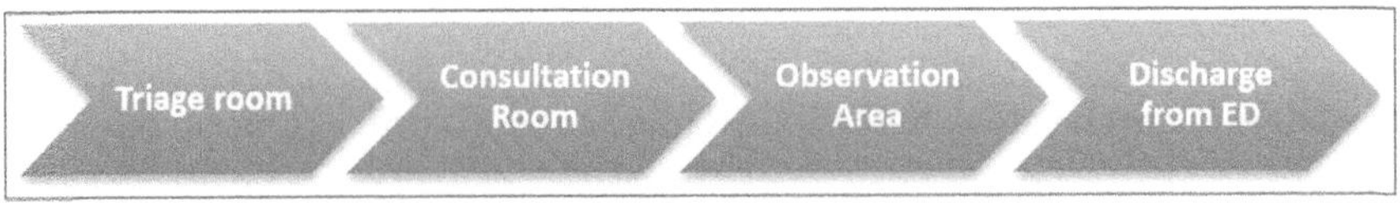

Figure 21.1. Patient pathway in sepsis care within the ED.

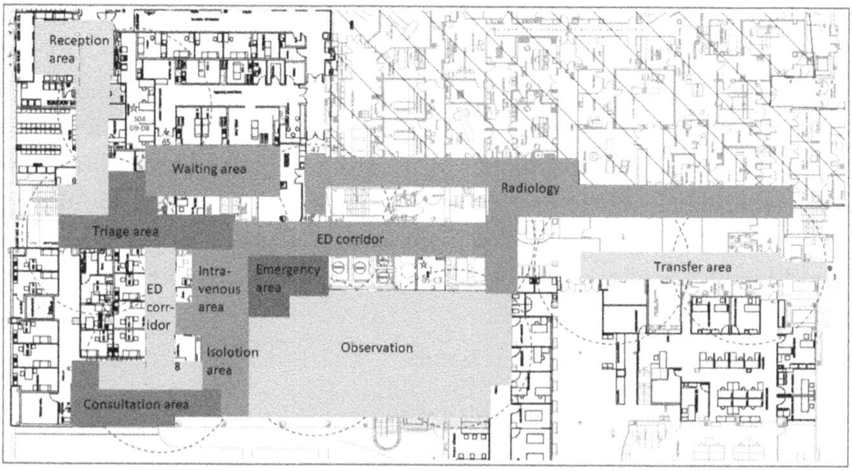

Figure 21.2. Distribution of the areas used in the sepsis care pathway within the ED. The dotted circular lines are the reception area of a "star."

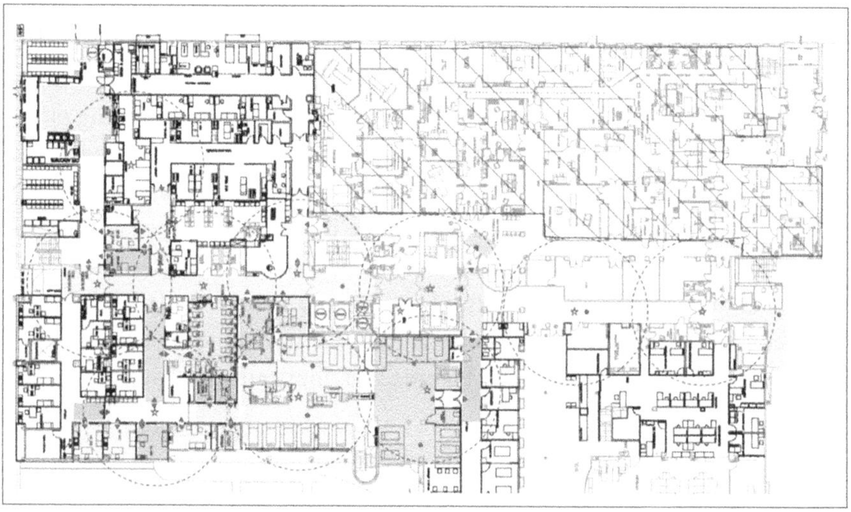

Figure 21.3. Distribution of the sensors.

were as follows: A: admission; IT: start of triage; FT: end of triage; PMC: first medical contact/consultation; AS: obtaining blood for lab test; ATB: administration of antibiotics; HC: obtaining blood for cultures; F: starting intravenous fluids; O: arrival in the observation room; and I: transfer to another hospital ward. The listing is not necessarily also the order in which they were performed.

The main time periods calculated were as follows: IT-FT: start to end of triage; FT-PCM: end of triage to the first medical contact/consultation; PCM-O: first medical contact/consultation to admission at observation area; and O-I time from admission at observation area to transfer to another hospital ward.

In addition: PMC-AS: first medical contact and obtained lab tests; O-AS: arrival in observation room to lab; PMC-F: first medical contact to initiation of administration of fluids; O-F: arrival in observation room and start intravenous fluids; O-ATB: arrival in observation room and administration of antibiotics; and A-I: total time from admission to ED to transfer to another ward. Furthermore, A-ATB: admission in ED to first antibiotics in observation room; A-F: Admission to ED to first IV fluids in observation room were calculated; as well as A-AS: admission to ED to lab workup; and A-HC: Admission to ED to taking blood cultures.

21.2.3 Ethical and Security Issues

The Ethical Committee of the Hospital Clínico of Valencia approved the research, and informed consent was requested from all patients at admission or within a period of 24 hours after admission if the physical condition at arrival was not appropriate. GDPR principles were applied.

The system deployed to perform the prospective study was the RTLS by CenTrak. This system tracked not only the patient flow but also the material resources and their availability. To do so, wristbands, tags/badges, and access points were deployed at the ED. All the information was uploaded to a corresponding platform designed by Phillips. This platform used Big Data tools to process the data and also helped in the data visualization, making it more understandable, the results obtained and the potential improvements to be made. Also, some alerts could be designed for patient safety and installation availability.

The data are accessed and processed in a secure manner; ATOS developed a secure network that monitors and audits all the external connections to INCLIVA's servers where the data are stored. Figure 21.4 illustrates the workflow for the prospective part of the study.

21.3 Results

21.3.1 General Characteristics of the Study Population

A total of 268 patients with a diagnosis of sepsis were monitored, 201 as a retrospective control group and 67 in the prospective study with both EMR and RTLS simultaneously.

The main characteristics of the prospective study patients are given in Table 21.1.

Transition times and clinical indicators prior to RTLS installation (retrospective) are shown in Table 21.2a.

The results for critical steps involving both RTLS and the EMR are shown in Table 21.2b.

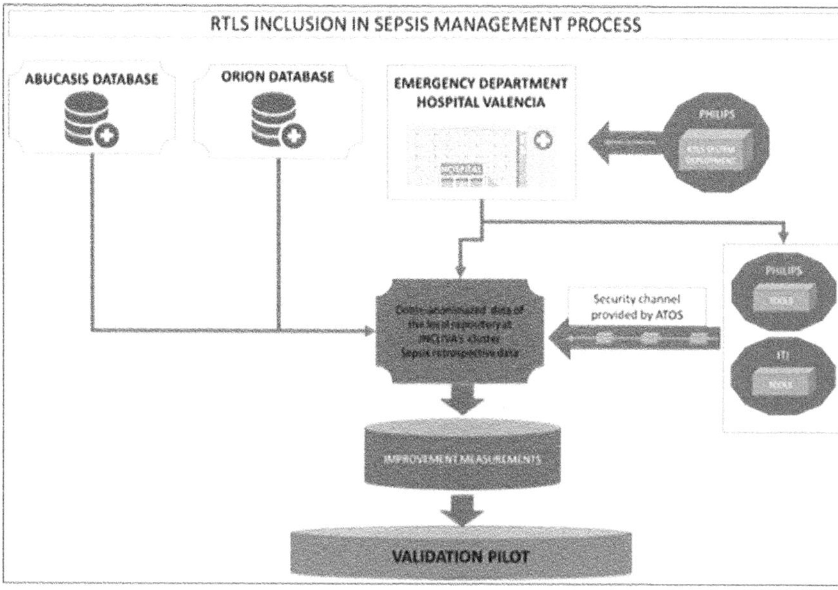

Figure 21.4. Data flow in the RTLS study at Incliva.

Table 21.1. General characteristics of the sepsis patients in the prospective study.

	Total (%)	Discharged alive (%)	In-Hospital mortality	Mortality in 3 months	*p* value
Total (201)	267 (100,0)	163 (56,5)	79 (31,5)	30 (12,0)	
Gender (male)	108 (53,7)	55 (27,3)	34 (16,9)	19 (9,5)	NS
Age (SD)	77 (11,9)	72,7 (10,9)	81,3 (12,3)	81,2 (11,3)	0,029
Diabetes	74 (37,0)	41 (20,5)	26 (13,0)	7 (3,5)	NS
Vital Signs:					
Temperature	37,5 ± 15,0	37,5 ± 1,4	37.0 ± 1,6	36.8 ± 1,2	0,021
SaO2 mmHg	91,9 ± 6,1	93,0 ± 5,0	92,0 ± 6,0	90,0 ± 9,0	0,011
FiO2 mmHg	0,26 ± 0,1	0,24 ± 0,11	0,29 ± 0,17	0,28 ± 0,14	0,016
Systolic BP (mmHg)	107 ± 29	109 ± 29	100 ± 30	108,0 ± 28,0	NS
Diastolic BP (mmHg)	61 ± 18	64 ± 18	62 ± 19	61 ± 17	NS
Heart rate (beats/min)	103 ± 25	100 ± 22	109 ± 29	99 ± 25	0,034
Respiratory rate ≥ 22 (resp/min)	72 (52,9)	33 (24,3)	29 (21,32)	20 (5,6)	0,013
Glasgow scale ≤ 13	64 (35,6)	20 (11,1)	42 (18,9)	11 (5,6)	<0,001

Table 21.2a. Main transition times obtained from the EMR before implementing RTLS system. Abbreviations: **IT-FT:** start to end of triage; **FT-PCM:** end of triage to the first medical contact/consultation; **PCM-O:** first medical contact/consultation to arrival in observation area; **O-I:** time from arrival in observation area to transfer to another hospital ward.

Time (min)	IT-FT	FT-PMC	PMC-O	O-I
Average	12,05	2,47	19,41	620,97
Median	8,00	2,00	7,00	541,00
SD	11,23	3,05	32,87	388,27

Table 21.2b. Main transition times obtained from the EMR before implementing RTLS system. Abbreviations: **A-ATB:** admission in ED to first antibiotics in observation room; **A-F:** Admission to ED to first IV fluids in observation room **A-F:** admission to ED to first IV fluids in observation room were calculated; as well as **A-AS:** admission to lab workup and **A-HC:** admission to taking blood cultures were calculated.

Time (min)	A-ATB antibiotics	A-F fluids	A-AS blood test	A-HC blood culture
Average	113,49	103,84	58,93	140,31
Median	53,00	53,00	41,00	56,00
SD	132,97	144,58	60,15	202,82

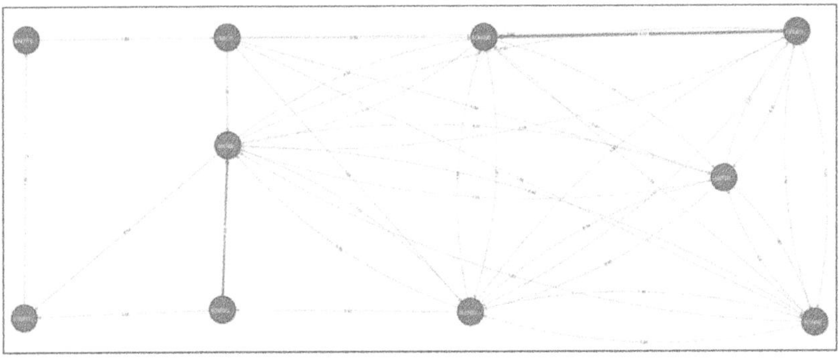

Figure 21.5. Real transition of patients.

Table 21.3. Times calculated with EMR timestamps were the following (retrospective part). Abbreviations: **A:** admission; IT: start of triage; **FT:** end of triage; **PMC:** first medical contact/consultation; **AS:** obtaining blood for lab test; **ATB:** administration of antibiotics; **HC:** obtaining blood for cultures; **F:** starting intravenous fluids; **O:** arrival in observation room; **I:** transfer to another hospital ward.

Time (min)	A-IT	IT-FT	FT-PMC	PMC-O	O-I	PMC-AS	O-AS	PMC-F	O-F	O-ATB	A-I
Average	8.0	2.0	5.0	34.0	340.0	15.0	18.0	17.0	21.0	21.5	378.0
Median	6.6	2.0	12.0	74.8	245.4	7.9	72.0	54.6	80.1	84.5	251.4
SD	9.4	2.7	8.6	52.3	371.7	15.7	38.1	36.6	39.8	43.3	431.6

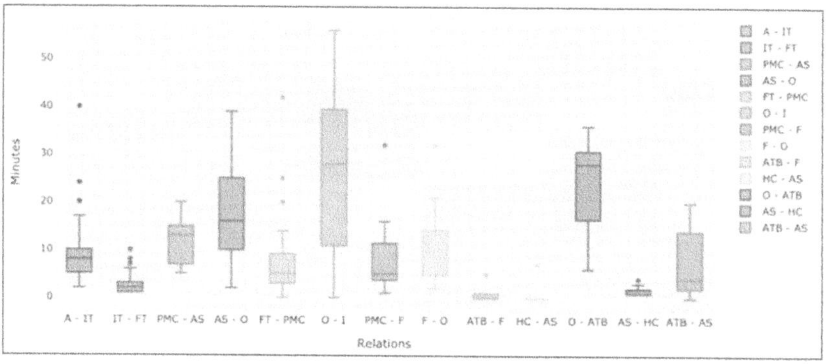

Figure 21.6. Graphical image (dashboard) of the distribution of times. Abbreviations: **A:** admission; **IT:** start of triage; **FT:** end of triage; **PMC:** first medical contact/consultation; **AS:** obtaining blood for lab test; **ATB:** administration of antibiotics; **HC:** obtaining blood for cultures; **F:** starting intravenous fluids; **O:** arrival in observation room; **I:** transfer to another hospital ward.

21.3.2 First Approach: Assessment Using EMR (Retrospective Study)

The transitions identified are shown in Figure 21.5, and the times obtained from the EMR are in Table 21.3 and Figure 21.6.

Having the transitions detected above, the Boxplot of Figure 21.6 allows the user to visualize the time distribution between stages in the workflow and detect anomalies in time measures. For example:

- O-I transition is the transition with a higher variability and a greater mean time.
- FT-PMC has three anomalies (outliers = dots) for the time required.
- ATB-AS has an asymmetric distribution for time which means that usually it requires a lower quantity of time, but sometimes, the required time could increase considerably.

In an analysis done on the EMR data of the patients included in the study, it was possible to understand the correlation between all the transition stages of the pathway. Looking at the EMR data also provides insights into clinical steps that cannot be monitored using RTLS (such as administration times of intravenous fluids or antibiotics). Figure 21.7 provides an overview of the correlation between the different stage transitions of the sepsis pathway. Where negative values mean that spending more time in one of the contrasted transitions implies requiring less time for the other.

The following graphs of Figures 21.8 and 21.9, from the prospective part of the study, allow for the visual identification of the parts of the process that require more time and the ones where there's a greater possibility for improvements.

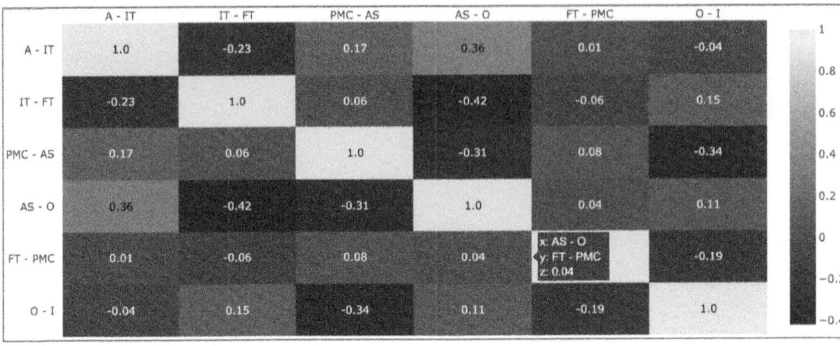

Figure 21.7. Correlation between stages of the sepsis pathway. Abbreviations: **A:** admission; **IT:** start of triage; **FT:** end of triage; **PMC:** first medical contact/consultation; **AS:** obtaining blood for lab test; **ATB:** administration of antibiotics; **HC:** obtaining blood for cultures; **F:** starting intravenous fluids; **O:** arrival in observation room; **I:** transfer to another hospital ward.

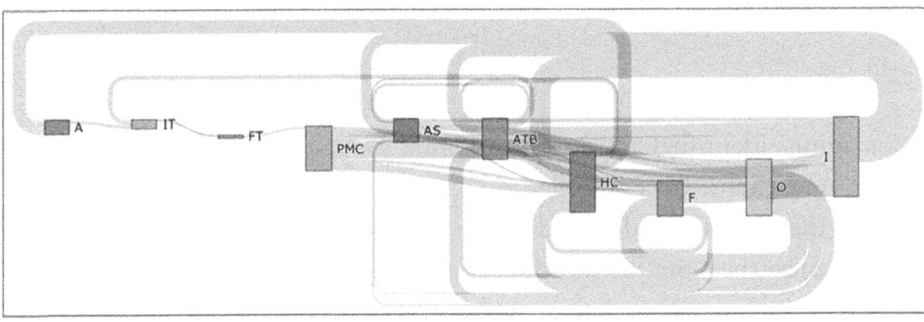

Figure 21.8. Mean time required per directed transition. Abbreviations: **A:** admission; **IT:** start of triage; **FT:** end of triage; **PMC:** first physician contact; **AS:** lab tests; **ATB:** antibiotics; **HC:** blood cultures; **F:** intravenous fluids; **O:** observation room; **I:** admission hospitalization.

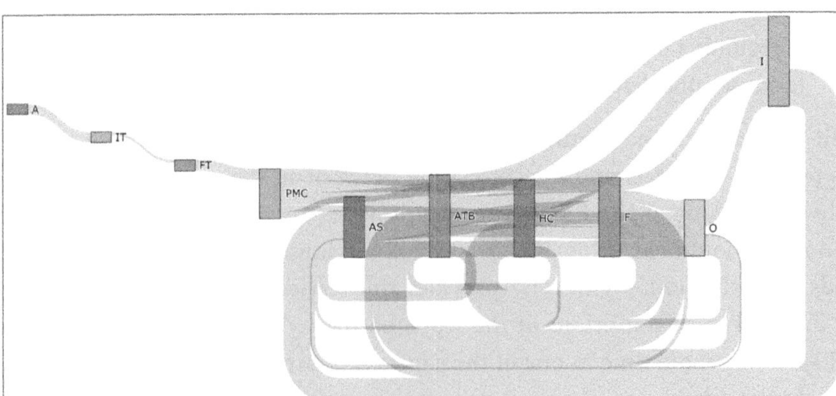

Figure 21.9. Standard deviation between transitions. Abbreviations: **A:** admission; **IT:** start of triage; **FT:** end of triage; **PMC:** first physician contact; **AS:** lab tests; **ATB:** antibiotics; **HC:** blood cultures; **F:** intravenous fluids; **O:** observation room; **I:** admission hospitalization.

Table 21.4. Times of Transitions between different RTLS areas calculated with RTLS timestamps. Abbreviations: IT-FT: start to end of triage; FT-PCM: end of triage to the first medical contact/consultation; PCM-O: first medical contact/consultation to arrival in observation area; O-I time from arrival in observation area to transfer to another hospital ward.

Time (min)	IT-FT	FT-PMC	PMC-O	O-I
Average	1.0	2.5	49.0	352.8
Median	4.6	23.2	22.5	331.2
SD	2.6	6.8	51.2	442.9

Table 21.5. Times calculated with EMR and RTLS timestamps combination. Abbreviations: A: admission; IT: start of triage; FT: end of triage; PMC: first medical contact/consultation; AS: obtaining blood for lab test; ATB: administration of antibiotics; HC: obtaining blood for cultures; F: starting intravenous fluids; O: arrival in observation room; I: transfer to another hospital ward.

Time (min)	PMC-AS	AS-O	PMC-F	F-O	O-ATB	A-I
Average	13.9	31.1	13.6	25.9	25.4	427.9
Median	10.0	26.4	60.5	29.4	30.0	324.3
SD	16.1	37.8	37.7	33.5	30.0	497.0

The Sankey graph (Figure 21.8) shows the mean time required per directed transition. The wider the edge, the greater the mean time required for the transition. It allows a visual identification of the part of the process that requires more time.

The Sankey graph (Figure 21.9) shows the standard deviation of time between transitions. The wider the edge, the greater the variability of the time found for the transition. A great dispersion indicates possibilities for improvement in the transition that should be studied.

21.3.3 Second Approach: Assessment Using Both EMR and RTLS (Prospective Study)

We observed an average difference of circa 60 minutes between the time of transfer recorded in the EMR and the actual time the patient is moved from the Observation Area of the ED to be admitted to another ward or discharged. Further investigations have shown that this disparity reflects the way in which the EMR is used at the ED. In some cases, the timestamp shown in the EMR refers to the time in which a request for transfer to another Ward was made and not the actual time of transfer.

This supports the idea that the EMR alone can lead to less accurate results for KPI and target measurements at the hospitals (Table 21.4).

Combining data sources has also been shown to have an impact on the calculation of Pathway indicators that include clinical steps of the pathway that cannot be calculated using RTLS data alone (Table 21.5).

21.4 Conclusion

We observed an average difference of circa 60 minutes between the time of transfer recorded in the EMR and the actual time the patient is moved from the observation area of the ED to be admitted to another ward or discharged. Further investigations have shown that this disparity reflects the way in which the EMR is used at the ED. In some cases, the timestamp shown in the EMR refers to the time in which a request for transfer to another ward was made and not the actual time of transfer.

This supports the idea that the EMR alone can lead to less accurate results for KPI and target measurements at the hospitals.

References

[1] Azkárate I, Sebastián R, Cabarcos E, Choperena G, Pascal M, Salas E. Registro observacional y prospectivo de sepsis grave/shock séptico en un hospital terciario de la provincia de Guipúzcoa. Medicina Intensiva. 2011. 36:250–256 (Spanish).

[2] Napolitano LM. Sepsis 2018: Definitions and guideline changes. Surgical Infections. 2018. 19: 117–125.

[3] Chaplin S. NICE guidance on the diagnosis and early management of sepsis. Prescriber. 2016. 27: 13–18.

[4] Rhee C, Klompas M. New sepsis and septic shock definitions: Clinical implications and controversies. Infectious Disease Clinics of North America. 2017. 31:397–413.

[5] Giamarellos-Bourboulis EJ, Tsaganos T, Tsangaris I, Lada M, Routsi C, Sinapidis D, Koupetori M, Bristianou M, Adamis G, Mandragos K, Dalekos GN, Kritselis I, Giannikopoulos G, Koutelidakis I, Pavlaki M, Antoniadou E, Vlachogiannis G, Koulouras V, Prekates A, Dimopoulos G, Koutsoukou A, Pnevmatikos I, Ioakeimidou A, Kotanidou A, Orfanos SE, Armaganidis A, Gogos C. Hellenic Sepsis Study Group. Validation of the new sepsis-3 definitions: Proposal for improvement in early risk identification. Clinical Microbiology and Infection. 2017. 23:104–109.

[6] Sartelli M, Kluger Y, Ansaloni L, Hardcastle TC, Rello J, Watkins RR, Bassetti M, Giamarellou E, Coccolini F, Abu-Zidan FM, Adesunkanmi AK, Augustin

G, Baiocchi GL, Bala M, Baraket O, Beltran MA, Jusoh AC, Demetrashvili Z, De Simone B, de Souza HP, Cui Y, Davies RJ, Dhingra S, Diaz JJ, Di Saverio S, Dogjani A, Elmangory MM, Enani MA, Ferrada P, Fraga GP, Frattima S, Ghnnam W, Gomes CA, Kanj SS, Karamarkovic A, Kenig J, Khamis F, Khokha V, Koike K, Kok KYY, Isik A, Labricciosa FM, Latifi R, Lee JG, Litvin A, Machain GM, Manzano-Nunez R, Major P, Marwah S, McFarlane M, Memish ZA, Mesina C, Moore EE, Moore FA, Naidoo N, Negoi I, Ofori-Asenso R, Olaoye I, Ordoñez CA, Ouadii M, Paolillo C, Picetti E, Pintar T, Ponce-de-Leon A, Pupelis G, Reis T, Sakakushev B, Kafil HS, Sato N, Shah JN, Siribumrungwong B, Talving P, Tranà C, Ulrych J, Yuan KC, Catena F. Raising concerns about sepsis-3 definitions. World Journal of Emergency Surgery. 2018. 13:6.

[7] Maitra S, Som A, Bhattacharjee S. Accuracy of quick sequential organ failure assessment (qSOFA) score and systemic inflammatory response syndrome (SIRS) criteria for predicting mortality in hospitalized patients with suspected infection: A meta-analysis of observational studies. Clinical Microbiology and Infection. 2018. 24:1123–1129.

[8] Vincent JL, Sakr Y, Sprung CL, Ranieri VM, Reinhart K, Gerlach H, Moreno R, Carlet J, Le Gall JR, Payen D. Sepsis in European intensive care units: Results of the SOAP study. Critical Care Medicine. 2006. 34:344–353.

[9] Martin GS. Sepsis, severe sepsis and septic shock: Changes in incidence, pathogens and outcomes. Expert Review of Anti-Infective Therapy. 2012. 10:701–706.

[10] Keep J, Messmer A, Sladden R, Burrell N, Pinate R, Tunnicliff M, Glucksman E. National early warning score at emergency department triage may allow earlier identification of patients with severe sepsis and septic shock: A retrospective observational study. Emergency Medicine Journal. 2016. 33:37–41.

[11] Hargreaves D, de Carvalho JL, Smith L, Picton G, Venn R, Hodgson L. Persistently elevated early warning scores and lactate identifies patients at high risk of mortality in suspected sepsis. European Journal of Emergency Medicine. 2020. 27:125–131.

[12] Silcock D, Corfield A, Staines H, Rooney K. Superior performance of national early warning score compared with quick sepsis-related organ failure assessment score in predicting adverse outcomes: A retrospective observational study of patients in the prehospital setting. European Journal of Emergency Medicine. 2019. 26:433–439.

[13] Mellhammar L, Linder A, Tverring J, Christensson B, Boyd JH, Sendi P, Akesson P, Kahn F. NEWS2 is superior to qSOFA in detecting sepsis with organ dysfunction in the emergency department. Journal of Clinical Medicine. 2019. 8:1128.

[14] Royal College of Physicians. National Early Warning Score (NEWS): Standardising the assessment of acute-illness severity in the NHS. Report of a working party. London: RCP, December 2017.
[15] Zhang Y, Luo H, Wang H, Zheng Z, Ooi OC. Validation of prognostic accuracy of the SOFA score, SIRS criteria, and qSOFA score for in-hospital mortality among cardiac-, thoracic-, and vascular-surgery patients admitted to a cardiothoracic intensive care unit. Journal of Cardiac Surgery. 2020. 35:118–127.
[16] Green SL, Smith MTD, Cairns C, Clarke DL, Bruce J, Bekker W, Kong V, Laing GL. The combined SIRS + qSOFA (qSIRS) score is more accurate than qSOFA alone in predicting mortality in patients with surgical sepsis in an LMIC emergency department. World Journal of Surgery. 2020. 44:21–29.
[17] Augustinho FC, Zocche TL, Borgonovo A, Maggi DC, Rateke ECM, Matiollo C, Dantas-Correa EB, Narciso-Schiavon JL, Schiavon LL. Applicability of Sepsis-3 criteria and quick Sequential Organ Failure Assessment in patients with cirrhosis hospitalised for bacterial infections. Liver Int. 2019. 39:307–315.
[18] Costa RT, Nassar AP, Caruso P. Accuracy of SOFA, qSOFA, and SIRS scores for mortality in cancer patients admitted to an intensive care unit with suspected infection. Journal of Critical Care. 2018. 45:52–57.
[19] Tusgul S, Carron P, Yersin B, Calandra T, Dami F. Low sensitivity of qSOFA, SIRS criteria and sepsis definition to identify infected patients at risk of complication in the prehospital setting and at the emergency department triage. Scandinavian Journal of Trauma, Resuscitation and Emergency Medicine. 2017. 25:108.
[20] Vicent JL, Sakr Y, Sprung CL, Ranieri VM, Reinhart K, Gerlach H *et al.* Sepsis in European intensive care units: results of the SOAP study. Critical Care Med. 2006. 34(2):344–53.

DOI: 10.1561/9781638282372.ch22

Chapter 22

Technological Support for Paramedical Asset Management in a Hospital Setting: Opportunities for Efficacy Enhancement and Cost Reduction

By Job Gutteling, Heleen Nelissen and Marijke Vulink

22.1 Introduction

(Para)medical assets, such as syringe pumps, volumetric pumps, mobile 'snapshot' blood pressure/saturation monitors, IV poles, or special needs mattresses, are rarely used continuously. There are always assets 'in reserve', as they may be needed for emergencies, changing patient needs and workflow among nursing staff. However, it is usually less clear how the numbers and availability of the assets actually relate to the total number available and their physical location.

Optimal use and availability of assets can contribute to the efficiency of the medical technology department in several ways. If a smaller number of assets are required, this would lead to reduced investments and also less assets requiring maintenance.

A distinction must be made between types of medical assets: (1) relatively small or low-cost assets are typically present in bulk, e.g., perfusion or volumetric pumps and special needs mattresses, and (2) smaller numbers of more expensive, complex assets like ultrasound carts—for the latter, more specific requirements with regard to utilization apply, such as immediate availability, which is outside the scope of this project.

The bulk assets are used in many places, with a frequency dependent on variable patient needs and with potentially high peaks. Little is known about 'hoarding' assets and also departmental/ward-specific purchasing (budgets) are not necessarily known to the department of medical technology. A strong driving force is the perception of needs as opposed to actual use. Due to the large numbers of these assets, the ease with which they 'settle' in a departmental/ward storage room strongly supports that a possible efficiency gain here is at least as interesting as with the expensive assets.

Previous studies have shown that nurses can spend up to 10% of their total work time searching for misplaced paramedical assets [1].

European hospitals invest some 100 billion Euro per year in medical technology – a measurable fraction for replacing mobile equipment that has been lent to another department and not returned or which is hidden by staff in their own department to assure they have it available for urgent situations, leading to specific assets utilization as low as 30% [2–5]. In addition, costs other than purchase, such as maintenance and general operational costs, must also be associated with the number of assets available, regardless of their actual usage.

Two separate studies, using different paramedical assets and different wards, were performed in OLVG, to investigate both the flow of these assets and the usage of a centralized storage facility (nursing paramedical assets storage facility). Despite the presence of a nursing assets warehouse with a pool system, and emphatic attention to reducing the ward-level closeting, OLVG was convinced that paramedical equipment could be used more efficiently.

The goals of these studies were to assess the ability of RTLS to provide knowledge and insights from the hospital point of view into nursing workflows by the implementation of an area-wide track and trace system. Secondary goals focus on the ability to implement and support the RTLS infrastructure in a vibrant environment and use Big Data technology for analysis.

The hypothesis in the OLVG is that RTLS can show that the number of bulk paramedical devices can be significantly reduced by device tracking.

22.2 Methods and Materials

Two studies were done successively. For simplicity, they will be described as Study 1 (pumps) and Study 2 OB-GYN ward.

The local Ethics Committee designated that project did not fall under the Medical Research Involving Human Subjects Act (non-WMO) and qualified it as a quality assessment and improvement study without clinical consequences, and therefore waived the need for informed consent. Data collected through RTLS focus on location data of assets only, and no patient data were involved. All data are securely stored on a local server at the hospital. As no patient data are involved, ethical approval was waived. The study was approved by the hospital's research board. A data-sharing agreement with Philips Research was in place to jointly work with the data.

22.2.1 Materials and Methods—Study 1: Pumps

Study 1 involved installing and use of RTLS in the central assets facility and in the halls of nine clinical wards within OLVG. The study tracked all 183 pumps resourced from the nursing warehouse and clinically used on nine nursing wards with active RFID tags (company CenTrack). These pumps, volumetric ($n = 107$), syringe ($n = 57$), and enteral feeding ($n = 19$), were monitored for 5 weeks by a dozen transmitting/receiving stations (circa one per department). No other pumps of these types were used in these departments during that time.

The stations were able to trace the position of the pumps via triangulation. A pump was defined as 'in use' when it was more than a few meters from the storage space, wherever the station was located. For the purpose of the study, it had previously been agreed with the departments that assets that are not in active use would be returned to the storage facility. In addition, every day nursing warehouse employees actively searched for assets that were not in use but had remained on the ward.

Steps in this project included:

- RTLS localization of pumps
- Active return to storage policy, supported by staff
- Analysis of pump logs to validate actual usage duration

22.2.2 Materials and Methods—Study 2: OB-GYN

Study 2 assessed the process of finding and managing mobile paramedical assets within OLVG. It sought to validate that improved productivity could be achieved by decreasing time spent looking for assets and that the hospital organization could utilize mobile assets more cost-effectively by identifying utilization patterns and by limiting surplus assets. This is by implementing an RTLS system.

Steps in this project included:

- Placement of software showing the actual location of mobile assets on the computers on wheels (COW)

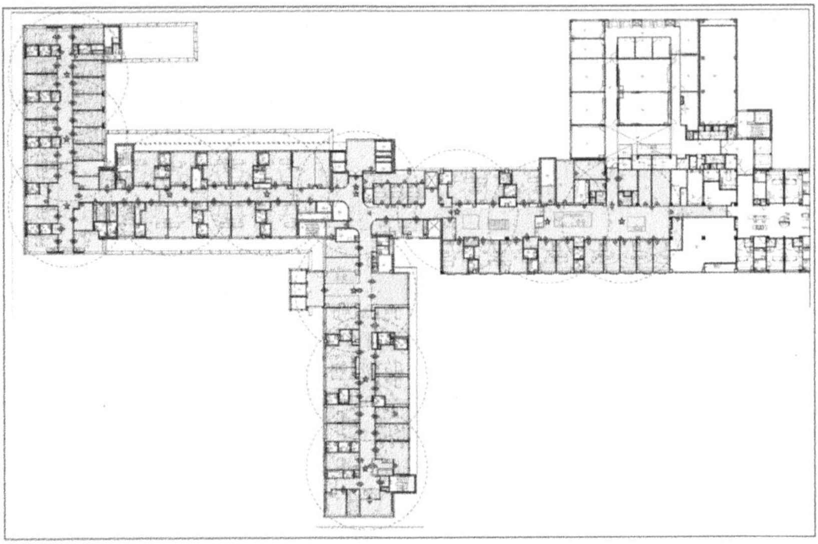

Figure 22.1. Star, device, and zone layout design at OLVG East (OB-GYN).

- Inventory of actual search time by nurses and their satisfaction using RTLS and questionnaires
- Labeling and following the distribution (usage) of mobile assets

A before–after study design was chosen. Initially, data collection was conducted through surveys and an active search time measurement for assets using RTLS. RTLS infrastructure was deployed in the OB-GYN department at location OLVG East (Figure 22.1). This department was chosen because it has a large floor area, it is a closed environment, its assets mostly do not leave the department, and it has a large number of assets and many private patient rooms with closed doors. At the department, the majority of mobile assets received a tag connecting to the RTLS. Three wards were covered by RTLS with room-level accuracy.

We employed a real-time Big Data analytics solution that received streaming data from an RTLS to track mobile assets. The RTLS technology includes InfraRed (IR), Wi-Fi, and Radio Frequency (RF)-enabled tags that are placed on any assets which needed to be tracked. An application on a COW was available for staff, especially nurses, to accurately see the real-time location of mobile assets. Daily and monthly data analytic reports were created on the location of mobile assets to be able to make real-time decisions. In Q3, 2019, a prototype of the application was introduced and the staff was trained using presentations. The project team was available by phone or e-mail for questions.

One year later (Q3, 2020), the prototype was replaced by production software. Staff was retrained at a higher frequency than with the prototype. Additionally,

Table 22.1. List of assets at the OB-GYN department by base location.

Potential for reduction in number of assets		Types of devices/assets	
		Storage room (mobile)	**Patient room (semi fixed)**
Yes		Category 1 (n = 12)	Category 2 (n = 5)
		Incubator (Type A)	CTG-device
		Incubator (Type B)	Ultrasound
		Breast pump	Delivery bed
		Volumetric pump	Blood pressure device
		CTG (wireless)	Blood pressure device (manual)
		Blood pressure device (automatic)	
		Blood pressure device (mobile)	
		Bladder scan	
		Phototherapy lamp	
		Vacuum pump	
		Heat lamp	

project staff was regularly present at the department for support related to the solution, as well as through e-mail and phone.

To evaluate our objectives, room-level location data of target mobile assets (Table 22.1: assets suitable for tracking) was continuously collected through the RTLS using IR. These data were exported and analyzed to estimate assets utilization on a daily basis. We focused on the 12 asset types that had the potential for reduction based on the number of assets in the department and their main storage location (Table 22.1, Category 1).

Time investment by staff: To monitor time invested in searching for assets, staff badges were distributed and connected to the RTLS network. Staff working at the department were instructed to wear the badge and to press the button when they started searching for an asset and again when they found what they were looking for. Two periods of data collection were conducted with these RTLS badges. Feedback on the results was provided on a daily basis. In addition, surveys were used to evaluate the time invested and subjective staff satisfaction with efficacy (Figure 22.2).

Utilization of assets was estimated using the asset's location information by defining that assets were in use when they were in a patient room. For this assessment, we looked at the number of assets currently available in the department and the number of assets simultaneously in use. Note this was a selection of the paramedical assets available with the OB-GYN department.

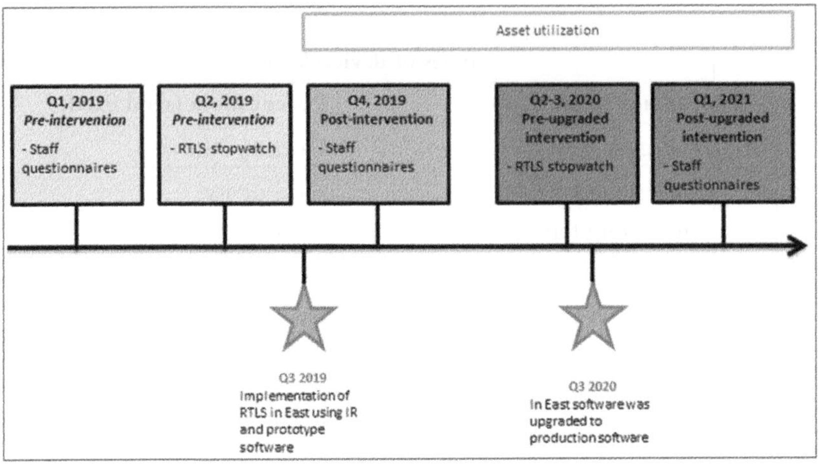

Figure 22.2. Timeline RTLS (RTLS data on COW).

Real-time location on COW: To facilitate staff in finding assets, we placed prototype software (pre-intervention) on the COW. Prior to this, surveys were conducted and search time was measured through RTLS badges. The software enabled staff to see the location of the assets in real-time. After the intervention was implemented, a second round of surveys was conducted (post-intervention).

Device usage: To calculate the usage of, e.g., a pump, the following calculation strategy was used: a department that uses an infusion pump for 8 hours during one a day and then puts it back in the storage room for 16 hours generates a usage rate of 33% for this pump.

22.3 Results

The concept of tracking mobile assets in terms of paramedical devices was readily accepted and recognized as logical by OLVG. Cooperation was without resistance. Technically, the RTLS systems worked well, compliance with badge wearing was acceptable, and staff were interested in the concept and feedback.

22.3.1 Study 1

22.3.1.1 RTLS localization of pumps

Table 22.2 shows that the utilization of the pumps is not optimal. The volumetric infusion pump is best utilized at an average of 65%. This is significantly higher than the syringe and enteral feeding pump, although clinically one would expect that therapy would continue on a 24/7 basis.

Table 22.2. Utilization rate of pumps during the measurement period.

Pump type	Week 1	Week 2	Week 3	Week 4	Week 5	Average
Volumetric infusion pump	65%	65%	62%	66%	67%	65%
Syringe pump	39%	37%	37%	33%	40%	37%
Enteral feeding pump	25%	23%	27%	29%	26%	26%

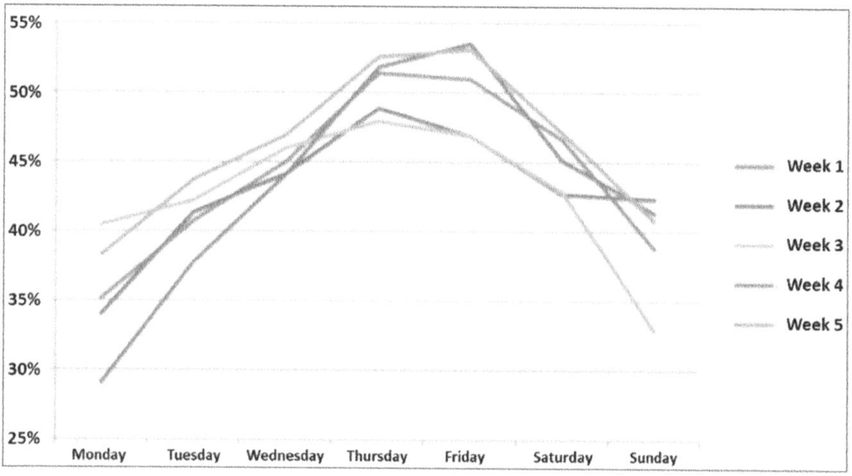

Figure 22.3. Variability of usage during one week for volumetric infusion pumps.

A striking aspect of the results is the variability during the week: utilization is low on Monday, rising during the week, and then falling again at the weekend (Figure 22.3). A possible explanation for this is that more patients are admitted during the week and they are then allowed to go home at the weekend, after which the influx will start again from Monday.

22.3.1.2 Active return to storage policy, supported by staff

In addition, a day/night pattern was sought, but this turned out to be almost a constant, probably because most therapy continues during the nightly hours. It should be noted that no active searches were done during the night for unused pumps, which might have caused an overestimation of the usage rate. Despite the careful methodology, a certain uncertainty remained about the utilization of the equipment being traced from the RTLS data. A pump present in a patient's room is not necessarily in active use and proactive removal and return to the storage facility only took place during office hours.

The three types of pumps are not used equally in the different departments (see Table 22.3).

Table 22.3. Use per type of pump per department.

	Volumetric infusion pump			Syringe pump			Enteral feeding pump		
Department	Avg.	Lowest	Highest	Avg.	Lowest	Highest	Avg.	Lowest	Highest
Nursing ward 1	3,9	2,1	6,1	6,4	2,3	9,7	0,4	0,0	1,0
Nursing ward 2	5,8	2,2	11,6	4,6	2,7	9,4	0,9	0,0	2,0
Nursing ward 3	7,7	3,7	12,2	4,2	1,9	6,3	1,9	0,3	3,7
Nursing ward 4	2,8	1,1	5,0	1,3	0,0	2,8	1,0	0,0	4,0
Nursing ward 5	11,1	6,9	17,3	3,8	2,0	5,2	2,0	0,0	3,7
Nursing ward 6	19,2	12,8	23,7	2,5	1,5	4,2	1,1	0,0	2,6
Nursing ward 7	1,4	0,0	3,5	5,9	2,2	8,6	2,5	0,0	4,5
Nursing ward 8	7,7	5,2	11,0	4,0	1,3	7,5	1,2	0,0	3,0
Nursing ward 9	5,7	2,6	9,4	1,0	0,0	2,9	0,7	0,0	1,9
Nursing	9,5	5,5	11,6	7,2	4,0	10,0	3,4	1,3	4,6

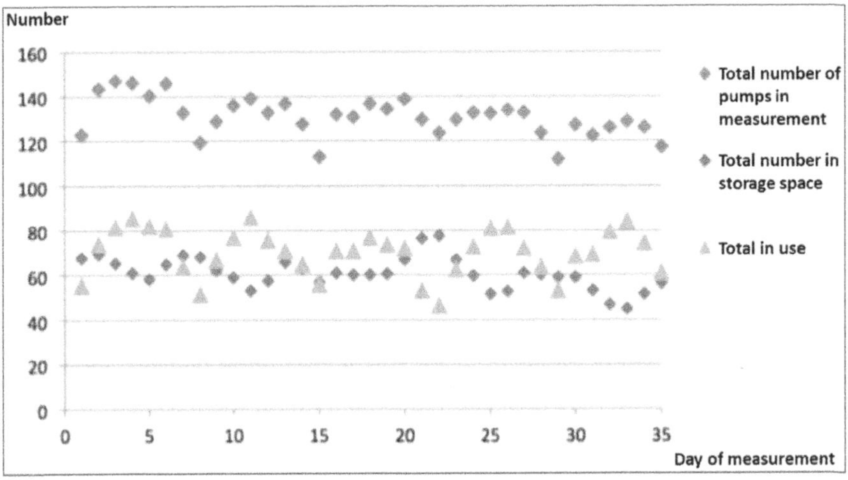

Figure 22.4. Actual pumps in circulation and use per day of measurement.

Figure 22.4 shows that the actually required (total) amount of pumps varies much less than would be suspected on the basis of the department-related lowest and highest values (from Table 22.3). There are between 46 and 86 pumps in use every day and between 45 and 78 pumps in a storage room. Based on these figures, it should be possible to take such a quantity of pumps out of circulation that the number in storage areas is minimal. However, this requires a system that allows departments to quickly obtain a pump if needed, to avoid unnecessary search times.

22.3.1.3 Analysis of pump logs to validate actual usage duration

The log files for a period of 2 weeks during the study of a random sample of 47 pumps were accessed and downloaded. The log files have a capacity for more than 24 days, depending on usage (each log has a fixed number of lines). From these log files, it can be calculated when and how much time a pump has actually been used.

On average, this usage appears to be 37% of the total time in the downloaded period. This varied greatly per pump from 6% to 74%. This suggests that the RTLS estimate of 65% overall utilization for these pumps is high. However, note that the study was designed to investigate the parallel usage of pumps, as this could be an independent limiting factor in the potential for reduction.

Study 1 suggests that there is an overabundance of pumps available and that centralized storage is a strong strategy. Discipline to avoid localized hoarding and returning the pump whenever it is not in use requires more support.

22.3.2 Study 2 in the OB-GYN Setting

22.3.2.1 Placement of Find-it software showing the actual location of mobile assets on the COW

Through surveys and communications, we were informed that utilization of the find-it software was limited. A significant departmental organization and structural change just before the introduction of the asset management system software in the COW may have been distracted from its use. Searching for mobile devices was suggested to be less of an issue following these changes. Before the change, the obstetric department and the neonatology department shared three wings, and assets were used on all wings. After the change, one ward was no longer used by the department and the obstetric and the neonatology care received their own wards. As a result, the assets were less susceptible to sharing and moving around. Moreover, assets were given a designated storage location per ward.

Because of this low utilization and a planned upgrade of the software, it was decided to conduct a second assessment on search time with the RTLS badges before the software upgrade. This also enabled data quality improvement. After the upgraded intervention, a third round of surveys was conducted (post-upgraded intervention). Figure 22.5 shows a print-screen of the layout of the upgraded intervention.

22.3.2.2 Asset tracking

An animation video on how the RTLS solution was implemented at OLVG can be found on the BigMedilytics website [6].

In the post-upgrade, monitoring of a period of 6 months estimated efficiency in Category 1 asset utilization as low averaging around 41% overall (i.e., the breast

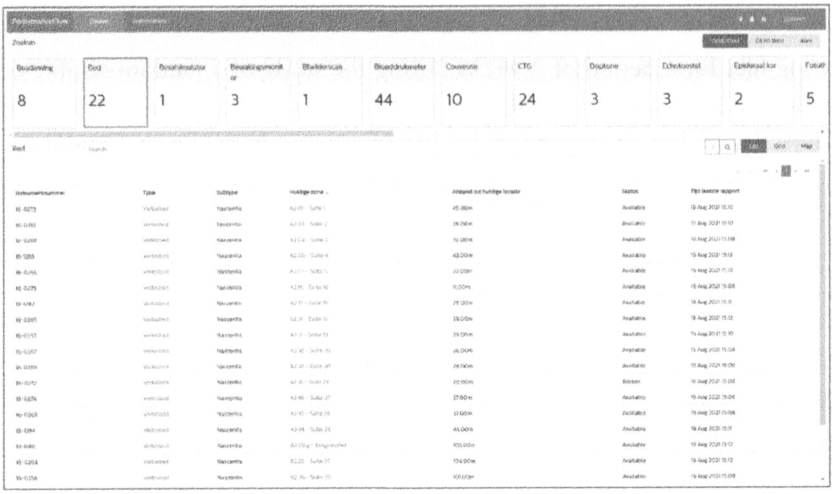

Figure 22.5. Print-screen of the upgraded solution (PerformanceFlow).

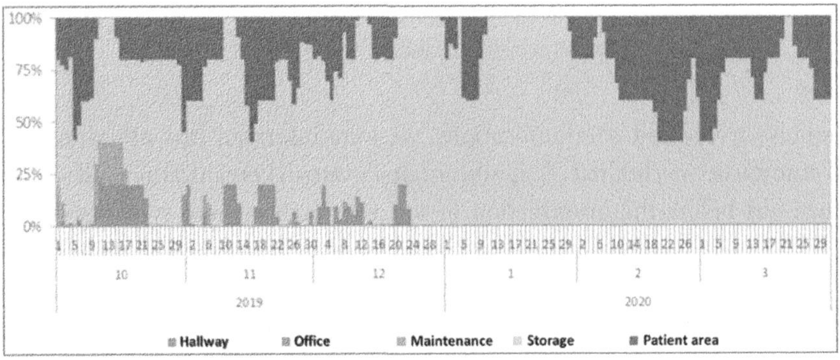

Figure 22.6. Average daily location information for incubator type B.

pump). We observed that, for 5 of the 12 asset types, all these assets could be in use simultaneously.

Figure 22.6 shows the location data of one asset type (incubator type B). The graph can be generated for any asset type, single asset or combination of assets. It distinguishes five locations: hallway, office, maintenance, storage, and patient room, and shows the percentage of time these assets were in each of the locations.

Table 22.4 shows the results of four asset types as an example. We choose to show these assets as an example as they are in a storage room when they are not in use and the initial investment is expensive. Based on this example, a potential saving of €82.500 was identified. When looking at all 12 asset types, potential cost savings could be as high as €93.000, a full 30% of the total asset value in this department.

In addition to the 12 Category 1 asset types, there are five additional Category 2 asset types that have the potential to reduce in number. These assets, for example,

Table 22.4. Asset utilization for four asset types over a period of 6 months.

	# of assets	Costs per asses	Average time in patient room	Maximum assets in patient rooms at the same time		Potential reduction	
			%	*n*	(%)		
Incubator (Type A)	4	€25.000	2%	2	50%	2	€50.000
Incubator (Type B)	5	€17.500	22%	4	80%	1	€17.500
Breast pump	20	€1.500	41%	14	70%	6	€9.000
Volumetric pump	7	€2.000	8%	4	57%	3	€6.000
					Total	**12**	**€82.500**

Table 22.5. Self-reported search times through surveys.

	Pre-intervention	Post-intervention	Post-upgraded intervention
# Searches per shift per nurse	0,6	0,5	0,5
Duration per search per nurse	3,6 minutes	4,7 minutes	4,3 minutes
Total search time per shift for shift staff	11,9 minutes	14,5 minutes	13,5 minutes

a CTG and echo device, are generally fully prepared and ready for use in patient rooms for acute situations, even if they are not in use. Only RTLS location data to estimate asset utilization are therefore not possible. Potential remediation could be to cross-reference whether a patient was in the acute care room and/or to access data logging files with the specific assets.

22.3.2.3 Inventory of actual search time by nurses and their satisfaction using RTLS and questionnaires

Using questionnaires, the average self-reported search time for the breast pump, CTG device, incubator, infusion pump, phototherapy device, and resuscitation table remained unchanged during the study (Table 22.5). Forty pre-intervention surveys were completed. Sixteen and 27 post-intervention and post-upgraded intervention surveys were completed, respectively.

Separately, two search time experiments were conducted using RTLS, one before the intervention and one after the (prototype) intervention. During the

Table 22.6. Queries used in the staff satisfaction experiments. Their responses were free text.

1	I am satisfied in how the use of mobile devices is organized in the department
2	I always find a mobile device immediately when I need it
3	To do my job well there are always enough mobile devices in the department
4	I can perform my work better when I would spend less time looking for mobile devices
5	At the end of my shift, I often feel flustered because I couldn't easily find mobile devices
6	I get enough information to quickly find mobile device
7	I get enough information to know if a device is available or still in use
8	The information I get about the location of mobile devices is reliable
9	They way we handle mobile devices in the department can be imporoved

first experiment, 146 searches were registered, with an average of 13.7 minutes per search. This compared to 24 searches in the second experiment, with an average search time of 4.9 minutes per search.

22.3.2.4 Increase staff satisfaction in using mobile assets

Surveys on staff satisfaction were conducted at the same time as the search time surveys. Table 22.6 shows the questions that were used to calculate an average staff satisfaction score on a scale from 1 to 10. Questions were completed on a 5-point Likert scale. The results show that staff satisfaction in handling mobile assets slightly increased during the study from 4.9 (N = 59) pre-intervention, to 6.1 (N = 17) post-intervention and 6.3 (N = 29) post-upgraded intervention.

22.3.2.5 Labeling and following the distribution (usage) of mobile assets

The main metric of interest when assessing assets is the utilization of all assets of a particular type across time (utilization score). Utilization information allows a hospital to determine whether they are under- or overstocked on a particular asset type. The utilization score can be calculated by measuring the total time a class of assets is in storage over a particular timeframe. A utilization metric was calculated per each individual asset and averaged over the entire group to form the final metric for that asset class.

In Figure 22.7, an example of (daily) utilization can be seen in the (upper)purple line. Due to the nature of RTLS data, the graph contains more data for context. The red line shows the number of assets available to calculate the metric.

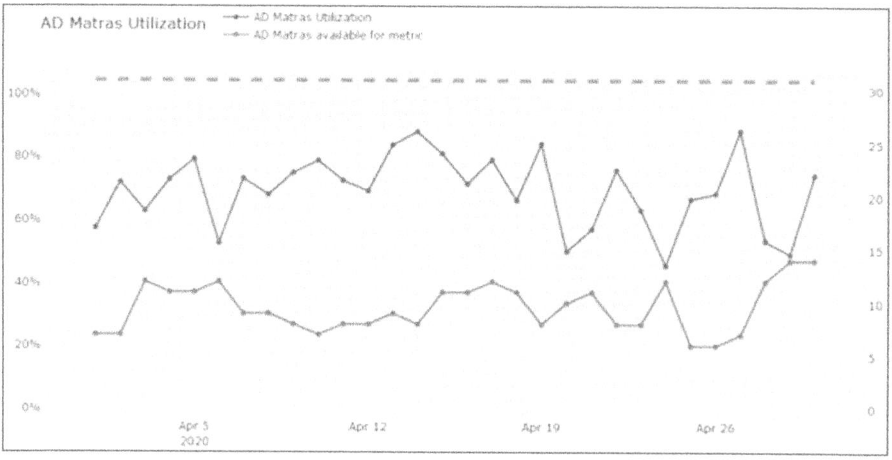

Figure 22.7. Utilization of anti-decubitus mattresses (purple line), assets available for the calculation of the metric (red line), and the maximum supply (blue dotted line). The low number available for calculation may indicate low reliability in the calculation.

It often happens that there are not enough data to reliably report a utilization metric for a particular asset. A common reason for this is so-called 'occlusion' (i.e., due to the covering of the IR sensor: the RTLS system knows the asset is within the system but cannot accurately define its localization. This is due to the different types of signals used). As utilization is reported as a percentage, it is crucial that the number of assets that this percentage is applied to is also known.

22.3.2.6 Time spent in room metric

While utilization gives information regarding the usage of (a class of) devices, it may also be useful to know the total time an asset spent in different types of rooms. This offers a lower level of granularity to the movement patterns of assets.

Additionally, this view is a nice alternative to room-based utilization when the assets rarely change rooms. For example, some ultrasound devices are always in specific (acute care) patient rooms. Therefore, using location to determine utilization is ineffective. However, it may still be useful to view the distribution of assets across rooms to spot anomalies. In Figure 22.8, each bar represents one unit of time (i.e., hour) and is split into multiple room types. Each asset is assigned by the majority of time spent in one room in each unit of time. The final result is that the bar then shows the distribution of assets (of the same type) across room types.

Similarly to the previous graph, there is a line to show the assets available for the analysis. In this case, this same information is also represented by the 'Missing time' category of the bar.

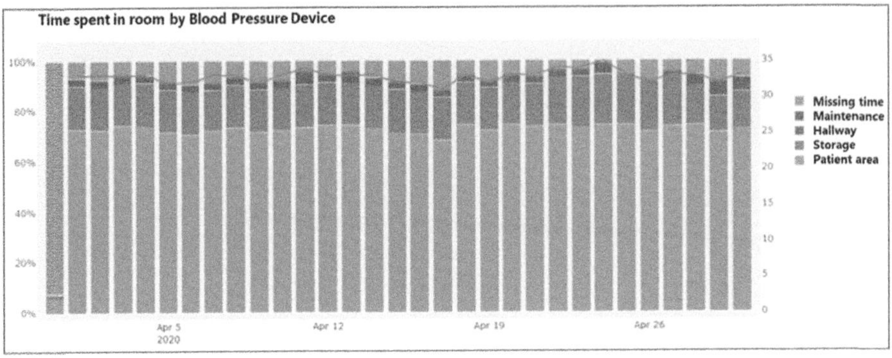

Figure 22.8. The time spent in different room types of blood pressure cuffs.

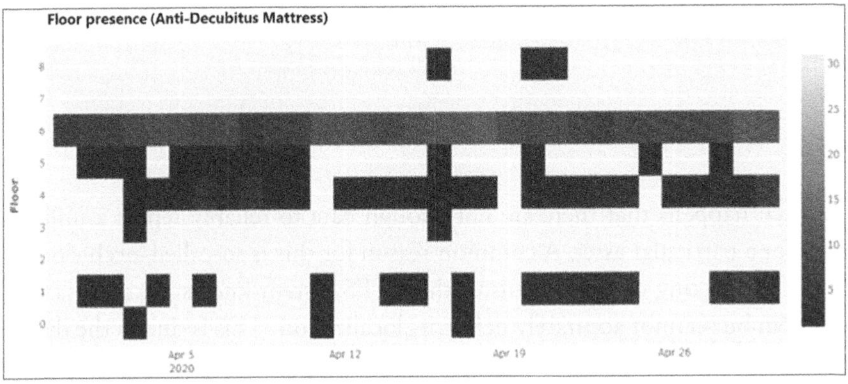

Figure 22.9. The number of mattresses staying predominantly on each floor. The bar on the right shows color coding for the duration.

22.3.2.7 Floor presence

Another potentially useful insight regarding assets is floor distribution. Often, asset types are shared across multiple departments and these departments may be on different floors. This graph allows visualization of how this spread across floors may evolve over time. As in Figure 22.9, the floor per asset is determined by the majority of the time spent somewhere by each asset. For example, if an asset spent more than 50% (on a per hour granularity that means over 30 minutes) of its time on the third floor, then it would be assigned to the third floor on the graph below.

22.3.2.8 Floor transition graph

To further attempt to understand the movement of assets across floors, it may be useful to understand not only where they most often are but also which floors they transition to most often. This is visualized using a network graph from RTLS data. For example, by integrating the 'floor presence' graph from Figure 22.10, we can

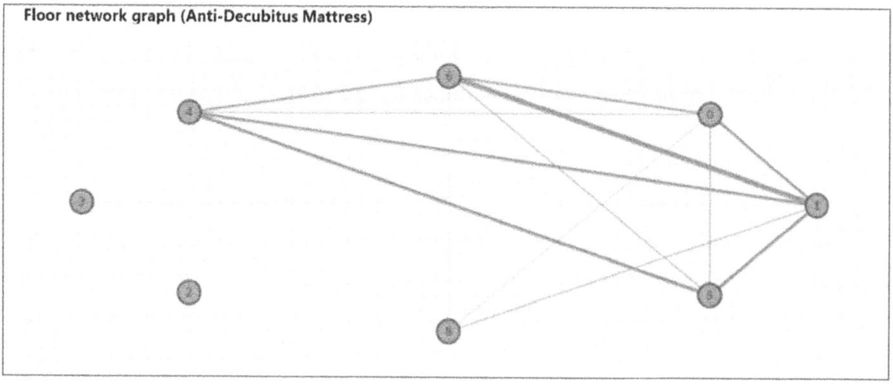

Figure 22.10. The floor transition graph for anti-decubitus mattresses.

see that most of the assets on the first floor come from the sixth floor. This may be an inefficiency in the process that could be worth pointing out to clinical staff.

22.4 Discussion

22.4.1 Study 1: Asset Management

The RTLS system worked well but should have had a higher granularity, to reduce or alleviate search for the assets to return them to the storage area. In addition, while RTLS shows location, it does not show usage in our study design. Pushing a button on the RTLS asset tag when the use is actually started and twice when the use is stopped could alleviate this concern but was not designed for our study. Overall acceptance of the concepts, the need, and the use of the RTLS system was high.

Knowing that the resources are not used fully efficiently is one thing, but attaching consequences to it is a separate challenge entirely. For example, an average of one and a half feed pumps were used full time per department, but in a department itself, that number can still vary from an average of less than one pump to four pumps per day. For syringe pumps the spread is between 1.0 and 7.2 per department and for volumetric pumps even between 1.4 and 19.2. This means that, even if there are 'too many' pumps in total, a department with only one pump cannot easily return it.

Another problem with interpreting the data in this way is that the lowest and highest values per department are measured independently of time. For example, sometime in the measurement period, departments 1 and 2 had the busiest periods with 6.1 and 11.6 volumetric pumps in use, respectively. However, this probably was not on the same day. Figure 22.4 shows that the various departments partly complement each other in terms of equipment utilization. One aspect that needs to be addressed is the 'occlusion' (the blockage of a tag signal) as this makes data analysis difficult, requires one-by-one analysis, and limits a big data approach.

22.4.2 Nursing Warehouse

The results also support the potential return on investment for the careful development of centralized nursing warehouse(s) in helping to reduce the number of assets required. In a model where each department would have a fixed number of its own, it is logical to expect that the highest values from Figure 22.2 would be needed at least. After all, these are the actual pumps required, as evidenced by a measurement period of 5 weeks (longer measurement would probably have yielded an even higher number). Summing up all the high values across the departments yields an enormous number of 209 pumps, while Figure 22.3 shows that the actual maximum is 147, a difference of 62 pumps or 30%. The one-time investment of correct location(s), support staff are likely to offer return on investment and increased satisfaction plus reduced search times for staff.

This does not alter the fact that even with a nursing warehouse, there is still more cost reduction achievable by monitoring and optimizing the use of pumps. Probably, this is certainly the case at the OLVG; this requires a new working method in which pumps are ordered and returned instead of maintaining small storage spaces locally. A system based on active RTLS tags with which users can see where a pump can be obtained will have great added value.

22.4.3 Study 2: OB-GYN

The RTLS study in the OB-GYN and neonatology setting is seen as successful, despite organizational changes that impacted ground area and staff team needs and wants. The study was welcomed and generally accepted by staff in answering questions and wearing the RTLS badges.

The RTLS data provided us with new insights into asset utilization which can help with future investments in mobile assets. Through the data, we identified a potential overall cost reduction of €93.000, which is 30% of the total value of the asset types studied. This may be a conservative estimate as utilization may be optimized, for example, by scheduling and better insights into actual use in addition to location. Yearly maintenance costs – averaging 6–10% of the asset value – would also decrease.

From the evaluation of staff search time and satisfaction, we learned that change management is important when rolling out an asset-tracking application. We observed low engagement and usage of the system by department staff for software on the COW as opposed to the willingness to participate. Moreover, a change management system can continuously monitor the process to directly intervene when adaptations are needed. During our study, we experienced that the departmental organization and structure changed before the introduction of the asset management system. This may be a factor in the low engagement with the COW system as the search area became smaller (and walking around is also a social-contact moment).

During the first round of the active search time experiment with RTLS, we learned that close monitoring of the data is needed to develop and maintain accurate results. During the analysis, we found a large number of unsuccessful searches, e.g., very short (<30 seconds) and very long (>30 minutes). During the second round, we improved our data collection by continuously monitoring the data through the RTLS. Our data quality became more realistic, but the number of searches also decreased. As the utilization of the intervention was low, we do not assume that the reduction in searches was impacted by the intervention. We observed a slight increase in staff satisfaction with handling mobile assets during the study.

22.4.4 Overall Limitations

Because the range of the transmitting/receiving stations was limited, a small part of each of the participating departments was out of range. As a result, the total number of (visible) devices in the results is lower than the actual total number of devices with a tag. Correction was attempted by taking a random sample in which devices seemingly not being counted were manually traced. Some 50% of these assets turned out to be in use.

Importantly, a tag cannot detect whether a device is on or off. In this way, a small overestimation of the utilization rate may arise, when some equipment is wrongly earmarked as in use for a time. However, this is not a problem for this pilot, as it was expected that there would still be sufficient profit to be made.

22.5 Conclusion

The first study with asset tracking with its goals of developing and implementing RTLS and using this system makes the process of finding and managing mobile medical equipment (assets) within a hospital more efficient. Productivity was to be improved by ensuring that staff invested less time looking for equipment and that a hospital utilizes its mobile assets in a more cost-effective fashion, e.g., by reducing unnecessary equipment, distributing, and/or scheduling usage. This will be accomplished by using an Asset Finding application that receives real-time data from an RTLS system to track mobile assets. In this case, electronic asset tags are placed on the assets that need to be tracked.

The study was able to demonstrate that RTLS can be used as a valuable tool in optimizing asset management, making visible staff work in finding assets, and in search for improvements. After establishing search times and utilization levels for the initial situation (baseline), as an intervention, a dedicated Asset Finder Tool was introduced.

In the second study, technical implementation for the different goals was successful. RTLS hardware and software were installed at the OB-GYN department, and assets could be tracked successfully up to room-level accuracy. Data collected through RTLS were centrally stored and could be exported to create (monitoring) reports. Acceptance was middling.

Hospitals are dynamic environments, and when introducing an intervention, this needs to be taken into account. Adoption of the tool on the Computer On Wheels (COW) by staff was more challenging due to changing conditions at the department. Also, participation in the research was lower than expected.

Moreover, the data collection period was long, especially data collection with RTLS staff badges. We did find that staff forgot to wear the badges and to take them with them when searching. The study confirms the usability of RTLS and demonstrates the need to carefully think out the system, its locations, and ways to avoid 'occlusion' and missing data. The potential benefits in investment and maintenance costs were clearly relevant.

The medical technology department is ideally situated to be a driving force and stakeholder in these processes, as they have an overview, distance to the user group, and strong process and safety insights.

22.6 Main Learnings

Our main learnings are as follows:

- RTLS-type systems are a potentially valuable tool to gain insights into asset management, leading to cost reduction in investments and maintenance costs. The medical technology department should be recognized as a major stakeholder in this process.
- Continuous data collection to evaluate the solution and training and awareness for the solutions are needed are essential factors in the success of an RTLS solution.
- Change management needs to be in place to realize potential advantages and savings.

- RTLS infrastructure can be expanded from Wi-Fi to a more accurate (IR) system based on the needs. A thorough analysis of the needs of the institution/department (e.g., bed, room, or floor level accuracy) should be done to decide which technology should be used: Wi-Fi, IR, and/or RF.
- A platform (IoT/data-integration platform) should be in place that integrates multiple data sources and combines this with RTLS data to get in-depth utilization figures but can also be used for other applications.
- Including data from Wi-Fi areas makes it possible to assess asset utilization enterprise-wide.

References

[1] https://www.nursingtimes.net/archive/nurses-waste-an-hour-a-shift-finding-equipment-10-02-2009/.

[2] MedTech Europe, The European medical technology industry in figures, 2015.

[3] http://www.beckershospitalreview.com/hospital-management-administration/3-ways-hospitalsunintentionally-waste-money.html.

[4] Mohr JJ. BMKT 460.01: Marketing of High-Technology Products and Innovations. 2016. Syllabi. Paper 390.

[5] Nurse X, Sheer Buffoonery: How Hospitals Kill Patients, Virtualbookworm.com (2006), ISBN 9781589398948.

[6] https://www.bigmedilytics.eu/.

Section V

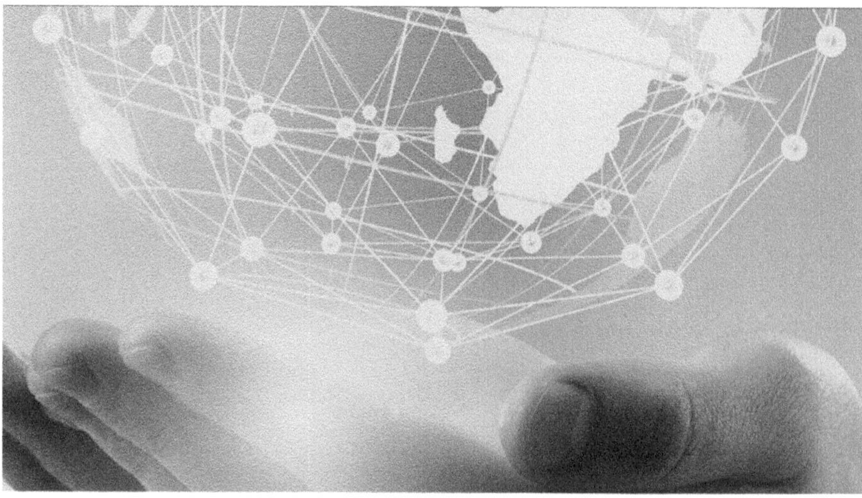

Big Data Technologies

DOI: 10.1561/9781638282372.ch23

Chapter 23

Introduction to Section V: BigMedilytics and Looking Forward

By Roland Roller

BigMedilytics (Big Data for Medical Analytics) was the largest EU-funded initiative to transform the healthcare sector. By applying state-of-the-art Big Data and AI technologies, the project intended to achieve breakthrough productivity in the health sector by reducing cost, improving patient outcomes, and delivering better access to healthcare facilities simultaneously. To do so, the project introduced 12 studies as testbeds exploring a large range of different problems and covered the three general themes: (a) Population Health and Chronic Disease Management, (b) Oncology, and (c) Industrialization of Healthcare Services. In addition to this, studies have been conducted with partners in 12 different countries. In various cases, partners from multiple countries contributed to one single study, for instance, a data provider (e.g., hospital) in one country and a technical partner to apply Big Data technologies in a different one. This, of course, increased the number of hurdles and challenges to overcome. The first section of this volume focused on the challenges associated with such cross-disciplinary and cross-jurisdiction collaboration.

The previous sections and their corresponding chapters presented the fine-grained view of the different contributing BigMedilytics studies. Each study reported the main idea, the solution, and the learnings they made. Those learnings can be valuable in initiating a similar project addressing a similar problem. On the other hand, many of the presented problems can be very study-specific. They might depend on a variety of aspects, such as certain regulations within a given country, particular company workflows that have been established over many years, and also the background and experience of the involved employees. This section instead tries to provide a more general and transversal overview of the project. More specifically, this section builds on the study-specific learnings and presents a more generally applicable overview according to different aspects. What can we learn from the experiences made?

The chapters in this section summarize the core outcomes and core learnings of the twelve study projects. The studies provided the opportunity to gather not only scientific results but also experiences and knowledge within the projects and across projects. Chapter 24 (The Interactive BigMedilytics Website) presents the BigMedilytics Blueprint Website, collected scientific results and learnings across all studies, but also transversal level, and can be explored interactively. The BigMedilytics Blueprint Website is considered one of the most crucial outcomes as it combines all relevant project data/outcomes and can be explored according to the perspective of different stakeholders, such as data scientists, patients, hospital decision makers, and privacy officers. Chapter 25 (Data Processing in Healthcare using CRISP) presents, based on the experience we made during our project, a blueprint to set up a Big Data project in healthcare. This blueprint is based on the CRISP-DM schema, a cross-industry standard process originally developed in the context of data mining. The chapter describes how CRISP-DM can be adapted to a Big Data healthcare project, including the different steps to take and which aspects need to be taken under consideration from multiple perspectives (e.g., business, legal, and technical). One of the significant features of the project was the collaboration of multiple stakeholders based on various technologies. At the same time, though, that technology can be disruptive and change the relationships between those stakeholders. Chapter 26 (Technology Acceptance in Healthcare) discusses the experience of technology acceptance during the runtime of BigMedilytics, and how traditional models of technology introduction can benefit from the experience of the project. Finally, Chapter 27 (General Learnings From the Horizon 2020 Project BigMedilytics) summarizes the key learnings across the BigMedilytics study projects. While each study presented its study-specific learnings in the previous chapters, Chapter 27 (General Learnings

From the Horizon 2020 Project BigMedilytics) presents 19 general problems, challenges, and learnings that occurred in multiple studies. Those 19 learnings are assigned to different high-level themes, namely, "general learnings," "data," "technology," and "validation," and might be valuable for future Big Data and AI projects in healthcare.

DOI: 10.1561/9781638282372.ch24

Chapter 24

The Interactive BigMedilytics Website: A Collection of Scientific Results, Best Practices, and Lessons Learned

By Holmer Hemsen, Roland Roller, Supriyo Chatterjea, Anne Marie Weggelaar-Jansen and Alexandra Muñoz Oliver

24.1 Introduction

The goal of BigMedilytics is, through the application of Artificial Intelligence (AI) technologies in combination with the analysis of Big Data, to transform Europe's healthcare sector and enhance patient outcomes and productivity. The European Commission (EC) funded BigMedilytics as a lighthouse project to foster this disruptive innovation effort, i.e., BigMedilytics should have a certain signalling effect for future projects.

One of the outcomes of BigMedilytics that stands out in comparison with similar Big Data Healthcare projects is the Interactive BigMedilytics Website. The Interactive BigMedilytics Website is a webpage that enables users to browse through a selection of aspects related to the BigMedilytics project. By navigating through the Interactive BigMedilytics Website, you cannot only find information on results and different aspects of the 12 study projects that participated in the EU lighthouse project but also read about lessons learned grouped by topics, such as ethical, legal, and privacy issues or with respect to validation, technology, and business impact.

The outcome of the BigMedilytics project consists not only of scientific articles describing concrete aspects of the application and its evaluation, e.g., system architecture, data (pre-)processing pipeline, application of (machine learning) methods, AI techniques, use of Big Data and evaluation, but it also contains more specific topics across these applications, such as ethical considerations and how compliance with relevant national and EU legislation (e.g., GDPR) can be achieved, as discussed in Chapter 3 (Using Causal Diagrams to Understand and Deal With Hindering Patterns in the Uptake and Embedding of Big Data Technology), Chapter 4 (Lessons Learned in the Application of the General Data Protection Regulation to the BigMedilytics Project), and Chapter 5 (Ethics). In addition, guiding principles, which facilitate the establishment of new healthcare projects in the domain, are incorporated by sharing practical experiences and lessons learned across the 12 studies and by disclosing certain pitfalls, for example, to establish a big data project in a hospital data scientists and medical staff have to work together. But working together requires a certain understanding of each other's field and methods and a common vocabulary to communicate with each other – an often time-consuming effort that cannot be avoided and therefore needs to be considered already in the project planning phase.

24.2 Related Work

Apart from the 12 BigMedilytics studies, various other projects have been carried out applying Big Data and AI in Healthcare. Several of them target a particular disease, for example, Big Data Analytics to improve cardiovascular diseases, [1, 2] kidney diseases, [3, 4] lung cancer, [5] or diabetes [6]. Some research also takes a specific Big Data in healthcare aspect under investigation, such as privacy and ethics or economic impact [7–10]. Hansen *et al.* present the results from a literature study on Big Data in Science and Healthcare [11]. Agrawal and Prabakaran studied Big Data initiatives in the United Kingdom and the United States and abroad to identify lessons learned and recommendations for general practice [12]. However, to the best of our knowledge, no similar website as the Interactive BigMedilytics Website exists to interactively explore the results from multiple Big Data and AI in healthcare projects including lessons learned and recommendations.

In the following, we discuss the selection of the content to present on the website and how we structured and organized it. We decided to use an existing web design template to present the content, so layout and interaction possibilities of course are predefined by this template. The choice of this particular template, among the many other templates available, is also briefly explained in the following paragraph.

24.3 Aim, Content, and Structure of the Interactive BigMedilytics Website

As already mentioned in Section 24.2, various projects have applied AI with Big Data analysis in healthcare projects. Some of them also reported lessons learned and recommendations for general practice. However, with its 12 study projects, the BigMedilytics project provides an exceptional opportunity to collect, compare, and report on lessons learned and promote recommendations across medical disciplines with an additional focus on business and privacy and ethical aspects.

The aim of the Interactive BigMedilytics Website is

- to provide users with an interactive way
  - to inspect and compare various aspects of the 12 studies carried out in BigMedilytics;
  - to read about lessons learned in BigMedilytics;
- to provide stakeholders with tailored information relevant to specific stakeholder groups;
- to link the new concepts and technologies developed within BigMedilytics to sections in a patient journey and to illustrate how these new technologies and processes can improve the healthcare system in the future;
- to support the development of future Big Data and AI in Healthcare projects.

In order to enable users of the website to compare certain aspects of the projects with each other, we asked each study participating in BigMedilytics to fill in a pre-structured template document. Via the template document, the following data on each study were collected:

- Key information: It provides information on involved partners and countries, keywords, and a task description.
- Building blocks: It contains information on system architecture including data flow, software components, and necessary hardware; processing of structured and non-structured data, containing information on data sources, data cleansing, processing of heterogeneous data streams, and real-time event detection; AI components used or developed including deep learning for NLP and image processing; and privacy and ethical issues;
- Learnings: It summarizes challenges and barriers, lessons learned, and main achievements.
- Output: A section providing information on published papers, open source, and demos.

In this way, we ensured that the projects provided comparable blocks of information.

The input for a chapter on general learnings (see also Chapter 27 – General Learnings From the Horizon 2020 Project BigMedilytics) is a direct result of the experiences of the 12 studies carried out in BigMedilytics as described in filled-in template documents, additional items that have been added manually are a result of manifold discussions within the BigMedilytics consortium. To present each stakeholder group with only relevant items, the information has been manually selected and clustered. To be able to link the new concepts and technologies developed within BigMedilytics to different stages in a patient journey, we first sketched and described a fictitious but realistic patient journey throughout four stages: 'at the GP', 'at the Hospital', 'at Home', and 'Follow-Up GP'.

In order to view the content of the website, five different entry points to inspect results, findings, and lessons learned gathered from BigMedilytics exist: 'Pilot View', 'Transversal Aspects', 'Stakeholder Perspective', 'Patient Journey', and 'General Learnings'. All views consist of a structured hierarchy of layers to be able to quickly navigate to the content of interest. In Table 24.1, the different views are presented in more detail.

24.3.1 Web Design of the Interactive BigMedilytics Website

The goal of the Interactive BigMedilytics Website is to present the selected and curated information in an interactive but also appealing and modern way. In the beginning, we discussed several web design options and prototyped some of them. A traditional, old-style, web design by simply transforming the study documents into HTML, adding menus and links between sections and studies' descriptions was quickly ruled out, because 'flexibility and efficiency of use' (Nielsen Usability #7 of usability heuristics) could not be achieved for both navigation within studies (Pilot View) and across studies (Transversal Aspects) [13]. We finally decided to use an existing web design called zoomable circular packing[i] to present study-specific information, transversal aspects between studies, such as system architecture, information relevant for a specific stakeholder group, patient trajectory-related information, and, last but not least, lessons learned throughout the BigMedilytics project. The chosen web design uses circles inside circles to represent hierarchies of information. While the outer circle and its label represent items belonging to the current level, circles inside circles represent the next level in the navigation hierarchy. Figure 24.1 shows the top layer of the Interactive BigMedilytics Website with its five different entry points for navigation.

---

i. See, for example, https://observablehq.com/@d3/zoomable-circle-packing for an implementation.

Table 24.1. The five views of the Interactive BigMedilytics Website.

Pilot View	The pilot view provides a theme-centric perspective on study-specific data. The elements of the first navigation level are arranged by study category, which is either population health and chronic disease management, oncology, or industrialization of healthcare services. At the second level, the user can choose a specific study to inspect, such as kidney disease or asset management. After selecting this study, the user can in the third level choose a particular aspect of the study to read about, which in the fourth level is shown. All studies provide an identical set of aspects that can be explored, for example, Business Aspects, Challenges and Learnings, or Achievements.
Transversal Aspects	In contrast to the Pilot View, as discussed above, the Transversal Aspects view shows the user a horizontal view (across studies) of the content. The elements of the first navigation level in this view are arranged by aspect and are similar to the third level in the pilot view but with the difference that the aspects building blocks, ethical and privacy issues, and security issues are further subdivided, so the chunks of information presented to keep a reasonable size to be inspected interactively. Building blocks, for example, is further split into the aspects data processing, system interaction, auditory and logs, Natural Language Processing, image processing, system architecture, and prediction.
Stakeholder Perspective	The Stakeholder Perspective organizes the information in such a way that relevant information for the specific target group is shown. In total, eight target groups are addressed: policymaker, hospital decision-maker, privacy officer, hospital IT/equipment, clinical staff, data scientist, health insurance, and patient. At the first navigation level, the user selects the target group of interest, and at the second level, the topic of interest. For example, policymakers can read about trustworthy AI, privacy measures, or learnings. In contrast, the information presented to data scientists is of wider scope. In addition to information about policies, also information about more technical issues such as natural language and image processing or information about access control is included for this group.
Patient Journey	The Patient Journey view organizes the information according to a realistic but fictitious patient journey and shows in the first navigation level four different stages in this journey: at the GP, at the Hospital, at Home, and Follow-up GP. After selecting a particular stage, the user can either read about studies including this stage in the patient journey or about applying BigMedilytics Technologies to this specific patient Journey stage.

(Continued)

Table 24.1. Continued

General Learnings	The General Learnings view presents lessons learned from the BigMedilytics project that are of a broader and less study-specific nature. The information presented in the first navigation level is grouped into eight thematic categories, such as Data, Technology, or Business Impact. For example, under the category Ethical, Legal, and Privacy, it is pointed out that consent gathering to use patient data is of major importance before the data can be used and analysed. Category Big Data Blueprint differs because it (a) links to the Blueprint document (see Chapter 25 – Data Processing in Healthcare Using CRISP) and (b) to a Blueprint Matrix table listing for a selection of aspects, e.g., Natural Language Processing, the studies contributed to.

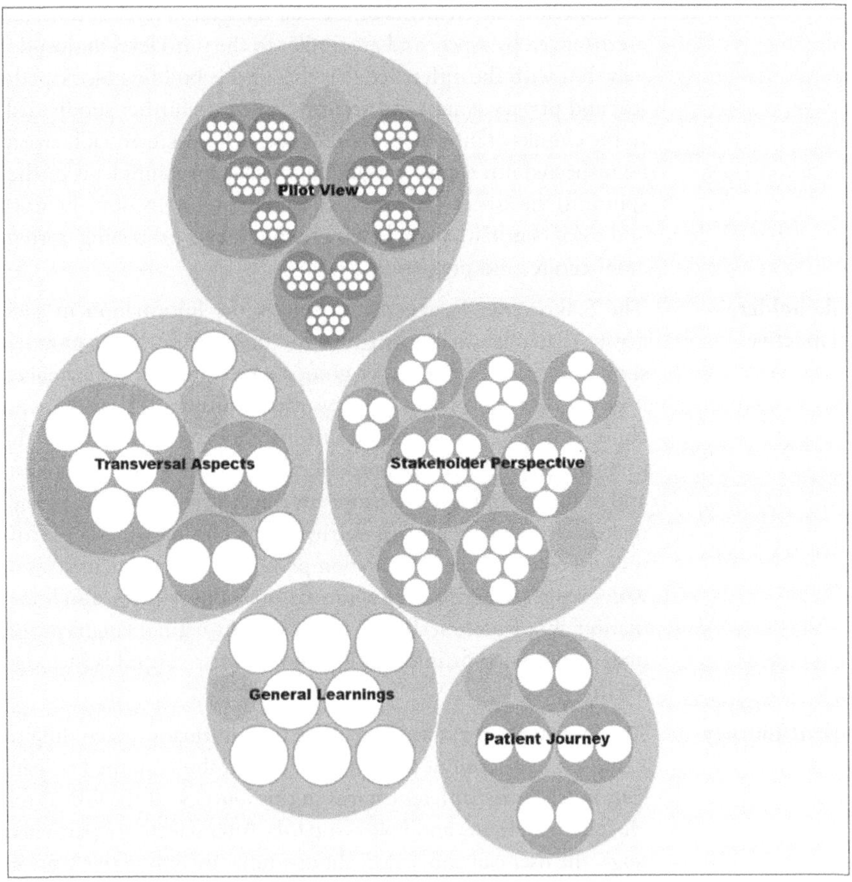

Figure 24.1. Interactive BigMedilytics website – the five different entry points to view the data.

During early tests of the Interactive BigMedilytics Website, we observed that the users anticipated the chosen web design quickly and rapidly learned how to navigate through the hierarchy to find the content of interest. But we also noticed that the web design is, especially for new users, not fully self-explanatory. Therefore, we added upfront, i.e., before showing the circular packaging design, a section with help texts, explaining the following aspects: "What is the Interactive BigMedilytics Website?", "How to navigate it?", "Who is it for?", and "What will you find?". To keep the help texts close to the interaction area (see Figure 24.1), initially, these help texts are collapsed and only the section title is visible to the user. In addition, the "How to navigate the Interactive BigMedilytics Website?" subsection provides two videos to show both the general structure of the webpage and second a tutorial on how to navigate the Interactive BigMedilytics Website. Furthermore, we slightly modified the standard zoomable circular packing web design as defined by the JavaScript library and introduced a circle with a special meaning and a distinct colour – the "About" circles. These circles only appear in the top-level view and, if selected, explain the view and its structure.

24.3.2 Structure and Content of the Interactive BigMedilytics Website

When a user clicks within a circle (see Figure 24.2), it reaches the next hierarchy level in the chosen view. Users can go back to one hierarchy level at a time by clicking into the surrounding circle (see Figure 24.3) or reach the top level of the hierarchy by clicking outside the circles area. The leaves of the navigation tree point to the content, presented in a classical, text-only, design (cf. Figure 24.2: No. 5 and 6). The web design therefore enables "user control and freedom" as Nielsen requires for good web design [13, #3].

Figure 24.2 shows a sample interaction path starting with the overview page (1), then selecting the Pilot View (2), choosing heart Population Health and Chronic Disease (3), and selecting Hearth Failure (4) and Business Aspects of this study to see the final content in (6). Please note that navigation is possible in both directions as shown in Figure 24.3. Starting with the pilot view (cf. Figure 24.1), a user can, for example, choose Oncology (2) and then inspect the next layer (3b) or go back to (2) and instead choose Population Health or Chronic Disease (3a).

The content presented in Pilot View and Transversal Aspects is based on the documents describing aspects of each study. The predefined structure has been mapped to the hierarchical web design layers, so equal sections, such as Key Information, can be accessed in a similar way within Pilot View (aspect shown for a single study) and Transversal Aspects (aspect shown for multiple studies) view. The structure presented in Pilot View and Transversal Aspects view differs slightly from the content

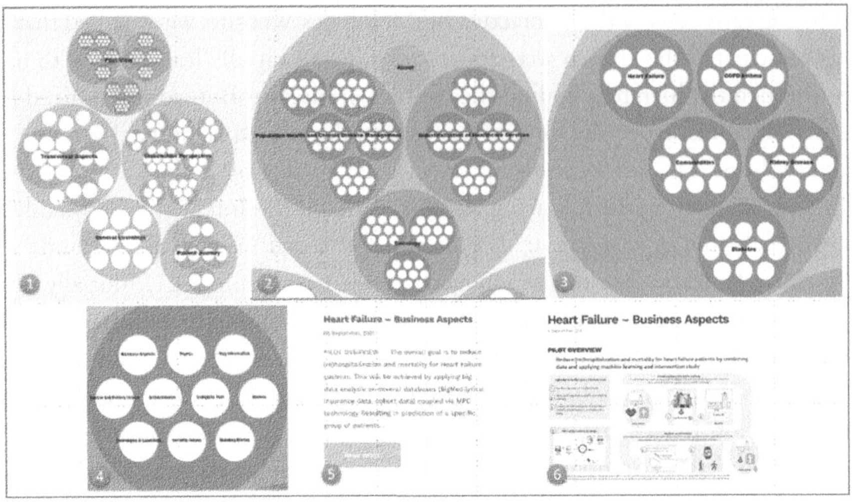

Figure 24.2. Sample Interaction - From the Top Layer (1) to Content (6).

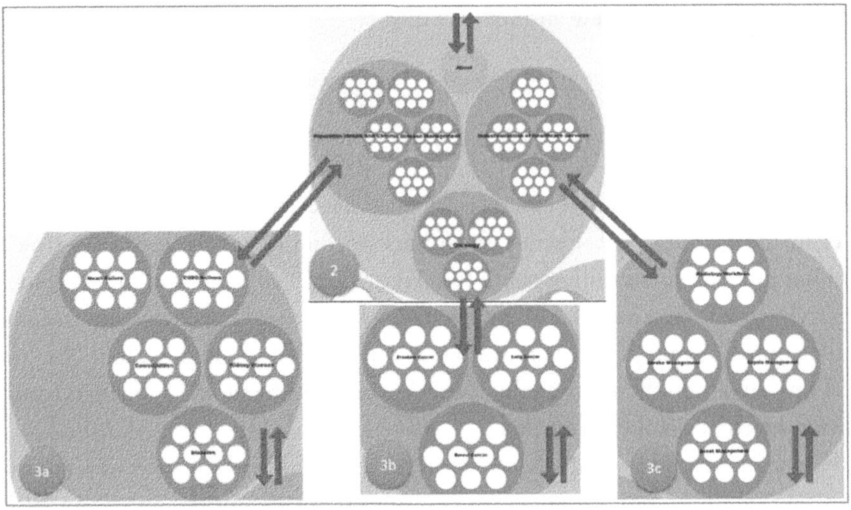

Figure 24.3. Possible forward/backward (zooming) interaction between layers.

structure in the template document (see Figures 24.4 and 24.5). This change was mainly done to balance the number of sections presented but was also necessary to make certain sections more easily to find, for example, Ethical and Privacy Issues. As, by splitting the study documents into separate content units (see Figure 24.2: No. 5 and 6.), the connection with the study itself is no longer visible, each content document is labelled with the study name in its title.

The intention of the Stakeholder Perspective is to address stakeholders in a targeted manner and provide each stakeholder with four to his/her group relevant information. We included the following stakeholder groups: Clinical Staff, Data

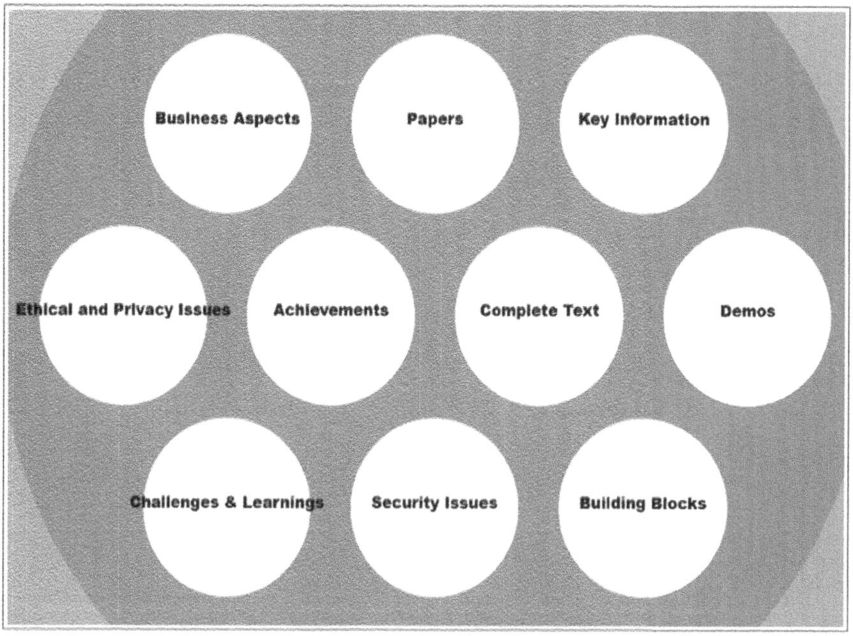

Figure 24.4. Pilot view: structure of contents.

Scientists, Health Insurance, Hospital Decision Makers, Hospital IT/Equipment, Patients, Policymakers, and Privacy Officers. For example, for stakeholders from Hospital IT/Equipment information regarding system architectures, access control, data processing, and learnings were considered relevant. In contrast, stakeholders from Privacy Officers are shown the findings with respect to trustworthy AI, privacy measures, and data protection.

To illustrate the Patient Journey, we constructed a realistic but fictitious medical case, as shown in Figure 24.6, in which a patient goes through the following four stages: General Practitioner (GP), at the Hospital, at Home, and at Follow-Up GP. The Patient Journey view of the Interactive BigMedilytics Website relates relevant studies and BigMedilytics technology to nodes in the sample patient journey. For example, for the At Home stage, the Interactive BigMedilytics Website lists all studies that use technology that supports telemedicine or remote patient monitoring, e.g., the Kidney study (Chapter 9 – eHealth and Telemedicine for Risk Prediction and Monitoring in Kidney Transplantation Recipients) that uses a web app for telemedicine and remote patient monitoring or the Diabetes study (Chapter 10 – Remote Monitoring to Improve Gestational Diabetes Care) that develops an integrated self-monitoring and self-management system for Gestational Diabetes Mellitus (GDM).

The General Learnings view differs from the other views/perspectives. While the other perspectives mostly focus on the presentation of the scientific results from the

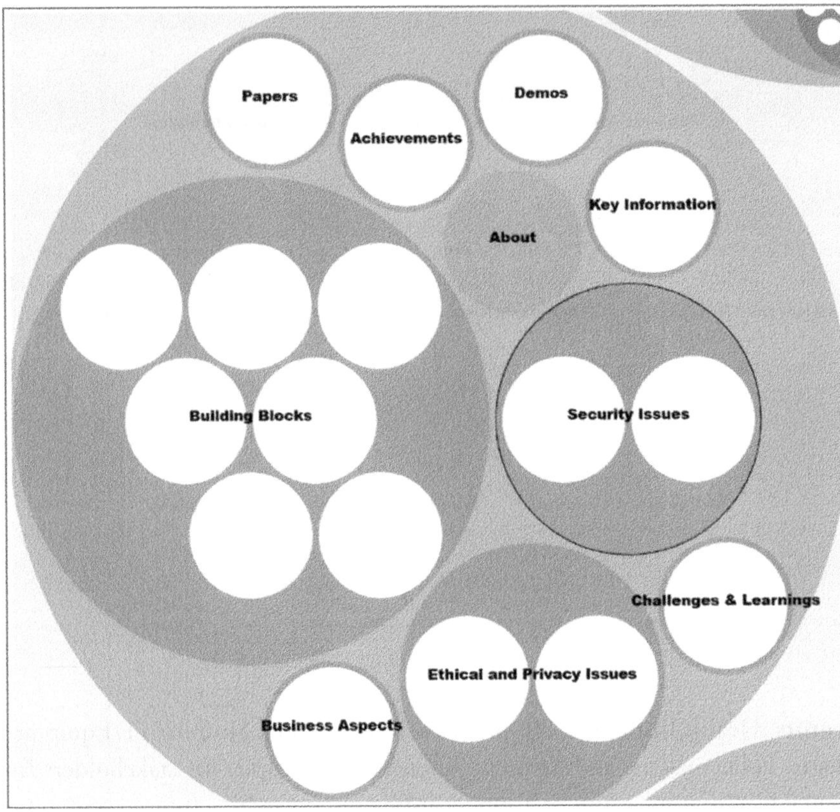

Figure 24.5. Transversal aspects: structure of contents.

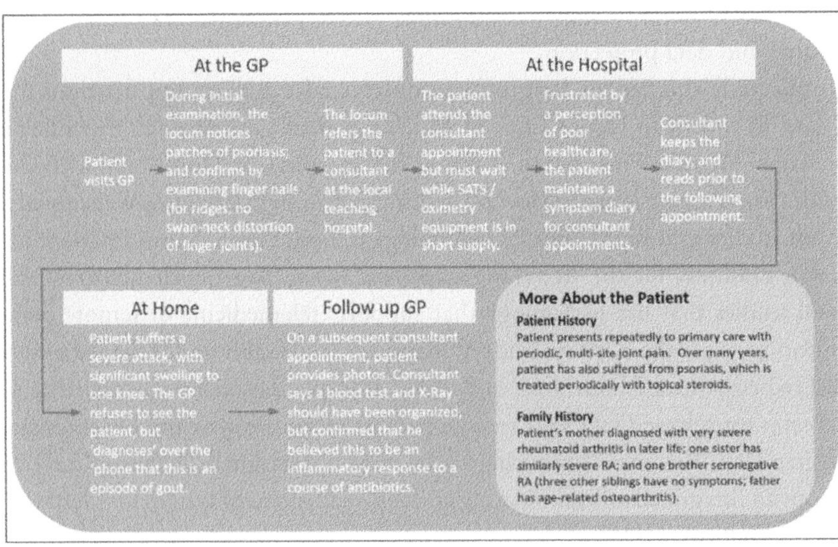

Figure 24.6. Patient journey.

BigMedilytics project and include practical aspects on how to carry out an AI and Big Data technology-based healthcare project, the General Learnings view mainly is a collection of pitfalls to avoid, and lessons learned gathered throughout the realization of the 12 study projects and that may be valuable knowledge for future projects in the area. The General Learnings that are presented on the website are included in Chapter 27 (General Learnings From the Horizon 2020 Project BigMedilytics).

24.4 Conclusion

BigMedilytics resulted in more the 50 scientific publications that demonstrate the disruptive potential of applying Big Data technology in combination with AI in healthcare projects (see Section II, Section III, and Section IV). But BigMedilytics with 36 partners and 12 studies covering several medical and healthcare domains (Population Health and Chronic Disease Management, Oncology, and Industrialization of healthcare services) due to its size also provided a unique opportunity to present a more holistic view and thereby support the implementation of forthcoming projects in the healthcare sector.

In this chapter, we have presented the structure and content of the Interactive BigMedilytics Website: a collection of scientific findings, best practices, and lessons learned from the BigMedilytics project. The Blueprint presents both facts about each of the 12 studies carried out in BigMedilytics, as well as information targeted at specific stakeholder groups, reveals general learnings from planning and executing the studies, and finally relates technology used and findings from the studies to stages in a sample patient journey.

To be able to compare the methods and technologies of different studies, we first asked each study team to describe their study in a document with a pre-defined structure. So, for the website, this information could be split into smaller, comparable chunks for Pilot View and Transversal Aspects. General Learnings from BigMedilytics (see also Chapter 27 – General Learnings From the Horizon 2020 Project BigMedilytics) have been collected partly based on these documents and manually extended by observations made by consortium members. To provide information that is relevant for a specific stakeholder group in Stakeholder Perspective, the content collected has been filtered, so only information is shown that is relevant for the specific group of stakeholders. The Patient Journey stands out a little bit as a realistic but fictitious story about a patient's journey provides the background and defines stages (At the GP, At the Hospital, At Home, and At Follow-Up GP) in the journey and exemplifies illness and treatment of the patient. The four stages are used on the website to explain how technology implemented in the studies can transform healthcare.

To sum up, with the Interactive BigMedilytics Website, we created a unique knowledge source containing facts and findings from the implementation of the 12 Big Data and AI healthcare study projects. Beyond that, cross-cutting topics that concern all project phases, such as ethical and privacy issues and general learnings, are included as well, so future projects in the same domain can benefit and learn from experiences from BigMedilytics and avoid common pitfalls. The content has been prepared in such a way that items of interest can be accessed quickly and easily compared between studies and persons from different stakeholder groups can find relevant information. To achieve this, a modern website design has been selected and implemented using an existing JavaScript library module. While the goal of the BigMedilytics Website mainly has been to provide a holistic view on findings and lessons learned from the BigMedilytics project, the chosen approach can also be used as a template for other lighthouse projects in healthcare or other domains.

The Interactive BigMedilytics Website can still be accessed online (https://www.bigmedilytics.eu/blueprint/). The main parts of the content of the Interactive BigMedilytics Website are presented in this book. Newly updated information regarding a selection of BigMedilytics study projects can be found in Sections II–IV, ethical and privacy issues are discussed in Section I, and general learnings are presented in Chapter 27 (General Learnings From the Horizon 2020 Project BigMedilytics).

Acknowledgement

We would like to thank the team from Inclivia that implemented the interactive webpage.

References

[1] Leopold JA, Maron BA, Loscalzo J. The Application of Big Data to Cardiovascular Disease: Paths to Precision Medicine. Journal of Clinical Investigation 130, Nr. 1. January 2020. 29–38. https://doi.org/10.1172/JCI129203.

[2] Dai H, Younis A, Kong JD, Puce L, Jabbour G, Yuan H, Bragazzi NL. Big Data in Cardiology: State-of-Art and Future Prospects. Frontiers in Cardiovascular Medicine 9. April 2022. 844296. https://doi.org/10.3389/fcvm.2022.844296.

[3] Thongprayoon C, Kaewput W, Kovvuru K, Hansrivijit P, Kanduri SR, Bathini T, Chewcharat A, Leeaphorn N, Gonzalez-Suarez ML, Cheungpasitporn W. Promises of Big Data and Artificial Intelligence in Nephrology

and Transplantation. Journal of Clinical Medicine 9, Nr. 4. April 2020. 1107. https://doi.org/10.3390/jcm9041107.

[4] Zeng XX, Liu J, Ma L, Fu P. Big Data Research in Chronic Kidney Disease. Chinese Medical Journal 131, Nr. 22. November 2018. 2647–50. https://doi.org/10.4103/0366-6999.245275.

[5] Rossetto, AM, Zhou W. Deep Learning for Categorization of Lung Cancer CT Images. IEEE/ACM International Conference on Connected Health: Applications, Systems and Engineering Technologies (CHASE). 2017. 272–73. Philadelphia, PA, USA. https://doi.org/10.1109/CHASE.2017.98.

[6] Rumbold JMM, O'Kane M, Philip N, Pierscionek BK. Big Data and Diabetes: The Applications of Big Data for Diabetes Care Now and in the Future. Diabetic Medicine 37, Nr. 2. 2020. 187–93. https://doi.org/10.1111/dme.14044.

[7] Price WN, Cohen IG. Privacy in the Age of Medical Big Data. Nature Medicine 25, Nr. 1. January 2019. 37–43. https://doi.org/10.1038/s41591-018-0272-7.

[8] Ferretti A, Ienca M, Sheehan M, Blasimme A, Dove ES, Farsides B, Friesen P, *et al.* Ethics Review of Big Data Research: What Should Stay and What Should Be Reformed? BMC Medical Ethics 22, Nr. 1. December 2021. 51. https://doi.org/10.1186/s12910-021-00616-4.

[9] Roski J, Bo-Linn GW, Andrews TA. Creating Value In Health Care Through Big Data: Opportunities And Policy Implications. Health Affairs 33, Nr. 7. July 2014. 1115–22. https://doi.org/10.1377/hlthaff.2014.0147.

[10] Bakker L, Aarts J, Uyl-de Groot C, Redekop W. Economic Evaluations of Big Data Analytics for Clinical Decision-Making: A Scoping Review. Journal of the American Medical Informatics Association 27, Nr. 9. September 2020. 1466–75. https://doi.org/10.1093/jamia/ocaa102.

[11] Agrawal R, Sudhakaran P. Big Data in Digital Healthcare: Lessons Learnt and Recommendations for General Practice. Heredity 124, Nr. 4. April 2020. 525–34. https://doi.org/10.1038/s41437-020-0303-2.

[12] Hansen MM, Miron-Shatz T, Lau AYS, Paton C. Big Data in Science and Healthcare: A Review of Recent Literature and Perspectives: Contribution of the IMIA Social Media Working Group. Yearbook of Medical Informatics 23, Nr. 01. August 2014. 21–26. https://doi.org/10.15265/IY-2014-0004.

[13] Nielsen J. Designing Web Usability: The Practice of Simplicity. New Riders Publishing, USA. 1999.

DOI: 10.1561/9781638282372.ch25

Chapter 25

Data Processing in Healthcare Using CRISP

By Roland Roller, Anne Marie Weggelaar-Jansen, Ricard Martínez Martínez, Sven Schmeier, Holmer Hemsen and Supriyo Chatterjea

25.1 The BigMedilytics Blueprint

The BigMedilytics Blueprint is based on the experience and lessons learned from the 12 BigMedilytics studies. It aligns them to an abstract level of common blocks based on their similarities. Big Data and AI are data-driven techniques that have many aspects in common with data mining, so instead of creating a new process model, we build our blueprint upon the cross-industry standard process for data mining, also known as CRISP-DM [1]. We use this well-established open standard process model, apply it to our healthcare domain, and incorporate our experiences and outcomes.

The CRISP-DM model is presented in Figure 25.1 and defines six phases, which will be described in the following paragraphs. As the figure indicates, CRISP-DM is not necessarily a fixed sequence of phases, as you can move back and forth if necessary. Moreover, the arrows connecting the different phases are not the only way to proceed. The outer circle shows a clockwise movement and highlights that the development of such a project is an iterative process. For instance, with the successful deployment and the completion of a project, previous problems or new ideas could be brought into a new use case, and the circle can restart. Also, the general process may continue after the end of the project.

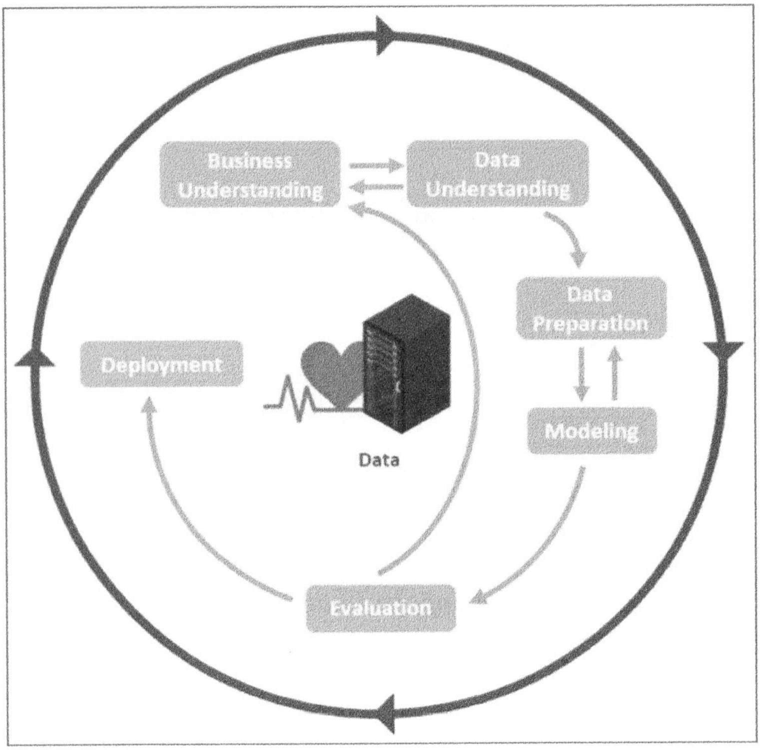

Figure 25.1. CRISP-DM—cross-industry standard process for data mining.

25.2 Business Understanding

An essential starting point in establishing a Big Data/AI project is a thorough understanding of the business, and the business goal(s), assessing the current and target situation, defining the technical task (Big Data/AI), and producing a project plan. Usually, this step results in a business model that describes how an organization creates, delivers, and captures value with the introduction of Big Data/AI technology.

Also, concerning business understanding, the healthcare sector behaves slightly differently. In healthcare, not all stakeholders are 'business' stakeholders, and a translation to our specific context is needed. Public, private for-profit, and private non-profit actors join forces to create value in the healthcare system. In addition, the value for patients is at least partly not only of monetary value. Still, it can be expressed in terms of quality of life, clinical outcomes, patient experience, and cost of treatment. Furthermore, value is also created for other stakeholders, such as healthcare professionals (better and faster decision-making and more efficient work processes), healthcare providers (higher productivity and better use of resources), and healthcare payers (better outcomes for the lowest cost). Also, value for the society can be discerned, e.g., a healthier population, increased labor productivity, and lower health expenses (in total or as a percentage of the GDP).

In BigMedilytics, all 12 studies developed a business model to describe what value their Big Data/AI innovation will create, which stakeholders, resources, and partners are involved or affected, and what activities are needed to create that value. Moreover, the business modeling process helps estimate which development costs and operational costs are related to the innovation and how such costs may be covered to ensure that the innovation action creates a positive value for the healthcare sector.

The classical 'business model canvas', a strategic management tool for developing and documenting new and existing business models, was part of BigMedilytics adapted for the context of Big Data/AI innovation in healthcare. The three main adaptations were as follows:

- Acknowledge the multi-sided market in healthcare and recognize that these innovations create value not only for patients but also for healthcare professionals, healthcare provider organizations, healthcare payers, and society at large.
- Acknowledge that 'profit' is not the main driver for innovating in healthcare. Still, it is a positive value in terms of better outcomes and/or lower costs.
- Acknowledge that, in the Big Data/AI context, rules and regulations play a key role and must be added as a separate player in the business model canvas.

Business modeling is not a one-time activity but often entails updates of the business model to finally meet the demands of all stakeholders involved in the activity. Therefore, it is rather a business modeling journey, moving from a business model of the pilot stage to the stage of scaling up and on to the phase of sustenance of the innovation.

In addition to that, compliance must be considered in this CRISP-DM phase as well. Therefore, the following requirements should be taken into account:

1. Integrate the Data Protection Officer and/or the Compliance Officer in the design team early.
2. Bear in mind that not only European legislation (GDPR) must be taken into account but also the following must be considered:
   - National laws regarding research in health
   - Laws of other member states in trans-European projects
   - Laws associated with international data transfers
   - 'Soft Laws' (such as Guidelines from the European Data Protection Board (EDPB), national data protection authorities, and so on).

3. In the case of multi-partner projects, roles should be defined in terms of GDPR (controller–joint controller–processor) and data use or access (data provider–data consumer). These roles can then be used to determine future agreements between the parties (joint-controller's agreement, processor's agreement, and data-sharing agreement).
4. Access to health system data requires considerations of ethical procedures(research protocol, ethical protocol, informed (ethical) consent, and ethics committee approval) as well as whether or not a clinical trial process of a medical device is necessary under Regulation (EU) 2017/745 of the European Parliament and of the Council of 5 April 2017 on medical devices.
5. Integrate the recommendations of the EU High-Level Expert Group on Artificial Intelligence, or depending on the location (e.g., the United States), alternatively the ethical principles of the Organization for Economic Cooperation and Development (OECD) and the ethical standards developed in the United States.

25.3 Data Understanding

The next phase is data understanding, which involves the sighting of the available data and the data collection. The data have to be explored and examined, particular characteristics identified, and the quality of the data assessed. This analysis needs to ensure that the data can help tackle the problem. If not, the aims within the business understanding must be amended, or other data sources must be found or incorporated.

Particularly in the medical domain, this phase can be challenging: Getting access to data can be time-consuming, for example, in case the data scientist is not associated with the data provider or is located in a different country. Also bear in mind that access to data requires having been able to comply with regulations in a way that allows you to demonstrate:

- The legitimate origin of the data
- The patient's consent, where necessary, and the guarantee of his or her rights
- The different requirements that each country imposes on retrospective and prospective studies.

In addition, data typically cannot be easily understood without medical (or additional) expertise from others. Therefore, interdisciplinary work is essential, which typically requires extra time, as different stakeholders use different terminology and understand the problem differently.

Furthermore, already in the data understanding phase, the problem of anonymization emerges. The position of the data protection authorities of the EU in Working Party Opinion 5/2014 on anonymization techniques is clear: irreversible anonymization must be achieved. Afterward, each data protection authority usually publishes its own guidelines.

The project has taught several lessons:

- De-identification and anonymization are not synonyms.
- Resources must be foreseen to verify the risk of re-identification and to perform second anonymization when health system data have been 'deidentified.'
- A double layer of additional measures should be implemented:
  - Technical: a controlled platform environment with appropriate security measures should be designed. Among these, the traceability of users is particularly relevant.
  - Legal: data-sharing agreements and non-identification commitments of partners and/or users of the platform should be formalized.

25.4 Data Preparation

In the next phase, the data have to be selected and integrated. Then, based on the previous analysis, data have to be cleaned and often converted into a different format to be used in the next stage. However, although data preparation and understanding might sound trivial, these steps usually take up most of the time within the overall project.

Often, in the healthcare domain, the creation and selection of digital data, such as electronic medical records, has grown over time, and so the quality, even of a single data source, may vary over time. However, missing and/or wrong information in the data is a common phenomenon that must be dealt with. Possible errors and inconsistencies might not be directly obvious to an outsider, emphasizing the need for interdisciplinary work on data cleansing. Moreover, valuable information might be "hidden" in not only structured but also unstructured text data, which makes it necessary to apply additional Natural Language Processing (NLP) techniques to access these data, which can raise additional challenges as those techniques need to be often adapted to the language and particular domain.

The limitation to working with the data only on-site, within a secure environment of the data provider, may also create additional challenges that need to be considered (e.g., limited user rights and old infrastructure).

25.5 Modeling

The next phase in CRISP-DM describes the modeling phase. In this phase, it needs to be decided which AI algorithms to use and which test procedure to follow. For example, we may choose to train a classifier based on the mathematical concept of linear regression and use a 10-fold cross-validation training strategy, i.e., we will perform the fitting procedure ten times, each time a training set of 90% of the data is randomly selected, keeping 10% of the data for validation.

Regarding Big Data, we also need to decide if we follow a batch (the data are collected and stored first and then in one or more batches analyzed) or a streaming approach (data are generated and analyzed continuously). In this respect, and especially with AI, a combination of both approaches is possible. For instance, a model may be trained in a batch but used with streaming data.

One of those lessons our 12 studies taught us is that due to the rather specialized data, the evaluation of the result of model training can only be interpreted successfully by a team of medical experts and data scientists.

As CRISP-DM focuses on data mining, there are certain aspects of modeling that, from a software engineering part, need to be taken into account concerning modeling but that are not addressed by CRISP-DM, such as modeling of the software architecture or domain modeling that may need to be considered in a healthcare project. Modeling involves the application of data protection by design principle. Usually, it starts with the data protection impact assessment from which the risks to be eliminated, mitigated, and reduced will be derived. Lessons learned from the project in this area include the following:

- The emergence of lists of criteria and methodologies of data protection authorities are similar but different. For example, the French National Commission on Informatics and Liberty (CNIL) offers a multilingual tool with a very open methodology. At the same time, the Spanish Spanish Data Protection Agency (AEPD) defines a comprehensive checklist of controls with a complementary guide of controls for AI.
- It is essential to train the whole staff.
- It is essential to consider the requirements of Regulation (EU) 2017/745 of the European Parliament and of the Council of 5 April 2017 on medical devices.
- Decisions must be taken on developing an ethical impact analysis on AI.

25.6 Evaluation

In this phase, an evaluation is performed if the previously defined business success criteria are fulfilled and supported by applying Big Data and AI technology.

If this is not the case, a thorough analysis of all previous phases is required. The reasons for not reaching the final goals may be manifold. For example, insufficient data are available to successfully train a model, and too much missing information or relevant data have not been collected. When all fails, it may even be necessary to amend the business success criteria in the business understanding phase. Moreover, this phase will review the overall work (e.g., were all steps properly executed? Summarize findings, and so on) and determine the next steps.

To measure the impact of Big Data innovations, business and research projects frequently rely on Key Performance Indicators (KPIs). In BigMedilytics, the three core KPIs were as follows: (a) improving the quality of the healthcare system by improving its effectiveness, (b) providing more people access to the healthcare system, and at the same time (c) reducing the costs by applying Big Data and AI technology.

But which KPIs capture the impact of Big Data innovations on healthcare in general? In the BigMedilytics project, we learned the following:

- First-order KPIs outline how Big Data innovations change the information provided.
- Second-order KPIs shed light on how Big Data innovations change the decision-making process.
- Third-order KPIs capture the perceived usefulness of the data and how far value is attributed to the information.
- And fourth-order KPIs reveal whether Big Data innovations might affect patient experience, population health, costs, and professional satisfaction in the long run.

However, KPIs might differ not only in their order effects but also in their function. Some KPIs can have a temporary function and can be revoked and revised as one sees fit. However, core KPIs remain relevant over time. Consequently, KPIs are an iterative, recursive process of moving back and forth between finding out which indicators are feasible, acceptable, measurable, and informative.

While assessing how Big Data affects long-term health outcomes, one needs to remember that long-term outcomes depend on a sequence of decisions and exogenous factors. How far changes in long-term outcomes can causally be attributed to Big Data innovations is therefore dependent on how rigorously one can establish the counterfactual scenario of what would have happened if the Big Data innovation had not been developed and implemented.

For evaluating Big Data and AI in healthcare, we also should keep in mind that the impact of applying the trained models for healthcare often can only be validated with new patients, i.e., over a longer period.

25.7 Deployment

The final phase defines the deployment of the model. This includes planning, roll-out, monitoring, and maintenance. Planning of the deployment should already be considered in the business understanding phase as the deployment of the Big Data/AI technology may create costs, such as additional hardware, for example, buying a cluster for handling Big Data or purchase of a fast computer with GPU support for training AI models. In addition, organizational structures may need to be changed or adapted. For example, if telemedicine data are automatically monitored, it requires a team of medical experts to check and decide if further actions need to be taken in case the system triggers an alarm.

Already in this phase, an ethical and legal governance model must be implemented that should be able to:

- Ensure that the AI system respects the values of human rights, human centric-approach, and human oversight, explainability, and fairness
- Ensure transparency at two levels:
- Internal:
    - Clearly identifying and notifying the roles and responsibilities of users, particularly concerning those uses involving the adaptation of decision-making processes subject to the risk of bias
    - Ensuring the involvement of users in continuous improvement
- External:
    - Providing adequate information to patients
    - Designing dialog methodologies with all relevant stakeholders
- Regularly audit the system from a legal and security point of view
- Maintain adequate incident management procedures, particularly those relating to security breaches and those identifying reliability issues in AI results.

Governance models may involve, depending on the characteristics of the entity:

- Adopting and implementing ethical codes
- Promoting and adopting the codes of conduct and/or certifications provided in the GDPR
- Defining governance bodies for the systems

In this phase, how information is presented and reported is also important. This also includes the development of a Graphical User Interface (GUI). Additionally, planning the deployment should include a fall-back strategy in case the new technology is not working as expected and interferes with the day-to-day operation.

This applies, in particular, to disruptive technologies, such as asset management technologies that replace older techniques.

The deployment of the developed Big Data/AI technology (the roll-out) should happen after the model at the IT infrastructure using the model and attached components, such as a newly developed GUI, has been thoroughly tested and evaluated. In contrast to most companies at which a roll-out of a new system can take place after a (partial-) shutdown of some services; in hospitals, usually, the IT system has to be running all the time and must only be interrupted for a short period and therefore should not be interfered by erroneous systems. If a backup twin system is available, it would be a good idea to test the system there first.

The team using the new system should be informed about the roll-out timely. Also, the outcomes of the model need to be communicated with the decision-makers, which were mainly included in the business understanding phase.

Monitoring is necessary to see how the newly integrated Big Data/AI technology behaves over time. Regarding Big Data, an aspect of monitoring is how fast the assigned storage is filled. Regarding AI models, an aspect of monitoring can be how the prediction or classification based on the new model behaves over time with new and, thereby, unseen data. For example, in a hospital, these data are usually based on patients (vitals, lab values, and so on), so monitoring may be necessary over a longer period because only a few new patients are being hospitalized every day. In addition, the deployment infrastructure should support the automatic collection of key KPIs that detect the performance of the solution being rolled out. This would allow AI models to be adapted after rollout and even detect any drifts that might impact the models' performance to make predictions. This also implies that it is critical to think about what KPIs need to be measured to accurately impact the system's rollout. This might also result in the need to integrate with other IT systems, which needs to be considered before deployment.

Maintenance may mean that a trained AI model is outdated and needs to be replaced either because the algorithm calculating the model has been significantly improved or due to a larger sum of new data collected, a new training, testing, and deployment of a model make sense. With regard to Big Data, the hardware infrastructure may be evaluated, and depending on the result, a Big Data cluster needs more computing power.

Reference

[1] Shearer C. The CRISP-DM model: the new blueprint for data mining. Journal of data warehousing. 2000. 5(4), 13–22.

DOI: 10.1561/9781638282372.ch26

Chapter 26

Technology Acceptance in Healthcare

By Brian Pickering

26.1 Introduction

Traditional approaches to the Technology Acceptance Model (TAM) see the characteristics of the technology itself as the main predictors of acceptance and adoption, namely, the perceived ease of use and the perceived usefulness [1]. Around the same time, the Diffusion Of Innovations (DOI) model introduced the willingness of potential adopters, the implementational context, and communication channels as significant factors beyond the technology itself [2]. Later extensions to TAM have sought to account for differences in adoption by different user types, which moderates perceived ease of use and usefulness, such as the Unified Theory of Acceptance and Use of Technology (UTAUT, [3]). For healthcare specifically, the Health Belief Model (HBM) focuses on patient perceptions alone [4]. While broader stakeholder engagement, including patients, clinicians, technologists, planners, and policymakers, is said to be required to ensure the long-term adoption and sustainability of an intervention, [5] the complexity of the technology and the process of deployment are perhaps even more significant than specific features of the technology itself. Indeed, direct collaboration and cognitive buy-in of patients and clinicians are a prerequisite to rolling out technology or other interventions within healthcare [6].

The BigMedylitics (BML) project provides a unique opportunity to explore the attitudes of those directly affected by the deployment of advanced technology in healthcare settings. In this chapter, I report on two empirical studies that aim to provide additional evidence for how advanced technologies are likely to be received by those stakeholders – patients and clinicians – directly involved in the provision and receipt of care.

26.2 Challenges

Figure 26.1 illustrates the potentially disruptive effect of technology introduction into healthcare (for a more detailed discussion, see [7]). The left-hand panel shows the simple relationship between patients and clinicians which is based largely on trust. In the behavioural sciences, trust involves an acceptance of risk: the patient expects the clinician to cure them, [8, 9] whilst appreciating that this may not be possible. This relationship, that is between patients and clinicians, may be guided and monitored, of course, by a relevant authority.

The studies in the BML project (Sections II–IV) sought to introduce technology in different healthcare contexts. For instance, Chapter 9 (eHealth and Telemedicine for Risk Prediction and Monitoring in Kidney Transplantation Recipients), Chapter 10 (Remote Monitoring to Improve Gestational Diabetes Care), and Chapter 11 (Monitoring Wellness in Chronic Obstructive Pulmonary Disease Using the myCOPD App) introduced Remote Patient Monitoring (RPM) solutions for self-monitoring and thereby for patients to engage with their own care. Chapter 14 (Usability of Enhanced Decision Support and Predictive Modelling in Prostate Cancer), Chapter 15 (Monitoring and Decision Support in Treatment Modalities for Lung Cancer), and Chapter 16 (Artificial Intelligence to Support Chooses in Neoadjuvant Chemotherapy in Breast Cancer Patients) provided support to clinicians during diagnosis and treatment. Finally, Chapter 19 (Implementation and Impact of AI for the Interpretation of Lung Diseases in Chest CTs) and Chapter 20 (Innovative Use of Technology for Acute Care Pathway Monitoring and Improvements) focus on hospital operations to improve efficiency.

The right-hand panel of Figure 26.1 shows the effects of introducing these technologies into a healthcare context. Now, the trust relationship that accepts and assumes an element of vulnerability, overseen by a relevant healthcare authority, is replaced on the one hand by reliance on advanced technology and on the other by an ambivalent response by the patient as a member of the public to advanced

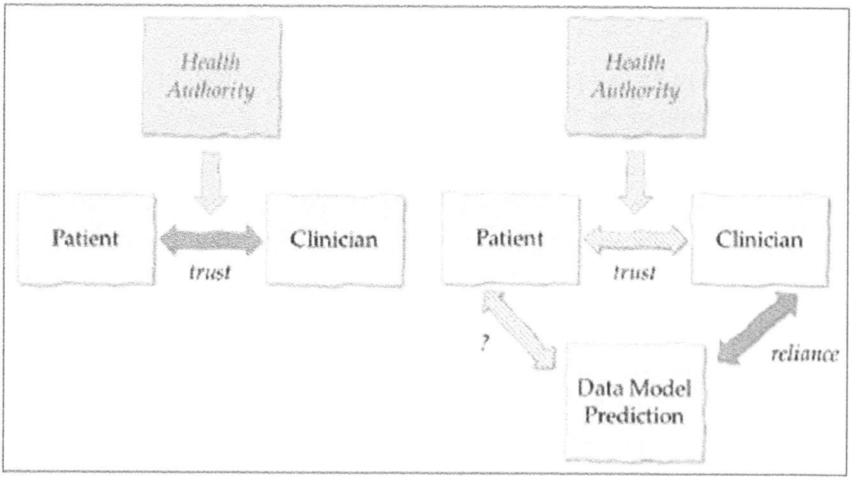

Figure 26.1. Schematic representation of the delivery of healthcare without technology (left) and with advanced, AI-enabled technology (right).

technology. First, the patients assume that the data used to build the model that the clinician is relying on are relevant to them: the sample used is representative and inclusive. Second, they are unsure about AI technologies per se[i] [10].

26.3 General Public's Views on Technology in Healthcare

In this section, we summarize the findings from an online survey targeted at the general public; as UK residents, they are UK National Health Service (NHS) patients. So, their perceptions reflect their expectations and experience with a free-at-source health service. A little more than half (53%) do not currently use an app; the others do. The survey was intended to explore the general public's perceptions of using an app in healthcare, rather than specifics of the technology as highlighted by TAM or user demographics as suggested by the UTAUT. It does, however, seek to explore user decisions in adopting apps in much the same way as the HBM. Further, adopter willingness from the DOI theory is represented to a limited extent in trying to cover both existing app users (Early Adopters) and non-users (perhaps the Late Majority).

i. Similarly, in the BML project, one of the conclusions of Chapter 10 (Remote Monitoring to Improve Gestational Diabetes Care) was that interpretability is crucial for trusting AI models, and reliability strongly depends on the correct usage of the app.

26.3.1 Method

The HBM seeks to predict patient willingness to engage with an intervention based on the combination of the following factors:

- The perceived vulnerability to a given condition and its impact
- The cost/benefit assessment of adopting the proposed intervention
- The self-efficacy resulting from adopting the proposed intervention.

An anonymous online survey was developed based on assertions associated with the HBM factors, adopted specifically for the use of an app to monitor a health condition (see Chapter 11 – Monitoring Wellness in Chronic Obstructive Pulmonary Disease Using the myCOPD app). These were supplemented with statements derived from a Patient and Public Involvement and Engagement (PPIE) discussion with patients who have a COPD diagnosis. Specifically, reports that patients could feel isolated and a little ignored and the potential for a self-reporting app to provide social contact with other patients.

This resulted in a survey containing 28 items, grouped into three sections: the first dealing with perceptions of participants' own health, the second about app usage, and the third general attitudes to healthcare. Participants were asked to respond on a four-point Likert scale (Strongly agree to Strongly disagree). Some assertions were reversed to try and avoid participants selecting the same response throughout.

26.3.2 Participants

A total of 400 UK residents were recruited via a crowdsourcing platform (Prolific.co) and were paid a nominal amount (£3.00).[ii] The average time taken to respond to the survey was 4 minutes and 7 seconds. Table 26.1 summarizes the demographics of the survey respondents.

The respondents correspond to current UK census data.[iii] In addition, 187 respondents reported that they were regular app users, whereas 213 were not.

26.3.3 Results

I focus here solely on the 13 assertions that refer directly to app usage. Using 67% – or roughly two-thirds – provides a threshold to identify significant (dis)agreement among respondents. Namely, percentages above 67% indicate significant support

---

ii. This study was approved by the research ethics committee of the Faculty of Engineering and Physical Sciences at the University of Southampton, reference: ERGO/FEPS/65003.

iii. See https://www.ons.gov.uk/. 2011 figures are available; 2021 figures are in preparation.

or rejection of an assertion. Table 26.2 summarizes those assertions where responses from both app users and non-app users coincide: Columns 2 and 3 in the table are percentages over 400.

The first two assertions relate to self-efficacy: both app users and non-users agree that healthcare app usage provides a sense of doing something positive. Even though I suggested above that an app might disrupt the healthcare ecosystem (see the right-hand panel of Figure 26.1), the general public in the United Kingdom accepts that healthcare apps increase their feeling that apps give them the opportunity to do something positive and take responsibility for their own health. The last three records in the table show general disagreement with the assertions. Neither app users nor non-users believe that a healthcare app is too difficult to use nor too time-consuming. Interestingly, nor do they believe that app usage is a way to replace traditional clinician-provided healthcare: the general public does not believe they are being fobbed off and left to fend for themselves.

Table 26.3 summarizes cases where private citizens did not agree about the importance of the assertion. In all cases, with the exception of the first assertion in the table, responses for both app users and non-users are around the 50% mark: there is no clear (i.e., greater than 67%) indication that citizens either agree or disagree with the statement. Other assertions suggest that privacy and trust are not issues, nor that the potential social-interaction benefit of using a healthcare app (the last two assertions) seems to be so important.

The final app-specific assertions are shown in Table 26.4. For Using an app regularly would identify problems earlier, the app users seem to agree with the statement (70% versus 30% disagreement), whereas the non-users appear to be undecided. This suggests that the app users can see benefits to app usage once they start using them which the non-users don't yet appreciate. For Using a healthcare app means that I can show a doctor what's been going on for me if needed, private citizen responses are reversed: app users disagree (85%), whereas non-users agree (82%). Expectations from healthcare app usage are therefore different once apps are being used. Indeed, these two statements suggest that app usage helps the patient identify

Table 26.1. Participant demographics (Total N = 400: 187 App Users, 213 Non-Users).

Age Group		Gender Identity	
18–29	82	Female	203
30–49	153	Male	194
50–69	152	Non-binary/third gender	2
70 or over	13	Prefer not to say	1

Table 26.2. Private (UK) citizen perceptions of healthcare app usage (Total N = 400).

Assertion	Agree	Disagree
Both Agree		
Using an app regularly means I can do something positive to take care of myself	85	16
Using healthcare apps makes me feel that I'm taking responsibility for my health	81	19
Both Disagree		
Using an app takes too much time	16	85
I don't know how to use apps	11	89
Using a healthcare app on my own means I'm being fobbed off	21	80

Table 26.3. Ambivalent private citizen perceptions of healthcare app usage (Total N = 400: 187 App Users; 213 Non-Users).

	App Users		Non-Users	
Assertion	Agree	Disagree	Agree	Disagree
It is hard to remember to use an app regularly	44	56	59	41
A healthcare app is not necessary if you get regular health checks	39	61	58	42
I don't trust healthcare apps will get it right for me	40	60	52	48
I'm worried about my privacy when using healthcare apps	47	53	58	42
Using healthcare apps would mean I could get in touch with other people like me	48	52	56	44
Using healthcare apps means I'm not so alone	46	54	52	48

Table 26.4. Disagreements among app users and non-users about healthcare app usage (Total N = 400: 187 App Users, 213 Non-Users).

	App Users		Non-Users	
Assertion	Agree	Disagree	Agree	Disagree
Using an app regularly would identify problems earlier	70	30	55	45
Using a healthcare app means that I can show a doctor what's been going on for me if needed	15	85	82	18

issues not that they wish to alert a clinician. It is about self-awareness rather than part of the general healthcare context, but only once users have experienced (are using) healthcare apps. This suggests that users will make their own decisions about the benefits they get rather than any particular preconceived usefulness, such as an aide-memoire between consultations (see [11] which provides some evidence of cognitive support for rheumatoid arthritis sufferers).

26.3.4 Conclusion

From the survey completed by a representative sample of the general public (in the United Kingdom), there is general agreement that healthcare app usage provides patients with a sense that they are engaged in and taking responsibility for their own health (self-efficacy). Apps are not difficult or intrusive, nor are users particularly concerned about trust and app reliability, and do not see potential social connectivity as a motivator. Importantly, though, app users differ from non-users in that adoption seems to be about making the individual aware of their health status for existing users, whereas non-users are unsure. Further, current app users do not see healthcare apps as an aid in interactions with clinicians, whereas non-users seem to believe that apps would provide useful information to the clinician. The survey sheds some light, therefore, on the complex expectations of patients when offered a healthcare app. Perceived ease of use does not appear to be an issue. Perceived usefulness depends to some extent, though, on the existing app usage experience of patients.

26.4 Stakeholder Perceptions of Advanced Technology

In the previous section, the focus was on patient perceptions of healthcare app usage. Here, I turn to consider other stakeholders within the ecosystem as represented in the BML consortium. Partners were drawn from not only different disciplines but also different roles. This would allow a practical view on the complexity of introducing advanced, AI-enabled technology into healthcare, much as set out in the NASSS framework.

26.4.1 Method

A previous three-round Delphi study involving around 10 experts (12 in Round 1 and 8 in Round 3) focusing on the adoption of advanced technologies identified a number of key areas [12]. Although not specifically targeted at healthcare technology, the types of issues raised are pertinent to the domain. These were used therefore to derive 30 assertions across four areas as described in Table 26.5.

Participants were asked to respond on a four-point Likert scale as to whether they agreed or disagreed with the statements.[iv]

26.4.2 Participants

The survey was distributed to partners in the BML consortium. A total of 47 responses were received, but after the initial review, one had to be removed since the respondent did not rate 10 of the 30 assertions, leaving 46 responses in total. Table 26.6 summarizes how participants described themselves.[v]

26.4.3 Results

Tables 26.5 and 26.6 provide two sources of variability in responses. A two-way ANOVA (Category x Role) was performed on the ratings to establish whether there were any significant effects due to category or role. Category accounts for some 50% of the variance in responses (from the partial η^2 p-value):

$$F(3, 1121.97) = 373.930, p < 0.001(\eta_p^2 = 0.501)$$

The greatest differences in opinion, therefore, relate to the area Requirements, Design and Responsibility, Ethics and Governance, or Transparency. Further,

$$F(4, 103.846) = 25.962, p = 0.006(\eta_p^2 = 0.085)$$

In total 8.5% of the variance is attributable to the self-reported role. So, role has some effect also. The interaction between category and role—that is, how different roles in Table 26.6 respond differently to each of the categories in Table 26.5—is

Table 26.5. Assertions relating to the design and deployment of advanced technologies.

Category	Description
Requirements	What do stakeholders expect from advanced technologies?
Design and Responsibility	How should advanced technologies be designed?
Ethics and Governance	How should advanced technologies be managed?
Transparency	How should advanced technologies operate?

iv. This study was approved by the Faculty of Engineering and Physical Sciences research ethics committee at the University of Southampton, reference number: ERGO/FEPS/65194.A1.

v. Note that the lines in the table do not align: so not all clinicians work in chronic disease, and so on.

Table 26.6. How participants described themselves.

Self-Reported Role		Self-Reported Domain	
Clinician	4	Chronic Disease	10
Data Scientist	18	Oncology	3
Social Scientist	5	Organisational Effectives	14
Vendor	5	Other	19
Other	14	–	–

not significant:

$$F(12, 82.854) = 1.012, p = 0.440(\eta_p^2 = 0.069)$$

In the following, I focus only on responses to individual assertions within each category. Pooling the responses provides an overview of the kinds of concerns that the stakeholders represented in the BML consortium perceive related to advanced technology being introduced into healthcare. Figures 26.2–26.5 summarize the responses received from BML consortium members. Each figure should be interpreted as follows: first, there is the assertion that participants were asked to rate agreement with (on a four-point Likert scale). "Strongly Agree" responses are shown to the right in pale orange, "Agree" in yellow, "Disagree" in green, and "Strongly Disagree" in blue. Overlaid is a rectangle that represents 25% agreement on the left-hand edge and 75% agreement on the right-hand edge when reading left to right. The opposite is true if reading from right to left (25% on the right-hand edge and 75% on the left-hand edge). The hashed centre line represents the 50% mark.

To illustrate, in Figure 26.2, for the assertion "There's too much data available now for humans to be able to process and understand", "Strongly Agree" (pale orange) and "Agree" (yellow) were selected by more than 50% of respondents: together, these two boxes exceed the hashed line in the middle. For the assertion, advanced technologies help people do their jobs better, the two "agree" boxes (pale orange and yellow) exceed the 75% mark: so over 75% of respondents agreed with the statement. Any boldface black assertions are those where more than 75% of respondents agreed with it; items in boldface red (see Figure 26.4), then more than 75% of respondents disagreed with the assertion.

From Figure 26.2, the response to the assertion I trust the person I get to talk with understands the technology they're using suggests that those using the output from advanced technologies may not always understand that technology. This may reflect that these stakeholders do not expect clinicians, for instance, to be able to understand the technology they rely on. Other than that, especially given the

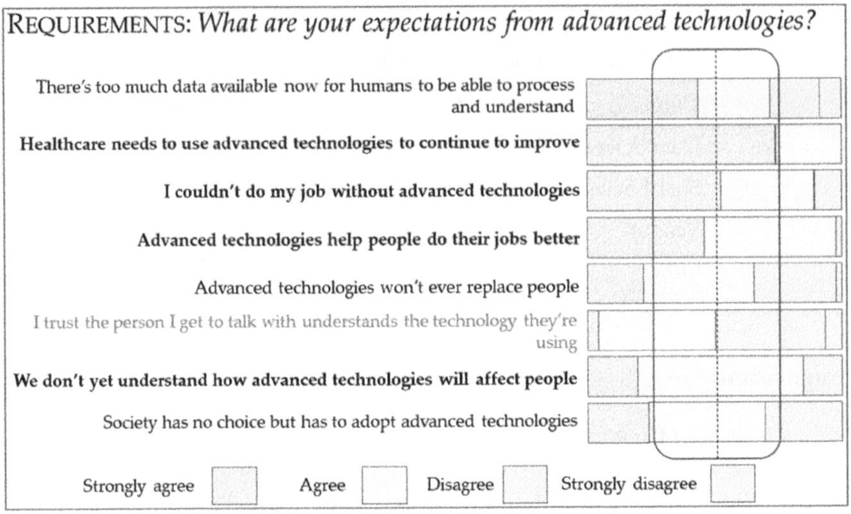

Figure 26.2. Stakeholder perceptions about the requirements for advanced technologies in healthcare.

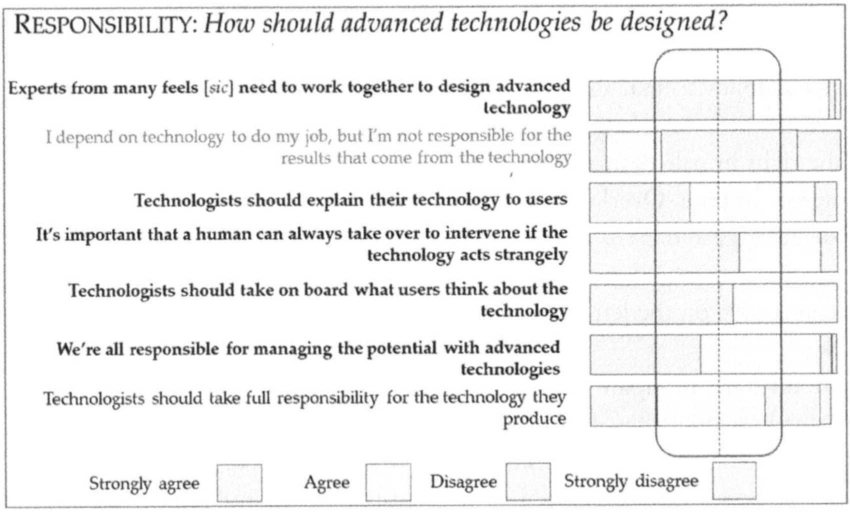

Figure 26.3. Stakeholder perceptions about who is responsible for advanced technologies in healthcare.

number of cases where there is overwhelming agreement (those items in bold), it indicates the perception that advanced technologies—however, they are defined—are seen to be essential for the future.

From Figure 26.3, taking both the assertion that stakeholders do not agree with as well as those with overwhelming agreement, it is clear that partners in BML believe that responsibility with advanced technologies is shared across many stakeholders. This includes those developing the technologies, such as data scientists,

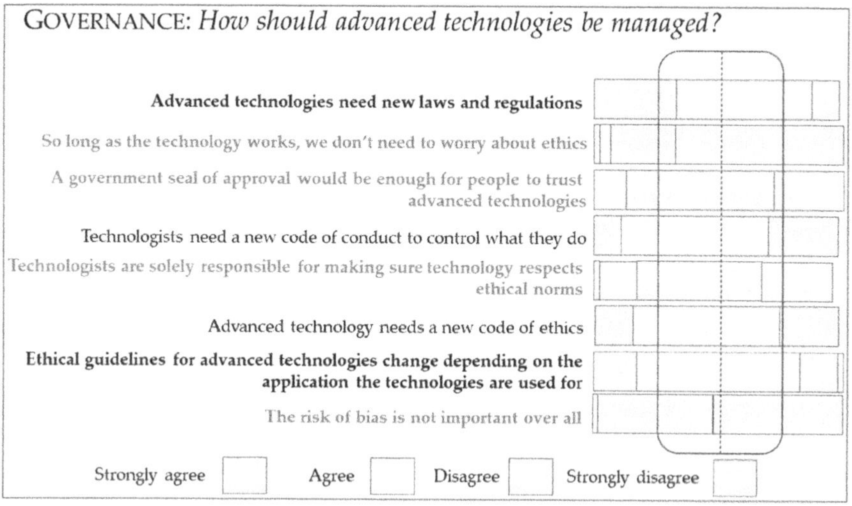

Figure 26.4. Stakeholder perceptions about the ethics and governance of technologies deployed in healthcare.

those reliant on them, such as clinicians, and those affected by them, the patients. Whereas previously, technology would simply be delivered and expected to fulfil its function, advanced technologies require ongoing collaboration from all those stakeholders.

Turning to Figure 26.4, it is clear that a new type of ethics is required (as highlighted in [12]). Moreover, the definition and oversight associated with such governance is the responsibility of multiple stakeholders: different agents within the healthcare context must collaborate for effective governance once the ethical framework has been established.

Finally, as regards transparency (Figure 26.5), there is general agreement that understanding how a decision is reached – such as a prediction in many of the studies in BML – is not only desirable per se but would potentially lead to greater insights and advances. This is not solely about ensuring defect-free operation (respondents disagreed with the assertion "Understanding how a technology works means we can make sure a problem doesn't occur") but also about deriving additional benefits.

In addition to the ratings summarized in the figures here, some participants provided free-form comments as follows:

- "Technicians and "other people" need to find or develop a common language to be able to discuss the pros and cons of AI". This highlights the need for different disciplines to collaborate on the basis of a shared understanding or a common language.

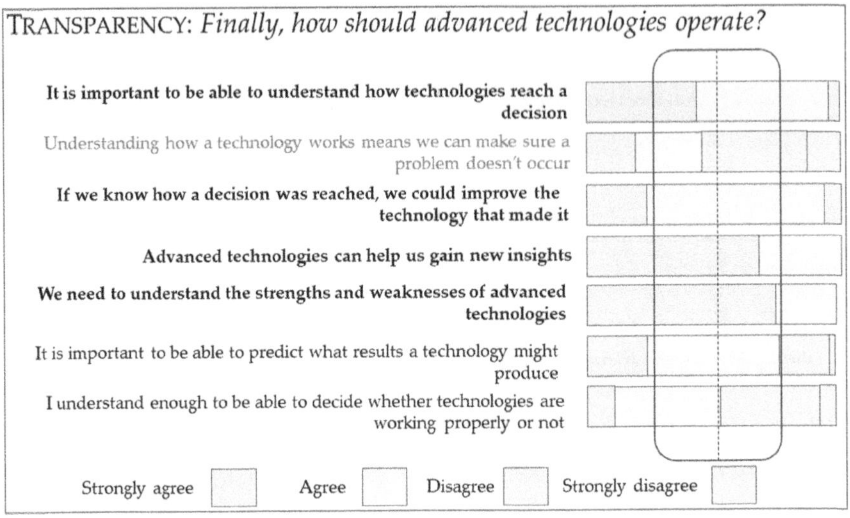

Figure 26.5. Stakeholder perceptions about the need for transparency regarding advanced technologies deployed in healthcare.

- "Advancing technology may become a new field in which multi-disciplines work together". Taking the perspective of collaboration from the previous comment forward, this recognizes the importance of projects like BML to encourage cross-disciplinary work, and, of course, to share experience.
- "We need to start viewing the world as a socio-technical system where humans and technologies are networked together and inseparable [from] each other". This comment highlights the complexity of the ecosystem around and dependent on advanced technologies. It is essential (as highlighted in the survey responses themselves) to rethink how all actors and stakeholders need to be and can be involved or at least be appropriately represented.

26.4.4 Conclusion

The BML project survey on advanced technologies in healthcare derives from the practical experience of the project partners but has thrown up some common themes recognized in the area of responsible AI (see [12], but also the DARPA project and related work, e.g., [13], but also [14]). In the context of technology acceptance, the survey outlines the concerns of the main stakeholders. As such, it not only provides further material for the definitions of complexity in adoption models like NASSS but also highlights some of the communication problems – like a common language, and the need for multi-disciplinary approaches – identified in DOI. The BML consortium has therefore provided a significant use case for considering how technology can and should be introduced into healthcare.

26.5 Learnings

This leads to a set of 18 recommendations regarding the introduction of advanced technologies into healthcare. The first set of five relates to the ethical treatment of all those affected by the technology.

1. There is a clear need to engage in further discussion about the ethical running of advanced technologies in healthcare.
2. Advanced technology testing should include an ethics audit along with standard testing.
3. Advanced technology deployment and operation needs to plan for and resource ongoing monitoring, especially regarding the ethical treatment of those affected by the technology.
4. An acceptability framework should be developed, including checks for bias and how to remedy it.
5. Advanced technologies require a new set of ethical norms, developed in consultation and by agreement with all relevant actors and stakeholders.

Note that the general public did not express any concerns with privacy (often conflated with ethics) or trust in the technology and how it may work for them as individuals. The next seven recommendations relate to the involvement of all stakeholders and facilitating communication between them.

6. Multi-stakeholder involvement is essential to ensure that all perspectives are understood and can be factored into the exploitation of advanced technologies.
7. Where advanced technologies are to be deployed, all main actors (those directly involved with the technology) and all other stakeholders (those affected by the technology) should be consulted.
8. All actors (and stakeholders) need some visibility and oversight of advanced technology deployment; it is not enough to have a separate certification authority.
9. All those affected by technology need to be considered and to be engaged, including assuming responsibility for technology once a choice to use it has been made.

10. There needs to be a code of conduct established for all relevant stakeholders.
11. Technology in healthcare is one component within a broader, complex network. Focus needs to be given to how technology can affect or even disrupt existing relationships.
12. To support and facilitate cross-disciplinary understanding, there needs to be a common language in place so that all relevant stakeholders can engage and contribute.

This is entirely consistent with models such as DOI, NASSS, and NPT, especially in recognition of the complex ecosystem that healthcare relies on. The online survey with the general public showed some discrepancies in expectations around what an app could provide. This is precisely the sort of area in which good communication and a person-centred approach to design are important. Indeed, the next two recommendations cover design:

13. There needs to be a new way of thinking around the development, testing, deployment, and ongoing monitoring of advanced (AI-enabled) technologies.
14. Advanced technologies should be designed and deployed from a human-in-the-loop perspective.

This is precisely what the BML project sought to achieve: with prospective studies involving key stakeholders to identify the benefits of technology for the ecosystem as a whole.

15. Moving forward, there needs to be more focus on how advanced technologies will affect society and individual people.
16. It is important to consider if and how advanced technologies may affect significant current relationships.
17. How advanced technologies work needs to be understood in the context of the ecosystem where they are deployed.
18. Advanced technologies offer much potential beyond immediate needs. If they are explainable as well as functionally adequate, this will lead to greater potential benefits.

The final set of recommendations highlights the broader effects of advanced technology as it is introduced into healthcare. The BML project partners were aware of this, not least as highlighted in their comments. However, the general public is already demonstrating what they derive from using healthcare apps as reported in the online survey. PPIE-type engagement moving forward is one way to maintain oversight of how apps are used. For instance, current users identified that app usage would help them identify issues early. However, at the same time, they were less clear that they intended to use that information to share with clinicians. This might suggest that a more complex relationship is developing in the healthcare context (see, for instance, [15]).

26.6 Discussion and Conclusion

In this chapter, I have cited empirical evidence gathered during the BML project to identify the challenges associated with introducing advanced technologies into healthcare. The focus was mainly on self-reporting apps used by patients as part of their health regime, though the survey with BML partners also provides insight into broader advanced technology issues. I started with the traditional view that for a technology to be adopted, it should be perceived as easy to use and useful. Traditional models such as TAM and even UTAUT fall into this category. However, especially in healthcare, other researchers have highlighted the complexity of healthcare intervention and technology acceptance. Innovation in general requires willing and innovative participants and appropriate communication channels (DOI). However, there is also a significant need for multi-stakeholder involvement and an appreciation of the complexity of the technology, but also the ecosystem into which it will be deployed (NASSS and NPT). Taken together, though, the surveys reported here demonstrate an awareness of these challenges as well as generate some recommendations as to how to address them. Most importantly, perhaps, is that the survey carried out with the general public seemed to suggest that healthcare app users as well as non-users are not so concerned with reliability and privacy. Instead, they want to feel able to engage in their own healthcare: perceived self-efficacy is essential, alongside all of the ethical and design issues with advanced technologies. Potential healthcare app users want to use and derive benefits from those apps. They do not simply want to maintain the existing status quo. As such, they are perfectly capable of engaging with other stakeholders: they need to be part of the conversation in terms of the NASSS framework, and they have already developed cognitive participation as described in NPT from their own understanding of healthcare apps.

References

[1] Davis FD. A technology acceptance model for empirically testing new end-user information systems: Theory and results. 1985. Massachusetts Institute of Technology.

[2] Rogers E. Diffusion of Innovations. 1962. 1st ed. NY, USA: The Free Press.

[3] Venkatesh V, Bala H. Technology Acceptance Model 3 and a Research Agenda on Interventions. Decision Sciences. 2008. 39(2): p. 273–315. DOI: 10.1111/j.1540-5915.2008.00192.x.

[4] Champion VL, Skinner CS. The health belief model, in Health behavior and health education: Theory, research, and practice. 2008. Jossey-Bass: CA, USA. p. 45–65.

[5] Greenhalgh, T, *et al.* Beyond adoption: a new framework for theorizing and evaluating nonadoption, abandonment, and challenges to the scale-up, spread, and sustainability of health and care technologies. Journal of medical Internet research. 2017. 19(11): p. e367. DOI: 10.2196/jmir.8775.

[6] May CR, *et al.* Development of a theory of implementation and integration: Normalization Process Theory. Implementation Science. 2009. 4(1): p. 29. DOI: 10.1186/1748-5908-4-29.

[7] Pickering B. Work with me, don't just talk at me: when "explainable" is not enough, in Future Health Scenarios: AI and Digital Technologies. Global Healthcare Systems. 2023. Taylor & Francis Group, LLC: Boca Raton, FL.

[8] Rousseau DM, *et al.* Not so different after all: A cross-discipline view of trust. Academy of management review. 1998. 23(3): p. 393–404. DOI: 10.5465/amr.1998.926617.

[9] Schoorman FD, Mayer RC, Davis JH. An integrative model of organizational trust: Past, present, and future. Academy of Management review. 2007. 32(2): p. 344–354. DOI: 10.5465/amr.2007.24348410.

[10] O'Neil C. Weapons of Math Destruction: How Big Data increases inequality and threatens democracy. 2016. New York, NY: Crown.

[11] Hooper C, *et al.* TRIFoRM Final Report: TRust in IT: Factors, metRics, Models, in IT as a Utility Network+ working papers, J. Frey and S. Brewer, Editors. 2015.

[12] Taylor S, *et al.* Responsible AI – Key themes, concerns & recommendations for European research and innovation. 2018. DOI: 10.5281/zenodo.1303252.

[13] Gunning D, Aha DW. DAPRA's Explainable Artificial Intelligence Program. AI Magazine. 2019. 40(2): p. 44–58.

[14] Rohlfing KJ, *et al.* Explanation as a social practice: Toward a conceptual framework for the social design of AI systems. IEEE Transactions on Cognitive and Developmental Systems. 2020. p. 1–1. DOI: 10.1109/TCDS.2020.3044366.

[15] van Riel N, *et al.* The effect of Dr Google on doctor– patient encounters in primary care: a quantitative, observational, crosssectional study. BJGP Open. 2017. 1(2). DOI: 10.3399/bjgpopen17X100833.

DOI: 10.1561/9781638282372.ch27

Chapter 27

General Learnings From the Horizon 2020 Project BigMedilytics

By Roland Roller, Supriyo Chatterjea, Brian Pickering, Holmer Hemsen, Dimitrios Vogiatzis, Ricard Martínez Martínez, Georg Langs, Simona Rabinovici-Cohen, Wiebke Duettmann, Alex Sangers, Maria-Esther Vidal, Ernestina Menasalvas Ruiz, Marga Martin Sanchez, Josep Redon, Ana Ferrer-Albero, Alexandra Muñoz-Oliver, Gerrit J. Noordergraaf, Igor Paulussen, Per Henrik Vincent, Arne IJpma, José-Ramón Navarro-Cerdán and Santiago Gálvez-Settier

Big Data, in combination with Artificial Intelligence (AI), has the potential to change and improve processes in medicine. However, these activities/technologies must be developed to promote the trust of all stakeholders: patients, healthcare professionals, private and public providers, and businesses. Providing a trustworthy AI – lawful, ethical, and robust – requires significant efforts. Although technological development is moving quickly, testing, validation, and integration of such innovation may take many years. The reasons that slow down this process are manifold. However, some barriers and pitfalls are foreseeable and, therefore, can be taken into account or avoided. In order to support future development and integration of AI and Big Data technologies, we present technical challenges and lessons learned from our previous project, BigMedilytics, involving clinicians and data scientists. This chapter considers the challenges data scientists providing advanced technology in the healthcare domain may face, along with some suggestions to address any related issues if applicable.

27.1 Introduction

Sharing experiences can be helpful to make others aware of problems, to learn how to overcome them, and, therefore, to take those difficulties into account. In the context of a technical project, this would enable such projects to plan ahead and save time. This chapter will present possible and common problems and pitfalls while setting up and implementing a Big Data and AI project in the healthcare domain. More specifically, we would like to share the experience of the 12 different BigMedilytics studies. As each study tackled different problems, used different datasets, and dealt with different challenges, the broad variety combined into one project provides much potential to learn from.

Most studies in the project were set up within a hospital to support clinical staff, while only a small number directly targeted patients. The data used in the different studies cover a wide range, including Electronic Medical Records (EMR), clinical text data, images, real-time data from different sources, smartphone data, insurance company claims, biomedical literature, ontologies, and open structured or semi-structured data sources. The studies generally involved a data provider, the custodian of the health-related datasets, and a technical partner processing the data. In most cases, a health register in the community or a hospital represents the data provider, and at the same time, a different external partner carries out the technical implementation. In one instance, data from a hospital were combined using multi-party computation with health insurance claims data, thus, maintaining the security and privacy of the data. Also, in some cases, data providers and technical partners were located in different countries within the EU. Topic-wise, most studies target the prediction of particular outcomes, such as complete pathological response to treatment, risk of cancer recurrence, mortality, risk of hospitalization, infections, exacerbations of Chronic Obstructive Pulmonary Disease (COPD), or heart failure. Others focus on monitoring, for instance, to detect bottlenecks in the usage of particular medical devices, glucose levels, or patient adherence to drug intake. Various studies provide tools to analyse and/or navigate more easily through the given data with the help of AI and Big Data.

Of interest to all stakeholders working on data-driven healthcare propositions, we present the biggest and most crucial technical challenges across the project, along with some lessons learned and solutions. In particular, we discuss the different challenges and consider what would be done differently if we were to do it again. Challenges will be presented, with examples taken from the different studies, and a possible solution or lessons learned. We present information at different levels, namely: general, data, technical, and validation.

27.2 Prerequisites

Expanding on the general perspectives in response to the internal survey, partners provided specific comments and feedback relating to their studies and their experiences during the project. The main common themes are discussed here.

27.2.1 Interdisciplinary Teams Require Time

Working on Big Data and AI in healthcare involves interdisciplinary work. The stakeholders typically include hospital CEOs, department managers, privacy officers, medical and laboratory staff, system administrators, data scientists, and researchers. This means that people with different educational and professional backgrounds and perspectives need to communicate with each other. It is already difficult to explain the work to a peer when working on complex topics. However, trying to do this with people from totally different backgrounds can lead to miscommunication, frustration, and ultimate failure of the endeavour. Further, bearing in mind that people might use different terminologies for similar things, a language and cultural barrier may exist. Although most people can understand and speak English, they may not appreciate contextual factors or domain-specific jargon. So, it is essential to allocate sufficient time and to have many meetings, particularly at the beginning, to find and then maintain common ground and a common understanding.

27.2.2 Regulatory Protocols that are Incompatible with the Iterative Nature of Scientific Research

In exploratory projects, the clarity on what data are needed to meet a particular objective may evolve over time. There is a fundamental disconnect between regulations and how scientists work. In the hypothetico-deductive tradition, scientists develop a hypothesis, gather the initial data, perform experiments, and derive conclusions that support or question that hypothesis. This might make them realize that they need to collect different data points. In other words, what is needed to address a particular problem may not always be apparent from the start. This is especially true for problems where Big Data is involved.

Different from the financial sector, designing sandboxes in health research is impossible. The sandbox provides a controlled testing environment to enable the implementation of innovative technology projects. It would mean defining confined environments to conduct data-driven research with the elimination or appropriate mitigation of potential risks. For projects involving partners from several EU Member States or non-EU Members, however, differing legislation must be harmonized and balanced. In addition, effective compliance with GDPR is only possible if it is based on the formal approach. The definition of data protection by design and, by default, legal compliance by design implies a material process appropriate to the conditions of each processing operation and a risk-based approach. The compliance maturity model achieved by GDPR compliance decisions is not theoretical. They involve decision-making by the controller or the processor and generate auditable evidence.

BigMedilytics incorporates valuable lessons learned that inform debate in building the European Health Data Space. At present, legislative asymmetries only allow trans-European research with anonymized data. While many countries exempt consent for retrospective research with data, the requirements for prospective research are diverse. This has the consequence of constraining the design of federated data analytics strategies. In this model, data processing would take place locally, on-premise at a given hospital in a given country, and the results would be shared in the cloud, duly anonymized. In practice, this hampers the possibilities that a European Cloud should provide for data analytics and deploying a common AI strategy for healthcare systems.

27.2.3 Established IT Structures Meet New Requirements

Often the IT infrastructure in hospitals has grown organically over the years and cannot be changed radically due to the need for high availability of services, inherent interdependencies, and external (e.g., government) regulation. While data scientists might be used to powerful computer clusters, Linux machines, and admin rights to quickly install the tools they need, two different worlds collide here. The most significant of these aspects is computational power; the others make the working environment less convenient. However, in cases where the hospital does not provide a powerful enough computer cluster or access is restricted, it may be necessary to buy separate servers, sometimes with GPUs, and integrate them into the existing hospital IT infrastructure. Be aware, this will increase the project (capital) expense, and the integration of new hardware might take time and will doubtless require approval from different departments. Overall, it is essential to be flexible and be able to find quick workarounds to make your system work. In addition, a cloud solution makes the situation easier for the developers. On the other hand, this raises issues related to de-identification, security, and GDPR safeguard. Thus, a hybrid (private) cloud approach might be the optimal solution.

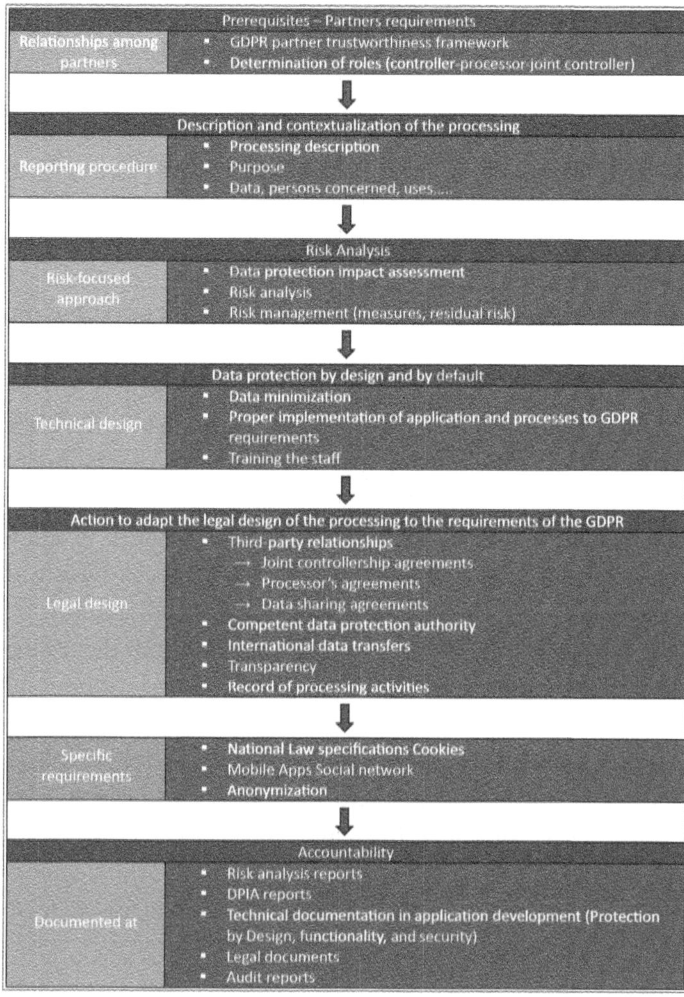

Figure 27.1. Compliance workflow.

27.2.4 New Tools and Clinical Acceptance

Although results might be good within an experimental setup, how can the target group be convinced to use a new model? For instance, certain patient groups may have less experience using apps, such as older or less digitally aware cohorts. Alternatively, clinical staff may be under time pressure and are focused on immediate patient care rather than technological advances. Therefore, they may be reluctant to test or deploy additional tools within their daily routines. At all events, the end user (either patient or clinician) must be convinced of the benefit of a given tool. There are standardized models (e.g., normalization process theory [1][i]),

i. http://www.normalizationprocess.org/.

frameworks (e.g., non-adoption, abandonment, scale-up, spread, and sustainability [2]), and programs (e.g., personal and public involvement[ii]) to encourage and facilitate discussion, understanding, and ultimately adoption of new technologies into healthcare contexts. These take time, require significant planning to engage appropriate stakeholders, and may be constrained by existing institution-specific procedures. On the other hand, they depend on good cross-discipline communication and, therefore, can encourage a common language and understanding early on in the project (see above).

From our experience, we achieved good acceptance by preparing introductory material in the form of text or video, including on occasion as part of an app, having direct personal briefings, or including the personnel in the process. Visualization certainly plays an important role. However, it turned out that instead of providing a new tool in addition to all the existing apps and programs, integration into existing working environments, e.g., as an additional feature, might make it easier as medical staff already uses multiple programs daily and may not be open to adding another one so easily unless it is presented as part of existing practices. Finally, trust in the technology might play a crucial role depending on the application. It is important here to see the app as part of a broader sociotechnical context: the technology itself may be robust and completely reliable. However, if the agency promoting its use has lost patient trust, then this will affect take-up negatively.[iii] Make time to cater to all of these aspects, especially by doing user experiments and engagement. It should be remembered that for healthcare, there are at least two main user groups who need to be collaborated with: first, the clinicians themselves who may have other priorities and may not understand the subtleties of the technologies themselves, and second, the patients who may be suspicious of technologies where they do not see immediate and personal healthcare benefit.

For example, implementing a new study protocol that includes commercial smartwatch technology to track patient activity runs into several security concerns by the data security officer and GDPR compliance officers. Data security officers must contact the commercial provider to validate if proper data security processes are in place. Data of these devices might be stored in the cloud on a different continent, running into GDPR compliance issues. The company selling the commercial devices might be bought by another company during the study, potentially triggering novel GDPR concerns. All these complexities can add significant time delays to a study.

---

ii. https://www.health-ni.gov.uk/topics/safety-and-quality-standards/personal-andpublic-involvement-ppi.

iii. This was observed during the COVID-19 pandemic with varying levels of adoption of contact-tracing apps, regardless of each app's reliability, because of suspicion of government or the attitudes of particular groups of users.

27.3 Data

27.3.1 Data Access Across Institutions and/or Countries

Access to data is of fundamental importance to the success of any data-driven initiative. Traditionally, a patient's care has primarily depended solely on the data available to the care provider. However, it is evident that in today's hyperconnected world, the data that could positively impact a patient's health could typically reside across multiple entities and even in multiple countries. Experience gained from the BigMedilytics project has shown that while individual research studies can get access to data after very lengthy procedures, such strategies would not scale in the real world. In fact, even the innovation carried out in research studies would proceed much further if data access mechanisms were more streamlined. For example, in BigMedilytics, there was an instance where a hospital simply could not arrange to have data shared outside its physical boundaries due to privacy/security issues. This prevented it from collaborating with another research institute and resulted in lengthy, drawn-out negotiations. Finally, to resolve this issue, the hospital provided temporary 'visiting researcher' contracts to researchers from the research institute so that they could process the data on the hospital's premises based on its terms and conditions.

Such a construct would be impossible to scale up in the real world and is a clear example of how siloed the world of healthcare is. In fact, the different silos in the healthcare sector are the greatest hurdles that prevent the widescale adoption of Big Data-driven solutions. These silos can exist at different levels: within a hospital, across care providers and other entities (profit/nonprofit organizations), or across countries. Silos within a hospital can be overcome by adopting open platforms that integrate data from different systems. However, for silos beyond the hospital, the technical challenges are less of an issue, and instead, regulations play a more significant role.

In recent years, several techniques for privacy-preserving data analysis (Privacy-Enhancing Technologies or PETs), which could circumvent the problems highlighted above, have received much attention. BigMedilytics has focused on one of these techniques, Secure Multi-Party Computation (or MPC for short), to demonstrate how sensitive healthcare data can be securely shared and processed across multiple organizations. However, MPC (and other privacy-preserving techniques) do not constitute a universal panacea that solves all problems related to data sharing. This is due to several factors, ranging from a technical level – in that designing and implementing an MPC solution is far from trivial and often requires more computational power and running time than a conventional solution – to a more legal and societal level, in that jurisprudence on the usage of these techniques is extremely scarce. Moreover, the exact privacy properties of these techniques often present non-trivial nuances, and ensuring that data owners and controllers properly understand these nuances takes time and effort.

Therefore, there is an urgent need to streamline regulations to improve the competitiveness and innovation potential of the EU at a global level. The following are some points that could help:

- Clearer and updated guidelines (from the European Data Protection Board) on the concept of personal and non-personal data. The EU Member States do not hold a unique and aligned position on the legal concept of personal data (and non-personal data). This limits the capability to re-use health data.
- Clearer and updated guidelines (from the European Data Protection Board) on anonymization techniques. In addition, a code of conduct on anonymization (or anonymization of personal data concerning health) and re-identification risk is also needed.
- Clear guidelines on using privacy-preserving techniques, such as MPC (mentioned above), differential privacy, or federated learning. This point is strongly related to the one above in anonymization, as it often needs to be clarified to what extent these techniques can be seen as forms of anonymization.
- Reduce fragmentation of local conditions on data processing for scientific research purposes, given that member states have leveraged art. 9 (4) GDPR to introduce further limitations to the processing of health data for scientific research purposes, such as the concept of 'public interest of the research', the 'impossibility or disproportionate effort to obtain consent', or the concept of 'research institute or body'. This fragmentation limits the capability to process health data in the context of research. In this respect, a code of conduct, followed by harmonizing the local GDPR implementation acts, would be beneficial.
- Reduce fragmentation of local data protection/healthcare rules applicable to health data, particularly in cross-border transfers of health data within the EU.

27.4 Data Access Needs to Comply with Highly Complex Rules and Regulations

As data scientists are not necessarily associated with the data provider, accessing sensitive (special category personal) data in the first place might bring challenges. In our project, some data scientists and data providers were even located in different countries, which did not make the situation easier. The introduction of the General Data Protection Regulation (GDPR) was intended to harmonize member-state regulation and therefore facilitate well-founded and managed data sharing. However, in practice, it has resulted in many difficulties and further delays.

- Regulation: Periodically, as demonstrated by the pandemic, regulators may announce specific programs to facilitate the sharing of healthcare data.[iv] It is worth exploring any such opportunities that may apply.
- Governance:
    - Approvals: The sharing of medical data is tightly controlled with oversight, usually from multiple agencies. It is essential, therefore, to begin the ethical approval process as early as possible and especially to be explicit about what data are required and for what purposes.
    - Data curation: Although approval, especially research ethics, will still typically be needed, de-identified or fully anonymous data have reduced risk to the data subject/patient. It is useful, therefore, for members of the team to discuss the appropriateness and impact of fully anonymous data. Further, if data are de-identified or pseudonymized, this should be done by the (clinical) data provider before sharing.
- Technology:
    - Infrastructure: Data are usually protected by special dashboards for computer scientists, which must be programmed, if not already available, or by contracts. Even so, contractual arrangements between medical healthcare providers and guest scientists are difficult to secure and require long processing times. This may also include separate discussions and approvals for any infrastructure to be used to store and process data. Our recommendation would be to engage with a Trusted Research Environment (TRE)[v] which conforms with the 5+1 Safes.[vi]
    - Remote visitation: One approach to this challenge is to use a model-to-data paradigm, where all the data remain within the data provider infrastructure. All computations are applied on a secure server that resides at the data provider premises, and various docker containers and pipelines of analytics models are transferred to the server and executed there. So, if data queries and algorithms are well-defined, the structure of the data they

---

iv. See, for instance, the COPI Regulations in the UK; https://www.legislation.gov.uk/uksi/2002/1438/contents/made.

v. https://www.hdruk.ac.uk/wp-content/uploads/2021/04/Goldacre-Review-TREResponse.pdf.

vi. https://www.ukdataservice.ac.uk/manage-data/legal-ethical/access-control/fivesafes.

are to be run against is known. It is worth considering whether the clinical partner (the data provider) can host and run the queries/algorithms the data scientists developed. That way, the raw data are not shared, just controlled access. This requires careful planning and governance but may reduce the administrative burden considerably.[vii]

- Federation: For a project in which privacy-sensitive data from two or more institutions needs to be combined, privacy-preserving techniques such as MPC (which BigMedilytics used, albeit on synthetic data) offer a potential solution. However, as these are relatively new technologies, conveying the data-security aspect to the respective data security officers is not straightforward. Nevertheless, if multiple datasets are to be used together (collated or cross-correlated), then running a complex query that remotely accesses and temporarily links different data from different sources would again leave the raw data with the data provider and covered by standard operating procedures. Standardized formats and interface 2 are required in this setting as well.

27.4.1 Complexity of Data Rises for Non-experts

Data scientists usually are not medical experts. In addition, real (clinical) data might include many errors (partially due to human input errors, for example, misuse of predetermined fields or use of non-standardized codes) and missing values. Datasets can grow organically over time, and historic design decisions influence the data, but these are not obvious to an 'outsider'. Thus, in most cases, it is impossible to test methods and directly get excellent and meaningful results. In most cases, there needs to be close interdisciplinary work. Each stakeholder needs a specific understanding of the work of the others in order to achieve satisfying results. For this reason, it is essential to plan frequent technical meetings to share results, foster ongoing and mutual understanding, and ensure that no apparent errors have been made.

Discretizing some variables for anonymization and usability purposes could require different dynamical ranges depending on the considered populations in the study. Moreover, not all clinical measures are obtained at the same time and some of them must be assumed from other heterogeneous past periods related to the dynamics of the corresponding variable. Besides, different and heterogeneous imputation techniques to fill in the empty values for some features in individuals must be applied for a great part of machine learning models to work. The chosen

vii. Care must be taken, of course, that the results of such remote query/execution do not increase the risk of re-identification.

imputation technique depends on some feature properties such as feature nature, probability distribution, and feature relation degree among all related features.

Moreover, the data of the medical domain are of different types and include structured data, text data, genomic data, and imaging of different modalities (e.g., X-ray, MRI, ultrasound, CT, pathology, and so on). Understanding all these modalities and different types of data is complex and requires special expertise. Furthermore, even within the same modality, different medical centres create different data. For example, MRI has no standardized protocol for scan acquisition and high variance of image resolution, voxel size, and image contrast dynamics. This diversity of modalities increases the data complexity and requires special pre-processing and selection of different methods per modality.

27.4.2 Limited Data

While from a medical perspective, a data source may be large, data will likely be too small and with many missing values from a data scientist's perspective. This is because many modern machine learning models are data-hungry. The small data size may introduce biases and not represent the real-world distribution. Also, it significantly decreases the data size if the events you want to detect are seldom. The difficulty of data access for data science in the medical domain is often that the relevant data are distributed across hospitals. This stands in contrast to the majority of data science projects, where the data to analyse is usually either in a single place, can be accessed without restrictions, or is a public source that can be integrated freely. Despite national- or European-level legal regulation for data access, each country and in some countries, even each state and hospital, has its own rules on how data scientists can access and process the data. Moreover, in cases where the goal is to introduce new technology to collect data, e.g., a remote patient monitoring app, work starts from scratch. Beginning to develop methods without data is almost impossible. Where it is necessary to wait until the size of the data increases, rule-based approaches or simple models at the start might help, as well as the generation of some synthetic but representative data. Further, exploiting some additional existing and similar open-access data sources can be beneficial. In such cases, we can either start on that data to develop your first baselines, or blend the data, or pre-train our models.

27.4.3 Data Quality

Data quality in the biomedical domain and clinical care can be critical, as it will inevitably affect patient outcomes, as well as the costs of care. Data quality issues can manifest at multiple steps along a data science pipeline, originating from raw data but affecting inferred data. To maximize data quality, we recommend supporting standardization at best. For instance, if any clinical staff can enter information freely, the evaluation is complex and requires efforts to standardize afterwards. Furthermore, to standardize diagnoses, we recommend using SNOMED CT; to standardize laboratory values, we recommend using LOINC, and to standardize outcomes, we recommend using PROMS.

Information from biomedical articles or clinical text can support processes and use cases in healthcare. Information about treatments, medications, or adverse drug effects might influence the treatment decision of a caregiver or medical doctor. Thus, methods that extract information should attach a quality or trust score to the extracted information. Regarding the extraction of information from biomedical literature, the publication date of an article, the impact factor of the journal in which it is published, and possibly the authors' affiliations should determine the information's reliability. Investing time in a systematic literature review and a meta-analysis of relevant work may be worth investing time. This should be carried out by experienced personnel.

27.5 Technology

27.5.1 Remote Patient Monitoring

Implementing remote monitoring requires time and patience. We recommend involving all parties (e.g., patients, medical doctors, and nurses, depending on the use case) in the development process (design and such). Standard approaches (NPT, NASSS, PPIE, and so on) have been mentioned above, which would be run in parallel with traditional software engineering processes such as user story analysis. In addition, programming requires time, especially if new features and functionalities need to be implemented. Some extra time should be considered where patients are involved so that the software works well and to agreed standards before the release. This may involve additional testing beyond functional verification. Depending on the use case (e.g., monitoring life-threatening aspects), we do not recommend monitoring patients solely by AI tools, which certainly would also raise legal concerns. However, for those cases, we suggest putting humans in the loop, e.g., in the form of a telemedicine team.

27.5.2 Image Processing

Analysing medical imaging is generally done via deep neural networks with millions of parameters that need to be learned. Training such a network requires thousands of image data and some annotations on the images relating to thousands of patients. However, the imaging data available for analytics are scarce and confidential, and access to data is protected and limited. Nevertheless, access to the data for machine learning purposes and permission to display images to radiologists as part of guidelines or as examples can be obtained through approval by an ethics board and suitable anonymization of the images. Moreover, in medical imaging, the annotations require medical expertise and are expensive, time-consuming, and inconsistent. Sometimes multiple modalities are needed as different features are exposed in different modalities. For example, breast density shows up on mammography images but not on ultrasound images, and breast calcifications show up on mammography but typically do not show up via ultrasound and never show up on MRI. Finally, in the medical domain, there is a diversity of populations, genetic variations, and environmental differences that may impact the features exhibited in the imaging. This effect is not quite understood yet. As a result of all these challenges with analysing medical imaging, the creation of robust AI models needs to consider new advanced approaches. Multimodal algorithms that analyse multiple modalities (e.g., CT, MRI, and X-ray), pre-trained models, and transfer learning that reuse models trained on external datasets, as well as federated learning that trains simultaneously on multiple protected datasets, can be beneficial approaches to increase the usable dataset and address the medical imaging AI challenges.

27.5.3 Accessing Information in Text

Much information within Electronic Health Records (EHR) is encoded in semistructured clinical text, such as the well-being of a patient, medication changes, or particular findings. In order to unlock this information, appropriate Natural Language Processing (NLP) tools suited for the clinical domain are required. Overall, we recommend using or building upon existing NLP tools and libraries. Unfortunately, nearly all such tools exist only for English, as are nearly all existing clinical text datasets, which could be used to train a new model. Therefore, working in multilingual Europe on clinical text processing is a major issue and will slow development. While a rule-based approach, such as NegEx for negation detection, can be translated, machine learning-based approaches for more complex problems require labelled training and evaluation data. However, the creation of a new labelled dataset is very time-consuming. Technically, some ways to overcome this challenge are as follows: (1) Research groups working in this field need to publish data or models to contribute to the community. Publishing data, however, is more complicated, as data include sensitive (special category) information, even if de-identified. One solution, for instance, would be merging all de-identified text files and randomizing the sentences [3]. Publishing models trained on de-identified data might be easier, as models are more abstract. (2) A second possibility lies in modern machine learning techniques such as zero-shot or few-shot learning – training new models on, for instance, similar English data and applying the model to the new target language.

The processing of scientific literature, such as text from PubMed, instead includes, in most cases, English text. However, depending on the use case, the quality of the information provided in publications can be problematic due to outdated articles (information and facts might change over time) or publications from untrustworthy institutes and journals. To this end, when harvesting scientific literature to extract, for instance, related information (e.g., build up knowledge graphs), it is advisable to use specific filters:

- Quality of the journal, check, for instance, h-index or the Scimago Journal Rank (SJR) indicator.
- Filter for particular institutions or authors which are known for their contributions.
- Publication type: Different types of articles are defined according to the different levels of evidence (e.g., scientific review or clinical trial) based on where the represented knowledge is derived.
- Publication year: The recency of a publication allows an expert to decide if the results reported are still relevant.
- The number of citations for a specific publication is a sound measure of its quality and trustworthiness.

27.5.4 Data Quality for Workflow Characterization and Optimization

In order to characterize and improve hospital workflows, hospitals usually only have access to data derived from EMRs. However, while EMRs are excellent for managing patient data, they are not optimally designed to optimize hospital workflows – especially for the ones requiring fine-grained timing information. This is primarily because most data are entered manually in the EMR system. A direct consequence is that data entry is rarely performed exactly at the time a particular action is taken. For example, discharge details of a patient might only be entered into the EMR at the end of a shift. The care provider entering this information thus can only make estimates about the discharge time. Data gathered from BigMedilytics studies have shown that timestamp errors can sometimes be in the order of several hours. To accurately gather timing information, it is essential to understand that many processes within a hospital workflow are closely related to location. For example, in the Emergency Department, the triage, treatment, and discharge processes can be detected based on the location of a patient. Because of this, data gathered from a Real-Time Locating System (RTLS) can be used to gather accurate timestamps of particular processes automatically. Thus, the RTLS timestamp not only helps to improve the data quality of timestamps but also reduces the burden on staff as the process of entering timestamps can be fully automated.

27.5.5 Strategy to Grow RTLS Infrastructure

Real-time, outdoor location information has radically transformed the way society functions by not just allowing us to locate a position on a map but also by enabling people to perform a wide variety of tasks such as navigating traffic, picking out restaurants, and shopping at a store when it is the least busy. Similarly, real-time indoor location information can transform how healthcare is delivered in hospitals. More specifically, location information from an RTLS infrastructure can significantly improve hospital workflows ranging from asset management to optimizing patient flows. However, an important point to realize is that as most patient and asset trajectories are not limited to a single department but span across multiple departments, any RTLS should ideally be deployed on an enterprise-wide basis.

However, a common misconception is that an enterprise-wide system requires a uniform high-resolution RTLS deployment that can locate any tagged entity down to a room. This is not only expensive but is (in most cases) unnecessary. Instead, a more cost-effective approach is to try and re-use a hospital's existing Wi-Fi infrastructure to act as an RTLS. While a Wi-Fi-based RTLS may only deliver department-level resolution, it does help cover the entire building without investing additional dedicated RTLS infrastructure. Furthermore, once the enterprise-wide Wi-Fi-based RTLS has been rolled out, a hospital can opt to upgrade specific departments or areas that can benefit from more fine-grained location information by using higher-resolution RTLS technologies (such as those based on infrared or Bluetooth). For example, the Emergency Department might be equipped with an infrared-based RTLS to monitor all ED patients or pay special attention to hyperacute (e.g., stroke/sepsis) patients. In addition, Wi-Fi-based RTLS could be used to track ED patients admitted to the hospital and also track mobile assets that move around the hospital. In other words, adopting an open, real-time platform that allows the tagged entities to be seamlessly tracked across multiple high- and low-resolution RTLS technologies is important. This heterogeneous, stepwise approach would allow a hospital to monitor and optimize processes along the entire trajectory of patients while keeping costs in check. Using an open, real-time platform is also a future-proof strategy, as it allows a hospital to build up its capabilities over time and meet its changing needs.

27.5.6 Security

As medical data, by definition, are regarded as a special category of personal data (GDPR, Art 9[viii]), there are additional requirements on those holding and processing such data to ensure its security. There are standards (e.g., ISO 27001[ix]), and certification programs (e.g., Cyber Essentials[x]; NHS Digital Toolkit,[xi] in the United Kingdom) which provide assurance as to the appropriateness of data storage environments. We recommend that those hosting medical data should explore the options in their context[xii]: external accreditation of this sort takes some time and may affect budgets. However, they provide an objective indication that the data will be appropriately handled and secure once obtained.

If privacy-preserving solutions such as MPC are used, another challenge rises from the fact that these solutions need to be installed on the IT infrastructure of the data owners, which may pose significant technical and governance challenges, especially given that these solutions often start from a low Technology Readiness Level (TRL) and need to be interfaced with different systems and infrastructures.

27.6 Validation

27.6.1 Comparability

At some point during development, it is important to establish whether the results are sufficient. This may be difficult as development may depend on a single restricted database and even aim to provide insights where no other work has been carried out to date, meaning there are no comparative studies available. Papers on similar tasks, which report results on their data, which can often not be accessed, are only helpful to a small extent, as small differences (task definition, the proportion of positives/negatives, quality/underlying population, and so on) can have a strong influence on the outcomes of your model. A continuing bias exacerbates this situation in the literature to publish only positive findings, not those

viii. Art. 9 GDPR – Processing of special categories of personal data |General Data Protection Regulation (GDPR) (gdpr-info.eu).

ix. https://www.iso.org/isoiec-27001-information-security.html.

x. https://www.gov.uk/government/publications/cyber-essentials-scheme-overview.

xi. https://www.dsptoolkit.nhs.uk/.

xii. Note that, in some cases, such accreditation is essential to process certain datasets. This should be checked as part of planning.

where an approach did not yield useful results. In this regard, we recommend three approaches:

(1) Try to find a dataset with a similar task and a corresponding benchmark system and test the approach.
(2) Put sufficient effort into a simple but strong baseline, possibly with the help of domain experts.
(3) Try to evaluate the system with the end users – although this may be time-consuming. However, the use of systems such as the Observational Medical Outcomes Partnership (OMOP) would solve some of these problems.

27.7 Clinical Validation

In some cases, the AI models can be used in clinical practice only after conducting a clinical trial. AI models that may affect the treatment selection have a direct impact on the patient's health and must be first validated and tested in clinical trials and then approved by regulatory authorities such as the FDA in the United States and the EMA in Europe. This makes clinical validation long and complicated; thus, only a few validation cycles are possible. Additionally, these models need to be interpretable and explainable to increase the acceptance of the AI models. The stakeholders need the ability to interpret the models and understand their reasoning.

27.7.1 Study Design

The study designs should be planned with the help of medical experts and relevant statisticians so that the impact on patients can be evaluated sufficiently and in a way that other medical experts would readily understand and accept the methodology and the findings, leading to their use of technological innovations. It is important to contextualize a given innovation activity within the existing literature and procedures. Clinicians will be used to reading and assessing various trials; they may not so easily follow typical data science publications.

The design of studies involving workflows in hospitals requires some additional considerations. Hospitals are highly dynamic environments. In addition, it may not be possible to control or influence all factors that can impact the outcome of a study. To take these characteristics into account, when executing pre-post studies that focus on evaluating the impact of a particular intervention, it is important not to obtain only two sets of KPI measurements before and after the introduction of the intervention. Instead, tools and procedures should be in place to monitor KPIs continuously at regular periods before and after the introduction of the intervention. In addition, it is crucial to keep a daily log of all events (e.g., with the help of consultants) that could impact the selected KPIs, as the collected information could prove to be critical in retrospectively explaining the characteristics of the KPIs. Tools to continuously monitor KPIs can also help to check if the introduced intervention is being used correctly or if further training is needed to ensure that the end user (care provider/patient) derives maximum benefit from the solution.

Where multiple partners engage on a project, as with the BigMedilytics trials, ethical approval is likely required from multiple bodies: a relevant health research body and the institute that any academic or data scientist is associated with. Approval should be sought as early as possible and may involve dependencies between different agencies that need to be catered for.[xiii] Where secondary data are to be used, that is, data collected previously and for another purpose, the data controller or data steward must be consulted to ensure that the data can be used for the proposed trial.

27.7.2 Consent Gathering

The human subjects (e.g., patients) who will participate in a research study need to provide explicit consent before their data can be used for scientific approaches or forwarded to third parties (e.g., data hosts). Thus, the participating medical institutions will need to compose a consent form that requires filling in the name of the patient, the name of the doctor that informs the patient about the study, information about the subject of the study, and the ability to withdraw from the study. The consent form will need to be signed by the human subject. In Germany, for instance, additional consent is required if data are used to establish Big Data and AI tools, especially if the data are used by other medical subspecializations (scientists from the radiology field cannot use data from patients with heart diseases). In addition, it is prohibited to use an established prediction model in another context, for instance, in the same patient group but in another hospital. There is the possibility to forward data to third parties (data hosts) if the patient agrees to discard medical privilege in this particular topic (written consent necessary). Better would be to sign contracts with third parties to become a data order processor.

Generally, patients can withdraw their consent at any time without giving a reason. Still, hospitals are advised not to delete data, as they have to provide medical data for at least ten years after production.

---

xiii. In some countries, for example, the research sponsor will need to approve first. Universities may act as sponsors in this way, but equally, a local health authority may be the sponsor and therefore need to provide approval before the university ethics review board.

Discussing informed consent as a requirement in trials and research studies is common. However, it is important to be clear about what consent is being requested and for what purpose. Briefly, consent may refer to a research participant's agreement to participate in a study, a patient's agreement to undergo treatment, or one legal basis for collecting personal data. By definition, for the consent to be informed, the person giving consent must understand which of these it is. From our experience, we recommend the following:

1. Primary data collection: where you collect data, there are specific requirements:
    a. A research participant/data subject should be fully informed about the planned purposes, that is, what the data will be used for and who will have access. Make sure, at this stage, that any purposes you are aware of are covered.
    b. Of course, it may not always be possible to predict how data will be used. It is important, therefore, to let the participant know that future, ethically approved purposes may be found and to give them the option to refuse any such future use, even though they agree to the specific use you have identified.
    c. Because data are so valuable, it is recommended, wherever possible, to obtain agreement from the research participant for their data to be used, albeit anonymized, in future research.
    d. Consent should be recorded for audit purposes; research consent does not require a written record.
2. Secondary data use: where you do not collect the data but use data from a different source (an online research database, for instance), then:
    a. You must check that your intended use of the data complies with the conditions of the data steward.
    b. You should also check that your intended use of the data is consistent with the original consent provided by the data subject.
    c. You should make a judgement as to whether the data subject would expect their data to be 'private'. For instance, social media content is not necessarily public domain: there may still be an expectation that content is quasi-private, shared only with trusted others.

Local ethics committees will be able to provide guidance. Most importantly, though, (research) consent should be sought in good time, and any data protection consent could be associated with the potential future assertion of data subject rights (such as withdrawing consent).

27.8 Conclusion

In this document, we presented different challenges along with possible solutions and lessons learned we experienced in a large Big Data and AI project in healthcare. The findings should guide, from a technical perspective, all stakeholders working on data-driven propositions in healthcare.

References

[1] May CR, Mair F, Finch T, MacFarlane A, Dowrick C, Treweek S, Rapley T, Ballini L, Ong BN, Rogers A, *et al.* Development of a theory of implementation and integration: Normalization process theory. Implementation Science. 2009. 4(1), 1–9.

[2] Greenhalgh T, Wherton J, Papoutsi C, Lynch J, Hughes G, Hinder S, Fahy N, Procter R, Shaw S, *et al.* Beyond adoption: a new framework for theorizing and evaluating nonadoption, abandonment, and challenges to the scale-up, spread, and sustainability of health and care technologies. Journal of medical Internet research. 2017. 19(11), e8775.

[3] Kittner M, Lamping M, Rieke DT, Götze J, Bajwa B, Jelas I, Rüter G, Hautow H, Sänger M, Habibi M, *et al.* Annotation and initial evaluation of a large annotated german oncological corpus. JAMIA open. 2021. 4(2), ooab025.

Index

Printed and bound by CPI Group (UK) Ltd, Croydon, CR0 4YY

15/09/2026

14962365-0005